BEATING THE FASCISTS

The Untold Story of Anti-fascist Action

BEATING THE FASCISTS

The Untold Story of ANTI-FASCIST ACTION

by Sean Birchall

FREEDOM PRESS
LONDON

Published by Freedom Press, 2010

Freedom Press
84b Whitechapel High Street
London E1 7QX

ISBN 978-1-904491-12-5

For information on all Freedom Press publications visit our website at www.freedompress.org.uk

Design and DTP by Jayne Clementson

Printed on recycled paper in the UK by
Imprint Digital

This is a controversial book. It has to be. It is about controversial issues that still resonate today. *Beating the Fascists* is an account from one point of view, albeit one at the heart of the struggle. However, thousands of others also took part in that struggle and inevitably some will disagree with the views and conclusions expressed here. We think the historical value of this narrative outweighs the risk of re-opening sectarian differences, but we understand that some people involved may feel that their story has not been told.

We hope that this book will encourage other histories, open the debate and ultimately strengthen the fight against fascism.

"The fascists, backed up by Loyalist elements, were still rubbing their wounds after an abortive attempt to invade an Irish meeting at Conway Hall two nights before the march. Richard Edmonds of the BNP led the attack, and the attackers included members of the Fields' family from Islington and the mad bomber, Tony Lecomber. But despite having nearly 100 'fighting men', they were soundly beaten off."
Searchlight magazine, December 1988

"We have to advertise our gigs by word of mouth. If they get to hear about it they want to turn it into a blood bath."
Ian Stuart, lead singer of Far Right band Skrewdriver, London Evening Standard's ES magazine, April 1989

"Remembering the outrageous unlawful violence used by the BNP members to attack an anti-apartheid meeting in Blackburn in March, it is obvious that the party has standards and policies that decent people are happy to condemn. But they prefer their condemnation to be confined within the scope of law and order and the ballot box. And that is what these anti-fascist thugs must learn, or be tarred with the same brush. It is a mad policy that sets out to smash the opposition and ends up being likened to it."
Lancashire Evening Telegraph, 1992

"... the total failure of the authorities to take any measure against this group, or others involved in attacks on BNP members during the May election campaign, suggests that state security agencies which are supposed to act in defence of democracy are not doing their jobs very efficiently."
BNP leader John Tyndall, Spearhead magazine, July 1994

"I started to become actively involved against the National Front in the middle of 1974... we carried on a campaign 'till the end of the 70s. By then the National Front had splintered and broken off. I suppose the most significant part of that was the actual demonstration in Lewisham where they were literally smashed. They got a terrible pounding, literally a pounding on the streets. Their whole philosophy did seem to be working... it was the philosophy of one Adolf Hitler: controlling and ruling the streets.

"The National Front became very aggressive. It started off by the obvious thing, people selling newspapers in the streets. Not only Socialist Workers Party; they attacked people selling the *Morning Star*. They attacked people selling *Militant*... and we decided that we'd have to stop it.

"We formed a system where people would have a telephone and we used to be waiting and if there was a presence of NF either in Barking, Stratford, Upton Park, East Ham, between ten or twelve of us used to go over there and try to, if you like, remedy the situation.

"I'll be perfectly honest with you, I was very surprised when we started coming into physical contact, and I mean physical contact, with these people. I was very, very apprehensive at first. Most of 'em used to look very, very aggressive. Some of 'em used to wear military uniforms which don't mean nothing... none of 'em was ever in the military. To use an East End terminology, they weren't very good on the pavement and we started getting a bit more confident. These people were not supermen, you know what I mean? In our opinion they were putting forward poison. They were putting forward ideas about people's colour. Racist stuff that was poisonous and if people like that are allowed to do as they please, then they become acceptable.

"So we've gone then from a situation of complete defence to being in front by having a demonstration that went right through the middle of their heartland and wasn't attacked. We considered that we were in front and it was then that the idea [from the opposition] came across about having a big march by the National Front to counteract that balance.

"They were losing their momentum. They were smashed to pieces and unfortunately a lot of people in the Left side of politics thought it was a disposable item. That the issue had gone away. It might have gone away for them in particular but it certainly didn't go away for Asian families in Brick Lane or in Cannon Street Road, or even around here [Bow, East London].

"It's all very well saying that people have got a right to express their own opinions. Altab Ali, a young Asian worker, was coming down the bottom of Brick Lane. He was stabbed to death by two skinheads for no apparent reason. Just because he was Asian, and if you allow those people to sell that sort of muck, that is the end result."

Interview with anti-fascist veteran, Micky Fenn,
for BBC2 documentary on AFA, May 1992

CONTENTS

Section 3: 1990 onwards

INTRODUCTION

Sensing a threat to the political status quo, something approaching hysteria touched sections of the press in the run-up to the local elections in May 2002. Screaming front-page headlines, even denunciatory editorials in *The Sun* newspaper, were not uncommon as the BNP sought the endorsement of neglected sections of the population, particularly within the former mill towns in the north west of England. Even the *Daily Express*,* with a pornographer as a proprietor, temporarily suspended its campaign against refugees to concentrate on demonising the anti-immigrant BNP instead.

Afterwards, the BNP breakthrough was restricted to single figures, and to just one town, Burnley. The media smear campaign (which included widely broadcast allegations of rape against a BNP 'chief', who was in reality a fringe member, while the conviction was more than 25 years old), was publicly lauded a triumph by the architects.

Back-slapping replaced hand-wringing as the Far Right, and the former mill towns they had targeted, instantly became yesterday's news. And with the crisis deemed to be over, the state of complacent invulnerability exhibited by the liberal establishment for the two previous decades returned. Within months one left of centre columnist was lauding the campaign as "a near total victory for Searchlight and the ANL" (Nick Cohen, *Observer*, 13th October 2002).

But just three months down the line he and his liberal contemporaries were again filled with dread. *Guardian* columnist David Aaronovitch noted that "all over the place now you find people discussing a possible vote for the BNP. Perhaps in the past it would have been the Conservatives, but now they discuss the BNP and what it could do as they might discuss the plot of a Hollywood movie. Oh yes, politics is alive and exciting. That's the bad news" (*Guardian*, 29th January 2003).

In the *Independent*, Yasmin Alibhai-Brown, while continuing to describe the BNP as "pitiful", nonetheless felt that Britain was now "a more hate-filled place than it was during the days of Enoch Powell" (*Independent*, 27th January 2003). A year on, even with the capture of an additional 13 council seats by the BNP, anti-nazis were again congratulating each other for "having corralled the BNP at the eastern end of the M65" (*Guardian*, 10th May 2003).

---

* A survey the following year (2003) revealed that in one 31-day period the *Daily Express* "ran 22 front page leads about asylum-seekers, becoming fixated on the so-called 'crisis' with alarmist stories, many of which rested on statistics from unofficial sources that were no more than guesstimates" (*Guardian*, 30th May 2005).

However, when yet more seats fell to the BNP in a number of hotly contested council by-elections, even the Home Secretary David Blunkett warned against liberal complacency: "In this country there is a tendency to dismiss these [Far Right] trends as continental politics, far removed from the tolerance and diversity which has characterised UK society and always ensured the BNP has remained a fringe party. But we should have no truck with complacency. Last week a report showed that the proportion of people who regard themselves as racist has risen for the first time in 20 years to 31 per cent" (*Observer*, 14th December 2003).

Following the general election in 2005 this note of caution had again been cast aside, with complacency or its approximate again becoming the order of the day. When the BNP – with 224 fewer candidates than the NF – surpassed the total vote accrued by the NF in 1979, the lead headline in the anti-fascist magazine *Searchlight* read "Hopeless".

Within days of European election results in 2009 one-time film actress and Labour MP Glenda Jackson announced that the election of Nick Griffin and former NF chair Andrew Brons to the European Parliament was, contrary to appearances, "not the breakthrough that Griffin craved and many of us feared". It was rather yet another triumph for *Searchlight* "for without their campaign, the nightmare of a dozen BNP victories could have become reality" (*Independent* 9.06.09).

True to form, when in the following year's general election the BNP vote actually climbed threefold, from 192,746 in 2005 to 563,743, outpacing both the Greens and the Scottish National Party in the process, Weyman Bennett, joint secretary of Unite Against Fascism (UAF), nevertheless insisted the BNP return was "paltry", and that "the party has gone backwards" (BBC News, 7th May 2010).

This book then has a number of purposes. It is on one level a straightforward history of militant anti-fascism from the late 1970s up to the present day. But within that story there is the explanation for why the BNP is now in a position to profit from the pattern discernible across much of mainland Europe, where, for a second time in under a hundred years, reactionary forces are once again driving the political centre remorselessly to the right.

Today, as was the case in the 1920s and 1930s, the nature of the threat from the Far Right is either totally misunderstood or wilfully misrepresented. From the early 1980s to the late 1990s political analysts in Britain, with encouragement from many so-called anti-racist and anti-fascist experts, arrived at a fateful and fundamental miscalculation, which led them to believe that the political potential of the Far Right could be gauged most accurately by keeping an eye on the numbers of actual card-carrying members. This misconstruction reached its zenith with Home Office Minister Mike O'Brien's claim that tough new measures to tackle racial violence would "send out an unequivocal message to racist groups such as Combat 18", thereby implying that the tens of thousands of race attacks a year could reasonably be laid at the door of a group that never reached more than a hundred members. Reality was less reassuring.

For, as the experience of both Austria and Italy has demonstrated, the Far Right has risen, albeit to be junior partners in government. So the real potency of the fascist renaissance across Europe is far better judged by how easily its appearance on a national stage can first panic, and then stampede, an erstwhile political centre to the right. It is also worth noting that a fascist organisation does not have to be large to do this. Gone is the need for a private army, as 'strength on the street' is no longer obligatory. Unlike its 1930s forbears, what characterises fascism today is not the 'putsch' but what anti-fascists have referred to as 'the drift'.

A case in point is Denmark. Courtesy of the baleful influence of a small ultra-right party wielding just over 10% of the national vote, Denmark has the harshest immigration laws in Europe. With absolute conviction these latter day fascists can declare: "we are satisfied – for the time being" in the knowledge that, when push next comes to shove, other principles previously held to be inviolate by the centre may be abandoned as well.

In Britain the election of just three BNP councillors in 2002 was enough for the Labour Home Secretary to self-consciously appropriate the totemic term 'swamping' in a vain attempt to assuage popular disenchantment with government policy. Five years later another cabinet minister, Margaret Hodge, once notorious for flying the red flag from Islington Town Hall, went further. In an article in the *Observer* she called for "indigenous families" to have priority in housing. Tellingly, Hodge drew praise from other Cabinet colleagues – as well as the BNP – for daring to "raise a taboo issue" (*Observer*, 27th May 2007). Shortly after being installed as Prime Minister, Gordon Brown appropriated a former NF slogan in calling for 'British jobs for British workers', while a senior Tory spokesperson declared that "BNP voters have some very legitimate views". On 5th October 2007, a senior government minister, Geoff Hoon, legitimised the party itself when he addressed a meeting in his constituency chaired and organised by a BNP councillor. Totally squaring the circle, Trevor Phillips, the former head of the Commission for Racial Equality, even urged ministers to positively discriminate in favour of "young whites". A failure to do so would see Britain "end up with the same kind of conflict as we have seen in Austria, Belgium and Holland where anti-immigrant parties get a big boost" (*Daily Mail*, 28th October 2008).

Evidently, 'ignore them and they will go away', the establishment's trusted mantra for the best part of 30 years, no longer seems such sound advice. With the all-pervading complacency dispelled, it does seem a good time to review the influence on events of fascism's direct opponents. It is necessary to take on board why the BNP breakthrough did not happen earlier, not only for reasons of historical accuracy but in order to remedy what has gone wrong.

In March 1994, seemingly totally out of the blue, the largest British fascist party, the BNP, took everyone by surprise when it called a press conference to announce its abandonment of the 'politics of the punch-up'. The Left did not know what to make of it. But almost from that moment, their rise to national prominence has by their own standards been meteoric. It is a climb crystallised by the nine votes a BNP candidate took in Burnley in 1993 at the height of the conflict with militant anti-fascism, and a near 10,000 differential there less than a decade later. All in the teeth, it should be stressed, of concerted efforts from the major political parties, many of the 'red tops' and of course, legal anti-fascism.

Nonetheless when compared to our European neighbours – France, Holland, Austria, Norway, Denmark, Sweden, Germany and Switzerland – pundits continue to insist Britain remains a veritable paradigm of tolerance. But if, as the Home Secretary seems to believe, 'tolerance and diversity' were always what had previously forced the Far Right to the fringes, then why, at a time when the UK has never been more self-conscious in promoting diversity, does the BNP tax government strategists at all? No doubt many of them would have subscribed to the view that the British had largely been inoculated against the Far Right by cross-party sympathy for the continual pressure from an anti-racist lobby that sought to foreground race at every opportunity. It is almost inevitable, therefore, that they visibly struggled to explain this apparent outbreak of extremism at a point when, as far as they could see, the economy remained healthy. But it is precisely because the BNP success seems inexplicable, that it becomes unexplainable and thus untreatable. The politically motivated attempt to prosecute BNP leader Nick Griffin, not once but twice, illustrates the lack of establishment understanding of the challenge posed.

It is, perhaps, fortuitous that there is a straightforward explanation, though admittedly not one that many who might otherwise genuinely express an antipathy to fascism will probably find palatable. For, as we explain in the book, British nationalism was sidelined for almost a quarter of a century not by tolerance and diversity, but by the insurrectionary strategy pursued by fascist groups and the cold-eyed counter-measures adopted by their direct opponents. Basically, from the 1970s onwards, while race awareness took the plaudits, it was a strikingly illiberal militant anti-fascism that did all the heavy lifting. Or putting it another way, the essentially conservative argument, that cross-party support for all things multicultural supplied so unbreachable a dam of tolerance that it all but drove fascism out of business, is clearly phoney.

Though formed in 1982, the BNP up until the mid-1990s was steadfast and loyal to the Oswald Mosley strategy commonly known as 'march and grow'. Distilled, it was in essence the same impatient, and even insurrectionary, argument for a popular political uprising against the political elite, 'the Old Gang'.

Indicative of the impatience of many right-wing activists during this period was their fondness for army surplus trappings, a paramilitary trend that was, we can assume, not wholly dictated by fashion. "A state of war" was exactly how BNP leader John Tyndall described the relationship with his direct opponents in 1991 (*Sunday Express*, 7th July 1991).

Nevertheless, right up until January 1993, the BNP sought to attract recruits precisely on the basis that "it must first win power on the streets if it is to achieve power at the ballot box." It maintained the "advantage of greater manpower" would have "a positive effect on the morale" of the passive support of the movement. Large numbers of "disciplined campaigners on the streets" in addition to providing hope would encourage a "trust" that would be "reflected" in votes for "the Party" at elections (BNP recruitment leaflet).

Perhaps. But if this analysis was ever true then the obverse must carry equal weight; humiliation on the streets would have a disproportionately negative effect on the morale of activists and supporters, and this too would be reflected in support for party policies at elections.

In 1992 while straining all sinews to 'win power on the streets' the BNP took a pitiful 7,000 votes in the general election. Battered and bewildered, the BNP began describing its militant opponents as 'terrorists' and even 'storm-troopers'.

In March 1994 the BNP leadership blinked when it confessed to both its own supporters and the general public that the insurrectionary approach had failed. Their inability to 'out-violence' militant anti-fascism had in essence caused the more direct route to power and influence favoured by fascists since the 1930s to be cast aside in favour of a more circuitous pathway to their objectives. And with the adoption of this 'better way' the previous strategy was put into complete reverse. Now, rather than seek confrontation, it was to be avoided at all costs.

The first of what would be a number of down payments came in the council elections in 2002 when, along with the three council seats won in Burnley, the BNP came within one place of being elected in seven other wards, and overall the party collected votes from 28% of the electorate there. In Oldham, four out of five of the BNP candidates came second and the party took 27.3% in the seats contested. In one ward it came within 90 votes of overturning a huge Lib-Dem majority. In Stoke a BNP candidate came within 70 votes of being elected. In another six wards the BNP secured the vote of one in five voting. Later that year the same candidate took 8,000 votes in the mayoral election there. Not long after, the party took council seats in Blackburn and Halifax. In May 2003 it added a further 11 council seats, as well as taking 14% across 25 wards in Sunderland. In June 2004 the BNP took over 800,000 votes in the European elections. More importantly, steady pressure from the BNP inched the mainstream further to the right. "Having receded as a decisive electoral issue for the best part of a quarter of a century, 'immigration is back'. In a Populus Tracker poll in *The Times* last week immigration and asylum emerged as the fourth most likely issue to influence votes. At the same stage in the elections of 2001 and 1997 it did not rank at all" (Gary Younge, *Guardian*, 25th April 2005).

Other supporting data, plus a series of high profile by-election victories by the BNP since 2002, seemingly convinced Tory Party strategists that their route to power lay in making immigration-related subjects their primary policy, or as some complained, their only policy in the 2005 general election. With UKIP and Veritas also thumping the same tub, the effect was to steal votes from the BNP at the cost of legitimising them. By 2006 the BNP had doubled its intake of councillors to 55. Now, instead of gauging BNP potential in terms of card-carrying members, it is being calculated by focusing solely on the actual number of BNP councillors. All in all, unless some evidence is produced that the BNP has peaked, then Britain can no longer credibly claim to be immune to the 'European disease'.

Unsurprisingly for liberal democracy the lessons are disturbing. For the best part of twenty years it has turned its face from the problem and now, through force of circumstances, when it can identify the problem it finds it lacks a remedy. By and large it has responded to the situation with a pout.

Up until the BNP clambered on to the national stage, the liberal consensus was that rigorous anti-racism, and in particular the British take on multiculturalism, was the faultless foil, with aggressive anti-racist legislation acclaimed in some quarters as the epitome of anti-fascism.

Decades of this type of wishful thinking, culminating in 1999 with the establishment's public embrace of the notion of 'institutional racism', convinced many that a corner had been turned in race relations. Such was the sense of euphoria that from within the heart of the Macpherson inquiry there was wild talk of finding ways to outlaw 'racist thinking'.

To a large degree this reckless self-assuredness was based on the utter folly of believing that, in a Europe driven by the agenda of the nationalist right, Britain was, and would remain, immune. In addition, and paradoxically, British politicians of Left and Right had somehow come to regard multiculturalism as a uniquely British panacea, "a small reason for national pride" as one columnist put it. "Britain is better than most EU countries. They vote neo-fascist. We don't." Even the acting head of the CRE (Commission for Racial Equality), who one might have imagined had a duty to be less self-congratulatory, announced just four months after the BNP signalled a breakthrough that when looking "at North America and all parts of Europe, the UK is way ahead of any society" (*Evening Standard*, 19th September 2002).

Such bellicosity is especially mysterious as, throughout the 1990s, repeated surveys had exposed the chauvinism behind the boasting. For instance, in 1997 a European survey described Britain as being responsible for rearing the most "racist youth" (almost 30% disagreed that all races were equal) of any country (*Guardian*, 6th February 1997).

Together with a deep loathing for all things liberal, complementary data showed a Britain with race attacks on a par with Germany, where neo-nazi skinheads were numbered in tens of thousands. A year earlier an ICM poll for the *Daily Express* found that the "creation of a party supporting repatriation and a 'whites first' policy would be on course to becoming Britain's top political force ahead of the Liberals" (*Daily Express*, 8th August 1996).

But without this antipathy taking tangible political form, few apart from the militants took much heed. Right up until BNP leader Nick Griffin grabbed the highest vote ever recorded for a Far Right candidate in June 2001, the political invisibility of fascism seemed to justify liberal self-righteousness and middle-of-the-road indifference. A certain responsibility for such smugness lies with the scholars, described in *Anti-Fascism in Britain* by author Nigel Copsey as "disinterested historians". Disinterested not in history as such but in the extent to which anti-fascism shaped it. Notwithstanding the huge numbers who, over the generations, have rallied to the banner of anti-fascism (far more, incidentally, than either fascism or communism), it is indeed striking that Copsey's own research, which traces anti-fascism from the early 1920s to the late 1990s, is the first and only book ever published where anti-fascism as a mass movement is studied for its own sake. In the many hundreds of books devoted to either fascism or communism, anti-fascism where it intruded at all invariably appeared as a footnote. What other historical literature on anti-fascism there is, is restricted to several local studies, autobiographical accounts written by former anti-fascist activists and specific chapters in books where the radicals on the Left or Right remain the main issue under consideration. In other words, it is an area that is fatefully under-researched, a scholarly lapse that has caused opinion formers to conclude that anti-fascism can have been of little historic importance.

So over the years prejudice has continued to grow. Some historians, like Lewis and Thurlow, when they deign to address the issue, only grudgingly allow anti-fascism any influence in the marginalising of British fascism at all. Others, such as Roger Griffin, go further in divesting anti-fascism of any impact whatsoever, insisting: "what marginalises fascism, then, is the irreducible pluralism of modern society, and not the strength of liberalism as such, let alone the concerted opposition of anti-fascists."

Safe to say that it was widely felt the triumph of liberal values had also inoculated the less educated lower orders against any possibility of nationalist or racist infection.

"There has sometimes been an assumption, albeit explicit in some cases, that the indigenous population has been, or is, characterised by the extent to which it has imbued 'liberal' values. So from this perspective the primary reason for fascism's failure to take root has been/is the pervasive tolerance and forbearance of the British population. This approach although comforting is clearly inadequate and other factors have undoubtedly had a more significant effect... it would be a mistake to accept uncritically the notion of British exceptionalism" (Dr Mark Hayes, *Soundings*, issue 14, spring 2000).

Prominent among those "others factors" are the activities of fascism's direct opponents. So as well as assessing the impact of the physical force tradition on the growth of British fascism, Copsey also foregrounds the "overarching divide between 'radical anti-fascism' – with its emphasis on physical confrontation – and 'legal' forms of anti-fascism, a tactical division between, but also within, those forces actively engaged in opposing British fascism". Genuinely welcome though the Copsey study must be, there is also a need for a certain caution, for while in relative terms he allows 'radical anti-fascism' a fair crack of the whip, his objectivity is seriously compromised by a conclusion that loftily dismisses the radical anti-fascist analysis from 1995 onwards. By so doing, he lays himself open to the charge of an *ipso facto* rationalisation. In addition, while assuming to speak as an authority on the overall efficacy of physical force anti-fascism throughout the 1980s and 1990s, he never once consulted the activists themselves. Although it is true London Anti-Fascist Action (AFA) is given some recognition, he fails to take into consideration extensive AFA activity stretching from Oxford to Edinburgh where the impact on the Far Right (due to the smaller numbers involved) could sometimes be seen with greater clarity. Overall, however, Copsey's greatest error is his absolute rejection of the militant prognosis which, a full seven years prior to the election of councillors in Burnley, forecast the breakthrough as inevitable – and began to plan accordingly.

In the final paragraph this loss of objectivity steers Copsey toward what must now seem an embarrassingly upbeat conclusion: "As the 1990s draws to a close, barring an improbable reversal in fortunes at the European elections, the BNP's bid for electoral credibility looks almost certain to have ended in comprehensive failure." With literally his last word he goes even further, questioning whether "the public's ever wider acceptance of multiculturalism" might in time "marginalise fascism to the point that the need for anti-fascist activity will eventually disappear altogether?"

As a historian, it is Copsey's misfortune that his book was published prior to the 1999 European elections he refers to, because by taking over 100,000 votes in a 20% turnout it represented for the BNP a breakthrough of sorts. Though representative of a voter base of less than half a million nationally, it was nonetheless a near fifteen-fold increase on their vote in the general election in 1992, which ought really to have caused Copsey pause for thought.

But if the ill timing of the publication is put to one side, what the summary says about Copsey himself is also revealing. For while most definitely a very 'interested historian', his wildly optimistic final chapter merely reflects the same trust in the self-correcting ability of the political system that obviously serves to sustain the indifference of his contemporaries. This is not to try and argue that physical force anti-fascism has no limitations. Violence of the first resort can never be anything but an artificial and temporary remedy, but there are reasons other than mere activity that serve to make its validation provocative and compelling.

As early as 1995 AFA began to publicly warn that electoral penetration by the Far Right was something that could be expected and ought really to be prepared for. Needless to say, it was an analysis that was widely disparaged, and yet the militants had come to realise that the extreme lengths they were forced to go to in order to prevent the breakthrough happening earlier had exposed some startling and as yet unspoken truths which are applicable both to Britain and to mainland Europe. These are:

1) Multicultural arguments that place race and identity over class are being appropriated by euro-nationalism to devastating effect both here and in Europe.

2) Legal anti-fascism is impotent in dealing with the new Right.

3) If the absence of any Far Right electoral presence between 1977-2002 made Britain appear unique in Europe, it was chiefly because the application of militant anti-fascism was for much of the period also unique in Europe.

If only half true, as unsettling as things might appear at present, we may actually be in a lot more trouble than we think we are, which is why in writing this book we set out to make the case for militant anti-fascism without apology. Indeed when doing the research our original argument was that the preparedness of anti-fascists to use violence was not only historically legitimate but was largely unrecognised as *one* vital component in the democratic armoury. But given the other factors usually cited, the media, mainstream political opposition and mass demonstrations have proved to be impotent against a latter day BNP, so it can be argued that physical force played the more decisive role.

Of course we are happy to acknowledge that the impact made by anti-fascism, even outright victory, is often objectively hard to quantify, largely because it is attempting to prove a negative. Damning anti-fascism with faint praise has all too often been the result.

It is therefore fortuitous that, in the period we study, such a dodge is hardly possible, as it is only after the militant foot is removed from the fascist neck that the latter blooms politically. That is to say, the authority previously exerted by militant anti-fascism on events becomes that much clearer by what happens after it is no longer the foremost influence. Perhaps the key to fully understanding how we have arrived at where we are is to see the conflict between fascism and anti-fascism from the 1970s to the present day not as a series of victories and defeats, but as a continuum. So instead of representing one era marked by victories or defeats, the decades actually bleed into one another.

From this perspective the Far Right renaissance can be traced back not to 2001 but to 1981 when, with the electoral threat from the NF fended off, the victorious ANL was unceremoniously dumped by the Labour Party without any trace of gratitude or sentimentality. The response of the SWP/ANL leadership was panic. Overnight the strategy of open confrontation that had served anti-fascism so well previously was ditched. Thereafter when either the NF or the even more violent British Movement announced a demonstration, the ANL countered by holding a parallel protest but almost always in a geographically distant part of town – and, where the protest was mobile, invariably in the opposite direction.

Invigorated and emboldened, a vengeful Right freed from all electoral restraint stepped up the pressure. Race attacks spiralled. To some it had all the hallmarks of the Weimar Republic writ small. For at this stage capitulation on the streets would without doubt have granted the Far Right the 'free run' denied them only a couple of years earlier. That it never happened in this way is down to the militant anti-fascists in the shape of Anti-Fascist Action (AFA) who picked up the baton dropped by the Anti-Nazi League in 1982. From 1985 to 1997 AFA fought the entire Far Right including the NF, Blood & Honour, Combat 18, and the BNP to a bloody standstill.

Not too surprisingly, outside of the membership, AFA's hard-nosed methods won it respect, but few friends. Uniquely the organisation was routinely condemned by both Left and Right as excessively violent. In 1993 a *World in Action* 'exposé' denounced the organisation as "paramilitary", while BNP leader John Tyndall condemned MI5 "ineffectiveness" against what he described as "a criminal conspiracy". More extraordinarily a *Times* editorial called for "pre-emptive action" against militant anti-fascists "even if this means restricting rights of free assembly" (*The Times*, 18th October 1993). When asked by a *World In Action* journalist if AFA condoned the use of violence, "No…" came the laconic reply from the militant representative, "… we don't condone violence we – *promote* it."

It goes without saying that even the most just of causes are never entirely innocent. But with characteristic single-mindedness the militants ignored both the brickbats and bouquets and ploughed on.

On 17th March 1994 the BNP, by now the largest Far Right party, controversially but decisively, turned its back on all forms of paramilitary activity and fully embraced electoral work as the way forward instead.

Today the BNP is 'sexy'. In terms of latent electoral support the Far Right is back to at least the level of popularity the National Front enjoyed when it briefly threatened to become the third biggest political party ahead of the Liberals in the mid 1970s. And while it might be true that the vestiges of 'Powellite'-style racism, symbolised by the call for forced repatriation, appear to have abated, for the time being at least, the essential fairness previously identified with the anti-racist cause has suffered from slippage too. With large sections of the population unconvinced by the logic of 'equal opportunities' and flummoxed by arguments fashionable in liberal circles that condemned any form of assimilation or integration as 'racist', racism was always going to reappear in one electoral form or another, once offered a credible opportunity to do so.

By the early 1990s some in the BNP leadership began to understand that, to appear credible to the electorate, the battle for the streets would have to be transformed into a battle for hearts and minds. And yet they hesitated to broach the subject openly for the simple reason that here was a political strategy reversal so complete it could only come about where the BNP tacitly admitted, to itself first of all, that the physical struggle had become counter-productive; a lost cause.

But if lost cause it was deemed to be, this was in no small measure a result of the pressure put on the BNP by AFA. This in turn raises an interesting question: in forcing the Far Right to abandon violence, did the militants also force the Far Right to find 'a better way'? Well, yes and no. As evidenced by developments, the BNP is now tapping into the 'reservoir of reaction' militants long argued existed, a theory substantially supported by the ability of the BNP to take on all comers, even in by-elections and with a membership (by no means all of them active) totalling just 3,487 in 2002. To be able to compete and win against the mainstream parties up and down the country despite such a handicap indicates the level of support for Far Right solutions being generated is way beyond the capacity of party activists alone.

With the benefit of hindsight, there are probably very few who would now argue that such a pool of support does not exist. A view endorsed by Dagenham MP Jon Cruddas who after the BNP vote went up by a further 20% in the local elections in 2007 said: "We have to accept that something palpable is happening here. The BNP is tapping into people's latent fears and disillusionment with the mainstream parties. The fact that the BNP achieved these levels of support despite the fact that the vast majority were paper candidates who did not put out a single leaflet or knock on a single door is particularly worrying."

But as we try to demonstrate throughout the book, to fully understand each stage of development it needs to be fully taken on board that the BNP did not actually create such a reservoir. All the evidence points to this latent support pre-existing the BNP reversal of strategy in 1994.

To a large extent the existence of such a reservoir was long accepted by both sides. Very likely it was only on this matter that there would be any genuine meeting of minds. As such, it goes some distance to explaining the motivation and level of commitment displayed by the individuals recruited to one side or the other. Contrary to the image of serial brawlers, this was always politics by other means. Or, as one AFA architect put it with it a straight face: "I never had any problem with the use of political violence, it was the *fighting* I didn't like." In other words, it was the political objective, not the methodology that excited.

At bottom what the militants achieved by taking up cudgels against the likes of the NF, BNP, C18 and Blood & Honour was to buy time for everyone else, by denying the Right the opportunity to properly tap into this reservoir five, ten, or even twenty years earlier. That they fought alone and their warnings were ignored is part and parcel of the militant's story and another reason for writing this book. It is a first hand account of what was largely a clandestine, almost subterranean, conflict that began as a holding operation that lasted for more than 15 years. Had the action been concentrated into a more limited time span (as was the case with the 43 Group or the ANL Mark 1) the battle for the streets could hardly have been ignored.

Remarkably too, unlike the 43 Group or the Anti-Nazi League who enjoyed tacit support from the Jewish community and Trade Union movement, AFA often had nothing more to anchor it than the sense of political responsibility drawn from its own analysis.

This sense of isolation could never have been more keenly felt than when three of their number were sentenced to a total of 11 years imprisonment in 1990, and the militant appeals to the Socialist, Labour and Trade Union movements of the time raised less than £10 for those jailed, their families and dependants. Yet the militants fought on, for and with each other, for the next five years, because they believed in the correctness of the cause, because they did not want to let anyone down, because they were aware of the price of failure and, if all else failed, out of sheer personal contrariness. If the level of resolve might seem scarcely believable today, it must be remembered that Britain in the 1970s, 80s and early 90s was a very different place. It was an era of industrial decline, flying pickets, insurrection in Ireland, the Cold War, state sanctioned killings, corruption amongst the police, conspiracies by the security services against the elected government, along with members of the establishment, retired generals and industrialists, allegedly considering trying to seize power in a coup. It was against this high-stakes backdrop that the fight for dominion of the streets was fought out.

What we try to do in this book is to convey the political thinking of some of the main anti-fascist players who, as late as 1996, current BNP leader Nick Griffin believed might need to be 'taken out' if new nationalism was to prosper. The qualities he feared were a preparedness to battle against the odds, an impressive stamina, unique vision, an ability to think the unthinkable and, on more than one occasion, to do the unthinkable.

In the telling of their story, although their names have had to be abridged or altered (one pseudonym is used throughout) for all the obvious reasons, the voices of the activists emerge unalterably authentic. By any standards it is an astonishing tale that is, without doubt, of legitimate historical interest. But it is also more than that. In truth, when looking at the confused impotence of anti-fascism across much of Europe, their story has a wider function, as it clearly has as much to say about the future as it has the past and, until the past is fully understood, the future will continue to be uncertain.

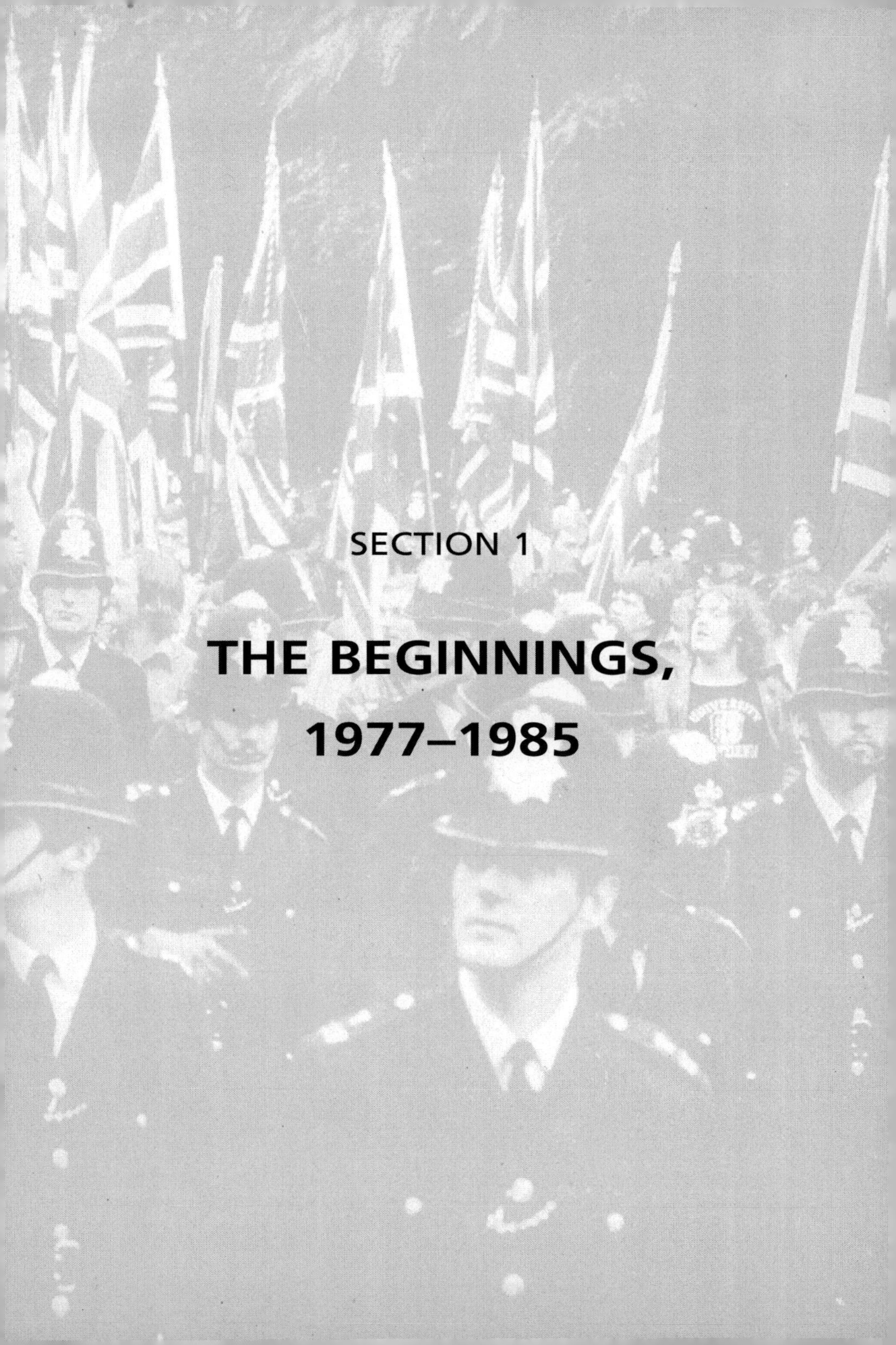

SECTION 1

THE BEGINNINGS, 1977–1985

Previous page: The National Front march in Lewisham on 13th August 1977, where riot shields were used by the police for the first time in England.

1.1

ROOTS, 1977–1985

Although AFA was formed in the summer of 1985, the roots of the organisation can be traced back to the anti-fascist squads of the late 1970s. The squads were in effect the all important physical force arm of the Anti-Nazi League (ANL), launched in 1977 to counter the growing threat from the National Front (NF).

The NF, itself formed ten years previously, had managed to bring together a number of small National Socialist groups alongside extreme right-wing Tories. The central plank of the party, which it made no attempt ever to deny, was openly racist: the repatriation of all Black and Asian immigrants from Britain. In the main, these were people who had been recruited to overcome the labour shortage after the Second World War.

While previous attempts at post-war organisation by the fascists had been decisively smashed by the 43 Group and subsequently the 62 Group, the NF proved to be a more robust opponent. And by linking up with, and recruiting from, existing community-based anti-immigration groups, as well as exploiting the electoral experience of disillusioned ex-Tories, the NF began to acquire public support. On the streets, too, the fascists made their presence felt and gained publicity through marches and meetings. As the post-war economic boom bust, the NF broke into the political mainstream, appealing to the middle classes with a traditional 'law and order' message on the one hand, and the working classes on the other by casting the blame for growing levels of unemployment onto immigrant communities.

And while the Left sought to depict fascism as an entirely 'petit bourgeois' movement, made up of and supported by the lower middle classes, the reality is the NF had inroads into the white working class, and in many areas had more support in these communities than the self-styled 'revolutionary Left' could ever dream of. For instance, in 1974 the NF Trade Unionists Association was launched and immediately became active in a number of industrial disputes. Needless to say, the growing evidence of support for the fascists amongst the white working class caused concern for Labour, who were worried about losing votes to the NF, which in turn led to increased opposition from Left groups and the Trade Union movement. Then in 1976 when the National Party, a split-off from the NF, secured two council seats in Blackburn, the scene was set for militant anti-fascism to make its entrance.

The Socialist Workers Party (SWP) in particular played a key role in the development of counter-gangs equipped to confront the burgeoning NF. Along with the NF they too began to attract trade union militants disillusioned by the Labour government, and through other fronts like the Right to Work Campaign and, later, Rock Against Racism also attracted young working class people with an instinctive hostility to fascism. This combination not only formed the backbone of a reorganised anti-fascist movement, but also meant from then on the fascists could expect to be challenged at work and on the streets. As the NF was to find out, the honeymoon period it had enjoyed up to about 1974 was definitely over.

1.2

LEWISHAM, 1977

For many the turning point came in 1977, when the NF sought permission to march through Lewisham in south London with the idea of provoking a response from the large West Indian community settled there. This was to a background of an escalating conflict locally between sections of that community and the police.

"In the early hours one morning, a large number of police, in a full-scale planned operation, descended upon a number of homes and arrested eighteen black youths. They were all charged under the notorious conspiracy laws, conspiring to commit crimes unknown with persons unknown. The code name for the police operation was P.N.H.20, which was reputed to stand for Police Nigger Hunt 20. Friends and associates of the accused immediately set up a defence campaign to assist them and publicise the case. Amongst other activities they started holding public meetings in Lewisham High Street. Very soon members and supporters of the National Front were subjecting these meetings to organised attacks.

"... A number of organised retaliatory raids were carried out upon the Front members involved, and large-scale stewarding operations were organised to protect Defence Campaign meetings and demonstrations. In an effort to counter this challenge to their ability to control the streets, the Front announced their intention of holding a national march and demonstration in Lewisham High Street.

"The SWP immediately called a counter-demonstration, calling upon their members to occupy the Front's proposed assembly point a couple of hours before they were due to assemble there ... On the day some five or six thousand anti-fascists turned out, making it the largest anti-fascist demonstration seen in this country since the war. A series of pitched battles followed as the police tried to force a path through the anti-fascists... Eventually, after managing to march just a couple of hundred yards, the Front were forced to abandon their plans. The counter-demonstration had been a complete success" (*Red Action*, issue 35).

The media outcry after Lewisham, the first time that riot shields had been used in England, was deafening; the *Sunday Times* asserted that "it was a frightening and tragic sight to see on a London street one group of extremists, backed by an artillery of bottles, bricks, rocks, staves and tins, advance on their rivals with such vicious intentions". Meanwhile the *Daily Telegraph* appeared to back the fascists by suggesting there should be a ban on "marches by the Socialist Workers Party, Communist Party and several sections of the Labour movement. Nor can native-born Englishmen properly be denied the right to march through a part of their capital city merely because it is settled by immigrants." For the *Daily Mail*, it was the police who were innocent victims: "In defending the right of the repellent National Front to march through the racially sensitive areas of Lewisham and Deptford, they presented themselves as the prime target for the Red storm troopers of the Left. But it wasn't bags of flour and placards and jeers they had to face this time. It was blinding ammonia and caustic soda."

While large anti-fascist mobilisations during 1976 marked an important watershed in the anti-fascist struggle, it was the events at Lewisham that really brought matters to a head. Soon afterwards, on the back of this successful event, the Anti-Nazi League (ANL) was launched.

Anti-racists in New Cross Road block the route of the National Front as they try to march from New Cross to Lewisham on 13th August 1977.

1.3

THE ANTI-NAZI LEAGUE MARK 1, 1977–1982

The official launch of the Anti-Nazi League in early November 1977 was not actually the first attempt to pull things together. Local and regional anti-fascist committees were already up and running throughout the country at this time, linked up through an umbrella organisation called the national Anti-Racist Anti-Fascist Co-ordinating Committee (ARAFCC). Though loosely structured it had brought significant improvements in intelligence gathering and also provided some insight into the fascists' overall strategic and tactical outlook. However, by the time it was decided to "create a national body to co-ordinate the AF/AR work" at a conference in June 1978, "to wage and help co-ordinate a struggle against racism and fascism in all their aspects," and to build "mass mobilisations against the racists and fascists," the more dynamic ANL was already setting the pace.

In addition, "coming as it did at a time of the escalation of the struggle and the relatively recent entry into it of women, gays, black organisations and trade unionists ... virtually everyone had different reasons for being there, and this proved to be more important than what we had in common. Given all these conflicts it is not surprising that this attempt to build a unified and democratic organisation failed." ('The Past Against Our Future, Fighting Racism and Fascism', 1980, *Big Flame*) It is interesting to note at this early stage how the national ARAFCC, an embryonic anti-fascist organisation, was hampered in its development by sectarian in-fighting, a scenario that AFA would later be made familiar with, but just as interestingly, overcome.

Right from the beginning the driving force behind the ANL was the SWP, buttressed as it was by prominent figures in the Labour and Trade Union movement and other Left groups. Popular bands, sporting celebrities and other individuals with a high profile were also used to endorse the anti-fascist message, ensuring that this had a far wider appeal than typical left-wing campaigns, while the ANL strategy of imaginative propaganda and physical opposition contributed to turning it into a genuine mass movement.

In a widely distributed ANL leaflet, *Don't Be Conned By NF Lies*, the Sex Pistols' Johnny Rotten said: "I deplore them. How could anyone vote for something so ridiculously inhumane?" Nottingham Forest manager, Brian Clough, added: "The Front are scum – scum of the earth. If you step in something dirty, you don't just say 'how nasty!' – you wipe away every trace of that dirt. We must fight the Front menace in every way that we possibly can!"

Using slogans like 'NF: No Freedom, No Fun, No Future', hundreds of thousands of leaflets were distributed, badges sold, stickers and posters put up. The message was simple: the NF=Nazis. In the Britain of the 1970s this simple message proved devastatingly effective. Of course the Second World War had only ended 30 years previously, which helped. As well as this, Britain was almost alone in Europe in having to deal with Left/Right violence, as elsewhere on mainland Europe fascist groups were numerically weak and politically isolated. Most could only dream of reaching the level of support that the NF had achieved in Britain. Indeed the French FN, led by Le Pen, actually sent activists over to Britain to study the *modus operandi* employed by their English counterparts, which they subsequently, with some important refinements, put to good use at home.

While accepting that ANL propaganda was central to pinning the nazi tail on the NF donkey, it would never have been enough on its own, given the popular support enjoyed by the NF, particularly within sections of the working class. It thus fell to the ANL 'squads' to provide the ANL with the cutting edge, by emphasising that fascism would not only be fought, but that the hard men of the Right could be beaten. The squads are rarely mentioned now, for reasons we will go into later, but at the time were integral to the credibility of the anti-fascist counter offensive. Officially sanctioned by the SWP leadership, they were tightly organised groups of anti-fascists whose job was to attack NF initiatives, as well as defend anti-fascist events.

One former squad member, Jim Kelly, recalls that prior to their emergence, "the SWP had been systematically attacked on their paper sales. John Deason, a SWP Central Committee member organised stewards to defend local activities. This led to a partial retreat by the NF. This was the beginning of the infamous 'squads', the 'squadists' as they were affectionately known, groups of party members organised to protect SWP activities. The success of this specialisation was later to become one of the most controversial issues within the party." For Kelly, it was, note, the very 'success' of the policy of counter-terrorism that later caused it to be so controversial.

"The acknowledged leader within inner east London was a PE teacher from Hackney, John W. Micky Fenn, a TGWU shop steward from the Royal Group of Docks, led the outer east London squad, whose core was a group of fellow dockers. Micky Fenn stood out; he was an excellent organiser and a wonderful public speaker totally committed to the struggle." Another and separate group led by a second-generation Irish bricklayer, Mick O' Farrell, Kelly describes as "legendary" (*Anti-Nazi League: A Critical Examination* by Jim Kelly and Mark Metcalf).

Inevitably clashes with the NF led to confrontations with the police. On one occasion Micky Fenn ended up in the Old Bailey charged with grievous bodily harm with intent, after a fascist suffered a broken leg, jaw and arm following a chance altercation in Newham High Street. Knowing he would eventually be identified, Fenn took the unusual step of actually turning himself in and making a statement. But when the trial came to court he pleaded 'Not Guilty', pointing out to the jury that as he, Fenn, stood at about 5ft 8in and the alleged victim at 6ft 7in was almost a foot taller, he not unreasonably feared for his life and fought back in self-defence. The strategy worked and Fenn, a thoroughly engaging character, was acquitted.*

The squads emerged against a backdrop of deepening economic crisis. Desperate to be perceived by the electorate as a 'party of action', the NF set out to physically disable the Left, and thereby prevent socialists offering any political alternative, either to the mainstream parties or to themselves. Hence, left-wing paper sales were attacked, public meetings smashed up, and demonstrations harassed as a matter of routine. In Manchester, for example, it was a joint fascist and Loyalist attack on a National Council for Civil Liberties meeting on Ireland held at UMIST (University of Manchester Institute of Science and Technology) which demonstrated the urgent need for anti-fascists to organise effective stewarding and, all importantly, take the offensive when the opportunity presented itself.

Denis: "Here John P. was the catalyst. He pulled together not just ANL/SWP members who were 'up for it', but also recruited from rival Left groups. Alongside them were a useful number of street fighters from outside the organised Left who came to the fore during this period. Within a short period of time 'the Squad's' reputation impacted on the confidence of both sides."

Between 1977 and the general election in 1979, the ANL squads systematically turned the situation around by launching retributive attacks on fascist paper sales, meetings and marches. Micky Fenn operated mostly in his own borough of Newham and, if the opportunity presented itself, went 'skirmishing' in Barking. The success of his outfit in these boroughs meant that when the SWP came under

* During the making of the AFA documentary in 1991, Fenn stunned the BBC crew arranging his interview when he recounted an incident that occurred after his acquittal. He started to receive threatening phone calls late at night: "You're a hard man Micky, you're a dead man Micky." More worryingly, the caller revealed certain information about his work on the docks that could only have resulted from fairly determined surveillance. All the calls came through at about 11.30pm. Eventually, Fenn made a guess at the identity of the caller. He rang Albert Chambers, a leading member of the British Movement. His wife answered. "Is Albert there?" he inquired. "No," the wife replied "he's in bed." "That's okay, don't wake him, but get a pen and paper – I have a recipe for him. First, you'll need a bottle, a milk bottle would be good but any bottle will do. Then you'll need a cupful of sugar or detergent, followed by a half-pint of flammable liquid and some kind of a rag. Tell Albert... tell him Micky rang." The recipe was for a Molotov cocktail. There were no more calls.

pressure in Lewisham in south London it was from east London that the political leadership sought advice.

"A problem arose then in Lewisham which was very, very serious and one of the Central Committee... John Deason, came round my house with another member of them and asked us what we should do. So we had to go over there, literally as advisers. Now at the time I'd already been arrested on fairly serious charges, so all I could do was go and tell them, you know, what we thought. And we had to go to a pub called the Oxford Arms in Southwark. When we got there the branch was upstairs. It was, I think, the Friday, before the actual operation, not the Friday before, but the Friday before that – they had a week to organise in other words. And we told them that we think they should [continue to] sell their papers. What had actually happened in Lewisham was that they were standing outside Lewisham Station, about four or five people – a couple of girls and a young black kid and somebody else – and about fifteen thugs had come out of the pub all dressed in military uniform and attacked them and seriously had them up. The week after that there was a counter-demonstration by the people in that area against this behaviour. That was immediately attacked by the National Front. They slung bottles of paraquat poison at them, slung bricks at them, iron bars at them and the whole of that area of SWP was literally in a state of disintegration. They were very, very worried, very frightened and rightly so. If I'd been in the same position as them I would have been very frightened. But we tried to calm them down and said we would have to do something.

"Now what we proposed doing to counter-attack was this. We got five groups, as I've already pointed out we used to operate in groups of five. We got one group from inner east London, one group from outer east London and one group from north London and the other two which I don't know where they came from; one came from west London and the other come from... sort of round Bermondsey area, and the only way we could do it was to get someone that knew all of them. Now these people would be fighting, there would be four people who all knew each other but might not know the other four, or the other four, or the other four, which could cause a tremendous amount of confusion (giggling). So what we did then was we got a fellow to co-ordinate the whole thing who knew all, who knew at least one from all the five groups. His name was John W. and he was particularly good. He was very good in that sort of anti-fascist work. And I didn't attend but I was listening to what was going on. Now we pulled out the best group we had in Newham, who were very, to use a cockney phrase – warm, very warm on the stones. And apparently what happened was this: they, these five groups, went to the station. Each one of them identified... the leader identified himself to John W. who was controlling the co-ordination of it and waited in the crowd outside Lewisham Station looking in the shop windows, etc. And these four or five reasonably brave people got up and started selling *Socialist Worker*.

"Sure enough after twenty minutes, like the genie out of the bottle, out come the fascists. And as far as I was told, fifteen, twelve, fifteen of them – all in military uniform – and immediately went to set about the paper sellers. They were immediately attacked by the group I used to be involved with in Newham… [and] were supported by the second group. In fact… only two groups got involved. In other words only eight people got involved. But, because they attacked so fast and knew what they were doing, I think about six or seven of the fascists went to the pavement and got serious, serious treatment. And the others dispersed, in other words, ran away. About four weeks after that we were in a demonstration right through the middle of Hoxton, and Hoxton wasn't a very nice place to be demonstrating at the time. And sure enough who was on the corner of Pitfield Street – there's a roundabout – but this little group. They were about fifteen-handed. Still in their military uniforms and still carrying, literally, scars and black eyes and everything. So we stopped and said to them, 'Didn't you have enough three weeks ago?' Once again I shouldn't have been there but I was. And they didn't do anything, they didn't do anything. They'd had one dose of it and they didn't do anything.

"So the next week after that, the Socialist Workers Party organised a demonstration in Lewisham where a lot of people turned up, not SWP, because the SWP couldn't pull out the crowds. We relied, everyone relied on other people, Labour Party, etc., and they had a march through Lewisham. It was very hot and we put over a hundred and fifty people there who'd stirred it. A very simple operation. In groups of ten, in blocks going down along the back of the demonstration, along the sides. Just to protect the march. Not to attack anybody because we couldn't see anybody there that was going to attack. The march went off, it was very successful, right, and that was the end of it. We were very pleased. There wasn't no trouble. There were a few people who come out of pubs, shouting and hollering, you know, 'Nigger lovers', etc., the usual sort of stuff. But nothing actually occurred. We were told by our south London organiser about three or four weeks after that that the National Front sent over a hundred people to attack the march. But because they could see there was discipline and order, and because they could see there were people not on the demonstration – we never went on the demonstrations – on the pavements and behind, they could see they were going to be ambushed and they withdrew.

"So we've gone from a situation of complete defence, complete defence, you know, in fact being devastated, to stabilisation, right, with the fighting outside the station when they were selling papers, to being in front. By having a demonstration, it went right through their… their heartland and it wasn't attacked. So we considered we were in front. And it was then that the idea came across about having a big march by the National Front to counteract, to balance. The National Front obviously had to, they could see, I mean people like Tyndall and Webster could see exactly what was going on. They were losing momentum. So they decided, they had this big march, to counteract the balance and I think everybody... knows what happened. They were smashed to pieces" (Interview with Micky Fenn, BBC transcripts, *Open Space*, 1991).

In this way the damage inflicted on the NF reputation and morale at Lewisham, and earlier at Wood Green, was systematically reproduced around the country with confrontations in Leicester and Birmingham making headlines. A most important, but largely unnoticed, consequence was the disproportionate impact on middle class supporters of the NF, who no longer felt comfortable turning out for marches or public meetings, with female supporters and the less physically robust regarding it as increasingly risky to attend public or private NF activity of any kind.

Robert Taylor was Sheffield organiser for the NF at the time of Enoch Powell's speech in 1968. The speech legitimised the NF to the extent that he was able to build a branch on the back of it with encouraging signs of support for the first time from the mainstream Right. "Before Powell spoke, we were getting only cranks and perverts. After his speeches we began to attract, in a secret sort of way, the right-wing of the Tory organisations" (Socialist Worker pamphlet, *The Case Against Immigration Controls*). Needless to say, for the more timorous recruits, the level of anti-fascist violence being visited on supporters of the party or even those who made contact with it, no matter how discreet, presented an an enormous psychological hurdle. They retreated.

Amongst the more combat ready NF recruits, anti-fascist victories caused a thinning of the ranks there as well. In this way the NF was gradually, but perceptibly, reduced to a physical and political hardcore with, eventually, the skinhead cult coming to be regarded as not just the physical, but even the cultural vanguard. To compensate for this turnover, along with recruiting directly from the football terraces, another area of working class culture the NF sought to dominate was the music scene. Large gangs of fascist skinheads would frequently turn up at gigs to influence, recruit and intimidate. A Rock Against Racism leaflet provides an indication of the flavour and scale of the offensive:

"Looks like the wonder youth of the National Front and the British Movement have suddenly discovered the joys of music. It's not so long ago that Fuehrer Tyndall & Co. were preaching against the evil of those naughty 'jungle rythumms' and 'degenerate' rock music. Now we've got the master race performing its own strange rituals in dens of degeneracy like the Rainbow and Hammersmith Palais ... Closing down SHAM's last stand with a bit of military formation dancing onstage, tufty club salutes to Stiff Little Fingers at the Palais, thrusting dirty bits of paper in yer hand in the bogs at the Electric Ballroom, having a go at the Ruts at the Nashville, getting well turned over by the Upstarts' roadies and bottling a few innocent faces at Conway Hall. All good clean fun for real men. When Jimmy P. told the audience at the Rainbow that he did it for them and all they wanted to do was fight, he was wrong. All right he was pissed off and with good reason. Sham was shut down by the same BM/NF music lovers that have been doing their SS intimidation bit at gigs recently. And they are doing their best to send the SUBS, REJECTS, UPSTARTS, SLF, RUTS, etc., the same way. ONLY IT WON'T BE SO EASY!"

"My first sighting of fascists in action," journalist Mark Steel recalled, "was when a punk band called The Lurkers played at Thames Polytechnic in Woolwich. There was nothing especially political about the event until some 50 fascists took their shirts off, revealing T-shirts displaying the British Movement logo. 'Sieg Heil', they chanted, and set about attacking everybody in the room. The band was attacked, and dozens of people were pummelled, left to lie in a corner screaming for help. Stunts like this were common, and a lesson in the tactics of fascism. One argument was that the way to defeat these people was by making their arguments look stupid. But it was doubtful whether it would have made much impact, as a 16-stone skinhead rammed his fist into your eyeball, to point out that he may well be descended from a Roman." (*Independent Review*, 20th March 2001)

Instructively, there was no call to arms by the Left as a whole. But when a relatively small gang of fascists, numbering no more than a 100 or so, led to the abandonment of an 8,000 strong anti-racist carnival in Brixton in 1979, elements in the rank and file again concluded that 'making their arguments look stupid' was probably insufficient.

Counter-gangs were organised to take the fascists on at their own game: intimidation. Popular venues like the Electric Ballroom in Camden and The Greyhound in Fulham played host to the politically motivated mayhem. The sense of dismay and incomprehension of onlookers caught up in such encounters is vividly captured in an account of one such clash carried in an anarchist magazine called *The Leveller*. So mixed are the emotions in this article, it could read as a parable for a strata of the Left who made it plain they considered the cure to be at least on a par with the disease. Certainly, when considering what *The Leveller* honestly admits was already happening prior to the intervention of the small group of 'squadists', the sneering condescension and political ambivalence is still pretty extraordinary.

The title of the piece is 'Crass – "heavy mob invade"'. Perversely the 'heavy mob' reference is not to draw attention "to the danger of the new fascist tactic of breaking up rock concerts" but to "a group of heavies claiming to be from the SWP" – who confronted them. Patently, even with each side so graphically painted, for many on the liberal Left, to be properly anti-fascist it was necessary to be something other than working class. So, with the anti-fascists being described as looking like a 'football gang' in dress and demeanour, it made it almost impossible for some, it seems, not to regard them with distaste and suspicion. There is a noticeable tone of satisfaction as the authors record that a complaint from *The Leveller* to the SWP had triggered "an internal inquiry into the evening's events".

For physical force anti-fascists, this ill-concealed hostility would prove a recurring theme. The concert benefit had been organised as a fund-raiser for the defendants in the celebrated 'Persons Unknown' trial, when a number of people were arrested and charged under Kafkaesque conspiracy anti-terrorist legislation. One of those on charges of 'conspiring with persons unknown' was the author Ronan Bennett. Previously he had served a year on remand, charged with the shooting dead of an RUC sergeant in Belfast. He was acquitted. Another was Vince S., who was actually hospitalised in exchanges at Conway Hall, but would a decade later, as a leading member in the Direct Action Movement (DAM), play a pivotal role in anarchists getting behind the AFA re-launch in 1989. Just as crucially, when a move to create an anarchist-only AFA emerged, he commited to staying in it.

"The gig featured Crass, Poison Girls and The Rondos. It had been widely publicised and by nine o'clock there were about 500 people in the Conway Hall. The atmosphere was repressive and brooding, strangely quiet, too, for a rock gig, as though the punters knew something was going to happen. There was no security at the door and the organisers had abandoned any thought of taking money. Perhaps 30 or 40 identifiably National Front or British Movement youths marauded through the audience, some of them wearing NF T-shirts, swastikas, and, in one noticeable case, an Ulster Volunteer Force badge. The fascists seemed to move in organised groups, congregating in the bar, the foyer and the body of the hall."

If indeed the fascists visibly congregated in three areas of the hall at the same time it does suggest that larger numbers were involved than indicated. Anti-fascists actually involved in the fighting put the figure at around 80.

"The violence started early with the fascist groups picking on people. In one incident a black youth was surrounded and beaten and kicked until he ran out of the hall. And a group of skinheads took over the men's toilets and beat up unsuspecting visitors ... the police were called to the hall at about nine to investigate complaints about noise but left after the organisers assured them they could handle the situation." Plainly, whatever else they did, the one thing organisers did not do was 'handle the situation'.

"Shortly after the Poison Girls came to the end of their set, the atmosphere deteriorated noticeably: two of the organisers left the hall, others were drinking in a nearby pub." Bizarrely, given the circumstances, the excuse given was that the "fascists were in such a minority that the rest of the audience would either ignore them or deal with them." Given that there had been no security to begin with, the 'ignore them/spontaneously deal with them' disclaimer is one that would become very familiar to militants, employed as it usually was to cover a multitude of personal and organisational weaknesses.

"The real violence started at about ten with a confusing series of incidents. In one, a youth, said by one witness to be a 'real nutter', ran into the hall and shouted, 'Come and get me' at a group of skins. After a shouting match they all went for him. Scuffles broke out in the darkened body of the hall, bottles and cans were thrown and a number of people hurt. In a separate incident, which started at the door, eyewitnesses described a group of between ten and fifteen youths claiming to be SWP members, some of who were wearing Rock Against Racism badges. Other witnesses said they thought they were a football gang."

"They came in shouting 'Fuck The Front' and there was bother at the door. Someone hit a kid wearing a Union Jack badge and then they all piled in on him." Another witness said: "The SWP gave a Union Jack guy a right beating but he was nothing to do with the British Movement. One of them had a knife out. They said they were the SWP – they weren't skins or punks, they looked fairly ordinary. Their leader was Scots. Having dealt with the youth, this group then marauded into the hall and joined the general mêlée." While the intensity of commitment displayed by the anti-fascists caused some of the fans to run away from the hall, others evidently inspired by the resistance, instead "ran to join in the mêlée", leaving "the floor of the hall and corridors covered with broken glass and there were at least six separate pools of blood."

Needless to say the 'heavies' were indeed attached in one way or the other, if not all actually members, to the SWP. It is highly probable the 'Scot' identified as the leader was in fact Mick O'Farrell, who hailed from a working class satellite town outside London called Hatfield. Though second generation Irish, rather than Scottish, dressed as he invariably was in faded Wrangler jacket and jeans, and with an unruly ginger mop of hair and trademark moustache, save possibly for the ever-present Manchester United scarf knotted at his throat, he might easily have passed muster as an archetypal stocky and combative Glaswegian. He enjoyed personal notoriety amongst the Far Right, who christened him 'Red Mick'. In one encounter in Hammersmith, at a music venue called The Greyhound, he was drinking in the bar when word circulated of his presence. A large muscular skinhead stripped naked to the waist emerged from the crowd and stepped up to his table. 'Is this him?' he inquired of a lackey. O'Farrell, meanwhile, was eagerly trying to catch the eye of his companions variously playing pool or otherwise engaged in the packed bar. 'Are we ready here?' he called out, as brawny arms pulled him from his seat. As he admits, the next he remembers is finding a broken beer tumbler in his hand and the fascist slowly sliding down his legs. The usual pandemonium ensued. A fascist who lost part of an ear ran around screaming inconsolably: 'Look what the commies did to me, Patrick!'

O'Farrell's reputation was cemented when he had organised and led a full-frontal, hundred-strong attack on fascist supporters during a Madness gig at the Polytechnic in his hometown of Hatfield in the spring of 1979. The attackers smashed their way through a glass door to get in. While there were many casualties, there were only ten arrests, which inevitably included O'Farrell.

From late afternoon, as unwary groups of NF supporters alighted from the train at Hatfield British Rail station, they came under attack from as many as a hundred locals in the town centre. One skinhead was slashed across the buttocks with a cut-throat razor as he tried to escape over a fence. During the gig, and afterwards too, as they made their way back through the darkened streets – the local council kept public lighting to a minimum in order to keep down the rates – even though accompanied by a police escort, the visitors suffered repeated assaults en route to the train station. Two youths wielding a heavy garden chain emerged from a darkened alley to impact on the convoy like grapeshot.

Suggs, the lead singer of Madness, publicly condemned what he saw as anti-fascist excesses. In news items and in radio phone-in programmes later, band members and right-wingers alike expressed dismay at the level of aggression on display. *Socialist Worker*, however, felt sufficiently sure-footed to capitalise on the growing ANL reputation for lawlessness, by publishing a centre-spread interview with Mick O'Farrell in which, among others things, he explained the attractions of football hooliganism for working class youngsters to its readership. And with more than thirty hooligan-related convictions to his credit he was more than qualified to do so. Writing from Brixton prison, while on remand on charges relating to the 1981 riots, O'Farrell commented on the period:

"Two years ago, the nazis conducted a large scale drive around the music circuit. It went from strength to strength, the high water point being the disruption and abandonment of the anti-racist carnival at Brixton attended by 8,000 people. A group of socialists organised together and in three sharp encounters opposed them on the basis they had been building on. Their committed supporters were beaten, but far more importantly the Left had proved to the nazis' periphery that they could be beaten on their own ground, and not merely proved wrong to a meeting of 20 people. The two results of these initiatives were that the nazi activity at gigs almost ceased, yet the people who brought this about were unanimously derided by the SWP leadership" (*The News Socialist Worker Forgot*, 1981).

Others who, like him, would go on to become founding members of AFA, learned their trade during this period, understanding perfectly how forceful a combination of mass propaganda, carnivals and physical confrontation could be. However, when the Tories won the 1979 general election, with no little help from Thatcher's anti-immigrant 'swamping' speech, the principle political casualty was the NF, whose vote and entire electoral strategy collapsed, causing the political situation on the ground to alter dramatically overnight. Pre-existing fissures in the NF leadership led to recriminations and organisational splits. All importantly, as we will see, this was not quite the same as total ideological rejection, which liberal anti-fascism would pass it off as later. In the meantime, for militant anti-fascists on the streets, it was very much business as usual. For, freed from the constraints of respectability, the NF, supplemented by a hard-line British Movement, was out for revenge.

1.4

THE MANCHESTER SQUAD

So determined was the onslaught from the Far Right that by late 1980 the ANL in Manchester, which had been wound down by the SWP, was re-launched by rank and file anti-fascists contrary to the wishes of the leadership. The reformed ANL contained many of the anti-fascist street activists of the late 1970s who had now embraced the concept of political organisation as well as street activity. When the NF in Manchester set up its own football team, 'The Lily Whites', they were quite literally kicked out of the park, and out of the league, by tough-tackling anti-fascists.

In response to increasing and virtually unchallenged attacks on left-wing paper sales and meetings by the NF, the Manchester Squad had been brought together in 1977 under the stewardship of SWP member John P. Initially the membership was drawn entirely from the orbit of the SWP, along with individuals from other Left and anti-fascist groupings, including Searchlight. In the early days the squad were driven to operating in secret, meeting only in safe areas like Hulme where, because of the Irish and black population, its members were unlikely to run into any un-catered for opposition. The existence of the squad was talked about in SWP circles; however, the likes of Denis C. only came to their attention following an attack by him and others on an NF paper sale outside Chelsea Girl. This, on a day when the squad, following their stewarding of an Irish event which had earlier been threatened by the NF, failed to confront them in the town centre.

Denis: "A team of lads from Hulme made their own way in, slipping past the police cordon which had discouraged the rest of the Left. Bobby, a black lad, and myself found ourselves to the fore and made a run for them, only to see police running straight for us, which prompted a quick re-route as we both ran through the doors of Debenhams. Unfortunately for us more police were parked in the side street and we proved to be their easiest nicking of the day as we were chased right into the back of an open Black Maria!"

The squad operated with John P. as strategic planner and undisputed leader. Around him a core of SWP members like Roy Mac, Mick B., Phil Pyatt (RIP), Ian Mackintosh (RIP), Steve Tilzey, Paul B., Chris W. and Steve C. were the business end of the unit. Outside of these a wider circle of operatives drawn from other groups on the Left provided the squad with the capacity to mobilise up to 50 fighters when required. The squad was a product of the Left and represented the intent by the Left to physically confront fascism. As a consequence all left-wing activity took courage from the ability of the squad to underwrite the staging of public meetings and other events without undue concern of attacks from the Far Right.

But also, by introducing a new dynamic into the political equation, it drew respect from a section of working class youth that would not normally be motivated by left-wing rhetoric, much less get in line to join the Party. Nevertheless, from their own experience they identified totally with the need to use violence against a violent party like the NF. The street capability these tough working class recruits brought with them was of obvious benefit in itself. Both broadening the squad's capability and ambition but, as well as that, copper-fastening its operational independence by subtly shifting the support base from itinerant Left groups to the geographical areas inhabited by these same militants. And in the same way they had been exploited by the Far Right in other areas in the past, the sudden emergence of local 'faces' as key anti-fascists secured the allegiance and reputation of neighbourhoods almost overnight. This, plus the network of contacts established through Borstal or football gangs, opened up the possibility for militants to extend their area of operations from the city centre to most of working class Manchester. With no 'no-go areas' for anti-fascists, there could be no fascist strongholds either; defence quickly became offence.

Another significant addition to the polarisation in Manchester was the impact of the H Block Hunger Strikes in 1981. In tandem with the battle of wills inside Long Kesh, the resurrected Manchester Hunger Strike Committee organised public meetings and street protests that inevitably attracted violent Loyalist/fascist opposition. The issue of Irish nationalism has always proved a great motivator for the fascists in Manchester, especially after 1974 when they had been successful in violently driving the historic Manchester Martyrs Commemoration off the streets amid much anti-Irish hysteria in the aftermath of the Birmingham pub bombings. And as much as fascists lined up with anti-republicans, worryingly for the SWP, physical force anti-fascists just as enthusiastically made common cause with the pro-republicans. As events over a decade later would dramatically illustrate, this crossover would indeed prove both enduring and combustible.

Denis: "Now, as well as drawing anti-fascists toward Republicanism, the events of 1981, to the dismay of the Far Right, also drew many second generation Irish into the orbit of anti-fascism. Lads like Dessie Noonan* and Paddy Logan, whose legendary street-fighting reputations, even back then, were fully justified, threw in their lot with us. Hugely charismatic, Dessie had the delivery and timing of a

* An estimated 15,000 attended the funeral of Dessie's younger brother, Damian. When, in turn, Dessie died prematurely in July 2005, after being stabbed in a street fight, his funeral featured on Channel Five News. "A powerful teenager," was how Michael Showers, head of the Toxteth based crime family who met Dessie on the remand wing of Walton Jail in about 1980, remembered him.

professional comedian. He was larger than life and everyone in Manchester knew him, or knew of him.

"Without fail every event organised, from prison pickets at Strangeways to black flag rallies, to meetings with Sinn Fein speakers would see the Far Right turnout, so there was no shortage of action. Sinn Fein speakers were such a guaranteed attraction, at one stage there was talk of setting up a meeting just for their benefit!"

Initially John P. was understandably concerned that some of the larger than life characters, such as Noonan, would prove a destabilising effect. It says much for the ruthless efficacy of the more overtly political leadership that characters like Noonan were easily assimilated and happy to work under existing command structures throughout. Yet another arena of conflict centred on football. Ironically it was City, whose home ground was in the mainly black area of Moss Side, that had the hard core NF group within its hooligan element. John Scott, Brian Slater and Mickey Carr were all well-known NF activists and City hooligans. At United it was very different. But 'Reds against the Nazis' was set up anyway to pre-empt any similar initiative getting off the ground. Thousands of leaflets were printed and former Celtic and Manchester United favourite Pat Crerand threw his weight behind the campaign.

Denis: "We were looking for maximum publicity for the launch, so we approached Piccadilly Radio who agreed to run a story in the run up to the game. I agreed to do an interview and for obvious reasons I asked them not to broadcast my name. 'No problem', they say. A couple of hours later someone rings me up to tell me they had heard me on the radio. 'How did you know it was me?' I ask. It turned out they had run the interview uncut! The leaflets were well received by United fans, but less so by police who sought to move us off the forecourt into Warwick Road. Pat Crerand intervened to remind them that they were on private property and stopped them taking us onto the street where it was likely the obstruction charges could be better applied."

The NF was routinely leafleting supporters at Manchester City's ground. And when 'Blues Against the Nazis' was set up, the anti-fascists were immediately attacked. One NF member, Karl Heald, was arrested after attacking a woman anti-fascist. He was less combative when squadists turned up for his court appearance. And even less so when they found out where he worked.

Denis: "We received a tip-off that he was working at the Grand Hotel in Manchester. We go take a look and there he is behind reception. We about turn and leave, not sure whether the recognition was a reciprocal experience, but nevertheless we did not want him to know for sure that we knew where he was working. The following week, another member of staff shows us a side door round the back that led to the staff kitchens. So as not to arouse suspicion, two of us would go in and help ourselves to the food on offer, and sit down for lunch. Our target did not come in while we had lunch. Unperturbed we attended every other day for two weeks, all to no avail. The food was great, but our target was definitely off his food."

At the next home game when a confident NF attacked again, they were counter-attacked by a black gang also aligned to City, known as the 'Kool Kats'. One NF member was chased into the club's souvenir shop and severely beaten. Manchester City Chairman, Peter Swales, later declined an invitation from the ANL to publicly condemn racism and fascism, citing the souvenir shop incident as proof that 'one lot was as bad as the other'. Nevertheless, when faced with the prospect of internecine conflict with City's black hooligans, the NF's ambitions at City were put on hold. This did not mean that the Far Right identification with City evaporated; it was thereafter so low-key, the crossover in the city between political and football loyalty became almost indivisible. On one occasion some years later, 200 'blues' marched from Rusholme and launched a full-frontal attack on The Whalley Hotel where a number of Manchester United fans irrevocably linked with AFA boasted they would be drinking prior to the game. The revenge attack was as a result of injured pride following an incident six months previously when just half-a-dozen well-known political/football hybrids walked into the same pub when it was packed with City fans.

Denis. "The sudden silence as we walked in told us we were recognised as Reds immediately. Craig was at the bar and when I told him the City NF boys were in he didn't believe me, until he looked round and saw Mickey Carr standing next to him at the bar. One of our boys started laughing; 'You can tell it's him, he's still wearing the scars from when it kicked off in the Cyprus Tavern!' Carr said nothing. He acted as if we weren't there. We took our beers and had a good look round and began to move outside where we would have more room to manoeuvre if things turned nasty. On the way out I was approached by Daffy, one of City's boys. 'Are they who I think they are?' I asked him, indicating the main group containing the NF. 'Yes', he replies, 'but they don't want any trouble with you lot.' Their body language bore this out but, as more and more City fans began turning up, we pulled out anyway rather than overstay our welcome. One of the lads nipped into a shop doorway while the rest of us carried on. Ten seconds later there was a muffled shriek as the spotter they had sent after us was plucked from the street and given a crash course in counter-espionage techniques."

When six months on City came for revenge, their targets had been and gone. Startled locals and ordinary 'scarfers' were forced into mounting a heroic defence using tables and chairs to hold the door. The front page of the *Manchester Evening News* carried the story. Proof of the confusion of loyalties as well as bragging rights is evident from the account of the same incident in the football hooligan book, *Guvnors* by Mick Francis. Francis is mixed race and yet, in his version, it is twenty heroic Blues defending The Whalley from 200 rampaging Reds!

Not long after the '81 riots in Moss Side, word reached the squad that the NF were again using a pub called The Pack Horse in Deansgate in the city centre for meetings. Previously when the NF had met there a bugging device had been used to record their meetings. However, anti-fascists also needed to establish if the information coming through was correct. So, just after opening time one Sunday evening, three anti-fascists drifted in.

Denis: "The downstairs layout was such that until you went into the back room, you couldn't see who was there. We bought our bottles of coke, old style, thick glass, in the front bar, moved into the back room, picked up the pool cues and casually played pool. Five NF were already in, but only noticeable once you had walked into the room. The three of us armed with pool cues and coke bottles, carried on with our game of pool, as we surreptitiously observed the dawning acknowledgement of the NF contingent that three members of the squad were playing pool right in front of them. As two more NF arrived it was clear to us, apart from the growing odds against us, that the meet was definitely on. We breezed out to a chorus of under breath curses from our friends in the NF. Without saying as much, both sides knew round two would follow very shortly and, as we set off to round up the troops, the NF faced a dilemma. We went back to Hulme, knocked up a few lads, told them to meet outside the Royce in 20 minutes to go and smash the meeting. Out of nowhere Mikey W. turned up with a crew of twenty lads. Within the hour we had added ten more and set off for The Pack Horse through the back of Hulme. When we got there the NF, fearing the worst, had 'done one', but the landlord, smelling the fear on them, had already rung the police anyway. Hoping to catch some late arrivals, we set off to do a tour of the area. Then the police riot vans appeared. As they closed in, a large amount of weaponry was despatched on to wasteland behind us. A game of cat and mouse ensued, with a rather anxious post-riot Greater Manchester Police shadowing what was a mainly black gang whose plan seemed to change from trying to shake off the police to drawing them ever nearer the middle of Hulme before dispersing into the labyrinth of underpasses and connecting high level walkways."

After such a close shave the NF could hardly book The Pack Horse with any confidence in the future, not least because the landlord would have had the wind up. Slowly the licence to legally operate was being revoked and with that the life was being squeezed out of the NF in the city. Yet up to the early 1980s there had been a determined NF attempt to establish and sustain a weekly paper sale in the city centre. Naturally this became a focal point for the squadists. Attack followed attack, with a near fatal blow delivered when the entire NF group was ambushed at their meeting point.

Denis: "A number of set piece confrontations outside Chelsea Girl had led to 'nickings' on our side, mainly as a result of the police backing up the 'legitimate' paper sale by the NF. For their part the NF turned up mob-handed to secure the pitch regular as clockwork. It was this knowledge of their reliability that allowed us the opportunity to ambush them en route and away from the watchful eyes of the police.

"The squad split into groups and took up position along Piccadilly. The idea was that as the NF passed the first group and were in the immediate proximity of the second group, that would be the signal to attack. However, as it turned out, a couple of them had spotted a couple of our lads and, suspecting something was afoot, advised that they split up into two groups. Their vanguard passed our forward group without incident, but ten paces on the ambush was sprung, anyway. Hit from both sides by our lads equipped with chair legs and carefully wrapped iron bars, the NFers scattered into the road in disarray. As anticipated, their rearguard, which contained the organiser, Anthony Jones, failed to engage, preferring as they later put it to 'stand their ground'! A number of NF supporters were hospitalised, including, according to the *Manchester Evening News*, a 'German soldier on leave from NATO duties'. An NF member, Charles Allen, defected to the SWP soon after and provided a graphic account of the near total collapse of NF morale as a result."

The SWP had organised a coach to attend a protest march against unemployment in Glasgow. Among all the regular Left travellers on board, one interesting new face sat near the back. One of the SWP took a leading squad member to one side and advised him there was someone purporting to be ex-NF on board. He was left alone for the day and casually observed: whom he made contact with, his mannerisms, and general demeanour. At the next Gorton SWP meeting the following week, two squadists turned up and discreetly extricated young Charles to the snug for a quiet chat about 'old times'.

Denis: "Charlie was very forthcoming and helpful about his past life, as he had undergone some kind of Damascene conversion. Fuck knows why. He was shown the mug shots, including some of himself attending NF activities; he put names to faces, some we knew, some we didn't. That Charles's departure came after the Piccadilly ambush was hardly surprising, and his version of events on that day provided us with an amusing insight into how effective our direct action had proved to be. Charley-boy confirmed that the NF had actually spotted one of the two anti-fascist teams lying in wait for them. As a counter-measure, the NF split into two groups so as to ambush the squad. However, their little bit of intelligence proved to be their undoing."

A psychological profile of Charles Allen at this time would probably have concluded that here was an insecure, emotionally neglected individual in great need of attention with a desire to feel wanted and important. Initially the NF had provided him with this but the effect wore off, just as the risk to his health from attending their events grew. Charles was a short, rotund individual, who would be running with a higher risk of capture, so to speak. The Piccadilly ambush demonstrated to him what would happen if, or rather when, his luck ran out.

In the early days following his change of allegiance, Charlie was made to feel important by the attention he got, both from the squad for intelligence purposes, and from the SWP as trophy value. He relocated to the fashionable left-wing suburb of Hulme, with some SWP members who were kind enough to share their habitat with him.

What triggered his eventual alienation occurred when news of a rather dodgy Oi band appearing at Manchester Poly, during the build-up to the Leeds ANL carnival, prompted a squad response. The arrival of a number of key players for a hastily convened meet proved of great interest to young Charles. His despair at being excluded was undisguised. As his star faded, his disillusionment with Hulme and the SWP grew in line with his newly acquired taste for amphetamines and various other herbal remedies. He needed a way out of Hulme, but his only guarantee of safety back in Levenshulme was by making peace with his enemies in the NF and to do so he would need to buy his safety with information on the Left.

Ambush in Piccadilly: Squad members on right of photo. Denis nearest window.

Denis: "He repaid Joan from the SWP who had put him up by ripping her off for the rent and legging it with her address books and diaries. The door was barely shut behind him before the NF were ringing Joan and others, variously gloating and making threats of imminent violent house calls. One night after repeated phone threats were made to Joan in the early hours, two of the lads decided to show the NF we were more able than they were to carry out their kind of threats. The lads went round to Bryan Nylan's house in Fallowfield (Nylan was on every NF committee going right up to national level) and put all his windows in.

"Ten minutes later they rang him to ask him if he was interested in buying any double-glazing. Nylan screamed about having 300 of our names and addresses. We told him to put a stop to the intimidating calls by his members to women whose numbers were in the stolen address books, or he would be wasting his time replacing the glass. Not surprisingly the calls halted immediately. After this Charlie went to ground, but following the delivery of numerous unwanted services, including three tons of ready-mixed concrete, his own cover he found wasn't standing up too well either!"

Coming to terms with their inability to sustain a regular paper sale, the NF adopted guerrilla tactics, turning up randomly, and dispersing early before any attack could be mounted. The SWP in seeking to fill the void both in Piccadilly and outside Chelsea Girl merely presented themselves as targets for NF attacks. This led to a variation on the old game of cat and mouse: this time with one victim but two predators.

Denis: "The SWP, numbering about 50 or 60, were being monitored by a useful looking NF team numbering fifteen, which was in turn being shadowed by a five man team from the squad. Just a car load; Roy Mac, Tilzey, Steve C, Doug R and myself. 'Little Roy', who had been doing 'obs' on the picket itself joined us later. We had taken up position in Piccadilly Gardens in readiness to attack the NF from behind, after they attacked the SWP outside Chelsea Girl, which all hinged on the SWP staying in position. On spotting the NF boys, the SWP vacated the pitch and sheepishly sloped away. The NF clocked their move, divert through Piccadilly Gardens to head off the SWP, which forces us to vacate our position. We make a quick exit next to Lewis's, and slip into the back of the SWP flock. As the NF cut across Piccadilly Gardens we are making our way up through the body of the SWP supporters, appearing on what was now the front line just as the fascists charge across the road to meet us head on in Piccadilly Plaza in what they thought was a textbook ambush.

"The fracas that followed was captured by a handy photographer who carried on snapping throughout as the startled diners stared open mouthed from ringside in the Plaza café. In anticipation of an easy victory the NF, seemingly intent on humiliating the whole SWP group began by attacking the women first and were psychologically unprepared for the lip-smacking relish of the squadists who tore into their main men. It was a catastrophe that accelerated the downward spiral of the NF in Manchester, whose only appearance in the city centre thereafter was the very occasional paper-selling cameo. An excellent set of photos subsequently appeared which showed not only the squad in action, but also destroyed the reputation of well known NF and Manchester City face, John Scott, who is pictured shouting the odds from across the road."

On a more regional level, the militants using 'Manchester ANL' as a nom de guerre also threw themselves into the campaign against NF Chairman, Andrew Brons, who was working as a lecturer at Harrogate Further Education College. Alongside the other regular interlopers – a group of young Asians from Bradford – Manchester 'ANL' left their mark on Harrogate NF on more than one occasion. 'Civic recognition' was finally bestowed on an unfortunate few with custodial sentences handed down by Harrogate magistrates after the British Movement were again attacked in the town. So, at a time when the SWP was thinking of winding up the ANL, the high profile activities of 'Manchester ANL' were understandably regarded with irritation, embarrassment and trepidation by the SWP leadership. When squadist trail blazing eventually led to eight of their number being arrested on conspiracy and kidnapping charges, the SWP was mortified at the constant ratcheting up of a struggle they desperately wanted shot of. However, one of the strengths of the squads was that, though organised by the SWP, many came from outside of the party. As with the set up in Manchester, the squadists from Hatfield, a working class town on the outskirts of London, were not all SWP members, and so did not always have tremendous respect for the party line or notions of political decorum. This, together with the reality that 'squadism' created a bond between the working class elements at a rank and file level, evidently made many within the Party hierarchy fairly uneasy, probably from the very beginning.

As far back as the 1920s, anti-fascism saw the employment of physical force as legitimate, if not entirely a matter of routine. The SWP initially followed in this tradition as well. With the dropping by the Labour Party of support for the ANL shortly after the 1979 election, the SWP leadership felt immediately isolated and vulnerable. Rather than acknowledge the problem, they sought to disguise their retreat by attempting to have this important aspect of the ANL strategy effectively scratched from the records. Not only was the efficacy of the squads called into question, but the reasoning behind their deployment was, and has been ever since, turned on its head. In this at least the SWP leadership has proved to be consistent. For over twenty years the line has remained steadfast: physical force anti-fascism is a dangerous and seditious diversion from the true line of march.

But as events since the mid-1990s indicate, the activity of the irregulars was at least as important an ingredient to the success of the ANL as the carnivals, the celebrities, and the propaganda work within the media.

Poster advertising the Rock Against Racism Carnival in Victoria Park, 1978.

1.5

SWP EXPELS 'SQUADISTS', 1981

Under the pressure of the general election post mortem, the NF now splintered into three smaller organisations, as the Far Right entered a period of reorganisation. Unbeknown to the rank and file, the leadership of the SWP also had some reorganising plans. There had been growing concern among a section of the leadership that their control of the organisation had been seriously diluted and there was now a need for some pruning to be done. Along with the punk tenor of *Socialist Worker*, other culprits deemed to be responsible were a myriad of rank and file groups that had sprung up in the trade unions. All naturally had sectional publications and leadership, none of whom, incidentally, ever had a hope of being co-opted on to the Central Committee. For differing reasons, other offshoots such as Women's Voice and the Right to Work Campaign also gave cause for concern. Ironically, it was this very decentralisation, typified by the likes of Rock Against Racism, that had caused many manual working class recruits to feel they had a stake in the SWP/ANL in the first place. But as far back as September 1978, when the leadership refused to deploy stewards from the second ANL carnival to help supplement a counter-demonstration against an NF march on the area of Brick Lane, there had been a growing tension between the political priorities and perspectives of the working class rank and file and a largely upper middle class leadership.

Among the latter there was a feeling the tail was wagging the dog. If reconciliation could not be brokered on their terms, a total clearout was considered the only solution. Some in the rank and file had begun to sense some such threat in the body language of the leadership.

Jim Kelly recalls: "An event took place a few weeks after Blair's funeral [a reference to an SWP member who was killed in clashes with police during an anti-fascist demo in Southall, west London, in May 1979] that sheds a little light on the leadership's thinking. Some local NF sympathisers threatened a comrade who worked in a pub in Bethnal Green. It was decided this had to be met head on. The following Saturday night comrades met in The Approach Tavern in Bethnal Green to sort out the matter. We then found they were drinking in The Rose and Crown in Cambridge Heath Road. It was decided to pay it a visit... a fight broke out and the pub was wrecked. After the following week's branch meeting I was informed by leading SWP member and college lecturer, Colin Sparks, that things were getting out of hand. The pub was situated around the corner from the SWP print shop in

Corbridge Crescent and was used by various nonentities on the Central Committee. As I remember, his words were 'It's too close to home,' which I took to mean the Central Committee, not the print works!"

For Kelly the death of Blair Peach was a defining moment for the Party. "His death, and injuries deliberately inflicted on Asian, black people and anti-fascists that night had a profound effect on the Party. Many comrades were shattered after almost two years on the front line."

Not too long after a leading member of the SWP, Alex Callinicos, came across an ANL leafleting operation at Chapel Market in Islington which looked under imminent danger of an attack by a larger group of fascists massing on the other side of the road. Recognised, he was duly invited to stand with his fellow members. "Not my role in the Party," came the curt reply, and on he walked. Though a relatively minor incident this did not, it seems, stop the leadership seeking to exploit it at a later date.* At the extremes, the gulf between the leadership and rank and file militants' understanding about what was politically acceptable was divided to a barely believable degree.

Ron: "One day in late October '79, I was sat in The Albert with one of the boys when J comes in. He pulls us to one side. 'There is something big going on,' he said, 'not the usual diet of booting the opposition we were used to.' We wouldn't be told the exact details until nearer the time. 'Are you in or out?' I'd known J. for a few

* A 'leaked' account of events in Chapel Market in 1981 features in a grotesque and vicious little essay in a pamphlet entitled *When this pub closes...* In it, rank-and-file anti-fascists are accused of regarding "many Front members more honest than Labourites and Trotskyites," and of being "good types really," and states that the "street-fighters" themselves "now serve as an inspiration to the currently fashionable gay nazi artists Gilbert and George."

Referring to Chapel Market specifically it went on: "In the early 1980s, as Tony Cliff was walking through Islington market, he stopped to watch some of his followers battling it out with the National Front, when something struck him as odd. His followers were on suspiciously good terms with the 'enemy' and the battle was obviously being conducted according to recognised rules. When the whistle blew for half-time, the antagonists bowed to each other and went to drink in the same pub (admittedly in separate bars). Cliff, a near teetotaller who genuinely detests fascists, ordered an inquiry ... it transpired that on a previous occasion, a rising young intellectual had been recognised by his own comrades and beaten up when he refused to join in the fun."

That this kind of nonsense was published in 1988, three years after the 'street-fighters' had been instrumental in forming Anti-Fascist Action, and written by someone who advertised himself as a critic of the SWP, exposes the near pathological loathing of the working class male ('gangsters molls' was the description for the female squadists) among sections of the orthodox Left that would disable, and then utterly destroy it, within a generation.

years and had become sort of his unofficial bodyguard – he was only a little bloke but lots of bottle – so I said 'I'm in.' The other lad looked from one of us to the other and said 'Me too.'

"On 4th November we travelled to London. We were to book into a hotel under the name of 'Mr Brown's party'. The next day, Bonfire Night, we were sat in the TV room, just us, no other guests, when a stranger comes in and inquires, 'Mr Brown's party?' 'Yep', replies A. 'Call me Derek,' said the stranger. He then produces photos of a building on an industrial estate located somewhere between London and Brighton. It was supposed to be a plastics factory but functioned as a print shop and GHQ for both the NF and BM. It printed *NF News* and a new book *Did Six Million Really Die?*

"Derek told us he wanted our help to break in and destroy the operation. We were there, committed and in. We hired three cars and fitted false number plates. Derek put a holdall in the boot of his car and we set off. It was dark by the time we got there. There was only one way on and off the estate along a circular road. We left a sentry with a walkie-talkie and a car at the entrance to warn of anyone coming. Some of the other factories were lit up working night shift, so once we broke in we deliberately put all the lights on, too. We opened up the loading bay doors, parking the two remaining cars there. Near the printing press were piles of *NF News* and copies of the book. The office was open. It was large and had filing cabinets all round it. Opening the filing cabinets, we came across names and addresses of fascists all over Britain and the continent. We began to stuff them in bags and loaded them into the car. On the far side of the factory, the wall was lined with metal lockers. We jemmied open the doors. What we saw astonished us. Hanging up in the lockers were Nazi uniforms, SS on the collars. There were guns, pistols in holsters and machine guns. We took them all, except for a few. The ones we left we hoped might help incriminate the owners when discovered by investigating firemen. Once the cars were loaded we poured petrol all over the place. Derek then opens his holdall and takes out some devices, black boxes with timers on the top. 'What have you got there?' I ask. 'A present from Mossad,' he replies with a grin. I didn't know if he was pulling my leg or not, but it was a professional looking kit. Derek put the devices in different places around the building. Then we closed the roller doors and drove off. Suddenly the walkie-talkie cracked into life. 'Police car heading this way.' 'Don't panic,' said Derek. About a minute later it passes us. We drove on in silence. As we came over a small hill about a mile away the sky behind us is lit up. 'That's the biggest fuckin' fireworks they'll have around here tonight,' laughs Mr B.

A month later we got sent a brown envelope. Inside it was a photo taken from the air. It showed a large blackened and charred patch of land. All that was left. On the back of the photo, "Well done lads, thanks." £50,000 was the estimate of the damage (the equivalent of about £200,000 nowadays). A former member of the 62 Group, Manny Karpel, was later arrested, charged and convicted for his role in the burning of the print works. He refused to name any accomplices and got two and half years.

By November 1980, when an 800-strong British Movement march was held from Marble Arch to Paddington, the mutual lack of respect between the rival philosophies was naked and ill disguised. In what would later become a familiar scenario, the ANL mobilisation had allowed itself to be barricaded into an alley by police. After the march had passed, some squadists looking for 'afters' ran into a hundred strong crowd of local youngsters, mostly black, with similar plans. They were delighted, as coupled with their know-how and the locals' enthusiasm they believed they formed a very formidable crew. Expectations were high until a member of the Central Committee, Pete Alexander, a tall gangly, bespectacled, sports coat-wearing graduate, suddenly assumed command and started giving orders. Local black youngsters looked bemused, as all offers of help with regard to directions were waved away while he short-sightedly pored over his A-Z in search of Paddington Station. By accident or design, the unwanted intervention meant that instead of the BM being confronted, the only item of note turned over on the day was an ice cream vendor's van. Small wonder afterwards that some of the militants present began to talk sedition with increasing fluency.

It was against this background that the leadership tentatively began to put the case that, with the collapse of the NF vote, SWP resources could safely be concentrated against the Tories; the 'Tories were the real enemy' and so on. But this done-and-dusted optimism did not tally with the experience of local activists. They regarded a total anti-fascist victory as somewhat less than complete, and so there were immediate rumbles of protest, particularly in Islington, just a few miles from Bethnal Green, which had become the centre of anti-fascist activity in London. Moreover, the splintering of the NF had brought what was described by Jim Kelly as "a violent criminal faction to the fore," who regarded Chapel Market "as their patch" and who "enjoyed considerable local support on estates like the Packington, as well as in the large Post Office District Sorting Office in Upper Street." When the grassroots activists, through the Regional SWP organiser, were instructed to pull up stumps, there was outrage. A mood of defiance soon swept the Party, sparked by the appeal from the local ANL organiser to put out an S.O.S. over the heads of the leadership to anti-fascists generally, to make up for the deficit created by the SWP withdrawal. Not only were SWP members from outside of the area drawn into the struggle, but, to the embarrassment of the leadership, rival Trotskyist groups like Militant and the Revolutionary Communist Party responded to the public appeal.

As Jim Kelly recalls, the result was that "Chapel Street Market became a violent battle ground on Saturday and Sunday mornings. Support for the struggle came from many different Left groups including Labour Party Militant supporters. The notable exception was the SWP. The few principled SWP members that turned up to show support were soon threatened with expulsion. The local SWP leadership also began a campaign of rumour mongering, accusing one leading ANL organiser of being mentally unstable. This method of character assassination was increasingly used instead of open and honest debate on the changing tactics needed to meet this more sinister new phase" (*Anti-Nazi League: A Critical Examination* by Jim Kelly and Mark Metcalf).

In the summer of 1980, thirteen SWP/ANL supporters were charged with obstruction in opposing the NF there. The defence fund gained considerable support locally. This enabled the issue to be taken up in trade union branches. Eventually, all but one of those charged was acquitted. Following weeks of pressure, one small and inaccurate report was carried in *Socialist Worker*. The further arrests and strip-searching of two women activists, and their subsequent acquittal a couple of months later, were totally ignored by *Socialist Worker*. In a small pamphlet, *The News Socialist Worker Forgot*, produced for distribution among Party members, John Newman, a local shop steward, wrote: "Increasingly, the idea of a broad movement against fascism has been falsely counterposed to the idea of taking on the nazis in their chosen territory – the streets. The words 'macho' and 'squadists' have been bandied about to describe any anti-fascist activity which CC [Central Committee] members didn't like or couldn't control. Incredibly, the more slavish of North London District comrades have felt justified in attaching these labels to activity at Chapel Market – which has included mass leafleting of estates, Right to Work and Save our Hospitals campaign, and two successful defence campaigns. On one week's notice, the Islington ANL 'squadists' organised a 400-strong rally in Islington Green ... which included Communist Party, Labour Party and International Marxist Group members, and was four times as big as a Nazi rally in Smithfield a week later." (*The News Socialist Worker Forgot*, 1981)

In what was starting to look embarrassingly like a mutiny gathering momentum, the SWP leadership, in order to stigmatise the activists among the rest of the SWP membership in particular, began also to define the dissidents as physical force 'specialists' with a limited understanding of, or fidelity to, wider socialist goals. This pigeon-holing was intended to politically emasculate them, but at the same time for many it was really only the 'squadists' who seemed to be taking the opposition to fascism seriously.

Meanwhile, though on a steadily downward curve electorally, the NF continued with intense activity at street level, with a greater passion in their violent attacks on the 'opposition'. Apart from just chastising political opponents they also maintained high profile paper sales at popular working class markets like Brick Lane, East Street and Chapel Street in London. Though smaller in number, provocative demonstrations also continued to draw recruits from among a seriously disillusioned young working class, as well as at football grounds and around the punk/Oi/ska music scene. And by maintaining a high profile they provided both motivation and political justification for the rapidly increasing level of racist attacks. On the other hand, situations as in Manchester and Islington provided the 'squadists' with the argument that, not only did the fascist gangs still exist, they could be confronted and beaten, and on their own terms.

For some time the parting of the ways was recognised by the SWP leadership as both welcome and inevitable, and a relatively minor incident at the annual SWP get together over the Easter Bank Holiday, at a miners' holiday camp in Skegness in 1981, was considered opportunity enough for them to show their hand. Following a scuffle late one night between members and roadies of a band called Oxy and the Morons, and a couple of people associated in the leadership's minds with 'Hatfield', which was by now a pejorative term, the leadership went out of their way to maximise existing disagreements.

One prominent 'squadist' from north London, who held his hands up to his involvement from the beginning, was ordered to a meeting with a couple of Central Committee members the following morning to explain himself. The accused was from a manual shop steward background, normally prized within the Party, and as such was more than capable of explaining his side of the story. In addition, he was contrite for what, with hindsight, he accepted might have been an error of judgement on his part. But the leadership had no intention of accepting a mere apology. The charges were listed and whenever he sought to correct various inaccuracies he was told to "Shut up!" Further attempts to clarify what occurred were greeted with a similar response. Finally he was confronted with an ultimatum: "Shut up! – Or you're off the site!" By now thoroughly pissed off, he responded with a challenge of his own. "So who's going to make me then?" Pete Clark, an upper middle class son of an industrialist, who had been sitting on a window sill with his arms wrapped around his knees, wondering bleakly, what 'the miners would say,' looked up startled. Both he and Deason exchanged worried looks. Clearly it had never crossed their minds that they might be personally expected to provide the escort.

And with sixty of his companions drinking in a bar nearby, calling for security and thus forcing the issue was out of the question. However once the ante was upped, the leadership saw an advantage in escalating it for the duration of the weekend, openly goading other squadists in order to net as many as possible. Recognising it as the stratagem it was, the squadists did not rise to the provocation, but not long afterwards five, including Mick O' Farrell, who had not been in the vicinity of any of the incidents, were named and suspended pending expulsion. The appearance at the Leeds ANL Carnival in July of some of those marked down for expulsion provided the leadership with due cause. Those targeted for the purge were accused of anything and everything. Predictably, accusations of sexism and racism featured prominently. A letter from Leeds District Committee, dated 6th July 1981, accused:

> "SWP members and supporters from Hatfield who arrived in Leeds on Friday night, ostensibly to assist with security (the invitation was from a Manchester squadist yet to be disciplined) and then proceeded to conduct a drunken rampage …
>
> A by no means complete summary of their crimes is as follows:
>
> - They alarmed, threatened and insulted the existing security team.
> - They attempted or threatened to do physical damage to SWP members, including Holborrow, Rudder, Marfleet, Parkin and Mulvey.
> - They subjected a section of the Leeds security team to insults, including a multi-racial group of young people who had slept on the stage every night.
> - They used grisly sexist profanities and most criminally of all, one of them referred to our black comrades as 'monkeys'.
> - Several of the Hatfield comrades were carrying knives which they threatened to use on us."

With the fingerprints of the leadership all over it, the party political nature of the summary rather gave the game away. "Clearly a very small minority of SWP members feel that the use of violence and individual terrorism is a preferable method to taking on the racists. The experience of mass movements such as the Carnival seem merely to offer an outlet for drunken behaviour which in style differs little from the macho loutish style of the nazis. We therefore call on the CC to firmly state the case against the concept of squads as a means of opposing the nazis."

After that any pretence of the accused ever being allowed a fair hearing was regarded as either pandering or superfluous. The appeal was instant, handled by a five man 'control commission', two of whom were personally on the SWP Central Committee (one of them, Pete Clark, had travelled the country prior to the meeting, speaking at branch meetings, explaining the leadership's view of events) while the rest were appointed by, and directly accountable to it. Laughably the actual chair, one Peter Bane, had previously been accused by the defendants of being directly involved in attempting to provoke at least one incident at Skegness himself.

Despite the mutual contempt now existing between leaders and led, the 'squadists' were surprisingly not prepared to go quietly. Instead, in the following months, both they and their supporters within the ANL continued to argue strongly that physical opposition was a vital component of any effective anti-fascist strategy, and anything else was tantamount to surrender. Inevitably there was considerable unease at the turn of events within the party generally. A decisive illustration of both the gulf between the two wings and their potential strength had been demonstrated

PIANOS FOR SALE OR HIRE
RUSSELL ACOTT

OXFORD MAIL

No. 15,903 MONDAY, JUNE 8, 1981 12p

HONDA MOTORCYCLES AND ACCESSORIES
HARTWELLS

Hospitals face one-day strike chaos

Gangs on the rampage as anti-Fascist demo erupts

Youths run towards the city centre after the attack at the Old Gate House.

SUPER! a dad at 85

Pub smashed by rioters

AN ANTI - Fascist demo erupted into violence in Oxford city centre.

A pub was wrecked, British Movement supporters beaten up, and St Aldate's police station besieged.

During the four - hour demonstration on Saturday:

STORY: ANNETTE HUMPHREYS, DAVID DUFFY, PETER McINTYRE and ALAN CARTER

PICTURES: CLIVE POSTLETHWAITE and PETER FLOYD

Rocks

Blood

Windows smashed by rioters at the Old Gate House pub.

The vandals' weapons — concrete blocks on the bar at the Old Gate House pub.

Noel Fitzsimons picks up abandoned placards near the Old Gate House.

A distraught Tom Rice, landlord of the Old Gate House, is consoled by fellow-landlord Archie Gordon, from the Kite.

THE OXFORDSHIRE BUSINESSMAN

BRIEFS

Murder case man in box

Advised

Walkouts hit payouts

Murder charge

Wife killer goes free

Couple murdered by armed intruder

Death of girl: soldiers quizzed

LOCAL WEATHER

TV—PAGE 2

'Benn's hit list'

Court told of clash at quiet pub

VIOLENCE and chaos reigned after five men started an affray in a quiet Oxfordshire pub, an Oxford Crown Court jury heard today.

By MARIA MARTWOOD

Crowd

Stampede

Benn tests

Background to conflict: Page 6

The Oxford Mail's front page on 8th June 1981.

a month earlier when the hard line British Movement called a march in Oxford. Immediately the ANL responded by organising a protest several miles away from the fascists, while two of those under suspension travelled to Oxford to help organise direct confrontation with the BM. With the help of an ANL flag they convinced sufficient numbers to stay in the town centre and then with the support of a large number of young locals, confronted the fascists, causing a number of casualties and wrecking their pub in the process.

Under the headline 'Pub Smashed By Rioters', the *Oxford Mail* reported on the fallout: "An anti-fascist demo erupted into violence in Oxford city centre. A pub was wrecked, British Movement supporters beaten up, and St Aldate's police station besieged ... The attack on the Old Gate House began as youths, most of them black, hurled lumps of rock through the windows and crashed through the locked door of the pub, brandishing sticks. Customers, including a group of up to 25 supporters of the Right-wing British Movement, fled for safety to the back of the pub, but some of the BM youths were caught, knocked to the ground and kicked" (*Oxford Mail*, 8th June 1981).

Contrary to media reports, the anti-fascist attackers were made up of two different groupings, each numbering between eighty and one hundred, who had assembled separately, and met quite by chance in the city centre. It was a moment of high tension precisely because, while one half was almost all black, the other lot with few exceptions were all white.

Joe: "In contrast to the official demo, which had headed out of town, we had stayed in the city centre. We even had, I remember, an ANL banner with us. Slowly the crowd built up. Then news arrived that the BM had been spotted. En route through the city centre we became aware of another mob walking in parallel to us about 50 yards away. When we came to the intersection there was a face-off. Naturally we could see who they were; however, our problem was to quickly convince them we were not BM!"

As introductions were being made and information exchanged, scouts appeared with news that the BM had been spotted. The joint gang, now about 200-strong, set off on a run.

Joe: "By the time we came around the corner the British Movement had already retreated towards the Old Gate House. I remember one of the London lads, 'MacSquirty', hot on their heels, chuck a bottle at a window which, instead of going through, hit the frame and rebounded with such ferocity that had he not ducked he would have been the first recorded casualty of 'friendly fire'. Frankly, not fancying going through the front door we thought we would skip round the back and surprise them. Jumping over a fence, Mick was lowering himself down when a shout alerted him that he was about to put his Dr Marten right down the throat of an enormous Alsatian waiting patiently for him at the bottom! There was nothing for it but to go through the front. When this information was relayed, I personally was delighted when a couple of large black gentlemen stepped forward to do the honours. The door practically flew off the hinges. Coming through the door I was 'twinned' with this black kid who took out this massive mallet and, with me watching his back, set out to demolish the pub. Everything in the pub that could be smashed was, including the optics. Those British Movement members who had not already taken refuge in the cellar and barricaded themselves in were swiftly dealt with. I often thought how they must have felt, with all the crashing and smashing going on overhead, particularly in view of the fact that many were black, with them trapped as they were like rats."

Unsurprisingly, despite threats to return to Oxford, the British Movement never did. Even had they done so, it is unlikely the Old Gate House or any other pub in Oxford would have knowingly played host to them. Lessons were being learned all round. The irony for the SWP leadership was that they had sanctioned the purge precisely to avoid being outflanked by the rank and file of their own party.

Further stung by the considerable criticism from around the country that the smears against those under suspension were without substance, and not wishing to fight on that particular ground as a result, the SWP Central Committee, who had hoped the issue could be euphemistically dealt with through the disciplinary procedure, instead decided to come clean. In an article in the pre-conference 1981 bulletin they outlined their utter political opposition to the squadists in an article erroneously entitled 'Fighting The Nazis'. In it they made clear to all concerned that 'fighting the nazis' was exactly what the SWP must at all costs avoid from now on.

And in order to justify the *volte-face*, they made an admission which by their standards was remarkably candid. In a complete reversal of SWP propaganda hitherto (and since), it was argued on the one hand that the battle for the streets had been completed, but contradictorily, if it continued, it was not the NF, but the SWP who would likely be left facing organisational ruin. Coming less than two years after history tells us the NF had been crushed for a generation, it was an astonishing confession that demonstrated how much the leadership felt was at stake.

Accompanying this appeal for moderation was an appeal to a social snobbery within their membership, which as *The Leveller* report on the clash at Conway Hall illustrates, played well within the wider Left. Accordingly, the Central Committee (CC) portrayed those who continued to support direct action as largely lower class thugs, with limited political commitment and motivated purely by violence. In the process, the baby was thrown out with the bath water, with the whole tradition of militant anti-fascism being dismissed as both gratuitous and incoherent: largely a matter, according to the CC, of "chasing small groups of nazis from one street fight or pub brawl to another." There was also reference to the militants as 'specialists', although the squadists were often the best all-round activists in their local branches, unlike many who supported the leadership analysis.

By now openly opposed to physical opposition in any form, the SWP leadership began to argue that: "They [nazis] have more, and more eager, street fighters than we do. By setting up repeated confrontations with them – even when we seem successful at first – we feed their appetite for violence as satisfying in itself, and we help them draw in those that want a good punch up, and for whom the Reds are as good a target as any ... Comrades will ask what practical applications these points have – what for example should we do in the face of a fascist attack on a regular paper sale?"

Which was a very good question in the circumstances. For, as far as many in the rank and file could see, the choice was straightforward but limited. Abandon the sales pitch to the NF, as they were recommending for Islington, or after striking a concordat, actually share the pitch and sell *Socialist Worker* along side *National Front News*, as the leadership would endorse a little later in Leeds.

On a wider note if the CC prognosis was believed to be accurate, why was it, militants began to ask, that an organisation like the NF, who were routinely presented as 'petit-bourgeois', was also deemed to have the more 'eager street-fighters' than the self-proclaimed vanguards of the working class? And if indeed such an imbalance existed, would that not be exacerbated by the leadership plans to dispense with its own street-fighting element? Moreover, where was the evidence of the fascist appetite for confrontation being actually stimulated by losing?

The answers to such questions were not forthcoming, but instead, pedantically, the CC mapped out the alternative to 'standing your ground'. Faced with fascist aggression SWP branches would be directed in future to respond only as follows: "Organise for the widest possible leafleting of the area – estates, workplaces, and the shopping centre or High Street where the incidents have taken place. That usually means writing a good ANL leaflet which spells out what fascist violence is all about, but also talks about local cuts and closures, unemployment and the Right to Work, the Tories and the bomb. We can ask what NF or BM policies are in relation to all these, we can connect the issue of the fascists to most peoples' problems, without directing everything towards the question of the physical presence of the fascists themselves. Of course there are fascist nutters who will have a go at any time, but if we are under a banner calling for support for the march on the Tory conference, some of them might find it that bit more difficult."

Immediately, militants who regarded removing the 'physical presence of the fascists' as anti-fascism's first and primary duty denounced the leadership declaration as the self-serving abandonment of principle it undeniably was. Paradoxically when the SWP was forced to again correct its analysis ten years later, connecting the issue of anti-fascism to 'most peoples problems' was exactly what the ANL would visibly fail to do. In truth, what the SWP leadership was really promising, and banking on, was that if they turned a blind eye to fascist initiatives, in a *quid pro quo*, the odd 'nutter' apart, the NF would desist from attacking them.

Now, ever since the 1920s it was broadly accepted within anti-fascist circles that a decisive component in the arsenal of their opponents was the securing of unfettered control of the streets by force. If this analysis was correct then the equation was a simple one: fascist violence had to be met with anti-fascist violence. Of course, there was nothing original in the stance taken by the SWP leadership. The argument for turning the collective cheek away from fascist aggression was heard many times before, even in 1930s Germany. There were uncannily similar arguments put forward by the Stalinist leadership to KPD (German Communist Party) rank and file. One young communist militant commented: "We don't care for the idea that, if we are murdered by SA (Brownshirt) men, a small part of the working class will carry out a half-hour protest, which only makes the Nazis laugh for having got off so lightly." Some fifty years later 'letting them off lightly' was not something militants were ever going to be impressed by, either.

When the expulsions were rubber-stamped in August 1981, quickly followed by the shutting down of complete geographical branches like Cricklewood and Clapton that were judged to be irredeemable, there were few who expressed surprise. What opposition there was around the country mostly reflected itself in the tearing up of the Party card. But if the leadership had imagined this would be the last they would hear of the squadists they could not have been more wrong. Opposition by the militants had never been restricted to mere polemic. In the six months from the period of suspension to expulsion they had increasingly been taking political responsibility for the conduct of the struggle. Oxford had been a bit of a test case. Now their energies were directed toward stifling NF potential at Chapel Market.

Undeniably Chapel Market, alongside the cleansing of metropolitan Manchester, was a testing ground for much that followed. When a follow up campaign was mounted against the fascist pitch in East Street Market in south London, the resolve of the Far Right totally collapsed – a surprise attack by a 30-strong Red Action (RA) contingent left almost all their paper-sellers needing hospital treatment. And though it would take almost a decade before the militants worked their way around to the national stronghold of both the NF and BNP in Brick Lane, East London, when that paper sale came in for the 'specialist' treatment, it would prove only a little more resilient. The particular circumstances pertaining on the ground aside, there was a growing suspicion by now among the ex-ANL squadists that, as well as being exposed tactically, the SWP leadership might not have a leg to stand on theoretically, either.

For, as much as the SWP were fond of quoting Trotsky, his writings on fascism suddenly seemed to be largely a mystery to them. In *Fascism, What it is and How to*

Fight it, Trotsky had observed "fighting squads must be created ... nothing increases the insolence of the fascists so much as 'flabby pacifism' on the part of the workers' organisations" and he denounced the "political cowardice" of those who argue "we need mass self-defence and not the militia. Without organised combat detachments, the most heroic masses will be smashed bit by bit by the fascist gangs."

Joe: "I remember someone giving me a copy of the [Trotsky] essay 'The Militia and its Opponents'. It was a critique of the situation in France in 1935 and a real eye-opener. The core of it dealt with the Stalinist critics of the militants. Trotsky utterly demolished the Stalinist stance. However fifty years on precisely the same arguments were being used by the Trotskyite leadership – against us. It was doubly ironic because none of us were Trotskyites. Personally I felt empowered. I mean, if we who were largely uneducated politically could be so right, and they who immersed themselves like Talmudic scholars could be so wrong, maybe there was more to this dispute than met the eye. Overall, their seedy behaviour certainly helped generate the suspicion that the dispute may have a far wider application beyond Chapel Market or indeed anti-fascism."

This political awakening, so much at odds with the caricature painted by the SWP leadership of the so-called 'squadists' as just mere street-fighters for hire, would go on to play a vital role in defining the more comprehensive political ambitions of militant anti-fascism some two decades later.

From the moment they were set on an independent course from both the SWP and the wider Left, the challenging of the traditional blueprint for progressive social change was also unconsciously set in motion. This challenge was possibly acknowledged by the SWP itself who, a couple of years after the initial expulsions, in a shock move suspended rank and file dockers leader Micky Fenn for, of all things, "crossing a picket line". During the original furore in the spring of '81, Fenn, while expressing political sympathy with the arguments of his fellow squadists, made it plain he intended to 'stick with the Party' in order to see how things turned out. True to his word he immediately set out to re-build links with the broad base of the working class he felt were needed if the SWP was ever going to fulfil its political potential. Slowly under his tutelage his branch, Bow, east London, actually began to reflect in terms of composition the working class community of which it wanted to be a part. As such it was a refutation of both the analysis and orientation to the colleges offered by the leadership. Had Micky Fenn been someone other than the charismatic figure he undoubtedly was, this eccentricity might perhaps have been ignored. But for a leadership that was either paranoid or simply biding its time, his enthusiasm in attempting to recreate a working class base within the Party, probably seen as a complement to others building a working class alternative outside of it, was in itself deemed a sufficient threat to justify his effective expulsion through a pre-emptive strike. When the decision was delivered to the Bow branch, his shocked partner had to be restrained from doing the messenger a serious mischief with a heavy ashtray. Following his sudden death in 1996, an obituary in the *Guardian* attempted to gloss over the circumstance of his departure from the SWP, presenting the parting of the ways as "a matter of principle" (*Guardian* 5th August 1996), though principle had long been regarded by the hierarchy as ridiculously archaic.

In December 1981 the growing rationale for the expellees politically striking out on their own was given impetus when just before Christmas 'The Rochdale 8', as they had been labelled, received sentences of up to fifteen months. (The unlikely presence in the ranks of the convicted of a Manchester University professor, John P., caused a right wing conspiracy novelist, Ted Allenbury, a sort of poor man's Robert Ludlum, at least in terms of popularity, to cite the incident in a novel as evidence of the beginning of the collapse of western civilisation!)

Their initial arrests followed the abduction by them in broad daylight of a young skinhead from a Rochdale street. Eight people were subsequently charged with kidnap. Five of the nine were members of 'The Squad', with the remainder inexperienced students who had been commandeered from the Poly Bar. The random nature of the recruiting was unusual, to say the least. What had happened was that a female student, the wonderfully named Michelle Mole, resident in Rochdale, approached Davey H., an extremely large gregarious Scot, and high profile squad member, with a plea for help. She claimed to be under threat from the NF in Rochdale and if expecting chivalry might not be enough to secure protection quickly, offered to supply information on the NF in Rochdale in return. It so happened that a large-scale activity involving anything up to fifty squad members, designed to neutralise growing NF activity in Rochdale, was already at an advanced planning stage. Because, or in spite of this, when news of the 'protection versus information' trade off was relayed back to the squad, nothing happened. But not long after she appeared tearful and bruised at the Polytechnic, phone calls were made to rendezvous there. Her story must have sounded both urgent and convincing, as five experienced anti-fascists saw fit to immediately head off to Rochdale without waiting for experienced back up, choosing instead to press gang four untested students to make up the numbers. She claimed to have been beaten up by NF skins so the lads toured the area looking for someone she could recognise. Before long she fingered a young skinhead. He was unceremoniously dragged off the street into the van. Passers by reported the matter to the police. The police duly pulled the van but the skin, under duress, said nothing. Shortly afterwards the skinhead was ejected. This time he called the police. All ten occupants were arrested along with a choice armoury of weapons. Instantly the aptly named Michelle Mole turned Queen's evidence, incriminating all the others. There was understandable suspicion that it was all a State sponsored op from the outset, but nothing could be proved. Whether they expected to scoop even more remains a matter of conjecture. One way or the other, it took five key operators off the streets for the best part of two years, having being confined to desk duties on their arrest, followed by the 15 months served following conviction.

With the imprisonment of J.P., the SWP seized the opportunity to purge their ranks of the squadists, be it those in jail, or still active on the out. As in London, the expulsions of what were regarded as ringleaders saw many others leave in disgust. In a further attempt to bring Manchester back under operational control, the SWP installed a new full-time organiser, Andy Strouthous, in order do the necessary hatchet work. Peripheral groups such as Women's Voice, Right to Work campaign, Troops Out Movement, instantly came under the axe, with the leadership talking of 'downturns' and the 'battening down of hatches'. But consistent with the hard line those in jail represented, the Rochdale Defendants Fund, with the support of the families, underscored the political division by asking for support only from those who fully endorsed the actions of the anti-fascists. This stipulation notwithstanding, there were contributions and donations from trade union groups, branches and shop stewards' committees.

Denis: "One particularly successful fundraising benefit brought together Manchester's top three reggae bands and showcased Mick Hucknall as guest DJ, while the chart topping UB40 donated autographed LPs for the raffle. Initially the Polytechnic socials organiser, Elliot Rashman, who went on to manage Simply Red, expressed scepticism that the necessary nine hundred needed to fill the hall could be found. But on hearing that Harlem Spirit, Tribal, and Divine Inspiration, had already agreed to jointly headline – for free – he realised he was onto a winner and thereafter gave us every support to ensure its success."

If militants were at all concerned support from the SWP might taint the campaign, they need not have bothered. Freed from any pretence of bi-partisanship, the SWP offered financial support to just two of the eight imprisoned. In their view, the activities of the others could not any longer be qualified as 'political'. The former squadists not unreasonably regarded the classification as the other way round.

But the SWP were not the only ones to see an opportunity. Searchlight, led locally by Mike Luft and Graeme Atkinson, fairly blatantly sought political control of the squad. This raised eyebrows because, apart from the Piccadilly ambush, which was a three-line whip, they personally tended to steer clear of street work, focusing more on intelligence gathering. However John P., the acknowledged squad leader, had grown chary of the quality of the Searchlight contribution on an intelligence level when, on more than one occasion, it collided with the assessment of working class recruits nearer the street.

Denis: "When I first got involved in 1978, I was introduced to Mike Luft, who invited me to scan a whole batch of photos for faces. One guy was erroneously marked down as Ged Williams from Salford. Pointing to a different guy I said 'That's Ged Williams'. 'No it isn't,' declared Luft confidently. 'Yes it is,' I replied. 'I should know. He went to the same school as me. And that's his brother there,' indicating another photo. 'No it isn't!' retorted Luft, face reddening. 'He lives in Fallowfield,' I reply. 'His dad's got a newsagent on Hart Road and he drinks in The Sherwood. What more do you want to know?' Luft was silent for a while before countering: 'Well, there must be two of them called Ged Williams then!' To date the 'other' Ged Williams is yet to put in an appearance."

However, with John P. safely out of the way, Luft and Atkinson now sought to fill the vacuum. Meetings were called and agendas set, but apart from political briefings nothing by way of action was forwarded. Inevitably those operating from Hulme took it upon themselves to initiate events, successfully taking on the BM in Harrowgate. After that the crunch was not long in coming. Searchlight dispatched a mini-van to go to Blackpool on the same day as a large NF demonstration and a promised counter-demo by the ANL in the town. To the dismay of the street operators, the Searchlight plan, they found out, was not to join up with squadists from London but to scan the local library for background information on local NF activists – on the same day as many hundreds of fascists were marching through the town centre. Reconciliation was hardly boosted when it was discovered that London, badly over-extended, had had their transport impounded and suffered a number of arrests. The simmering discontent boiled over.

A devastating verbal critique at the next meeting by Denis C. regarding Searchlight priorities and general know-how saw Luft and Atkinson retaliate by attempting to exclude him from further meetings, and thus future activity. But for the absence of the more senior figures, decidedly less active since May 1979, this would have been a sensible tactic. As events would prove Denis C. was the very street leader they should have been keeping on side. The attempt to sideline him saw the next 'squad' meeting boycotted by the squadists. This was something John P., on his return from jail, formally endorsed by drawing up a letter, counter-signed by all of the squadists, which proscribed Searchlight from future involvement in squad activity.

Logic demanded that the militants now set up their own organisations. Within the year, Red Action and The Socialist Federation – an umbrella organisation set up by John P., of which RA was a part – came into existence.

1.6

EARLY CONFRONTATIONS: CHAPEL MARKET, 1981

Joe: "When we assembled we only had about fifteen, which was just about enough for what we had planned. We'd had a good look at the terrain and decided how we'd get there and, just as important, how we'd get away. On the morning we arrived by van and pulled up at the back of the shops. The NF was already on the paper sale across the road. We came out opposite them and sent a couple of women and a few of the smaller ones ahead to encourage them. They were terrifically encouraged. A couple of them nearly got knocked down running across the road to get into us!

"They came onto the pavement. We stepped out and there was a momentary pause; a bit of a stand off. It was a wide pavement. The nearest NF member was a yard or two in front of me. To my right was a display of goods outside a hardware shop. As he looked to his left to check his back-up I reached into a bin, picked out a yard brush and just backhanded him across the head. It caught him over the ear and he collapsed into a load of metal bins with a satisfying crash.

"That acted like a signal and it was off. We had about the same numbers really, not odds, to be fair, I would fancy normally. I saw J. fighting with a geezer by the cars. I broke the broom handle over his head. Another NFer in an attempt to get away ran straight into a bus stop. Along with him and the two others already floored, I could see another to my right being booted on the pavement and yet another fascist lying flat on his back on the road. I felt we had made our point. But as we began the retreat back up the alley, disaster struck. Out of the blue, this big old boy, probably in his late forties appeared in the alley. Looking back on it he probably came out of a back door from the shop. As a non-combatant no one paid him any heed. Suddenly, he launches a huge haymaker and caught one of the lads flush on the chin. He slumped against the wall and slithered down onto his knees. Clean out. I couldn't believe it. The fascists at the mouth of the alley howled in anticipation. There could be no question of leaving him to get help and the police were very likely on the way. I choked down a rising panic. Just then his assailant bent down to pick him up by the collar. He wanted 'seconds'. I was wearing light Puma trainers and I knew I had to put everything into that one shot. I caught him with my heel directly on the temple. He threw his hands to face and fell back without a sound. The NF just stood and stared. I stared back. Then along came a couple of our people who just walked straight passed them. It was hard to believe the fascists didn't recognise them as they had been in the thick of it. Realising that something was wrong, another two came running back from the van. Between us, with me acting as back marker, we picked up our colleague and carried him off, feet dragging on the floor, to the van. We were half way to Kilburn before he properly woke up" (Kingsbury, 22nd August 1981).

It took just forty nine weeks between the clash at Kingsbury on 22nd August 1981 to the final clash at the Angel on 1st August 1982 for the former squadists, now in the shape of Red Action, to register their first triumph, when a stunned NF were driven off their prestigious sales pitch at Chapel Market in Islington. From the early 1970s, Chapel Market had been the scene of frequent clashes, initially between the SWP and the NF, and later between the ANL and the NF. What would generally happen is that the NF would sell on one side of the road, while the anti-fascists occupied the other side. Not unlike a bad marriage, each tolerated the existence of the other – most of the time.

Then one bright sunny Sunday morning in July 1981, the NF suddenly upped the ante at Chapel Market, supplementing their regular turnout with members drafted in from Brick Lane and elsewhere. This 60-strong mob led by Patrick Harrington, a member of the NF National Directorate, appeared suddenly at the bottom of White Lion Street, and taking up the full width of the pavement advanced quickly on the far smaller group of unwary anti-fascists.

Joe: "All I remember is one of our number leaning against a post box or something when this NFer came over and punched him straight in the head. He went down without a sound. It had the making of an utter rout, but a few stood and put up a fight. I had already vaulted into the road and was well away but what do I see looking back? J. and some others making a fight of it! Muttering curses, I reluctantly made my way back and joined in. Right away I confronted a leading NF member. He was armed with a broken placard handle. He waved it in my face threatening 'to take my eyes out'. I believed him. Some minor skirmishing followed but for some reason they did not want to push home their advantage. Eventually the sheer weight of numbers forced us to leg it up Chapel Market. A metal trader's trolley thrown into our NF pursuers slowed them down enough for most of us to get away. Still one of our lads got badly done outside Marks and Spencer's, and though we got away largely unscathed, we were far from happy."

As the anti-fascists re-grouped at a corner, Unmesh D. attempted to marshal the situation. He was shouting the odds when someone pulled him up a bit sharpish pointing an accusatory finger, "You ran first!" "No I didn't," he replied indignantly, "I ran fourth!" which drew snorts as well as amused grins.

When tempers calmed, the squadists realised this was a defining moment for them. Up until then, those who turned up had done so as individuals in solidarity with the picket and acted more or less entirely in a supportive role. Now, however, everyone involved was uncomfortably aware that after years of struggle the NF were finally on the point of securing Chapel Market and, in the process, winning a vital victory. Islington NF was already one of the strongest and most notorious branches anywhere in the country, and it is likely that, if a bridgehead was established in Islington, they had the potential to cut a swathe through the Left across the whole of north London. Another NF sale had recently been established in Kingsbury near Wembley and there had been reported sightings in the weeks before of yet another NF sale in Willesden, geographically situated between Islington and Wembley. A 'squadist only' meeting was called to work out a viable response.

Joe: "It was forcibly put to the meeting that the only possible way to recover the ground lost was to do a retaliatory 'hit' on the NF – and as quickly as possible. It was argued that unless we did so the counter-picket against their sale would prove unsustainable for the simple reason that, with their confidence so high, it was likely the tactic of 'blitzkrieg' would be repeated whenever the opportunity presented itself. To avoid this we felt we needed to restore parity, and quickly.

"But due to the likelihood of a heightened police presence in Chapel Market in the immediate future the prospect of anything coming off there had also to be ruled out. It was then noted that several members of Brent NF had played a part in the attack at Chapel Market and so the idea was floated to attack their recently established paper sale at Kingsbury in north-west London in order to level the scores."

Not all were in agreement. Already aware of a creeping isolation, some felt that it might make matters worse. A certain nervous scoffing at the word 'hit' betrayed the feelings of those who already felt out of their depth. The minority eventually either drifted out of politics altogether, or re-engaged fully with the SWP. In any event this would not have any bearing on what was planned for Kingsbury. In the two weeks prior the area was thoroughly scouted. No one was aware of it at the time, but a new leadership of the anti-fascist movement was in the process of announcing itself.

On 22nd August 1981, on the morning of the Charity Shield, the curtain raiser to the football season, the anti-fascists made their move. Quite by chance, one presumes, the presence of a freelance photographer recorded the incident in considerable detail. Along with a number of other papers in the region, the *Harrow Observer* gave the scoop a front-page splash. "These dramatic photographs show the scenes of hate and violence which shocked shoppers when National Front members were attacked and beaten in a bloody weekend clash. Four men were treated at Edgware General Hospital after the clash in Kingsbury ... Fighting began just after 11am when about six NF supporters arrived outside Kingsbury underground station to display copies of the *National Front News.*"

Graham John, the National Front's local organiser, claimed, "They ran out from an alley and assaulted anyone in their way – not just our people. It was a calculated and indiscriminate attack and it developed to a point where people were seriously injured. They could have killed one man." The chairman of Brent North Constituency Labour Party said he had no idea who the Front's opponents in the fight were. "Whoever they were, the people involved in the fight with the NF had absolutely nothing to do with us. As much as we abhor the views and politics of the NF, we defend their right to stand in a public street and sell their literature" (*Harrow Observer*, 28th August 1981).

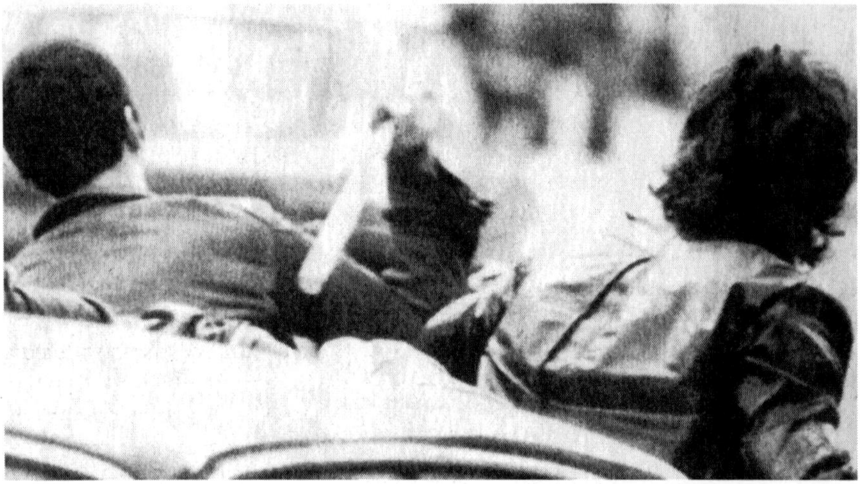

Above and right, images from the 'Kingsbury massacre' on 22nd August 1981.

National Front News, careful to avoid any speculation about the reasons for what was a retaliatory raid, feigned indignation. "A vicious attack on a small group of *NF News* sellers was mounted by a Red 'hit squad' in Kingsbury, North London, on Saturday 22nd August. The NF salesmen were assaulted with pickaxe handles, iron bars and shovels by the gang who suddenly emerged from an alley. Several NF salesmen were injured, including Mr Graham John, NF North and West London Regional Organiser. NF Haringey Organiser, Paul Nash, was hospitalised after his head was gashed open and one of his hands slashed" (*National Front News*, October 1981).

Whatever the opinions of the Labour Party, the local press and, of course, the NF leadership, the squadists were cock-a-hoop. Psychologically the organisers felt they had turned the tables. For this was not only a victory in its own right, something else of great significance had been spotted.

Joe: "What struck me on the day and particularly looking at the photographs later was the sight of three or four young lads, probably YNF [Young NF] fleeing as if for their very lives. This clearly was not what they had been led to expect. Perhaps they had been told all anti-fascists were like the local Labourites. If so somebody had clearly been telling them 'porkies'. If promising young recruits some action was custom and practice within the Far Right then counter-violence delivered with a bit of panache was likely to have a disproportionate effect on morale."

It proved a prescient observation. What is more, the unexpected raid, accompanied by crunching aggression, would go on to become the soon to be formed Red Action trademark.

The day following the 'Kingsbury massacre' over one hundred NF turned up at Chapel Market, including a heavily bandaged Brent NF organiser looking for revenge. The anti-fascists who had played leading roles in planning and executing the action, sought cover in bus queues and watched events from a distance.

Joe: "Coincidentally, that was the one day the Revolutionary Communist Party also turned up, all sporting flight jackets and looking very much the business – from a distance anyway. They were banging their gloves together very business-like, demanding to know where the fascists were, in complete ignorance of what had happened 24 hours previously, of course. Like the rest of the lads, I was keeping a low profile when one of them came up to me and goes all aggressive like, 'So where's the nazis then?' 'Well,' I say coolly, 'there's about a hundred of them mobbed up around the corner if you are really interested!' He must have had it checked, because a couple of minutes later he went into a huddle with some others and, next thing you know, they are practically running for their cars. They didn't even offer us a lift! As it was just the few of us versus the hundred-odd NF keen to settle the score we, sensibly in my view, adopted a tactic that consisted entirely of running away."

However as the squadists had correctly calculated, with it now considered 'one all' with each side recording a major victory over the other in short order, something like normality resumed at the picket. But the militants had no intention of settling for a return to the status quo. It would take until November some three months later, when the NF attempted to attack an anti-racist conference at Caxton House in Archway, that the NF would receive their second major lesson in street politics. Why the militants were particularly eager for contact was a result of an incident in the previous month when a very popular member of the squad, a diminutive Glaswegian, P. McL. (nickname, 'McSquirty') was ambushed outside a benefit in Clerkenwell. Stabbed three times, once through the lung, had it not been for a trained nurse being in attendance, the probability is he would have drowned in his own blood at the scene. A number of fascists were later jailed, with one NF member, Keith Rowley, receiving three years. As would be custom and practice over the following decade and a half of conflict, militant cooperation with the police was zero. The sole concession to convention was the provision of a skeleton account of events from the victim in order to qualify for injury compensation. From a militant point of view, Caxton House therefore presented an ideal opportunity for a settling of accounts.

Terry: "What happened was, this conference was organised by, you know, the usual do-gooder types. They made no direct contact with us at all and probably did not even approve of the picket of the NF paper sale at Chapel Market on the grounds that it was too confrontational. Anyway we guessed that, being a local event, the NF were almost duty bound to attack it. We planned accordingly. We just never told them."

The anti-fascists figured that the NF would appear shortly after closing time and when they did the anti-fascists would be waiting for them. As anticipated, at exactly 3.30pm the NF were spotted on the move and only then were the organisers of the anti-racist meeting informed of militant intentions. Weapons, which had already been smuggled into the building with the connivance of the caretaker, whose son was on the run for bank robbery, were produced and distributed, while the anti-racist organisers stood and stared wide-eyed and slack-jawed.

Joe: "We were positioned directly inside the door. Directly outside, the NF assembled. I watched them approach the door. The doors open, and whack! The first one got hit with a variety of implements. [He turned out to be a member of the Labour Party, a late arrival.] As we charged out, a smoke bomb one of the fash was carrying, went off which, of course, only added to the shock and confusion of the NF. For a moment they stood their ground until we got in amongst them. Then they were running everywhere. I remember chasing after this particular fascist I had taken a particular dislike to, only to be challenged by another who I liked even less! It must have been mutual because, unlike me, he was unarmed. I had a particularly heavy club. I immediately hit him over the head. I mean, what did he expect me to do with it?"

Undoubtedly what saved the NF from heavier reprisals was the presence in their ranks of a uniformed police officer. Apparently he had been ordered to escort the NF to the meeting. Once it kicked off he screamed down his phone for assistance. Despite the subsequent police intervention, the hard men of Islington NF looked shocked and mortified. Meanwhile as the anti-fascists frantically sought the security of the building to avoid arrest, they were met with a standing ovation from the anti-racists who, on witnessing the contest, realised possibly for the first time what a narrow shave they had had.

At no time did it even cross the minds of those planning the counter-coup to alert even the organisers, much less the Left or the authorities. There was the stabbing, of course, but also the desire to repeat and build on the victory at Kingsbury was a definite strategic attraction. Here then was anti-fascism stripped down to the tactic of violence as a first resort. It was an outlook the NF locally were clearly struggling to come to terms with. Up until then, even for a branch as notorious as Islington NF, their experience of anti-fascism, even when it manifested itself physically, would have been mostly defensive in nature. So this level of devotion was largely an unknown and unpredictable quantity. A particularly stressful aspect in the dealings with this new breed was the fact that being 'off duty' was no longer recognised or respected. All involved knew they were just as likely to be attacked out shopping as when hawking *National Front News*.

Behind this approach lay a profound impatience not to say embarrassment at how '*their*' side, the Left, conducted itself. In broad terms the rank and file anti-fascists believed socialism/communism had to return to being the moral, intellectual and, yes, the fascists' physical superior: and quickly. A by-product of the incremental gentrification of the Far Left had, they believed, resulted in the average member being far too sensitised to the use of violence to be of much value on the streets.

In an essay on violence, author Martin Amis provides an interesting insight into what the prospect of violence can entail for the uninitiated. Contrary to expectation, the adrenalin surge that accompanies a recognised threat does not always result in flight, much less fight. More often than not, the outcome is passivity and near paralysis. "In the moments leading up to violence, the non-violent enter a world drenched with unfamiliar revulsions. The violent know this. Essentially, they are taking you to where they feel at home. You are leaving your place and going over to their place." Now the fight for the streets meant a lot of work at close quarters. Eyeball to eyeball stuff. Any hesitation, the tiniest flicker, betraying either loss of appetite or unfamiliarity with that terrain, is instantly and gleefully sniffed out.

Accordingly, if the sort of 'scorched earth' approach recommended by the emerging militant leaders was to be applied, they themselves had to be psychologically equipped to put it into practice. "How far are you prepared to go?" was the question posed many years later by a *World in Action* reporter following the Welling riot for which militants were blamed. "How long is a piece of string?" came the unruffled reply. Of course by 1993 the anti-fascists had all but done for both the National Front and Blood & Honour, and had C18 and the BNP in their sights. So a certain sense of composure could be expected.

But in truth the foundation was arguably in place from the beginning. Of the five 'squadists' fingered in the first wave of expulsions in the London area, all had already been through the courts. Before 1982 was out, all five (including incidentally a female aged just 19), would have had first-hand experience, if for some only briefly on remand, of the prison system. Two prominent members from Hatfield had been marked absent at Kingsbury, due to already being in custody on charges of conspiracy to riot and arson arising out of the 1981 riots. Another two walked free from a crown court trial where the expectation of a lengthy jail sentence was so strong bail was refused on the grounds they might abscond. Affray, police assault, possession of an offensive weapon and grievous bodily harm with intent, studded the curriculum vitae of the remaining expellee. No angels these then, and unlike the archetypal left-winger, they tended to live and operate within a section of society where no quarter being asked or given was regarded as something of a by-law.*

Thus, while not entirely identifying with the respectable working class, they had little time for out-and-out criminals either, and their brushes with the authorities, though fairly constant, had more to do with rebelliousness and hell-raising than through any involvement in the systematic breaking of the law for financial gain. Although hailing from different parts of London, all were actively involved in the proceedings at Caxton House.

* On one occasion, a building sub-contractor defaulted on a payment to a Red Action building worker. He was beaten up on site and frogmarched to a café in Camden in order to borrow the money, while the rest of his workforce were actually held hostage. So confident were the RA members of the impression made on him, the £45 balance was accepted in the form of a cheque.

A case in point was Peter C., who had only been released on bail on the Friday prior to the Caxton House mobilisation. Armed with a meat tenderiser, he was in the thick of it. A few celebratory drinks afterwards and, with the good wishes from his fellow anti-fascists, he went back to court the following Monday morning and got three years. Yet within weeks of his release he would become involved in a no-holds barred brawl that left his opponent, a kick-boxing fellow parolee, nursing wounds requiring one hundred and fifteen stitches. O'Farrell we already know about, and it is hardly an exaggeration to say their Manchester comrades came from no less colourful stock. One leading activist had a brother in the British Movement who was later 'lifed-off' for a racist murder.

Another, Dessie Noonan, would himself be charged later with a capital offence, while a third would be shot dead by mystery assailants. One of the original Manchester Squad, Denis C., apparently made such an impression on the collective consciousness of the Far Right during this period that the infamous website Redwatch were still making inquiries as to his whereabouts as late as 2003, using a photo taken from the last verified sighting available which was in 1986.

But perhaps the more representative anecdote that best illustrates the thorough disregard for the forces of law and order is one that involves J. and G. In the summer of 1984 they were sharing a house in Kilburn Park in north-west London. Managed by Brent Community Housing, the rent due to lack of repair was cursory, £1 a week, yet much of the time the account was £200 in arrears. Another who had a room there was Peter Davies. A villain of the old school, he was a bear of man who, while only about 5ft 9ins in height, weighed over sixteen stone. He had served time for armed robbery in Wandsworth, and been deported as an undesirable from New Zealand. Aged about fifty, his tattooed frame was topped by a shaved head that, though more fashionable these days, was always likely to turn heads back then. Occasionally employed as a chauffeur for the wife of a Nigerian gynaecologist, or 'pussy mechanic' as Davies would respectfully describe him, he was dropping her off near Harrods one day when he was cut-up by another car. A dispute over parking space followed. After swearing profusely at both Davies and his passenger, the driver locked his Mercedes Benz and took a window seat in a restaurant opposite. Embarrassed for his passenger, Davies climbed out of his car, walked slowly over to the front of the Mercedes, put his right foot on the front bumper, hooked his fingers though the distinctive Mercedes badge on the bonnet and, with one savage yank, snapped the steel spring securing it. Putting the badge in his pocket, without further word or gesture he strolled back to his car and drove sedately away.

One evening Davies got into a disagreement with some local youths who had stolen a neighbour's keys. While attempting negotiations, he was smashed over the head with the edge of a house brick. Armed with a hammer, he pursued his attackers into a stairwell of a block of flats where he was again set upon and beaten with sewer rods and milk bottles. About 8.30 the following morning G., returning from his girlfriend's via Kilburn High Road, jumped out of his skin as a car pulled up sharply into the kerb beside him. Inside were J. and Davies. With the situation explained, G. promised to discover the identity of the attackers within the day. Actually, he did a little better than that, personally confronting the ringleader at about 11.30am the same morning. He fled. There were no further sightings for the rest of the day. But after closing time, as all three were returning from the pub, they walked into an ambush near the house. A local gang numbering up to fifteen, who had been hiding in the shadows at the gable end of the house, launched a pre-emptive strike. They set about the three with the regulation assortment of sticks, bricks, bars and bottles. Unknown to the two others, G. had placed some clubs just inside the door precisely for such an emergency. He now made a beeline for it. Spotting him, one youth ran to cut him off, screaming, arm pulled fully back, a brick aimed at his head. G. stepped between two cars, ducking only at the last possible second, causing the brick to whistle past his head by inches. To the sound of a car windscreen smashing behind him, he immediately straightened, sprinting for the door, all too aware that any fumbling with key or lock and it was curtains for all of them. To his delight the key slipped into the lock first time. A surge of adrenalin coursed through him. But, as he scrambled in the darkened hallway, he laughed to himself as the door swung shut behind him, locking a disbelieving Davies and J fighting for their lives in the pathway outside. A club in either hand, he soon re-joined the fray with considerable enthusiasm. The attackers scattered. Only when confronted by a youth armed with an axe, and fearing he might panic and throw it, did the counter-offensive come to halt.

Next morning at about 11am, as he and Davies headed off to sign-on, he spies one of the previous night's attackers walking jauntily towards them. G. nudges Davies, "There's one of them." Before waiting for a response, he crosses the road and fells the gang member with a single blow. Davies hurries over and begins to jump up and down on the prone but still conscious and, by now, near hysterical victim. There is some curiosity shown by occupants of the local bookies but, dissuaded by a grim-faced G., they think better of intervening. Unaware of developments, including the fact that, among other miscellaneous injuries, the nineteen-year-old had suffered a broken leg, J. is enjoying a lie-in when the front door crashes in. Throwing on a dressing gown, he snatches a huge sharpened screwdriver (a nostalgic memento from his teenage days) and bounds for the stairs just in time to meet a delegation from the night before led by 'Axe-man'. Battle is joined. When, at about 12.30, G. returns, he finds J. still in his dressing gown sitting on the stairs, chin resting on the handle of the screwdriver planted between bare feet. "Am I fucking glad to see you," he mutters. "I bet," G. replies, looking around at the evidence of battle. They both now knew they faced a serious problem. They could expect the house to be attacked once night fell and, to make matters worse, G. was due to fly to Belfast as part of the Red Action delegation that evening. It was decided they would need to get some of the boys in. "If the worst comes to the worst, save the leather jacket and the Crombie," G. instructed Davies, before departing. He would not get to wear either again.

About midnight, a mob of about forty assemble on a small green near the front of the house. The first night attacks are beaten off with relative ease but most knew worse was to come. The following night, the back lights of the police patrol car were still visible as it slowly cruised through the shopping precinct when the attackers, reinforced by a black gang from Paddington and now numbering about sixty, began drawing up crates of milk bottles filled with petrol. The battle lasted for hours. To the consternation of the attackers, as well as bombs flying in the windows, petrol bombs were also flying out. One black youth narrowly escaped almost certain death when, leaning back for greater velocity, a pair of garden shears hurled from an upstairs window by Davies skimmed his head and buried themselves in the tarmac behind him. The petrol bomb he released went straight through a second floor window and landed in a wardrobe without exploding. Immediately it was hurled back out at the expense of the net curtains, which were set alight. Downstairs as the main door began to visibly disintegrate under a volley of boots, Davies stood in the deliberately darkened hall, armed with a hatchet prepared to razor sharpness. As one of the attackers took a long run-up in order to smash what remained of the lock, J., hanging precariously by one arm from a first floor window, flung a brick with such brutal force that it knocked the attacker clear over an adjacent fence, missing not only the door – "but the whole fuckin' house!" as someone gleefully recalled later. Before the night was over, others also ended up in emergency in St Mary's in Paddington with serious 'head injuries'.

News of the effective demolition of his home was brought to G. via a shout from a window of a block of flats in the Divis. "G., your house has just been petrol bombed!" As bemused local Republicans looked at him inquiringly, "I told you this trip was just like a busman's holiday for me," came the off-hand explanation. By Saturday morning, concerned by the ferocity of the resistance being put up by the 'squatters' who they might reasonably have expected to have been run off some time past, local detectives finally decided to investigate. What they discovered troubled them sufficiently to order a belated picket of policemen that stretched across the park at the front of the house. The morale of the attackers was utterly crushed when on Monday evening they were on hand to witness the return of G., accompanied by a dozen unshaven desperados carrying gym bags. In actual fact, it was merely a detour for some of the RA delegation returning from Belfast, but to local tearaways it must have looked like reinforcements ready to move in. In any event, the siege was over.

Later, the house in Princess Road served as a safe house for a couple of fugitives who arrived there after midnight one Friday night, one still in handcuffs after an all-out brawl with the local constabulary at the Hilltop pub in Hatfield, during which a police car was overturned and a WPC knocked out. One of the visitors was hit by a Volvo in Kilburn High Road a few months later, and left with permanent brain damage.

Hardly any surprise, then, that even by the early 1980s the kind of working class self-sufficiency these former SWP members took pride in made them unique and somewhat controversial amongst the contemporary Left. And yet the hard-line approach toward fascism they fostered was not without precedent. Historically, for militant anti-fascism to follow a line of attack that was often neither liberal nor legal was hardly unknown. In the 1930s the Communist Party of Great Britain membership drew their inspiration from being involved in a worldwide movement, a movement, as they saw it, of destiny. After the war, for the largely Jewish paramilitary 43 Group, the indignation of having to fight fascism all over again, even with the existence of the death camps being common knowledge, served as a considerable spur. In both cases, objective circumstances created a climate whereby the rule of law, from an ethical standpoint, was a matter of indifference. With the new crop of militants, this essential dynamic was instinctive as well as political. In order to guarantee momentum, simple pragmatism demanded militants would continue to be recruited from a social stratum where a disregard for legal niceties was a cultural standard.

In an interview with a national newspaper many years later, the practice of recruiting 'ready made street-fighters' was explained in a matter-of-fact way by Joe Reilly: "If they come from football they know how to deal with the police, they understand the gang mentality, they know how to fight and understand the psychology of the other mob" (*Independent on Sunday*, 25th November 1994). Or as a character in the acclaimed film *LA Confidential* put it, the sought after recruits were those who already understood that "violence is an adjunct to the job".

Following the Caxton House debacle, spirits within Islington NF had hit an all time low. One wet blustery Sunday morning, as anti-fascists took shelter in doorways, half a dozen NF turned up proudly sporting smart new swastika armbands. Shoppers gaped. And while it may have been intended as a show of defiance or to intimidate, it was almost immediately recognised by anti-fascists as a signal of despair, and a measure of an ebbing of political discipline. With characteristic ruthlessness anti-fascists began to turn the screw.

Joe: "Without fail we would turn up every Sunday morning, rain or shine. It was always pretty nervy and tense, as you couldn't really know what the opposition might have up their sleeve. But after Caxton House we knew we were in the ascendancy, and so what we worked into the act now was, if say, we were early enough or had superior numbers, then instead of politely staying on our, by now traditional, side of the street, we might just go and take the NF pitch. Not always, of course. But simply not knowing what might happen, and what they might have to cater for, we could see was wearing them out."

Almost a year to the day since the NF looked set to crush anti-fascist resistance for good came the third and final clash, which saw the issue resolved alright, but not on terms anyone could have imagined twelve months previously. On Sunday morning, 1st August, around 11am, when Red Action arrived in Chapel Market they were confronted by a large group of NF activists, nearly all fresh faces, mainly shipped in from outside the area, and already in occupancy. As a mark of how valuable the NF nationally regarded the pitch, deputy chairman Ian Anderson, was the hands-on organiser.

If the numbers were not so unusual, what immediately struck anti-fascists as more than a little odd was the marked absence of uniformed police, as it was hardly as if the appearance of either the NF or their opponents was something not to be catered for. So, as a priority, Red Action scouts were sent to check the area for signs of police, or possibly fascists lying in wait nearby, awaiting developments.

Terry: "We had been there for about ten minutes and the NF, who had heard all the stories and had expected the worst, were just beginning to relax when the scouts returned. One I remember had just begun putting his glasses back on. Possibly he saw no significance in the brief conference that took place just yards from them on the wide pavement. After a few seconds the cluster broke and Ian Anderson, who was deputy Chairman of the NF, was sent hurtling to the floor by a right-hook. He was a boxing blue from Cambridge, or so he claimed, but he never got much of a chance to display the finer aspects of the noble art that day."

Within seconds the visibly stunned fascists, who had been standing in a line with their backs to the shop front selling papers, were individually engaged: every man for himself. A number were felled almost immediately. Those who could ran.

Joe: "A small group from Brick Lane in east London who had, in fact, escaped, saw a small group of likely looking lads, some in paramilitary type jackets, getting off a bus and understandably assuming they were local NF, beckoned them over, and in near absolute despair – took their second beating before breakfast that day."

In total fourteen anti-fascists, many of whom had come to Chapel Market directly from an all-night party, which may have played a part in a general lack of alertness in regard to getting away, were arrested leaving the scene. Three, O'Farrell, O'Shea and O'Rourke, all personally pointed out by Ian Anderson, were charged with affray and ABH. Interestingly, whether out of a wish not to get involved or out of enmity to the NF, not one of the market traders, many in any case Jewish, were produced by the prosecution. More surprisingly, not a single one of the literally hundreds of witnesses in the bustling market offered to give evidence on behalf of the prosecution, either. This rather marked failure meant the prosecution was forced to rely entirely on the credibility of Anderson and friends.

On the morning of the trial one of the defending barristers, Helena Kennedy, from a working class Glaswegian background ('a poor man's lawyer' was how her proud mum presented her success to neighbours), was seriously wondering whether she should ask the judge to clear the public gallery on the grounds that 'witnesses might be intimidated'. Still in two minds she decided to consult her clients. Smiling apologetically, the defendants informed her that the admittedly unsavoury looking individuals packing the public gallery, including one Peter Davies resplendent in a light blue suit and black shirt, were actually attending at their invitation. After three days at Snaresbrook Crown Court, two were acquitted outright, with the hung jury divided on Mick O'Farrell.* On the last day of the trial, two diminutive, wizened little old men were spotted in the public gallery studying events with a birdlike intensity.

With O'Farrell now facing the prospect of a re-trial, word came through an intermediary that, should the defence so wish, the prosecutor, a Jewish Orthodox woman, would be encouraged to stand down. It was an extraordinary but unnecessary intervention as the prosecution decided not to proceed with the case. A conditional discharge was later offered and gleefully accepted. Not long after, Red Action were tipped off by Searchlight that a 'contract' had been put out on leading elements, including two of those acquitted. Apparently this initiative was to be managed by Eddy Morrison, a fairly notorious fascist from the Leeds area. Notorious among traditional left-wingers that is, for 'glassing' someone in a student bar. Nevertheless, the militants took the threat seriously enough to do something about it.

* After the initial trial, barrister Ian Macdonald spoke to his client, Mick O'Farrell, in the corridor outside the court. He was convinced that the chasm between the sworn testimony of half a dozen prosecution witnesses, who repeatedly stressed his client had definitely struck the first blow, and the defence insistence that O'Farrell had not struck anyone at all, had resulted in the hung jury rather than outright acquittal. "Perhaps, Michael, if you had said you may have put your hands up to defend yourself...?" "But I didn't do it," O'Farrell protested. "I'm aware of that, Michael, all I'm saying is..." he gently berated. Again O'Farrell declared his absolute innocence. The exchange continued along similar lines, with the barrister growing increasingly exasperated. Then another voice interjected: "But Mickey didn't do it," – a pause followed to allow Macdonald to focus on the speaker. "I did." Macdonald looked round to see the slightly amused face of one of the two defendants who had, only moments earlier, been set free. A speechless Macdonald, his face visibly draining of colour, convinced his career was hanging by a thread, wheeled away and speedily put physical distance between himself and the guilty party.

Joe: "Not knowing what they knew, e.g. possibly addresses and so on, it was decided the best idea would be to let them know we knew. A young skinhead was duly despatched to convey the message to the leadership. What he did was to sidle up behind Patrick Harrington as the paper sale in Brick Lane broke up, and whisper 'Morrison is dead!' All colour instantly drains from Harrington's face. Presumably, instead of him [Harrington] taking it as an indication that they had been rumbled, which when you think about it was bad enough, he must have thought we had already done Morrision in! [Laughs]." Nothing more ever came of it, but it does give some indication of how jittery and unsettled, in a relatively short period of time, a battle hardened NF leadership had become. The major clashes at Kingsbury, Archway and Chapel Market, along with consistent and disciplined activity maintained on a weekly basis, unavoidably broke the back of the paper sale and the NF in Islington.

In tandem with the militant offensive, militant control was consolidated when eight members of Camden and Islington NF were sent down for a whole series of armed robberies not long after. (An estimated £200,000 was raised purportedly for the purpose of political funding.) This was a body blow, swiftly followed by the jailing of three members of the semi-criminal Fields family, for an aggravated gang rape that included the use of a broom handle. One got eight years. By now, unable to maintain what the NF considered a sufficient presence consistently (remember, a team of over twenty had been effortlessly turned over), by the end of 1982 support for the sale had entirely withered away. Operationally, it had become unsustainable. Not long after that the branch itself effectively ceased to exist.

This crumpling of spirits there caused a domino effect right across north London with the result that, within a relatively limited period, the NF ceased to have any organised presence in what for them, traditionally, had been one of their strongest areas of support nationally. Nor was it lost on the militants that they had achieved in a little less than twelve months what the weight of the SWP and the ANL had failed to do in six years.

Without doubt events surrounding the campaign at Chapel Market had set the tone for the development of militant anti-fascism in the years ahead. The militants had demonstrated that a violent party like the NF could be taken head on. The anti-fascists were well organised, disciplined and able to out-think and out-violence the NF at street level, an emphatic answer to the SWP leadership's critique of 'squadism'. Where was the NF's 'appetite for violence' now, was the inquiry?

Although clashes over the previous years were hardly uncommon, these resulted largely from fascist aggression, provocation, or encroachment. With the exception of some squadist operations, the absolutist mindset the NF now faced was largely a mystery to them. And, together with being prepared to get stuck in at street level, there was an ambition and determination to deliver results or, in salesman parlance, to 'close the deal'. Early on there was some speculation among the Far Right as to the real political allegiances of the opposition. Unable, or possibly ideologically unwilling, to accept their opponents as ordinary left-wingers, a recurring train of thought would be that the militarists were possibly fellow nationalists, albeit 'ethnics'. After Kingsbury, the talk centred on the 'hit squad' having possible 'Jewish' connections. After the arrests at Chapel Market, 'second generation Irish with a chip on their shoulder' became a favoured explanation. However, what may have been a throwaway remark then was soon to take organisational form.

1.7

RED ACTION IS FORMED

By early 1982, less than three years after claiming victory over the NF, the ANL existed in name only. It was by then regarded by militants as more of an embarrassment than anything else. What occasional activities it did organise were ineffectual and on the opposite part of town. Where effective action was still being organised, it was not by the ANL, but by the now politically 'independent' squads under the direction of Red Action.

On the 24th April 1982 the National Front held a St George's Day march in Blackpool and the ANL organised what would prove to be its last counter-demonstration for an entire decade. "A very half-hearted attempt was made to organise an Anti-Nazi League counter-demonstration which turned out to be a depressing failure. Ultimately a group of about 150 anti-racists held a short march around the town and were grateful to have the police between them and several hundred aggressive and confident fascists. And so the steady demise of the ANL goes on and on" (*Red Action*, No 4, 1982).

While this sort of non-confrontational activity had little impact on the fascists, other than to raise their confidence, it also failed to attract new recruits to the anti-fascist movement. "From the heady days of '77, '78 and '79, when thousands turned out in London, Leicester, Manchester, etc., and forced the Front to be completely dependent on the police to be able to march at all, we now see anti-racists needing police protection themselves. How – and why – has this happened?

"The ANL was founded in late 1977 and was soon riding the crest of a popular wave. It succeeded in uniting various shades of political opinion under one banner. Its specific aim was to expose the National Front (who, at the time, were attracting growing electoral support), as a fascist organisation, run by confirmed nazis ... The 1979 election proved how successful the League had been, when the Front completely failed to achieve their hoped for breakthrough, and for a short time retreated in disarray, the respectable image they were looking for firmly nailed. Since then the League has slowly but surely slid closer to oblivion, whilst the Front have re-emerged alongside the British Movement with a more openly aggressive violent character. The ANL leadership has totally failed to re-organise the League to face this new emergence. No-one would expect to maintain the massive carnival turnouts indefinitely, but there were still many committed anti-fascists up and down the country, who have been left high and dry with little or no direction or leadership" (*Red Action*, No 4, 1982).

Essentially what Red Action was arguing was that, instead of being wound up, it was more pragmatic to wind it down to a level appropriate to the nature of the challenge now being offered by the Far Right. But this argument was never going to be addressed objectively. Instead the ANL simply abandoned the field to the NF. In the absence of anyone else with the know how or appetite to pick up the baton, the political responsibility for confronting an increasingly aggressive Far Right rested with a relatively small number of manual workers who had never held rank in any party. And perhaps more instructively, were never likely to.

Against what was otherwise a rather ragged looking rearguard they had proved in the fifteen months from their suspension that there was more to them than a rough-hewn instinct. But, if they didn't know it already, an incident at Blackpool reminded them of the risks involved in taking the fight to the Far Right single-handed. A chance encounter with some Islington NF in Blackpool town centre led to a chase through the coach station, where one of the fleeing NF was felled by a blow from a tyre iron. Those in the queue for the coach were incensed by what they regarded as undue brutality and made moves to intervene before being warned off. As two of the anti-fascists retreated, they were followed by a hue and cry, only to emerge back onto the main road to be greeted by between fifteen and twenty skinheads looking for blood.

Joe: "To say it was a nasty situation was putting it mildly. Without breaking stride we wheeled round and headed straight back the way we had come. As we sprinted for the back of the station we could hear the shouts of our original pursuers but screened by the coaches we slipped passed them. Happily the skinheads never took up the chase. Perhaps hearing the hullabaloo made by the pursuing coach travellers bent on securing a citizen's arrest, they mistook them for more of us. Anyway, I thought we were home free when MacSquirty pulls up. 'I can't run anymore.' The double sprint coming so soon after the stabbing had done him in. His breathing was laboured and shallow. I knew that any second now the area was likely to be flooded by police, armed with our descriptions. We had to get off the street. Just then I saw a fish and chip shop. I dived in with an ashen-faced MacSquirty trailing behind. I could hardly believe it. It must have been the longest and narrowest restaurant in the world. And was entirely empty. We walked past the counter as if looking for a seat – but just kept going straight out the fire exit! 'I'll call the police,' the outraged woman behind the counter shouted after us, rightly suspecting we were up to no good.

"When we emerged we discovered to our huge delight that we had traversed the entire block and were now on the sea front. The tide was out and so we headed for the shoreline from where, as we strolled, we could see police vehicles whizzing up and down, and just occasionally the screaming sirens carried on the wind. We were safe for the moment. However, when after a number of hours we met up with some others who had escaped arrest, we found out that police sentries had been posted outside both the coach and rail stations, an operation that could only work if they had our descriptions. After lying low for a number of hours, we decided to catch the night train from Glasgow to Euston. This meant hiring a cab to Preston for sixteen pounds. We later found out Mickey had been arrested. When he was put in the line up, sensing he was about to be fitted up, he switched places with someone who had just volunteered to make up the numbers. Funnily enough it was actually the volunteer and not O'Farrell that was picked out by witnesses and led away."

While anti-fascism was undeniably a key element of the newly founded Red Action, it was not only on this issue that a radical departure from what was hitherto regarded as custom and practice could be discerned. In truth, what fundamental differences had arisen in this field were symbolic of a far wider alienation that, from the outset, caused the new grouping to look for fresh methods, and to dispense overnight with almost all conventional forms of agit-prop and recruitment along the way.

"It must be pointed out that confrontations rarely occurred as a result of political agitation, paper sales, marches, public meetings by us (by and large we hardly did any), but because we sought them out for retribution ... On some occasions, for tactical reasons (wariness of uniting our enemies), we neither claimed responsibility nor credit for these activities. The success of an operation contained its own political reward. As an organisation, our safety lay in our anonymity. There was little danger of infiltration at this time due to the camaraderie and intimacy that existed as a result of the semi-clandestine and security conscious way the group operated. Individuals were forced to remain politically anonymous at work and in the communities in which they lived for fear of identification and retaliation by fascists or their sympathisers. Practically our only other political activity at this time was taking part in and selling our paper, which was produced intermittently, at large left-wing demonstrations. For Irish or Republican demonstrations, we often provided stewards and helped with security, and so, for this and for the reasons outlined above, we rarely ever marched behind a Red Action banner. We sought neither recognition nor recruits" (*The Making of Red Action*, 1988).

A rationale that perhaps explains why, while militant anti-fascists were increasingly successful at street level, they simply were not equipped with strategies for tackling at a more political level the causes of support for the NF. Therefore, when the fascists were violently removed from a music venue, a paper sale, or their marches were attacked, there was no pro-active strategy to fill the political vacuum that had been fashioned. For the militants 'creating the space' by driving out the fascists was reward in itself. Right up until 1994 militant anti-fascists genuinely believed that the political vacuum created by them would be somehow or other filled by the wider Left. As events show, they were mistaken. This was not a case of them being 'too cynical of the Left'. Rather their mistake appears to lie in their not being cynical enough.

In the meantime, by providing a political identity for working class activists, many who had never actually been members of the SWP despite their activity within the 'squads', Red Action rapidly became a by-word for extremism within the Far Right. However, while its reductive role allowed the group to 'focus', it also allowed others to focus on RA. As early as 1983, within a year of being launched, RA personnel were informed by a Searchlight contact that Special Branch were making inquiries in regard to the group's motivation, composition, and *modus operandi*.

This did not come as a terrible surprise considering that, in one seven day period, RA had mounted successful attacks on three separate right-wing organisations, one of which resulted in the ill-named 'National Action Party' (a brainchild of would-be assassin Eddy Morrison) collapsing on the very day it was to hold its first national conference. Twenty years later when Gerry Gable recalled the incident, he mistakenly attributed the incident to AFA though it was an entirely RA operation. "When the assembled NAP masses spotted a large group of men walking towards them, Morrison announced that these were reinforcements. Unfortunately for him, they were Anti-Fascist Action supporters and Morrison's troops spent the rest of the day in the casualty unit of the local hospital" (*Searchlight*, April 2003).

Joe: "Much as we might have wanted to boast of our success, the fact is we simply couldn't afford to take the weight. Having taken point duty, we were always conscious of both the scale of the problem, and how utterly isolated we were, both physically and, as importantly, politically."

This political isolation did not for the moment intrude on operational matters. Red Action had the room to simply pick their targets. Almost casually the fascist presence in East Street Market in south London was irrevocably extinguished when, without warning or fanfare, the paper sellers were overwhelmed in less than five minutes of mayhem. As the grim faced anti-fascists massed on the other side of the busy road, waiting for an opportune moment to cross *en masse*, young mothers, sensing danger, swept up their children while fascists stood seemingly oblivious. As the fascists fled, a heavy glass door in a shoe shop snapped in two as they surged through seeking refuge. Some hope. They were pursued into a storeroom, while others, trapped among the displays, had a no-tolerance message literally hammered into their heads by stiletto-shoe-wielding opponents. So stunning had been the anti-fascist victory neither the NF nor BM ever returned.

But where the physical force strategy was undeniably successful, the Far Right continued to reorganise, and the alarming rise in racist attacks made it evident anti-fascism would sooner or later need to be put back on a wider agenda. By early 1984 militant anti-fascism in the shape of Red Action was at a crossroads. While its ability to win the battles it chose to fight proved effective in pegging back the opposition in the areas in which it was operating – like, say, the gig scene – a glance at the bigger picture revealed the Far Right steadily inching forward. The studied reluctance of the wider Left to take the threat seriously meant militants were fully conscious of the danger of either over-reaching or being outflanked. A more basic contradiction arose from the reality of a socialist group working full time as either the first or last line of anti-fascist defence. Two incidents, one in the summer of 1984 and the other at the beginning of 1985, illustrated there was only one way forward, and, as tellingly, no way back.

Poster advertising the free GLC festival in Jubilee Gardens, 10th June 1984.

1.8

GLC, REDSKINS AND HARROGATE, 1984

On 10th June 1984, in the midst of the Miners' Strike, the Greater London Council, led by Ken Livingstone, hosted a free open-air concert in Jubilee Gardens as part of a campaign against both unemployment and Tory government cuts. Thousands attended, with family groups making up a large part of the crowd. Halfway through the event, about 80 or more NF suddenly materialised and immediately set about the audience gathered around the main stage where the Redskins were playing. The boldness of the assault panicked the large left-wing gathering. Not all were cowed. Some elements within the crowd, including some striking miners, regrouped, and after some hand-to-hand fighting in which one RA member was slashed and another anti-fascist had his jaw smashed, the right-wingers, mostly skinheads, were driven off.

Peter: "I felt particularly guilty because we had spotted some fairly obvious NF types earlier but because of the size of the crowd and the fact they were youngish we decided to leave them. They, of course, were the spotters. All I remember as we headed toward the stage area was the shocked looks on the faces of what looked like thousands heading the other way."

But the NF had not finished. Again led by the 6ft 2in Nicky Crane, who had just completed a four year sentence for a similarly indiscriminate attack on a queue of black cinema goers, and buoyed up by the impact they had made on the many thousands of the left-wing enemy present, the rampaging right-wingers returned to attack the Hank Wangford Band on stage at the other end of the park. It proved to be a major blunder. Where the crowd had been taken unawares the first time, news of the second attack saw RA in particular more than eager for the unexpected chance of a replay. Armed with cider bottles, and anything else to hand, Red Action members sprinted toward the trouble. Their charge had the effect of further galvanising the crowd.

In attempting to make a getaway, Crane was felled by Peter C. and only by using a young female anti-fascist as a shield, survived the onslaught with cuts and bruises. Less fortunate was another skinhead who, to his evident relief, had been rescued from the crowd by two police officers who held off vengeful left-wingers with batons. The stand-off ended when a leading militant stepped out of the crowd and punched one of his benefactors full in the face. When the officer bent to retrieve his helmet, he was bundled headfirst into a concrete litter-bin. Terrified, the skinhead made a run for it with just time, possibly, to reflect on the shortcomings of huge steel toe-cap boots in such a situation, before being brought to earth and kicked unmercifully while the police, understandably putting their safety first, stood by and watched. Nearby another couple of skinheads, one male and one female were both booted on the ground, with police again unwilling to mediate.

One particularly unlucky individual, who up to that time had escaped the pogrom being visited on his compatriots, was attempting to leave the area of immediate danger when the attention of a keen-eyed member of a marauding RA crew, some now bare-chested, paused to study a lone figure walking toward them with eyes downcast and, though the day was warm, Harrington jacket fully zipped up. Challenged, he reluctantly revealed what it was he was anxious to conceal: a T-shirt bearing the legend 'Nicky Crane'. Add another customer for casualty. Events continued in this retributive fashion to the extent that the corridors of the local casualty department at St Thomas's hospital became the scenes of further clashes as anti-fascists and an increasing number of fascists queued for treatment alongside each other. When the news reached Red Action, the entire squad, along with a considerable number of fellow travellers, were dispatched to restore a menacing sort of order. For one young Redskin follower the arrival of Red Action proved an inspiring moment.

Andy: "I'd travelled up with a small group primarily to see the Redskins. While our sympathies were obviously towards the Left and anti-fascist, none of us were involved with anything formally, although we knew a few of the RA members who would turn up to gigs at the time. The day was a relaxed affair and we certainly didn't anticipate any trouble but, just as the Redskins were getting into their set, they were attacked by a large group of fascist skinheads. Our small group was near the front and, as this huge bonehead went to clamber onto the stage, my mate caught him with a great punch, clean to the jaw. He had always had a good 'dig' on him but this bonehead just stopped, turned, looked at my mate and then just carried on. I can only guess that, as my mate was also a skinhead,* he had thought it was a mistake!

---

* It is important to point out that RA/AFA was neither anti-skinhead, nor made the ignorant and lazy assumption many on the Left made: that skinhead equals fascist. In fact, militant anti-fascism always contained both skinheads and former-skinheads within its ranks throughout its existence. While it is used regularly throughout this book (mainly for the benefit of the casual reader), the term 'skinhead' was actually jettisoned from the language of AFA activists in favour of 'the boneheads' or simply 'the bones'.

This in itself was in recognition of the fact that by the late '80s, and the emergence of the Blood & Honour movement, fascist skinheads had dropped traditional skinhead fashion in favour of a semi-paramilitary uniform of shaved head, black flight jacket, Blood & Honour T-shirt, black combat trousers and black, almost knee-high, boots. And, of course, the traditional skinhead purists also insisted that a working class cult that had its origins in West Indian music and culture could never be, by its very nature, home to the fascist activist or racist bigot.

"By now a gap had opened up between the fash and the huge crowd. We'd all been caught on the hop, but this wasn't a lot different to what we'd all experienced many times at football, as far as we were concerned. Now everyone had sussed what was going on it was just a case of regrouping and 'steaming-in'. We urged those around us forward but their reaction shocked us to the core. Hundreds of 'lefties' were simply terrified and even more terrified of the idea that we wanted them to join battle. Five minutes ago these people were sing-a-long-a-revolution with the Redskins, now they were quaking in their boots. As the boneheads started backing off, we joined other groups who were arriving from all directions and gave chase. We thought that was it and were feeling pretty down when a little later the fash attacked once more. This time people quickly swung into action, we picked up empty cider bottles and headed towards the action. We were a mixed bunch of 'red skinheads', junior RA members and outraged miners [the strike was on at the time and many of them were down with their families].

"As the crowd opened-up, we saw the boneheads and immediately charged, catching some of them on the walkway next to the river. A number of them went

The Redskins

down but I prevented some of the 'trendy lefties' from putting the boot in as they lay on the floor. As far as I was concerned, they had forfeited that right by their display of cowardice earlier in the day. As the police intervened, we got word that a friend of ours, a DJ and fanzine editor, who was one of the least offensive people you'd ever meet and certainly not a 'combatant', had nonetheless had his jaw bust by the boneheads and was up at nearby St Thomas's hospital. When we got to the hospital it was pandemonium. Inside, two white males and a rather large black female RA member were kicking off with members of the Chelsea Headhunters (including Chris 'Chubby' Henderson) who were themselves demanding that the black security guard arrange taxis for them so they could leave the area safely. A couple of young lads wearing Celtic football tops and sporting RA badges sauntered into the hospital, sat down next to us and gave me a wink.

"Just then a large group of boneheads, who had obviously been visiting their mates, appeared from within the hospital. I was a bit worried but the boneheads clearly had other things on their mind. Through the window they could see a large group, a number of whom I vaguely recognised as senior RA people. One was doing press-ups on the steps as though he was warming-up for the main event. Others were pointing and laughing at the lead bonehead, debating whether he was the 'ugliest man they'd ever seen' and urging him outside for closer inspection. I recognised the bonehead in question as Matty Morgan, who had a bit of a reputation as a 'psycho' and was someone I'd seen throw his weight around at skinhead gigs at first hand. While some of the skinhead girls with him encouraged him to confront those taunting him, he simply looked petrified.

"It was like a scene from the Asterix cartoon books I'd read as a kid. Instead of being intimidated by the mighty legions of the 'master race', the RA group was in fact in high spirits, almost arguing who had seen the boneheads first and therefore had the right to land the first blows! After years of having to 'keep our heads down' in the presence of the Far Right, this was an eye-opener to say the least. Later on my small group was approached by one of the RA members and invited up to The Agricultural to continue the festivities. We declined. I think we'd all had enough excitement for the day by that stage and decided to retire to a nearby pub instead. That night, pint in hand, I watched John Barnes score his wonder goal for England in the Maracana but my mind wasn't really on the game. The day's events had given me much to think about. Obviously I didn't realise it at the time, but that day was my first in over a decade of involvement in front-line anti-fascism."

The pub in question was The Agricultural on Liverpool Road in Islington. It had become a meeting point for overtly nazi skinheads from all over London – and beyond. One wide-eyed visitor was a Belfast youth, Johnny Adair, later to be christened 'Mad Dog' by the media for his role in the deaths of an estimated 20 Catholics in the battle between Loyalists and Republicans for hegemony in the Six

Counties of Ulster. In the immediate vicinity, attacks on blacks and gays became commonplace. According to a biography of Adair, 'Mad Dog' himself, whilst in Islington, was part of a gang that "beat up and mugged a black man as they caught the tube [from the Angel] to Elephant & Castle where they went drinking with another nazi sympathiser" (*Mad Dog*, by David Lister and Hugh Jordan, page 40). That the black man in question had his teeth kicked out in the attack and was 60 years old was not mentioned.

By coincidence, anti-fascists had begun to use an Irish pub called The White Horse, also on Liverpool Road. It was run by a famous Tottenham football hooligan called Ronnie Parrish, and initially used as a retreat from the stresses of the weekly conflict at Chapel Market. Heavy drinking played a prominent part in the de-stressing, though imbibing while on duty was frowned upon. (Later on, although rare, it was not unknown for an individual to be stood down if considered under the influence prior to an operation.) With an RA centre for rest and recuperation in London sited only a hundred yards away from The Agricultural, scuffles and ambushes became more or less weekly occurrences. Occasionally some incident, like when an RA member slightly the worse for drink was kicked unconscious in broad daylight, would trigger a more concerted effort. The response on that occasion was a full-frontal assault by about fifty anti-fascists, which led to running battles involving over a hundred people that lasted for almost half an hour. One explanation for the tardiness of the police response was that they were no keener on the skinhead influx every weekend than were the militants. To repel one counter-attack, anti-fascists ripped off a nine-foot length of rusty pavement railing. Merrily a nearby building site was raided for bricks. Such was the ferocity of the ensuing onslaught that not only the windows, but also the actual wooden window frames in The Agricultural were smashed.

Attempting to rally the skinheads one shouted, "Get them, they are not English, they are Irish!" in a markedly foreign accent. When arrested, he was fined and deported back to Belgium the following Monday. Exploiting police antipathy, The Agricultural suffered another full frontal attack about 7pm on the evening of 16th June. Thereafter, the sounds of smashing windows, nonchalantly but nevertheless routinely broken, became a sound the owners and their neighbours came to be familiar with. After months of this unceasing hostility, the brewery had little option but to close down the pub altogether.

Meanwhile, media publicity following the attack on the GLC festival created the opening for Red Action. A leaflet, which followed their basic analysis, was quickly drawn up and widely circulated. It drew a warm welcome.

"The Anti-Nazi League was formed in 1977 to alert the public to the growing electoral threat of the NF. Its successful expose of the neo-nazi past of its leaders and the mobilisation of huge numbers to prevent the fascists marching led to the decline of the Front. The election of the Tory government in 1979 was another damaging body blow. Their policies on immigration and law and order were extreme enough to satisfy the right-wing nationalists on which the Front had previously relied for their support. Since then, there have been significant changes in the Far Right. The old 'constitutional' nazis like Tyndall have gone, and the NF is now dominated by a new group. They believe that 'controlling the streets' (i.e. smashing all potential opposition) is vital if they are to regain political credibility. They rely for their political and intellectual guidance on an Italian fascist terrorist group called the Third Position. They recognise that, as 'race warriors', the average NF member leaves a lot to be desired, hence the formation of the Instant Response Group. In the nine months since its formation, the IRG has been building the morale and experience of its members by attacking a series of 'soft' targets: student discos, Troops Out meetings, paper sales, and savage attacks on individual asians, culminating in the well organised assault on 10th June [GLC]. And they intend to continue these attacks throughout the summer. By operating in this way, they are aware that it will not have any electoral appeal, but consider it necessary to 'clear the way' if they are going to re-emerge as a political force. In the meantime, they present an immediate and personal threat to all left-wing activities. They must be stopped.

"Red Action has a credible record in dealing with fascists, but for obvious reasons we are not prepared to be the police force for the Left. We do, however, regard this 'new' initiative as sufficiently serious to launch this appeal to all unaligned anti-fascists and individual members of other groups to contact us through this leaflet. Our aim is to help form a mobile combat squad who would be on call to defend public meetings, gigs, paper sales, etc., of any left-wing organisation under threat of imminent attack. And to take the offensive when necessary. We are convinced that, at the moment, this tactic is the best response and the most effective way of preventing the fascists achieving their ultimate aim, 'controlling the streets'."

The leaflet struck a chord, and immediately generated debate within and among otherwise disparate groups, such as the Revolutionary Communist Group, who mounted a 24-hour anti-apartheid picket outside the South African Embassy and were under continual attack, and the likes of the Newham Monitoring Project, Class War and Searchlight.

If Red Action members had apparently been left "cursing ourselves for our reasonableness and moderation" (*Red Action*, issue 13) following the GLC attack, another act of aggression considerably closer to home reminded anyone irritated by the one-dimensional political profile the group was earning that, whatever the future, the possibility of any return to life as a conventional socialist grouping was already past. For one thing the fascists were not likely to ever let bygones be bygones and, equally, as there could be no retreat with credibility or honour, so for good or ill RA were now in it for the long haul.

Hard choices were also facing the militant irregulars in Manchester, some aligned to RA, some not. In part the strains resulting from the scenario outlined in the previous paragraph led to a call by founding members, John P. and Peter W. of the Socialist Federation – of which RA was a part – for Red Action to fully throw in their lot with the former and actually disband. This came as a surprise, particularly to militants in London. Eyebrows were again raised when Peter W. and Steve T. publicly sided with students at Manchester Poly following the latter being witness to a particularly violent encounter between leading squadists led by Denis C. and a hardy team of fascists in a pub in Harrogate. The criticism was not well received, to put it mildly, particularly as "but for our intervention, they would still be in comas and wheelchairs to this day," as one put it.

Denis: "A protest march through Harrogate by the students' union on an end of May bank holiday offered a promising day out. Harrogate had always proved to be a lively venue, as previous encounters against Andrew Brons and Steve Gaunt had shown, so the opportunity for the 'boys' to euphemistically 'show support' for the student comrades of Harrogate was readily taken, accompanied with free travel facilities provided by Manchester Polytechnic! Needless to say, this support did not involve actually going on the march. As soon as the students began marching through the town, we split off. The plan was to shadow the march through the town and see who came out to oppose it. Our team was only six strong, which meant we could be quite mobile without arousing too much suspicion. We slipped away to have a few quiet drinks whilst the march and its supporters and detractors assembled.

"Barely was the second pint launched before one of the Manchester students arrived to say that they had spotted a fascist scout. 'So what do you want us to do? All pile out and show him exactly what he's there to see? If it's only one, go back and sort him out yourself' was the gist of the conversation prior to him leaving, tail between his legs. As the march set off, we ambled along behind slowly, appearing almost casually disinterested. As the students meander past one city centre hostelry, the fash, already alerted by the approaching din, appear from a local pub 'sieg-heiling' and effing-off the students. Utterly confident in their ability to stand their ground against the student masses, they challenge them to come and have a go.

"However, they fail to look the other way, and by now we are in amongst them, expressing a strong interest in taking up their challenge. A minor exchange of blows takes place, prompting the fash to retreat into the pub; the police, now alerted, head over, as we seek cover in the body of the march. An inspector shouts out to his men to 'grab the one in the denim jacket'. Me. Immediately, the other lads begin to swap jackets with marchers, but I am told, 'Fuck off, I'm not getting nicked for you' by some student. Amid growls and threats, the police move in and pull three of us. Still unsure as to what exactly happened, the inspector proceeds to give us a pep talk, whereupon, one of the lads burst into a rant about how his dad was killed in the war by the Germans, and the sight of nazi salutes had triggered his emotions. Notwithstanding the fact that the lad in his middle twenties would need to be in his middle forties for this to be faintly realistic, and the sight of some onlookers spinning away, stifling giggles, the inspector sympathised with our war orphan, and tells him not to let them provoke him!

"The rest of the march passed off without further incident as we were under observation and had to go with the flow. There were a few fash milling around, no doubt holding back for easy pickings with the students. As people dispersed towards the coaches and the nearest pubs, we decided we would have one or two before departing. We went into this pub whose name escapes me, and noted there were about half a dozen people off our coach in an alcove having a quiet drink, totally oblivious to the fact that they were outnumbered by more than two to one by a likely bunch who had gathered on adjacent tables, and were lining them up. We sussed them the minute we entered but as their response to us was neutral, we knew they hadn't sussed us. So we engage them in a conversation that slowly but surely deteriorated.

"We are casually sat around the edge of their group, as they begin to put two and two together. Suddenly one of them stands up and declares, "I'm a fascist and proud of it!" He had a bottle in his hand. Unabashed and still sitting, Dessie Noonan responds, 'If you're thinking of taking this outside, you better bring that bottle with you – 'cos you'll fuckin' need it!' At which point Roy Mac launches one of your classic pub glass ashtrays to your man's head, which everyone took as the signal for hostilities to commence. The floor filled quicker than a Glen Miller comeback concert, as the fight set off at a belting pace. I was grappling with one lad when another one grabs the back of my denim jacket and tries to pull it over my head, a manoeuvre stopped abruptly by a precisely delivered chair leg to the head from Craig, which sparked him clean out.

"Some of the intended targets sat in the alcove also cut loose, and one fella, big Chris S., something of a gentle giant, led the charge. Tables, chairs, glasses, bottles, fists and boots flew in a wonderful free for all as the lads stood toe to toe, with odds of two against one, and fought the fash to a standstill. Above the din, the inevitable sirens catch everyone's attention, prompting both sides to professionally disengage and depart in a hurry.

"As the police come through the front door, we are filing out past them in the opposite direction, whilst the fash, armed with local knowledge depart through the back door. The police grab who they can as both sides disperse. We lose Roy Mac and the fash get two lads nicked as well. Fearing a nicking, as soon as the police arrive, Dessie makes a break for it and heads down the road to meet us back at the coach. It proves to be a mistake, as we regroup outside, do a headcount and make sure everyone is okay before we move off. Unbeknownst to Dessie, the fash who had departed via the back entrance were now heading in the same direction, via the adjacent road. As he gets within sight of the coaches on the green, he glances to his right to see about a dozen of them from the pub racing towards him, one armed with a screwdriver. Unable to double back he heads for the coaches at speed, as we saunter down the hill, unaware of Dessie's situation – a situation rapidly deteriorating as the driver deems it unwise to open the coach door. Incredibly, some of the students already on the coach, including Steve T., do their best to ignore his predicament. Somehow Dessie manages to force his way on to a coach and kick the door shut as the first arrivals of the mob reach the coach. As the rest of our lot appear heading towards the coaches, the fascists give up and run off.

"All that was left to do now was rescue Roy. The Harrogate police kindly provided bed and breakfast and booked him in for an appearance at the magistrates the following morning. Two lads went over to collect Roy, who was happy to accept breach of the peace on behalf of the team for the previous day's performance. Amid tense scenes in the court lobby, Roy walked calmly through his adversaries to leave the building, when one called out, 'Hey, Manchester… don't come back.' Roy turned, smiled and walked away."

Now, no one was pretending that this chance encounter was a major strategic victory, but it was well within militant guidelines of engagement and part and parcel of the ethos: 'Hit them wherever you see them'. In addition, in their eyes, the participants had, judging by the nature of the enemy, saved some students from what would likely have been a very serious beating. So there was genuine astonishment that, instead of congratulations, they were greeted with condemnation on their return to Manchester. They were accused of general indiscipline, leaving the march, drinking 'on duty', of using unnecessary and excessive violence and, worst of all, of provoking, then attacking, not a gang of fascists up to no good, but a group of ordinary football supporters. (This was a variation on the type of allegations that surfaced after the bloodbath in Conway Hall in London some years earlier.)

That colleagues like Steve T. and Peter W., neither of whom was involved on the day, saw fit to be critical of the level of violence used left many baffled. Backed by some, but not all, of the students actually present they insisted: "the opposition were, in fact, football supporters and not fascists". "What would football supporters be doing in Harrogate on a bank holiday at the end of May?" the militants countered. "And, moreover, if they were indeed football fans, you should have no trouble naming the team they were supporting?" With no answers forthcoming, the clamour for the calling of a more formal inquiry died. At the time it was put down to a couple of former comrades finally succumbing to the student lifestyle and in pursuit of student union office, but on a broader level it also reflected a general retreat from the streets.

1.9

RED ACTION NATIONAL MEETING, 1985

This isolationist course was further confirmed when in February 1985 RA, in an attempt to broaden its appeal, announced in issue 16 of the paper the meeting point and time of the annual 'Red Action National Meeting'. The meeting starts at 10.30am, the advertisement announced blandly. However, due to some unwelcome but hardly entirely unexpected early arrivals, it kicked off a mite earlier.

Joe: "Some of us felt it was a little foolhardy and an opposition response seemed pretty likely. So, to be on the safe side, a couple of us organised 'tools' to be made available if needed. Shortly after 10am that morning I turned up along with a few of the lads. We climbed the stairs to the meeting. At the end of the corridor I could see a queue of people. 'A good turn-out', I remember thinking. Suddenly one of them produced a large hammer and smashed straight through the glass panel of the door in which the meeting was to be held. Immediately, they were met with resistance from within, and so possibly when they saw us they thought we were an easier target and screamed, 'There's more of them!' and charged.

"For the briefest of moments I thought about holding the door and trapping them in the corridor. Then it dawned on me that the glass panel in this door was likely to be just as vulnerable to a hammer, as it was the same type as in the other door. Anyway, next thing we were all running. In the crush I actually got wedged on the narrow stairwell shoulder to shoulder with someone else. Literally stuck. It was almost funny, in a hysterical kind of way. Eventually we tumbled down and ducked back under the stairs and into the kitchen, looking for weapons. The fascists flashed past out of the building. So, along with a young lad, Eamonn, we picked up a few bits and pieces, a bread knife and some milk bottles and followed them. They were gone about twenty or thirty yards down the road. When they saw us trailing them they stalled and then stopped. Seeing there was only two of us to their dozen or so, one shouted: 'Let's get these two cunts, anyway.'

"Immediately, we began to back off. Time was on our side, I confidently expected, if we could stall them. Suddenly, Eamonn stepped forward and launched a bottle. Missed. Jesus! 'For fuck's sake, Eamonn, keep the other one,' I shout, a fraction of a second before he launches it. They came at us then. I threw a quick look over my shoulder. Sure enough to my intense delight, the boys were rounding the corner, on the run and armed to the teeth. So we stood our ground. Blows were exchanged. I took this tremendous punch in the forehead. Eamonn decked one of them; everyone was hacking away. A large bald fascist right in front of me took an iron bar straight over the nut. His whole face just went grey. Fractured skull for sure, I thought. Another one on his hands and knees on the floor dropped his iron bar – a great big silver thing with a screw through the top of it – and began shouting, 'Enough! Enough!' You'll be lucky, I thought, as blows rained down.

"People started chasing the others over walls and through gardens. I think the van pulled away with only about half of them in it. Three were left in the middle of the road. A taxi stopped, and a woman got out, screaming hysterically. Someone pulled her back in. Everyone else ignored her.

"Without much discussion it was decided to carry on with the meeting. Though it was unlikely they would come back, I volunteered for sentry duty outside, more to calm myself down than anything else. One of the women who worked in the kitchen was carted off in an ambulance with a suspected heart attack. So I'm standing there when Labour MP Jeremy Corbyn opens the door of the centre and peeps out. 'Have they gone?' he says. 'Yeah,' I say. 'Were they here for you or me?' he says. 'It was us,' I reply. You could see the relief visible on his face. 'Oh, good!' he remarked cheerfully. Then, with a quick look in both directions, he skipped off down the road. I remember laughing at the time. How ironic, I thought. Here we have a Member of Parliament, no less, having to skulk around his own constituency for fear of rampaging fascists everyone else seems determined to deny exist."

Later in the day at about 5pm, just as the meeting was concluding, the police turned up to make some casual inquiries. There were a number of men in St Thomas's hospital in south London with serious head injuries. Did anyone here know anything about it? Not unexpectedly, a collective 'No' was the reply. Apparently satisfied the police left, and so did RA. Twelve months later Jeremy Corbyn would be installed as the honorary president of the newly launched Anti-Fascist Action.

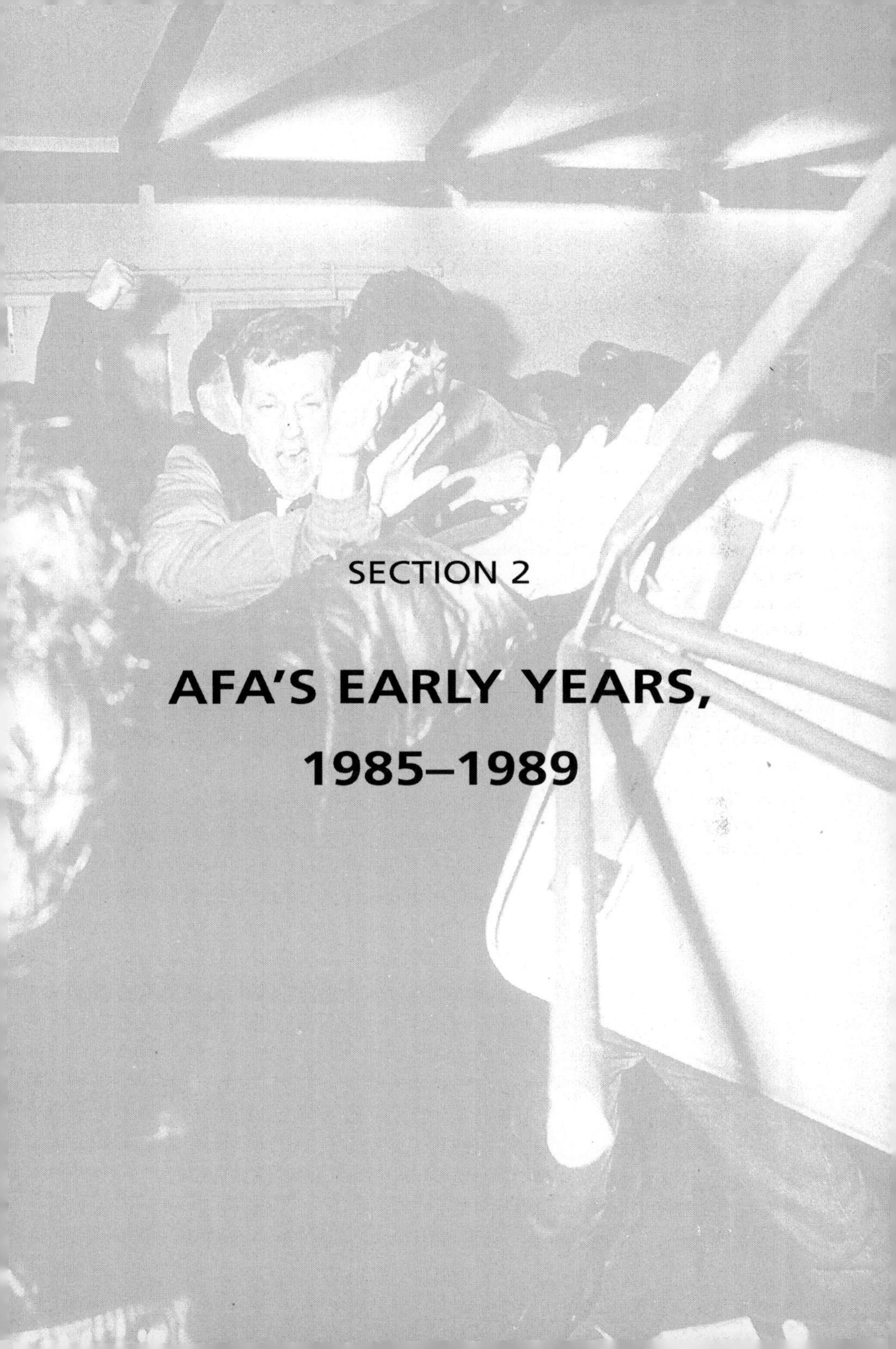

SECTION 2

AFA'S EARLY YEARS, 1985–1989

Previous page: The National Front meeting in Charlton on 21st February 1987.

2.1
AFA LAUNCH, JULY 1985

Though the initial proposal by RA was, on the face of it, limited to security only, in the discussions that resulted, a wider number of groups and individuals focused on the possibility of the launch of a new anti-fascist organisation. When, in May 1981, Searchlight had attempted to re-forge anti-fascism, it had proved an embarrassing flop, but that the call had not gone unheeded this time indicated the perspectives and concerns of Red Action were not exclusive to the document's authors. Eventually when a conference was called for the 28th July 1985, 300 people representing a wide range of groups attended.

The new grouping that emerged committed itself to a Statement of Aims: "This conference sees the need to build an anti-fascist front of groups willing to combat fascist activity in this country. We see the need to oppose racism and fascism physically, on the streets, and ideologically. We support the right of ethnic minority groups and groups under threat to organise for their physical self defence and see the need for us to organise in their support. This grouping should be organised on non-sectarian and democratic lines with equal representation for all groups involved."

These egalitarian principles notwithstanding, when Unmesh Desai proposed that Red Action ought to be allowed two delegates in recognition of their standing, it was the RA delegates who declined. This may have been the cause of some regret later. For, acting on information from Searchlight that a fascist 'commando unit' was planning to attack the conference, RA, two delegates apart, committed the rest of the membership exclusively to stewarding duties. Symbolically, as the organisation they had helped set up was founded, the militant wing of the new organisation were, for the most part, physically outside of the hall. From the very outset, therefore, the political orientation and agenda of the new group was open to be dictated by others: a basic misreading of the political chemistry at work it would take more than four years to rectify. Apart from groups like the Direct Action Movement (DAM), Class War, and RA, the bulk of support for the new organisation was comprised of elements drawn from anti-racist groups who, in the main, identified with the liberal left-wing of the Labour Party.

Joe: "To some this was a worry. But active anti-fascists were greatly outnumbered by the fascists at this time and, from Red Action's perspective, one of the aims of this new initiative was to alert the Left as to the scale of the tasks faced at street level, and to create a new organisation that would accommodate new layers of activists. So we were prepared to be patient."

Political naïveté also played a part in their thinking as well, as the militants assumed, wrongly, that regardless of what was decided in meetings, everything could be rectified on the streets. After the meeting when a BNP/NF ambush at King's Cross station, led by Tony Lecomber, was vigorously repulsed, with ambushers fleeing in all directions, this only helped firm up the militarist mindset. Not for the last time RA showed an ability to out think their street opponents. Anticipating that the fascists would be thinking to ambush O'Farrell and Co. as they headed back to Hatfield, the entire stewards group, once everyone else had safely departed, were instructed to travel to King's Cross where the Hatfield boys were to pick up their connection. Instead of the ambushers having the odds of up to four to one in their favour, as they might reasonably have expected, the odds were now reversed. As the first half a dozen AFA stewards passed through the barriers and began to mount the stairs, they were suddenly confronted by a far larger group of BNP members led by Tony Lecomber standing at the top of the stairwell screaming, "C'mon… Red Action!" Alerted by the shouts the rest of the RA stewards, many still on the other side of the barriers, began to systematically drop and unzip gym bags into which eager hands searched for weapons.

Bernard O'Mahoney, a young tough, who would later write a bestseller called *Essex Boys*,* was with the would-be ambushers. In his autobiography he recalls the day but for some reason he refers to RA/AFA as the 'RAF' (Red Army Faction), and also mistakenly believes RA were travelling from a march in south London, rather than a meeting in north London. He reveals that, rather than hole up in a pub somewhere, as would have been the norm, the presumably hand-picked crew had actually gone to the trouble of booking a room under a pseudonym in the Friends Meeting House in Euston Road.

"A BNP 'spotter' who was following them from south London rang on a mobile phone to say they'd just got on a train heading to King's Cross. One group headed over to the station. A skinhead with us produced a flare gun and promised to shoot a leading RAF member with it. Flares are designed to be used as distress signals or to illuminate targets. If they hit someone, the end result is horrific. A flare, unlike a bullet, doesn't smash its way through flesh and bone – it burns its way through.

There was a real air of menace that day, perhaps generated in part by the bloodlust speeches. Everyone felt something 'big' would happen. Instead of the usual fisticuffs, we thought at least one of the Reds would be seriously injured or even killed. There'd been a dramatic fall in the number of people supporting extreme right-wing parties. The feeling was that a 'spectacular' was needed to thrust

* *Essex Boys*, which told the story of three of his business associates shot to death in a Range Rover in 1996, was later turned into a movie, starring Sean Bean.

'the Movement' under the spotlight again and reawaken the public's interest. A Red maimed or murdered in such horrific fashion would fit the bill.

"The spotter phoned to say they'd be in King's Cross in 15 minutes. We went down to the tube station to meet them. The owner of the flare gun loaded it for us all to see, before putting it back in his pocket with a 'now we shall see' look. There must have been about 20 of us down near the ticket barrier as the first Reds came up the stairs. As soon as they saw us, they tried to turn and go back down the stairs. We advanced toward the barrier shouting, 'Fucking red scum! Come on! Come on!' Suddenly from further down the stairs came a great roar of manly voices. The Reds who'd been retreating were pushed back up towards us by the ones following. About 50 Reds were now advancing towards us. Everyone in our group was now shouting 'Stand! Stand!' but most were retreating as they said it. Adolf began shouting at the man with the flare gun: 'Shoot the cunts! Shoot the cunts!' But the man just turned and ran. Tony Lecomber was shouting, 'Stand! Stand!' too, but before long he was legging it as well. Only Adolf, Stan, myself, and two others remained as the Reds began clambering over the barriers to get at us. We looked around, looked at each other and said, 'Fuck this.' We legged it. On the stairs to the street Adolf stopped and said, 'We'll hold them here.'

"As the first Reds reached us, we began kicking and punching them but realised the space was too confined. As more Reds arrived, we'd be pushed back or, even worse, over. We ran up the stairs into the street. Adolf and I ran into the overground station. The other two men ran down the road. The leading Reds took off in pursuit of the other two. No one came after us. We sat on a platform bench to get our breath back. Adolf then began shouting abuse: 'We should have fucking done the bastards. What happened to the prick with the flare gun?' Stan looked at me and we both started laughing. Adolf didn't find it amusing. He stood up and stormed off, vowing to 'do some red bastard.' That evening in the pub, we learned that the two men who'd been chased up the street had been captured in a car park off the Caledonian Road. The Reds had kicked and punched them to the ground, then whipped them with a car aerial. As a final act of humiliation, they'd pissed on them" (*Hateland*, pages 98–99, by Mainstream Publishing).

Whether true or not, as the fascists were prone to embellishment, 'pissing on' the enemy in one way or another would prove to be a feature of the newly founded organisation's activity for more than a decade or more.

Later on in 1985, Tony Lecomber made the national news when a bomb he was ferrying exploded prematurely about "300 yards from the Far Left Workers Revolutionary Party's offices in south London," and when "Scotland Yard's Anti-Terrorist Squad searched his home" they "discovered a deadly DIY arsenal including hand grenades, two petrol bombs, detonators, timing devices and dangerous chemicals" (*Ilford Recorder*, 17th March 1994).

Meanwhile, for many in RA, DAM and Class War, the AFA Secretariat, with Unmesh Desai installed as public spokesman, were regarded as individuals who would effectively deal with the day-to-day bureaucracy of the new organisation: the people who would do the public relations work in the unions and the colleges and generally help facilitate an influx of new blood, all of which would help progress and provide a support base for the physical aspect of the anti-fascist struggle. It was not long before it became apparent that what was thought of as the support network saw their function in altogether different terms, and, while being happy to admit to the general indispensability of the stewarding wing, had distinct ambitions and, as importantly, politics of their own.

So within a matter of months there were the first signs of an unstated political tug-of-war between the militants, who aimed to build a larger militant pro-working class organisation, and the more liberal element, who were working just as busily to see AFA accepted as a respectable lobby group, though out of necessity protected by a disciplined security wing, which all importantly took orders only from the executive. Yet, despite this inherent contradiction, for the first time in over five years, it had become possible to confidently deploy large numbers in support of anti-fascist mobilisations and the new organisation quickly set about clocking up some impressive results.

2.2

REMEMBRANCE DAY, NOVEMBER 1985

The first of these mobilisations took place on 10th November 1985, when a contingent from the newly formed anti-fascist organisation, numbering less than a hundred, insolently occupied the traditional assembly point for the annual NF Remembrance Day parade. These parades were an important part in the NF calendar, attracting large numbers, an estimated 2,000 in 1986 for example, and generally providing an annual focal point for their supporters from around the country. The national media coverage that inevitably followed was hardly unwelcome, either. As the NF organisers had grown used to the absence of opposition, the response to the AFA challenge was not long in coming.

The AFA picket was in place for only about ten minutes when, led by Eddie Whicker, the eighty-strong Instant Response Group rounded the corner and approached at pace. Not unreasonably, they expected to run the Lefties everywhere. The pace quickened as the impact their arrival made appeared to send a ripple through the anti-fascist ranks. With police nearby making it perfectly evident they were likely to remain neutral, the sense of anticipation reflected in the faces of the NF's front line suddenly dissolved, as opponents of the more determined, not to say familiar, calibre stepped forward. Ian Stuart (pictured below), lead singer in the skinhead band Skrewdriver, was among the first to falter, slowing, stopping, then standing, before lining up behind members of a bus queue. The NF front line slowed as well and finally halted altogether, now no more than ten yards away. The two groups of approximately equal numbers, eyeball to eyeball, indulged in some near whispered baiting, without, though, any loss of focus. Watching on with equally avid interest, the police nonetheless stayed in their carriers. Impasse.

Eventually Whicker, after sizing up the situation for some minutes, ordered the NF stewards to turn on their heels and return the way they had come, no doubt aware that the difficulty involved in dislodging the AFA picket would inevitably force the main body of marchers to assemble somewhere else. This would result in confusion and delay, not to mention embarrassment for the NF, but there it was. But from the new organisation it was an unequivocal message statement.

Although the larger left-wing organisations did not join AFA, smaller socialist and anarchist groups, various organisations active within the race relations lobby, such as the Refugee Forum, *Searchlight* magazine, and many non-aligned individuals were enthusiastic. In purely political terms AFA was, from the beginning, a big tent indeed. Initially the contrasting and indeed competing agendas gelled. By the following year, London would see the biggest anti-fascist mobilisation since the 1970s.

2.3

INTERNAL AFFAIRS: CLASS WAR SUSPENSION, 1986

Notwithstanding the potential displayed at the Remembrance Day counter-demo, at the 1986 conference held in Manchester on Saturday 22nd February, just three months later, serious exchanges took place in what was set to become a constitutional war between the two camps that would last for the next three years. A blunt motion was tabled at the instigation of Searchlight to expel Class War. This initiative rested on the unlikely and unsupported charge that Class War had fostered links with the NF. Some months earlier at an AFA executive meeting, when asked by an RA delegate if there was any proof to substantiate the claims, Searchlight's Tony Robson struggled to convince. Nonetheless, at the next executive meeting the order suspending Class War was passed. On the morning of the conference itself, East London Direct Action Movement (ELDAM), one of the founding groups of AFA, produced a leaflet that drew attention to the glaring absence of proof.

"Our initial reaction, on reading a *Guardian* exposé on fascist infiltration of the group Class War, was one of amused contempt, and, knowing the article to be a tissue of lies and distortions, we assumed it to be the result of an over-tired and emotional journalist writing from the depths of El Vinos. (We did not know at that time that the story had been planted by Searchlight.) Our amusement turned to shock when, at the following AFA delegate meeting, it was announced that Class War had been suspended by the secretariat. This was announced in such a casual way that even delegates of groups not known for their love of Class War were forced to ask why ... At the following delegate meeting Searchlight produced not one shred of evidence saying the *Guardian* legal department had mislaid it. Yet, despite the absence of any verifiable evidence, the meeting voted in favour of suspension by 14 votes to two, with three abstentions."

The primary victims of the political attack, Class War, also produced a document which they believed accurately profiled the political character of their accusers: "We believe there have been systematic attempts to spread disinformation about Class War, quite probably in co-operation with Special Branch or MI5. We do not think, however, that such a simple explanation is adequate. Many of those on the AFA secretariat (including Gable) are part of the reformist Left – exemplified by the Labour Party and Communist Party – which believes conditions can only be improved via existing institutions: e.g. the state should pass more anti-racist laws, the police should take firmer action against racists, the GLC should set up more anti-racist quangos. Direct action is anathema to such people – any action should be left to the police, instead of us fighting the fascists. In Searchlight's case, opposition to the extremists of the Right has opened the door for extremists of the Centre, for whom Right and Left can be perceived as a threat to 'democracy'."

With the scene set, there was further polarisation between the camps when during the conference young Newham Monitoring Project (NMP) supporters were deployed to cheerlead the Searchlight line. Led by Unmesh Desai who shouted "Searchlight is my Bible," young Asians, none of whom were actually in AFA, paraded aggressively around the hall in a blatant effort to silence verbal demands for the evidence of collusion against Class War to be formally presented. None was forthcoming and the expulsion of Class War was ratified by the conference. Delegates from the DAM, by now the only remaining anarchist affiliates, and RA, led the walk out of the conference in protest. In light of the controversy, an internal investigation was launched "to investigate serious allegations made by a variety of groups and individuals against the Class War grouping."

Six months later, when an independent report was produced as a result of the investigation chaired by John P., it concluded that: "Searchlight's role in the affair was far from clear. The original allegations against Class War were contained in two *Guardian* articles by journalist David Rose. Most of the information for these articles came from the highly respected anti-fascist magazine, *Searchlight* ... We received a surprisingly small amount of written evidence, considering the scale of verbal or non-attributed accusations before and at the AFA conference. Class War sent us a lot of material. Some of the accusations against Class War (CW) were only made known to the commission via this CW submission! Despite the leading role of *Searchlight* magazine in the affair, and despite many approaches to the magazine for evidence, the sum total of material from Searchlight to the enquiry was nil. We are bemused by Searchlight's role in this affair."

Years later in a letter to a former member of the AFA executive, Tony Greenstein, Gable claimed that he had given 'a substantial dossier' on Class War to Unmesh Desai. In his reply Greenstein questioned the existence of the document. "I am in receipt of a letter of yours dated 11th September 1991 which makes exactly the same allegation. This is the same Unmesh Desai who persuaded me and the Brighton delegation to vote to uphold the Class War suspension at the 1986 Manchester Conference, who described Searchlight as the 'Bible' of the movement. I asked Unmesh about this allegation and he told me that all he had ever received from you were a few photocopies of existing newspaper articles, which AFA already had. Incidentally the journalist who broke the story in the *Guardian*, David Rose, also retracted the allegations saying you had misled him" (Letter from Tony Greenstein, 16th July 1993).

The enquiry recommended the lifting of Class War's suspension because the allegations "have not been proven." However, the damage has been done and Class War, along with the Direct Action Movement, refused to return. Decisively, though, Red Action did return. Even if the overall class character of the organisation lacked balance the unitary model offered by AFA had already shown its potential and was definitely worth persevering with. It did not go unnoticed, either, that during their period of self-suspension, AFA had effectively been paralysed without active direction from the security wing. So, from a RA standpoint, it was all to play for. As if to emphasise the point, Red Action's return to the AFA fold coincided with two dramatic victories for AFA at opposite ends of the country.

By the mid 1980s Nick Griffin was already warning of the threat posed by militant anti-fascism.

2.4

BRIEF ENCOUNTERS: STOCKPORT AND BURY ST EDMUNDS

As Red Action had always intended, low-level clashes were now beginning to take place on a regular basis between fascists and anti-fascists around the country. On 7th June 1986, AFA called a counter-demonstration against an NF march in Liverpool. The turnout from Manchester and London was considered to be impressive but no contact was made with the opposition. Any sense of disappointment was quickly forgotten when the NF and AFA clashed in Stockport outside Manchester.

"The SWP were strategically massed behind the police cordon outside the town hall, whilst the NF walked past waving banners. Two vans travelling in opposite directions pull alongside the nazis, whereupon anti-fascists emerged from the rear and engage in meaningful dialogue with them. The nazis and the police retreat to the shelter of the waiting room of Stockport British Rail station. A line of police moved in on the anti-fascists who, in turn, moved towards them, whereupon the police and dogs turn and run! Attempts to induce the nazis to leave the waiting room with the assistance of smoke bombs proved unsuccessful. Four fascists arrived late in a shiny new Saab (Daddy's?), and, on realising we weren't fascists, they drove off at high speed. The car escaped but only to a set of red lights, whereupon anti-fascists turned the car upside down complete with occupants, and some kind soul threw in a smoke bomb for good measure" (*Red Action*, No. 26). This report it turns out was not entirely accurate: the car was not actually turned over, though there was a determined attempt to do so.

Denis: "On the day we had about twenty fighters in two transit vans. The plan was simple. Each vanload was to operate individually and engage with whatever fash they came across whilst driving around the area, and then disappear. Hit and run, hit and run. As we drive up Wellington Street, we see the SWP and fellow travellers massed around a picket of about two hundred banner wavers. With the police cordoning off the picket with most of their manpower, all we needed was the NF to show. Suddenly, there they were; around twenty early arrivals, goading the Lefties – four traffic lanes and one police line away. By complete coincidence, our two vans travelling in opposite directions happen on the scene at the same time. Pull up, empty and headlong into the fash in seconds. Panicking, the NF bolt for the train station. As they turn a corner some put up a rearguard action. One, armed with a banner pole swung at my head. I take the impact on raised and crossed arms instead and deliver a boot to his unprotected groin. He resumes the retreat and others follow his example. Behind us the police abandon their positions and give chase, followed by the SWP. Surreal. One fascist, decked by one of our lads, is kicked into insensibility by the brave hearts of the SWP following up. So that's what they mean by 'mass action', I thought."

Somewhat overwhelmed by the unusual wildness of the assault, the NF were driven back into the train station, and then, for further sanctuary, into a large waiting room on the platform. With the help of a fireman's axe snatched from the wall, a wild-eyed Scouser, ably supported by leading London NF member Eddie Whicker, defended the door. Eventually, both were arrested. After trying to dislodge the NF with some smoke bombs aimed at the vents, AFA pulled back to concentrate on late NF arrivals. Many years later, current BNP leader, Nick Griffin would recall the day as his 'proudest moment'.

Denis: "Four short haired young men, including one known face, are spotted cruising the area in a Saab. Approached, they do a rapid U-turn and speed off, only to be forced to screech to a stop at a red light. Another team already in position at the lights on 'sniping' duty decide to intervene. In the ensuing mêlée one youngish police officer loses his helmet. It would end up as an auction item at a Manchester Martyrs fundraiser later in the year!"

No less dramatic, but arguably the more far-reaching, success was notched within a matter of weeks, when a National Front march in Bury St Edmunds, Suffolk, was attacked in the town centre. Originally alerted to NF plans by a local anti-fascist, who had lost most of his family in the concentration camps, and whose adopted son was, almost unbelievably, a leading light in the NF locally, AFA sent a delegation from London to Bury St Edmunds for the purposes of reconnaissance.

On returning, the delegation gave the go-ahead to mobilise. At 8am sharp, the AFA stewards assembled outside King's Cross Station on the day in question. Some were relatively new recruits. One of them approached a senior steward and inquired if there was "going to be trouble?" "I should hope so," came the relaxed reply, "otherwise we will be making the trip for nothing." The recruit then opened a bag. "So will we be needing these, then?" Inside, there was a fireman's axe and a machete. "I doubt it will be that rough!" the organiser chuckled. He ordered the weapons dumped.

Joe: "The arrangement was, we were to meet our contact at a junction near Bury St Edmunds station. But when we pulled up in the van he could not conceal his dismay on seeing there was only around half a dozen of us in it. 'Is this all of you there is?' he asked, crestfallen. 'No, no' I reassured him 'there are about sixty of us in the pub'. His face lit up. He later described the resulting turmoil as one of the best days in his life."

However, from the NF's point of view, the whole affair was as embarrassing as it was unexpected. NF supporters were attacked before, during, and after the march. At one stage, a Red Action led ambush from a building site in a narrow side street caused largely inexperienced police to rush forward, leaving the back of the march unprotected. The resulting free-for-all lasted a couple of minutes during which time the NF lost a banner, and a lot of their composure. The small market town of Bury St Edmunds could remember nothing like it. Such was the level of paranoia that, shortly after the anti-fascists appeared in court weeks later, the discovery of the 'mark of the ICF [Inter City Firm]', according to an over excited usher found scratched into the wood in the dock, caused the magistrate to order the court be cleared.

"The day ended on a high note when, while under police escort to the edge of town, we came upon a member of the Front's National Directorate, and a few of his lackeys on foot. As we swept past, to the utter astonishment of the local 'plod', one of the political soldiers was felled by a cheeky denim clad arm, swinging a blunt instrument. The motorised 'cudgel carrier' then sped off, hotly pursued by an outraged Old Bill, leaving current NF chairman, Nick Griffin holding his hands in the air, as if appealing for divine intervention" (*Red Action*, No. 26).

In all, just nine anti-fascists were arrested and charged with public order offences. This was a relatively low count, largely down to the local police sergeant having been kicked unconscious by the NF in the town square the previous Christmas, and thus understandably eager to see the fascists get their comeuppance. When the runaway van was eventually stopped, there followed a rather surreal exchange:

Joe: "By that time everyone had changed seats and the outraged local bobby demanded that the perpetrator give himself up. No takers. 'Everyone is under arrest!' he announced. Just then his sergeant arrived: 'What appears to be the problem, officer?' 'What?' spluttered plod. 'Have you got a complainant?' his sergeant insisted, straight-faced. 'He's in the ditch, sir… back there, sir,' pointing. The sergeant leant through the window, smiling slightly, then, for his colleagues benefit, shouted: 'Right you lot, on your way. I never want to see you again!'

"Along with the ritual condemnation in the local press by both NF and Labour, a private endorsement from a veteran anti-fascist, [this is a reference to the Bury St Edmonds AFA contact who had lost family members in the Nazi concenteration camps] who was himself arrested on the demo, described the tactics and attitudes of the London-based anti-fascists as 'inspiring'. Sufficient vindication for anyone, I would imagine" (*Red Action*, No. 26).

Shortly afterwards there was even greater reason for self-congratulation when news trickled through that, as a result of the debacle, the NF had split. However, as Nigel Copsey is careful to point out in his book, *Anti-Fascism in Britain*, this was in reality an organisation already beset "by ideological differences and personal rivalries." As the head of one faction, Nick Griffin had initially sought to explain away his personal responsibility for the security disaster that had unfolded by rather implausibly claiming the attackers were not actually anti-fascists, but members of the mythical 'Red ICF',* who, he insisted, were secretly working for his rivals within the NF. Unsurprisingly, there were few takers for the conspiracy fable. And the NF, which nationally still had a considerable following of thousands, split into two.

Ian Anderson headed the conventional Flag grouping, while Nick Griffin became leader of the 'political soldier' wing which, tellingly, stopped holding public demonstrations altogether. Later, in a pamphlet entitled *Attempted Murder – The State/Reactionary plot against the NF*, Griffin justified the retreat from the streets in stating: "all the politics of the punch-up had achieved in twenty years was to allow Red Action's influence to grow on the streets."

Though admittedly other wider differences were also at play, the AFA operation had, nevertheless, been the cause or pretext for provoking institutionalised division within their opponents. A defeat with such reverberations had not occurred since 1979 and the militants were heartened by the implications.

* Funnily enough, there was indeed an actual ICF (Inter City Firm) angle. One leading member of the West Ham ICF, John H., had made his sympathies for RA/AFA known around this time. However, he had not travelled to Bury St Edmunds on the day and, apart from one other ICF fellow traveller, Russell T., who was responsible for the graffiti incident in the dock, that was about the depth of the connection.

2.5

REMEMBRANCE DAY, NOVEMBER 1986

One of the many legacies of the winding up of the ANL was that the NF in particular was allowed to organise openly in many parts of the country, virtually without the threat of sanction. This immunity was reinforced annually at their get-together on Remembrance Day, when an organisation known to be violently racist could march through central London, thousands strong, in packed ranks without, literally, a murmur of protest from anti-fascists. For AFA it symbolised all that was wrong. In internal discussions following the counter-demonstration in 1985, it was decided to draw attention to this reality. But rather than confront the NF – and necessarily the police – head on, as in 1985, it was decided AFA would call a national demonstration of its own instead. To underscore and draw attention to the NF marching, it was decided that a wreath 'in memory of the victims of fascist violence, yesterday and today' would be laid at the Cenotaph.

Over 2,000 people responded to the AFA call, making it the biggest anti-fascist mobilisation seen since 1979. Not all were so enthusiastic. "Shame at the Cenotaph" read Monday's *Daily Mail* front page. "Last night, Home Office Minister, David Waddington, promised an immediate inquiry into the London demo, which happened only hours after the Queen had laid a wreath on behalf of the nation ... No one could have imagined that, when the royal ceremony was over, the nation would be insulted as the precincts of the Cenotaph were defiled." In the type of language similar to what might be found in *National Front News*, it blamed "a band of anarchists, Communists, homosexuals and students" for the insult (*Daily Mail*, 10th November 1986).

AFA, on the other hand, was greatly encouraged. The turnout had been better than expected, and any subsequent controversy merely helped, as they saw it, to place anti-fascism back on the national agenda. Front-page coverage in a national newspaper could only be regarded as a step forward and further underscored the necessity for active resistance. Although the march itself was widely recognised as a tactical success, not everything went exactly to plan. Elements at the open-air rally afterwards, perhaps fired up with the idea of physically confronting the NF on the day, circulated a rumour among the crowd that an attack by fascists on the ever-present anti-apartheid picket in Trafalgar Square was imminent. This led to platform speakers such as Labour MP Jeremy Corbyn being heckled: shouts of "We are the real anti-fascists," emanated from supporters of the Revolutionary Communist Group (RCG). As the picket was a brainchild of the RCG, the buzz may have been typical left-wing self-aggrandisement. But in any event the rally was disrupted to an extent, with a section marching off to 'confront' the fascists. Militants were far from impressed.

"Against the rumour of some possible fascist activity a couple of miles away, you had the absolute certainty that a large number of fascists knew exactly where an AFA rally was taking place, and the general direction in which most of those who had attended it would have to travel when they left. In such a situation, a 'real anti-fascist' doesn't just run off down the road shouting his/her head off. He/she does the job they have taken on, which on this occasion was to ensure that all of those who had attended the AFA mobilisation had safe conduct away from an area of possible danger.

"Apparently, many of those who did go back to Trafalgar Square found themselves confronted by large numbers of fascists, and there were reports that a couple of anti-fascists were stabbed. If this is the case, those individuals who were doing all of the shouting at the rally, stirring up a lot of people, many of them young and inexperienced, bear a heavy responsibility … I would have to say that the individuals who were making all the noise on this particular occasion did not strike me as the sort of people to strike fear into the hearts of, or be any match tactically or physically for, the street-wise working class gangs of the National Front" (*Red Action*, No. 29).

Later in the evening, one particular 'gang' of National Front proved itself to be anything but street-wise. Frustrated by the turn of events at the rally, a number of AFA stewards had been on the prowl for a number of hours, without any significant contact, and found themselves in the area of King's Cross at around six o'clock.

Joe: "We were all thoroughly pissed off, to be frank. Though the day itself had been a success, the RCG ruse had caused us to look like rabble. Moreover, the NF march had dispersed safely. I was just in the process of reluctantly sending everyone home, when one of the lads who formerly ran with the ICF at West Ham came flying back. 'They're here! They're here!' 'Where?' I asked. 'St Pancras Station.' And then 'How many?' 'We can do 'em!' he replied desperately. 'How many?' I demanded, knowing the form, you see. 'About twenty with flags.'"

A quick head count revealed the odds of two to one satisfactorily in the anti-fascists favour. Apart from the obvious value of greater numbers in helping secure victory, greater numbers also helped ensure that victory would be swift which considerably reduced the possibility of police intervention and arrest. The forty-strong group of anti-fascists headed directly for their prey. On some narrow, winding stairs between King's Cross and St Pancras stations, they came face to face with an impressively tall, heavily built man in a camouflage jacket. Militants were also on the lookout, always watching, never off duty. "We were forever," as one put it, "taking photographs in our heads." Thus, once seen never forgotten. Simultaneously, a number of stewards identified him from Trafalgar Square as the AFA march assembled earlier in the day. A pause ensued as people exchanged looks.

Joe: "To begin with we were not absolutely positive, but then it was clear from the look of apprehension on his face, he recognised us too. This confirmed he was connected but, as it was also unlikely we could do him without forewarning the actual NF colour party, we let him go."

The scalp of the colour party was the more politically prestigious. Years later, the lucky right-winger would come to national media attention as C18 groupie and serial killer, Colin Ireland, referred to later in Redwatch as the 'fairy liquidator'.*

Joe: "What always sticks with me is that, though just three of us came down the steps, admittedly fairly briskly, the boneheads assembled complete with flags outside the Wimpy just 'knew' we were the casuals they had been warned to look out for. Even though it was dark and the width of the Euston Road separated us you could see they were nervy. Then, obviously after some discussion, they began to shuffle into the restaurant. In doing so, they lost the advantage their bulk, not to mention their brass-tipped flagpoles, would have offered them in a street-fight. Dumb. Often when confronted with a situation like this, you might leave one door unmanned: 'a rat run' to create the 'prospect' of escape, thereby setting the scene where some would fight and some would run. This time I instructed the boys to go through both doors. I didn't want any of them to get away. So intent was Russ, our ICF recruit, to get into to them, I had to grab the back of his jacket to stop him running right under a bus."

As the anti-fascists entered through both doors, the colour party had grouped in an uncertain fashion near the counter, intermingling with the customers. In anticipation of what was to come, one anti-fascist sought to pick up a chair. "Sorry, that one is taken," came the prissy reply from a middle-aged customer, completely oblivious to what was about to evolve. At close quarters, it was a furious battle with flagpoles, metal trays and even chip pans brought into use. Customers and staff fled as the rivals battled. A scout posted outside to look out for police later timed the clash at a lengthy three minutes. When AFA departed, a number of nazi skinheads were left lying unconscious in front of and behind the counter.

Joe: "Even quite experienced activists within AFA did not always appreciate how demoralising for the NF as a whole such a calamity could be. Not only were the

* "At the time of the killing the identity of the killer was a mystery to us. It was only after his arrest that we recognised the killer. Colin Ireland was an old NF acquaintance who always tried to knock around with us. At the time of Combat 18's formation, he kept trying to get involved. We always thought he was a bit of a crank, so we kept him at arm's distance until last year, when, fed up with his pestering, we told him the only way to join C18 was to kill a queer or a nigger or a jew, thinking that his bottle would go" (*Combat 18*, issue no. 3).

colour party taken apart, but also each and every one of them would know a dozen or more people intimately. So within hours, hundreds would probably know of their humiliation. Then there are the personal and political recriminations that would inevitably follow: who fucked up, who stood, who ran and so on. Endless recriminations and all so corrosive to the discipline and good comradeship fascism set so much store by."

2.6

NF MEETING: CHARLTON, SOUTH EAST LONDON, 1987

AFA were again quickly out of the traps in the New Year with an emphatic victory over the NF on 31st January 1987 in Sheffield. An attack by a large mob of NF on the annual Troops Out Movement (TOM) march was thwarted when a sixty-strong AFA stewards group wrestled the initiative from them by breaking from the march, evading police and scattering the would-be ambushers among the shoppers. After the initial encounter one NF member lay face down in the middle of the road, as if comfortably asleep. Clashes continued until nightfall. *The Star* reported, "The demonstration itself, which was to be marred by violent clashes in the city centre leading to 19 arrests, and by bitter feuds between the marchers themselves, started with an impressive turnout in brilliant sunshine. About 3,000 of them, behind an army of flags and accompanied by two pipe bands, set off under heavy police escort from Cahorn Corner only minutes behind schedule. But as the procession reached the top of Haymarket at about 1.45pm, a mob of around 100 skinheads unfurled Union Jacks, shouted abuse and then attacked. One youth with a Union Jack pinned to his back, charged headfirst screaming into the demonstrators; he was quickly knocked to the ground and dragged off by the police. Others threw stones and bottles and shouted, 'Murderers,' before attacking again. Fights broke out as groups of demonstrators retaliated. For about ten minutes, stunned shoppers cowered as the police battled to keep the two sides apart."

Partly due to the trouble, and partly due to the unthinking decision to place one band bang in the middle of the march (that literally marched to the sound of their own drum), the procession gradually began to split into two. With the police concentrated at the front, the NF saw the opportunity but were thwarted by a number of Red Action members seeing the danger and taking command of the stewarding of what was by now almost a second separate demonstration. Instructions were then sent to the TOM leadership to halt the front of the march to allow the other part to catch up. They were ignored. When police, directed by plain clothes Special Branch men, began to send snatch squads into the body of the march, dragging out and arresting the militant stewards, the unofficial RA leadership decided to stop the march in protest. To the utter astonishment of both organisers and police, the march, all 3,000, suddenly ground to a halt in the middle of the city centre. For twenty minutes the police and TOM organisers pleaded and threatened in turn, but to no avail. Direct appeals to republican band members to lead off were met with Glaswegian stubbornness. "We don't move until Red Action gives the go ahead." Eventually pragmatism ruled, with the police officer in charge forced to deal directly with a leading RA member, who demanded an end to Special Branch provocations as the price for the embargo being lifted.

Afterwards, the TOM organisers, with noses out of joint, ordered the London coaches to leave without waiting for those arrested to be released. Dutiful as ever, when the marchers were released, militants were on hand offering both security and transport. As an added bonus an NF contingent also from London who had turned up to do likewise, ended up doing neither. After being attacked in a dark side street one leading NF member, Dave Thomas, from Newham in east London, fled into the night and hid himself in the stairwell of a local estate. Laughing AFA members shouted down: "It's OK, Dave, they've gone, you can come out now!" But less than a month later he was afforded the chance for personal revenge.

When a by-election was called in Charlton, south east London, the NF put up Joe Pearce as a candidate. This entitled them to use public buildings for any meetings they might wish to hold. The only legal caveat was that the 'public' had to be allowed in. They duly booked the local school for 21st February. On the morning, within minutes of AFA arriving, there were clashes. Pearce, the candidate, resplendent in an outsize rosette, was chased down the road. A less fleet-footed member of his entourage was tossed into the road where a passing van missed him by inches. Further light skirmishing, in and outside the meeting, led to other NF members taking second prize. Police were not getting to grips with events. Then, when the police commander announced that only 'thirty members of the public' were to be allowed in, not unexpectedly the militants were prompt in stepping forward.

However, NF security arrangements inside the hall meant the anti-fascists were forced to enter the hall one by one. Of the first sixteen to enter, nine were identifiably RA. Already alarmed, Dave Thomas, who was heading NF security, decided that was as many as he wished to handle. Spotting fellow Newham resident Unmesh Desai, in the queue, he decided to force a confrontation in the narrow corridor. This had a dual effect. With the help of police, Desai and the other anti-fascists were driven out, while the anti-fascists inside found themselves outnumbered three or four to one. And so, at the precise moment the disturbance began in the corridor it simultaneously erupted inside the hall. Hand-to-hand fighting involving about sixty people broke out in the low-ceilinged classroom.

Joe: "Initially, I had chosen to sit in the front row. The exit was at the back. In between, there were about fifty people fighting. I was already on my feet when I took a tremendous punch high on the cheekbone from behind. I turned toward the attacker. He backed off, probably surprised I hadn't gone down. To tell the truth, I was a bit surprised myself. But rather than go after him, I decided it would be more prudent to begin making my way toward the door. The instant I turned, I saw one of our boys on the floor already bleeding, with a 'Fronter' trying to inflict further damage. I pulled back my arm and smashed a full can of beer on the back of his head. He slumped. By now there were chairs flying everywhere. I got hit with one that even tore a hole through a heavy leather coat. I don't think anyone came out without a wound of some form of another, but it was worth it. "

A distraught NF leadership bitterly denounced the police, later going as far as to lodge a formal complaint. Aware the BNP were also holding an election meeting nearby, AFA stewards were not about to rest on their laurels. Alerted to what had happened down the road, police decided this time that, instead of the nominal thirty, a mere dozen AFA would be allowed into the hall. Together with the reduced numbers, and taking into account what had happened earlier, the AFA chief steward responded by rejecting the idea of calling for 'volunteers'. As it had not gone unnoticed that not everyone had been fully up for it previously, he decided to hand-pick the 'volunteers' personally. The studied choice of increasingly hefty looking characters drawn from the crowd left no one in any doubt of what to expect.

Joe: "I remember these two coppers grabbed a weedy protesting photographer, pushed him toward me, and said: 'Right, that's twelve.' I immediately threw him back and as he went he mouthed, 'Thank you, thank you,' and returned to the

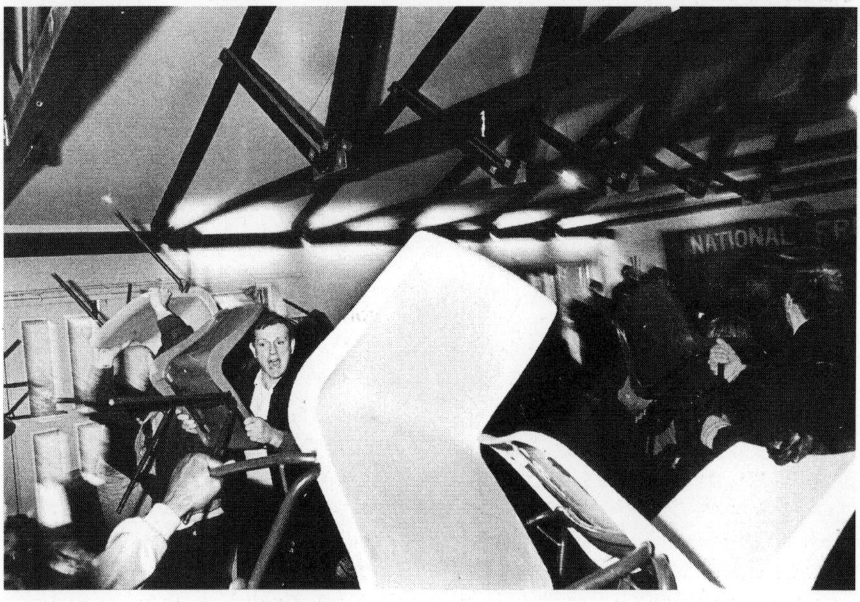

The National Front meeting in Charlton, south east London, on 21st February 1987.

safety of the crowd. My first choice replacement was 6ft 4ins with a broken nose, and covered in blood as a result of the earlier encounter with the Front. 'Me, me, me,' he gestured.

"The officer in charge looked at him for a moment and then, in alarm, at the cut of the other militants that had been assembled: 'Right, that's it, none of you are going in.' 'But it's a public meeting,' I protested. Then adding, 'What about the Representation of the People Act?' The police officer looked at me in the eye and said: 'Fuck the Representation of the People Act!' There was nothing you could do but laugh."

2.7

POLITICAL CLEANSING IN NORTH LONDON, 1987

Later in the summer, AFA turned its attention to the growing visibility of right-wing skinhead gangs in and around King's Cross, in north London. Intelligence indicated the fascists had established a relationship with a pub at the back of King's Cross Station. The grooming of the landlord by Ian Stuart meant he saw The Prince Albert as a successor to The Agricultural. Before making their move, AFA security stewards made sure they were aware of all the possible permutations. In order to carry as little threat as possible, female intelligence officers were directed to frequent it. When eventually fascist suspicions were aroused, it was the cool demeanour of the two AFA operatives, blonde hair pulled back in business-like ponytails, watchful eyes and no make up, that helped convince the organisers to allow them to leave unscathed. Not yet totally familiar with the nouveau working class militants, the skinheads had mistaken them for plain-clothes police. Still puzzling over how to deal with it, the strategists were unexpectedly provided with what they saw as an ideal opening.

"A firebomb attack which seriously damaged the home of a prominent anti-fascist activist is being treated as attempted murder by police. Three petrol bombs exploded at the home of Ms Anna Sullivan, secretary of Anti-Fascist Action's branch in Islington, north London, gutting a room which until a few weeks ago had been used as a bedroom ... Her son and his girlfriend had been with her in the house" (*Guardian*, 31st July 1987).

With the vicinity of the pub being little more than a mile away from the attack, AFA security instantly saw the chance to link the attack and the pub. A public meeting was called for 23rd September that was to be used to provide the mandate for a march or campaign. Only later did it emerge the attack in all likelihood was aimed not at Anna Sullivan at all, but at her son, who the attackers believed had been a witness to a murder of a relative at a party, but had failed to give evidence. The idea was for the public meeting to lay the basis for the march. But a one-off public protest, even with national media attention, would not, it was assumed, be sufficient to see the fascists removed.

So a plan was hatched for The Prince Albert to be attacked at 9am the following morning. In truth, the entire purpose of the public campaign, (the meeting, march and picket), was to provide a plausible denial for the 'usual suspects' who lived in the immediate vicinity, and whose doors would be the first on which the police would come knocking, should anything untoward happen. As would continue to be the case throughout, subterfuge was often the name of the game.

A constant by-product of such a stratagem was the tension between the human desire to reveal, in terms of positive propaganda, and the need to conceal in order to safeguard operational efficiency. Two young reporters happened to be doing a profile on Red Action for a magazine called *Blitz* at the time. In it, Joe Reilly, who was interviewed, along with others, is described as "tall and lean whose eyes stare confidently from behind tinted glasses." It so happens Reilly was one of the architects behind the multi-layered strategy to remove the NF from the King's Cross area. So the coincidence would have afforded Red Action, you might have thought, a perfect opportunity to promote itself and its message. But so circumspect and oblique were the contributions from RA, the *Blitz* reporters quite genuinely cast the militants as gatecrashers on events they themselves had conceived and organised. For, while describing Red Action as physically to "the forefront" during the picket of The Prince Albert, the conclusion reached was that "they're not invited but they're there." Subsequently, this became the theme of the article. Now, misrepresentation by the media is nothing new, but here the militants seemingly deliberately misled the reporters by playing down their influence, rather than risk any future operational efficacy. Red Action had many critics but few would ever accuse them of unnecessary grandstanding. At an editorial level, self-effacement bordering on false modesty was, rightly or wrongly, regarded as a desirable quality. This principal was taken to rather an absurd level, when, a couple of years later, a genuinely stunning victory against an international Blood & Honour initiative saw it written up in Red Action in less than a hundred words.

Although, on the night of the picket, Ian Stuart had cannily ordered a strategic withdrawal, causing the attack planned for the following morning to be abandoned, the skinheads soon returned – but, inevitably, so did the militants. One further visit, at opening time on the dot (5.30pm), by about fifteen activists, conveniently making them the only customers, was enough to convince the landlord that the loss of the skinhead custom which, in a conversation with two Special Branch officers overheard by an AFA supporter, he claimed was "worth up to £50,000 a year", was preferable to the loss of his business and possibly his home. However, his tacit surrender did nothing for the nerves of the owner of The Prince Albert in neighbouring Camden, who continued to receive blood-curdling threats by phone at all times of the day and night for many months afterwards.

By the end of 1987 those behind the strategy of tension employed against the Far Right had every reason to be pleased. In a series of set pieces: marches, meetings, paper-sales, AFA had shown itself able to demolish NF security. To avoid future fiascos, the NF leadership had to spend an increasing amount of effort in terms of logistics to mount even the most simple of events. This attention to detail now applied to every public outing. Every penetration of NF security increased stress levels. AFA was fulfilling its promise. Evidently, not all were nearly as impressed, for at the next AGM came the shocking call for AFA to be disbanded.

2.8

RED ACTION SUSPENDED FOR RACISM, NOVEMBER 1987

Militants approached the 1987 conference in Bradford in upbeat mood. But, as in 1986, they were met with yet another determined attempt to mould the organisation into an exclusive image, one that would specifically exclude physical confrontation. On this occasion the attack was led by Bradford, who tabled a proposed name change for the organisation, and with it a new set of priorities. 'Anti-fascism', they argued, was too restrictive an image, so 'Anti-Racist Anti-Fascist Action (ARAFA) was put on the table as the more fitting title. But much more than a cosmetic name change was at stake. As was made clear from the platform, the intention was a root-and-branch transformation, from a group equipped, as it had demonstrated, with a practical, sometimes physical, strategy that was meeting with growing success, into a politically conventional lobbying group, in time hopefully grant-funded and, out of necessity, both law-abiding and state-friendly. "Individual activists needed to concentrate more on the racism within", the stunned and disbelieving militants were informed. And consistent with the fairly outrageous attempt at re-branding were the tactics employed to achieve it.

Orchestrated by Geoff R., a local teacher, the first vote on the Bradford proposals was declared a victory by the would-be reformers, until it was pointed out, rather politely in the circumstances, that only one side of the hall had been counted. In a second ballot the Bradford proposal lost decisively. That should have been that, except, to growing dismay, the veracity of this vote was also called into question by the chair, Geoff R. So preparation for the third vote took inspiration from the mother of parliaments, with delegates being held in the lobby and counted as they passed through the doors of the conference hall. Significantly, third time round, the vote against was overwhelming. Desperate times seemingly call for desperate measures. During the break for lunch, a fairly outrageous attempt was made to provoke a particular member of Red Action into some form of violent reaction that would no doubt have been immediately presented as a racially motivated flare-up.

Joe: "Making my way to the canteen, I actually stumbled on the plot. The idea was to provoke an incident with J., not exactly renowned for his easy-going nature, by having a Bradford Asian jostle him in the dinner queue! I could hardly believe they were discussing this in the hall. Quickly, I got directions to the canteen and, sure enough, there was J. already engaged in an eyeball-to-eyeball confrontation with a thickset Asian, who was jabbing him aggressively in the chest. I walked up to him and whispered, 'Leave it, you're being set-up'."

Obviously, the plotters were working on the assumption that, in any such incident, the white working class male would be the one under suspicion which, they must have estimated, would have been enough to supply Bradford AFA with the necessary ammunition to demand RA's suspension/expulsion. It was a desperate gambit but, as so often within the Left of the political spectrum, when push comes to shove, reasoned argument and democracy are readily replaced with the grubbiest of politics.

Sure enough, within a couple of weeks of the conference, individuals identified as belonging to RA were duly accused of drunkenness, intimidation and – racism. Memorably, one of the Bradford tellers who happened to be black, had supposedly been asked if he "could count bananas". This was supposed to have actually happened inside the conference itself. At a subsequent National Steering Committee meeting called by Bradford, with delegates afforded only a few days notice, a proposal by Geoff R. to suspend Red Action was carried by votes of three branches to two. And, as with earlier manoeuvres to expel Class War the previous year, evidence to back up the allegations was regarded by the accusers as superfluous.

Though not always exactly seeing eye to eye with members of the security wing on the wider issue of political orientation, groups like the NMP (Newham Monitoring Project) and CARF (Campaign Against Racism and Fascism), who had previously backed Searchlight over Class War, felt obliged in principle to oppose such a blatantly clumsy and flagrantly dishonest effort to emasculate the working class base within AFA. And, as might be expected, this alliance between them and RA proved decisive.

A 1988 Red Action internal document assessed subsequent developments: "At the first National Steering Committee following the Bradford conference Red Action was suspended pending an enquiry into allegations of racism and drunkenness by unnamed members at the conference. We did not attend the Steering Committee meeting as we were not actually told of the meeting until three days before, and, as our delegates live in London and the meeting was in Bradford, we decided the notice was inadequate. Representatives of 18 other organisations registered an official protest by letter and did not attend either. Five branches of AFA were present – Bradford, Hull, Islington, Manchester and Liverpool. The last two abstained from any moves on suspension. At no time were we informed of the motion to suspend us, or the result.

"We disregarded the suspension by this body as invalid and lacking any authority, and continued as active members of AFA until the meeting in Leicester in July to discuss the matter. The allegations were again repeated and added to, and were rejected unanimously by the delegates present for the following reasons: lack of detail, substance and evidence; failure to identify alleged perpetrators; complete failure to link alleged perpetrators to Red Action; only one eyewitness whose written statement included all the weaknesses just mentioned; finally, and most satisfying from our point of view, was the total lack of credibility of the allegations in the eyes of the delegates present – largely due to the consistent work Red Action members have put in to the anti-fascist struggle over the years. Those of us present saw it as a cheap and incompetent smear on Red Action by those who, in presenting a non-negotiable document, hoped to bully the movement into accepting the policies that were largely rejected at the AFA conference. It was presented as an either/or scenario, either Red Action go or Bradford goes. They completely misjudged the situation and lost the gamble emphatically. They wandered off to form their own organisation, and if we ever hear from them again it will be too soon."

What occurred at the internal AFA inquiry, and with only a passing reference in the final paragraph, was indeed extraordinary. Essentially, the charges laid against RA collapsed in ignominy when the chair of the inquiry, Liz F. from the Institute of Race Relations, produced and read from a personal letter to her from Geoff R., in which he lobbied individuals he believed supported the effort to re-brand AFA, to "name their political price for getting shot of Red Action". Tellingly, the letter had been penned prior to the allegations of racism made by him at the Bradford AGM. Though Liz F.'s public censure of one of the architects behind the coup was most gratifying, RA members present were in awe at the cold blooded way the personal reputation of Geoff R. had been stripped away. It also bears testimony as to the gravity of the situation at street level that AFA was able to survive intact this second fairly desperate attempt to derail it.

Having been thwarted, Bradford 'AFA' departed, and, along with the Islington branch, set up Anti-Racist Anti-Fascist Action (ARAFA) and promptly disappeared into obscurity. At the time, a statement was issued explaining their departure: "We believe there is a fundamental political difference between those of us who see state racism and fascism as equal and complementary threats, and those who only recognise the threat of fascism in its organised form of the BNP and NF. We believe the consequence of this is that there is a failure by AFA nationally to build membership and support by and with the black community. This failure, in turn, means an emphasis on 'anti-fascist' specialists and physical force alone, rather than a complimentary political campaign to win support from local communities."

It is noteworthy that, in their condemnation of AFA, the emphasis and indeed language of ARAFA is largely indistinguishable from that of the SWP. But, as Nigel Copsey is at pains to point out, such tensions have proven to be systemic in anti-fascist circles; the same debate crops up again and again, and has done from the

1930s onwards. Here again was a manifestation of the historic either/or divide. But what was slightly different on this occasion is that the dispute between 'radical anti-fascism and its wholly legal counterpart' was not between, but within an organisation, one moreover wholly committed from its founding only two years earlier to exactly the use of physical confrontation now being condemned. What part, it must be asked, of the commitment "to confront fascism physically and ideologically" did the would-be reformers not understand? In other ways, it is an analysis that has echoes of the Stalinist position of the Thirties, whereby fascism and bourgeois democracy were presented as 'twins' which thus, in representing an equal danger, needed to be equally opposed. Like many other ultra-Left poses, it is presented as the epitome of radical commitment and analysis, when in practice it is a cop-out motivated mainly by, according to Trotsky himself, "political cowardice".

From the militant perspective, even if the theory of state racism and fascism were to be regarded as 'equal and complementary', in practice they remained very different and required different strategies. Fairly obviously, the tactics and, indeed, the type of people required for tackling what was condemned as a racist bureaucracy were, on the whole, woefully ill equipped when it came to directly confronting a violent political party. What's more, in the arena of the street where second place is nowhere, a thoroughly professional approach was required merely to avoid catastrophe against a numerically superior opponent.

Militants generally felt the liberal wing of the anti-racist movement wilfully failed to take this on board and, as a result, often lacked both the stomach and stamina to see things through. Funnily enough, the failed coup in Bradford was, in many ways, a precise expression of the amateur bungling that so often set militants' teeth on edge with regard to their involvement on the street. In addition, lobbying the state around issues of police brutality, deportations and institutional racism was an area of political work already extensively covered by the left-leaning liberals. "If numerous organisations exist to combat state racism, including some of the sponsors of AFA, why then does everyone seem so convinced one more will make a difference when the ground is already so well covered?" militants would counter, mischievously.

Naturally, ARAFA (or indeed the larger organisations which would follow them) would fail to address effectively what is referred to as state racism, much less recruit from the black community. By contrast, in the first two years of AFA's existence, the organisation had shown itself able to make an impact on fascist initiatives and had also given the rising level of racist attacks a high profile. Although a range of tactics were exploited, the fact remains that, between 1980 and 1996, British fascism was primarily a street-orientated and violent opponent and, in opposing them, it was incumbent on anti-fascism to counter-punch, or 'abandon the arena'.

As a complement to the intrigue emanating from inside, from the orthodox Left outside there came a studied indifference. Now, whether or not at this early stage there was some state encouragement in the various attempts to disable militant anti-fascism is a matter of conjecture. Either way, for militants the fact remained that, if AFA was to stay on course, all stratagems designed to cripple the organisation needed to be politically put down, whatever the origin. It was always inevitable – after first Manchester and then Bradford – that this apparent need to mount a political rearguard in perpetuity against elements *within* the organisation would have given those at the coal-face pause for thought. The principle of the 'big tent' was proving more problematic than many had imagined. Some began to wonder if an all-encompassing AFA aligned to a democratic structure was really what was required.

Though later it would be alleged that the 'hijack' perpetrated by RA and others was somehow always likely to happen, it was really not until the beginning of 1988 that the exponents of physical force, though resolute in their determination to keep AFA true to the founding statement, developed any ambition, much less a thought out policy, in order to secure absolute political control of the organisation for themselves. Hitherto, their political development had largely been a step-by-step response to events. But, coming on top of the evidence of continuing political manoeuvre behind the scenes, a number of incidents between the winter of 1987 and the spring of 1988 would cause what had amounted to passive resistance to be critically reviewed. The result of the discussions would see the militants take the political offensive, with far-reaching consequences for both Left and Right.

2.9

REMEMBRANCE DAY, HEADHUNTERS ATTACK AND FALLOUT, 1987–1988

As 1987 drew to a close, hoping to emulate the success of the previous year, AFA again called for a march on Remembrance Day. As part of what had become a ritual following the NF march, a large contingent of fascists would make their way to Trafalgar Square in order to attack the non-stop anti-apartheid picket outside South Africa House.

But on this occasion, at about noon, as large numbers of anti-fascists were forming in Northumberland Avenue just across the square from South Africa House, a section of a notorious football hooligan gang called the Chelsea Headhunters deserted the NF mobilisation in Victoria, and launched an attack on the AFA mobilisation instead. The back of the march was made up almost entirely of students who, seemingly without much hesitation, legged it. As the ripples spread it took on all the appearances of an embarrassing rout. Security stewards, who had been stationed all along the two thousand marchers, instinctively responded. But in the seconds it took them to get to where the trouble had erupted, they were puzzled to find the attackers had fled. Equally puzzled, the police approaching from the other direction, took one look at the AFA stewards and assumed they had caused the problem. A sergeant grabbed a leading RA member who angrily shook him off. "I'm the chief steward, you arsehole!" he snarled, pointing to his armband that did indeed say 'Chief Steward'. Quickly identities were properly established. And though about eighty Headhunters in all had charged the marchers, there was little or no evidence of any damage having been inflicted. But if physical damage was indeed imperceptible, the political fallout would not prove so insignificant.

Inevitably the AFA post mortem presented an opportunity for a consideration of current strategy and tactics, in particular from a militant point of view, the AFA orientation and reliance on student unions for numbers for prestigious set pieces. Conversely, with differing degrees of sincerity, sections of the liberal wing took the opportunity to try and sanction the stewards group for incompetence instead. It was suggested by some "more stewards were needed," while at times others insisted there were already "far too many who were far too macho" and "more women stewards" should be encouraged. Among the few not to flee were two RA women who picked up a discarded scaffold pole in order to defend the march. This was a repudiation of their analysis RA critics chose to overlook. Among the most vociferous of detractors was a stunning sixteen-year-old, Saffron Burroughs, now a Hollywood actress. One argument cited by her little group demanded that security should be feminised on the curious grounds of a male propensity to dither under pressure. Backing her up, a colleague spoke of how she personally had come across “over 100 skinheads on the Strand” that morning, and had duly brought news of the threat to the attention of Unmesh Desai who, in turn, had conveyed the information directly to the chief steward. But the chief steward, she claimed, “didn’t seem to know what to do about it.” With more than a little weariness, it was pointed out that, first of all, the attackers were in the main not skinheads, but Chelsea football casuals. And secondly, and crushingly, Unmesh, having flown to India on the Friday, was not even in attendance at the march. An increasing impatience with what RA saw as this endless middle class carping would not be long in finding a political outlet.

Instructively, the impact of the Red Action inquisition proved the more enduring. For all concerned, events surrounding the Remembrance Day march had been something of an eye opener. In effect, 2,000 anti-fascist demonstrators had scattered when confronted by a relatively tiny force of right-wingers. Students, patently, could not be relied upon. As one Red Action member put it, “What is the point of organising anti-fascists who, on sight of the enemy, abandon not only their position, but their principles and banners as well?”

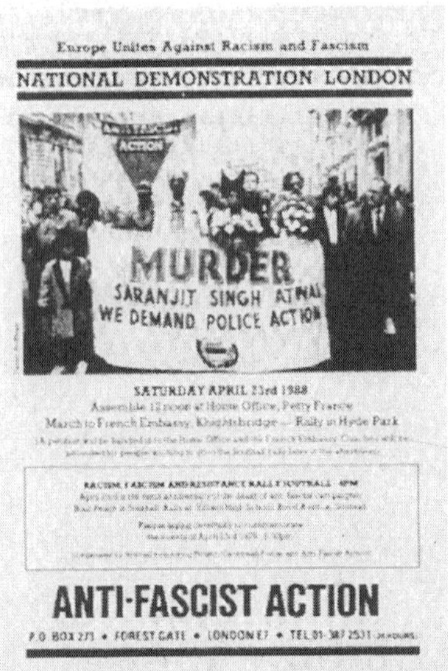

Flyer advertising the AFA national demonstration on 23rd April 1988.

Furthermore, if the Far Right were to be challenged politically for the white working class constituency, it was specifically within the indigenous working class where AFA needed to set up stall. Generally it was agreed a far greater degree of working class involvement was required. However, it was also noted that no sensible discussion around the working out of viable strategies for the organisation could take place in the political atmosphere that existed internally within AFA at the time. For this to happen structural changes would first need to be put in place.

But what finally signalled the end of AFA ‘Mark 1’ was a small incident on a little remembered AFA initiative that took place on 23rd April 1988. Under the title ‘The European Day of Action Against Racism and Fascism', the idea was that across Europe like-minded anti-fascists would protest about the emergence of the New Right. The AFA demo was sponsored by the British Labour Group on the European Parliament, led by MEP Glyn Ford, and was designed to draw attention to the growth of racism and fascism, specifically in France. The idea had been floated by Searchlight, and to announce the event AFA called a press conference. It was chaired by another Labour MP, Paul Boateng, who, in his victory speech after his election a year earlier, sought to establish his radical credentials by shouting: 'Brent South today, Soweto tomorrow!' – hoping thereby to draw a parallel between his success as a black candidate in his constituency, North West London, and the struggle against apartheid in South Africa. Red Action representatives scowled from the wings.

Broadly the idea of the march was for AFA to assemble at Petty France and proceed to the French Embassy, in protest at Le Pen's participation in the French presidential elections due to take place around this time. In short it was the kind of unremarkable gesture that would have found favour with most legal anti-racists. A thoroughly approving article in the *Guardian* claimed that AFA expected to "show its strength" by participating in a European Day of Action. But, before the day was out, the future of the organisation was itself in doubt, with talks of crisis and liquidation in the air.

Joe: "It was all very worthy, of course. There was even European money behind the initiative. But at the same time, it was now clear to practically all that elements on the executive were intent on using AFA to further very specific agendas of their own, regardless of the efficacy of the organisation as a whole. So great was the disenchantment on the militant wing, by the time we got to the Knightsbridge end of Hyde Park leading stewards simply walked off the march. They had had enough. The die was cast."

An injured policewoman is carried away after clashes between the National Front and anti-fascists at the Cenotaph in London, November 1988.

2.10

MILITANT ANTI-FASCISM DEFINED, 1988–1989

Within a matter of weeks, a set of proposals were formulated by Red Action and put on the table. The debate this document ignited would rage internally for the next eighteen months. The basic arguments outlined were as follows:

1. AFA had to recognise that fascism was a class problem and that a long term solution would not be obtained through prioritising state racism, and thereby appealing to sectional interests: the black community, immigrant groups and so on. Even without the existence of immigrant communities, fascist groups would still prosper, with their attention focused on left-wing, progressive and working class organisations – their traditional enemies. Appealing to good reason and conscience would never defeat the racism inherent in the country. This could only be achieved through gearing activities and propaganda toward assisting the white working class in reaching an understanding that fighting fascism and racism is part of a common struggle, the class struggle.
2. Propaganda should be aimed at the majority, the white working class. This is the recruiting ground for fascism, and AFA's job would be either to convince this constituency, through activity and propaganda, that fascism would not satisfy their short, medium or long term interests, or, failing that, to defeat or contain the committed activists through physical activity. Aiming propaganda, as suggested at the Bradford conference, at the victims of fascism was mistaken and patronising.
3. To attain any credibility, immediate and pragmatic help should be offered to besieged minorities to help them achieve, through activity and propaganda, the isolation of active racists and fascists within the community.

In short, 'state racism and fascism were very different opponents and required different strategies.' Uniformly, the liberal wing was appalled. For, despite the token socialist gesture, their politics were chiefly concerned with nursing and providing succour and support to the victims of racism and fascism. The idea that AFA should try and compete with the NF for hearts and minds of a section of the population with whom they had little sympathy or regard, and who, as was common across the Left, were regarded as more problem than solution, seemed to them faintly ridiculous. But if a progressive cause lacks sympathy for and from prominent sections of the working class poor, can it aspire to be anything more than a deluded self-regarding caricature?

Tangled up in what was, in many ways, fast becoming an ideological dispute were the emerging differences over the tactics most suited to Remembrance Day. According to RA, with the media fast losing interest, there was a danger of the march becoming nothing more than an annual pilgrimage, with little regard as to its actual impact on either Left or Right. Furthermore, it was argued, the nature of such a public event actually made it easier for police to prevent confrontations with the fascists, either before or after the event. However, for all the evident restiveness, the 1988 AFA march went ahead, but was engineered by leading stewards to end at Lincoln's Inn Fields rather than across the river. This was purely in order to allow AFA street-fighters quicker access to the area around Trafalgar Square where they knew the NF hard-men would head directly after their march and rally ended in Victoria.

So when the march ended, a 150-strong AFA force unobtrusively slipped back toward Trafalgar Square. A police officer on duty in a side street was startled by the almost magical appearance within yards of him of a large and entirely silent mob, and, all the more intimidating for it, obviously intent on mischief. After one disbelieving glance he took off at a run, shouting into his radio for assistance.

As if choreographed, the AFA arrival coincided with the Headhunters' charge from the opposite side of the square. When AFA were spotted, the war whoops died and the hooligans swung in a wide arc away from the picket toward the Strand. Not long afterwards, the protagonists came face to face on the east platform of Embankment tube station. Ostensibly, this was what the right-wingers were there for: 'to have a crack at the Reds.' An ideal opportunity seemed to present itself when a leading member of RA, accompanied by less than half a dozen anti-fascists, was spotted further down the platform. "It's the I-R-A!" one right-winger shouted. Some of the eighty-odd Headhunters who had crowded in the train idling on the platform stuck their heads out of the open doors to confirm the sighting. Curiously, none sought to take advantage of their huge numerical superiority, possibly because they could see it diminishing by the second. As more anti-fascists arrived, they piled in behind the first line of six, all remaining entirely silent.

When sufficient numbers were mustered, AFA attacked. Even though the train was still on a red light, the train guard quickly closed the doors. Not convinced by the ability of the toughened glass to withstand the pounding it was taking from the base of a fire extinguisher wrenched from the wall, though the real horror was reserved for an anti-fascist who was attempting to gain entry using his forehead, awed right-wingers began to clamber over each other in order to escape into the next carriage. This allowed some anti-fascists who had recklessly inserted themselves between the carriages to smash bottles on the heads that emerged.

As night drew in, the fascists suffered another, and final, humiliation. Having just successfully attacked and beaten unconscious one careless member of a smaller group, they rounded a corner only to run into the main AFA body standing calmly on the other side of the street.

Joe: "I genuinely think they intended to walk past pretending they hadn't seen us. So, to heighten their embarrassment, I whistled over. That they could not ignore. After a moment's uncertainty, they roared a challenge. As we strolled over to them, gingerly climbing over railings and traffic, one of their number picked up a dustbin as if to throw it, dancing about with it like a chimp, managing to tumble the contents on the heads of his fashion-conscious colleagues. When our boys charged, they cut and ran into Leicester Square and dispersed in the back-alleys and side streets fringing Soho.

"Particularly as it was night, I didn't fancy our fastest runners dealing with knife merchants in the back streets, so I pulled everyone up outside the Odeon in Leicester Square. One character in particular took my eye. Ignoring the decision, he kept urging every one on. Not recognising him, I challenged him. "What's your game"? I asked casually. He looked round, noticing hard stares, and altered his body language completely. "I'm just following you," he pleaded. "No, you're not," I answered, "You're leading us." Just then a police van screeched to a halt. He was beckoned over. With some mock threats he was sent on his way. Or, in other words, his colleagues* watched his back as he made his way out of the area."

The clashes continued into the evening. In King's Cross, following a number of encounters, a Millwall hooligan who had been seen with the Headhunters at Trafalgar Square was now spotted on a crowded bus. Anti-fascists barricaded the road while negotiations began with the bus driver, who happened to be black. After a moment or two, he opened the door and a leading steward boarded the bus to administer a beating.

"Police arrested 34 people during clashes between National Front marchers and an anti-fascist group after the Remembrance Day ceremony at the Cenotaph in Whitehall yesterday," the *Guardian* reported the following day. A chance conversation over a cup of coffee between two young building workers more realistically conveyed the flavour of events. In a typical Monday morning 'Do anything at the weekend?' type exchange, it quickly emerged they had, in fact, been

* During the 1980s and 1990s, the employment of police Special Branch/MI5 undercover agents was becoming increasingly apparent. Sometimes they were used as spies in the crowd, at other times to manipulate events to the satisfaction of unseen string pullers. The Poll Tax riots, the Miners' Strike and the Welling riot led to accusations that even military personnel had been used in such a capacity. Anti-fascist militants proved to be particularly skilled in sniffing them out.

on opposite sides on the day, with the now former Headhunter conceding: "We had been told Red Action were all old men in sandals and duffle coats. I was never so frightened in my life." Underestimating an enemy is never to be recommended, yet the depiction of militant anti-fascists as effete and middle class proved of enduring appeal within fascist circles, right up to the time the now BNP leader admitted that 'stopping AFA' was the key to eventual nationalist victory.

2.11

THE BATTLE OF CONWAY HALL, NOVEMBER 1988

"The fascists, backed up by Loyalist elements, were still rubbing their wounds after an abortive attempt to invade an Irish meeting at Conway Hall two nights before the [Remembrance Day] march. Richard Edmonds of the BNP led the attack, and the attackers included members of the Fields family from Islington and the mad bomber Tony Lecomber. But despite having nearly 100 'fighting men' they were soundly beaten off" (*Searchlight*, December 1988).

The meeting in question was a rally organised by the Troops Out Movement and featured Irish republican and former MP, Bernadette McAliskey, as guest speaker. The AFA involvement was on the basis of 'information received' from a BNP member called Alan Thompson, who would later become a founding member of C18. Quite inadvertently, his boasting to a work colleague had alerted AFA intelligence to the impending attack.

As so often with AFA, the secret to success was the element of surprise. To maintain the advantage for as long as possible, rather than tramp through Holborn station – which was the nearest, easiest and most obvious route – a Tottenham Court Road meeting point, which involved a twenty-minute walk under the cover of the Friday night rush-hour crowds, was selected instead. As there had not been an opportunity to extensively scout the area in advance, this meant that, while AFA knew the 'fash' and 'plod' would be on duty, no one knew precisely where. Further to the plan to avoid contact with either for as long as possible, the AFA stewards decided to approach the venue via the back streets. Seemingly, the police had come up with a similar idea for, on rounding a corner, the sixty-strong AFA group walked smack bang into about a dozen police wagons parked end to end in the ill-lit street. Being too late to turn back, it was decided to brazen it out, the only precaution taken being to 'dump arms', which is to say, all weaponry, bars, coshes and so on that could not possibly be otherwise accounted for, were instantly dropped.

Joe: "The racket – Clang, Bang, Bing – was unbelievable. I was convinced everyone was going to be lifted. Yet the police hardly raised an eyebrow. Thinking about it afterwards, and given what was to occur on the night, they must simply have presumed we were 'fash'. So, instead of arresting the lot of us for something or other, we were escorted the rest of the way by a lone policeman, in case, presumably, we got lost."

As AFA approached the hall, they had their first confirmed sightings of fascists. Small gangs of 'snipers' numbering no more than three or four were lurking, on the look out for unwary left-wingers or republicans. One outfit, with James Fields the former leading NF street fighter from Islington prominent, confronted the larger AFA group. "You're two bob, you lot," he snarled as AFA strode past. A promising tirade cut short when he was casually backhanded in the face by an anti-fascist using a truncheon wrapped up in a *Daily Mirror*. A confused police escort comforted him, as AFA continued on their way.

On arrival, an unusually large number of left-wing paper sellers hovered around the entrance of Conway Hall. As AFA merged with them, four men walked up the dimly lit street towards the hall. Excitedly, someone suggested they were BNP. As the BNP still had a distinctly limited political profile, even a leading figure like Richard Edmonds would not necessarily have been known to militants by sight. So as they tried to push their way through the crowd, they were challenged. "Are you republicans?" a voice inquired.

Joe: "The way they were dressed, car-coats and the like, they could have passed for middle-aged republicans of the more conservative variety. So I asked them again, 'Are you republicans?' One of them responded, 'It's a public meeting, we don't have to be'."

There was a pause, and they must have thought he had got away with it, when a voice shouted: 'You're fucking Richard Edmonds!' Shoving the weediest in his entourage violently in the back, Edmonds attempted a long-legged getaway, which was abruptly curtailed after only a few yards when a martial arts expert, who had been summoned from Manchester for the event, dropkicked him over some hoardings. His three companions, including *British Nationalist* editor, John Morse, and Derek Beackon, later to become the BNP's first councillor on the Isle of Dogs in 1993, if anything, fared worse. Morse, having been first trampled in the rush to get at Edmonds, was still prone when the attackers returned from chasing his companions and gave him a second going over. Eventually, he was rescued and delivered to hospital where he was treated, along with his comrades, for a variety of injuries, including gas inhalation and the odd broken bone.

This display of AFA efficiency was not greeted with universal approval. One *Socialist Worker* seller went berserk, screaming that AFA stewards were 'thugs', while a TOM organiser showed her gratitude by denouncing AFA as 'dickheads'. It took the appearance of a second and much larger wave of Loyalists and fascists moving towards the hall to interrupt the harangue. A strong AFA counter-attack led to clashes in the darkness of the square and the surrounding streets, with the right-wingers again forced to retreat. One leading BNP member, Tony Lecomber, ran straight through a hedge to get away. Emerging from the other side of the park he must have thought he was home free. Then, from out of nowhere, he was blinded by a blast of heavy-duty CS gas and saved from more serious injury by the sudden appearance on the edge of the action of some plain-clothes police.

When a head count revealed that TOM could muster the meagre total of six stewards, AFA assumed command. And, in the circumstances, there was nothing anyone wished to say about it. AFA surmised the original party comprising Edmonds and Co. had been sent to infiltrate the meeting with the intention of creating a ruckus in front of the media – not so much to inflict physical violence but to provoke trouble, by constantly interrupting until forcibly ejected by stewards. As well as feeding the BNP thirst for publicity, a rough-house expulsion would also trigger their 'rescue' by the 100-strong fighting-force assembled nearby. As the early encounter suggested, the police seemed keen to keep well out of sight until serious trouble flared. In the interim, if serious injuries were the result, what did it matter? After all, had not the likely victims been described by the Prime Minister, no less, as supporters of the 'enemy within'? And while the original plan had been thwarted, it was thought extremely likely something similar would be tried again.

Tony Lecomber

Terry: "Soon a latecomer approached the entrance. When asked who he was looking for, he replied that he had come for 'the meeting'. 'Which meeting mate?' 'Bernadette,' he replied. Under the watchful eyes of the stewards, he walked straight past the entrance to the meeting and headed up the stairs to the toilets. When he reappeared, he turned to walk out through the back door, but was blocked by visibly nervous TOM stewards. Indignant, he demanded to be let out, but they told him they were under instructions not to let anyone in or out. 'Under instructions from who?' he snarled. 'From them,' the steward replied, pointing in an almost apologetic way to a group of about a dozen or so standing placidly behind him.

"The look on his face was one of pure terror. It was not helped by the Irish accents of some of his captors. After a brief interrogation, it became evident that he had lost control of his bowels. And then he started to howl. A member of Sinn Fein, being interviewed by a foreign journalist nearby, suggested they continue the interview elsewhere, much to the relief of the journalist, who was clearly alarmed by this sudden turn of events. When stewards from the hall said the 'noise' could be heard inside the meeting and was causing concern – some actually thought he was being tortured!

"Despite knowing what was going on, when police turned up, following a report of someone being seen on the roof, a TOM steward invited them into the building. Luckily they were confronted by a senior steward and sent packing, otherwise we could all have been done for kidnapping. It was then decided to release the prisoner. Unfortunately the prisoner did not want to be released, convinced that his removal meant something far more sinister was about to take place. When the back doors were opened and the stewards, considering his previous accident, rather carefully tried to remove him, he wouldn't go. The more the stewards pushed, the more rigid he became, the howling intensified, and two policemen over the road, presumably not relishing the paperwork, looked the other way and strolled off. Finally, although he hadn't been physically harmed in any way up to now, considerable force had to be applied to get him out of the building. Once out, the door was bolted, the stewards washed up, and people wondered how he would explain the state he was in when he finally got home [Loughton in Essex], before undoubtedly having words with Mr Jarvis, his BNP friend, who had told him it would be a 'piece of piss'."

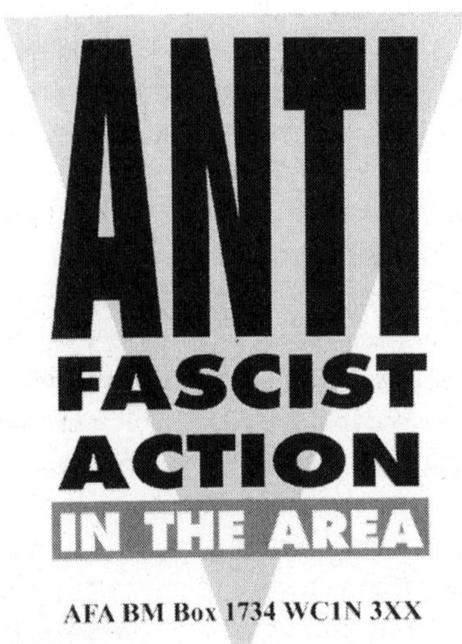

AFA sticker.

After the meeting, AFA stewards had to escort the audience, many of them Irish women, some elderly, out the back door, away from a very large, rough looking and vengeful mob, including Ulster Loyalists and British Movement members, that had gathered near Holborn station, hoping for rich pickings as the meeting broke up.

Joe: "As it was obvious to all what was going to happen once out on the street, we were faced by a dilemma. On the one hand, the people at the meeting could not be abandoned; on the other, I personally didn't fancy walking into a sea of bottles and glasses coming out of the night sky, while looking after someone's granny."

An offer was made publicly from the platform to escort people to safety. While many of the Left sneered and departed in 'groups', the working class Irish present, both young and old, perhaps more attuned to the danger, readily accepted the offer. A Belfast woman who saw an AFA steward arm himself with a hammer commented approvingly: "Thank fuck someone knows what they're doing." After a brisk and nervy march to Russell Square tube, the crowd was advised to remove any badge or item of clothing that might betray their allegiance, as it was not unknown for the fascist gangs to prowl the tube looking for victims. "Good luck, lads," someone said as the groups parted. Expecting the fascists not to be far behind, AFA decided to make a stand in a nearby 'lads' pub. Desensitised to the sense of menace they exuded, they pressed to the bar eager to get down at least one pint before battle was joined. Most of the locals were only too keen to make way for them. Some actually began to leave, preferring to stand in a sullen huddle in the rain outside. Another, unable to deal with the tension, finally blurted out, "Okay, Okay, I know you're after me – but I didn't do it!" The steward to whom the confession was mistakenly directed, laughed before accepting the offer of a pint.

Meanwhile, the Troops Out organisers, having effectively ceded all political responsibility to AFA on the night, quickly left the area with the speakers in cars. The following week, the local *Camden and St Pancras Chronicle* led with an account of how "Police intervention stopped an ugly attack by 100 fascist thugs on an Irish civil rights meeting on Friday night." And, while a TOM spokeswoman was quoted as saying that "there were enough people who looked like fascists at all the doors for our stewards to be sufficiently alarmed" (17th November 1988), the rather dramatic goings-on thereafter warranted not even a single line in the next issue of *Troops Out* magazine. Informally, however, the attendance of Red Action/AFA, rather than the BNP/UDA/NF, was being identified as the problem.

In a letter, one of the TOM stewards, Mark M., wrote afterwards: "Subsequent reports on events have bordered on the ludicrous. Perhaps the most stupid is the claim that violence puts people off attending future meetings. It is as if Red Action and others like myself were responsible for the violence. The facts are that one hundred fascists turned up to wreck a meeting. A number of people were 'tooled up' with iron bars, etc. In such a situation, how else can you 'persuade' people that they are not welcome? By telling them to go away? Not bloody likely. It really is time that some political activists began to take seriously the activities of the Far Right. This ostrich-like view that 'they are no threat' isn't much use to those black people who experience the attacks. It also isn't much use if we intend to raise the issue of the Irish struggle wherever we can."

Spearhead was by comparison unusually candid. Bemoaning the fact that "a strong body of British Nationalists about 100 in number ... had been unable to confront the subversives in one formation," it ruefully admitted one of the smaller groups had been "set upon by 30 or 40 IRA supporters ... Messrs Edmonds and Morse sustained two black eyes each and the latter also a broken wrist." More in hope than expectation, the article concluded that the operation "served to strengthen links between the BNP and various Ulster Loyalist [paramilitary] groups who have agreed to work more closely and regularly in the future." In truth, such was the scale of the debacle, it would be another five years before Ulster Loyalists would dare to venture on the streets with the Far Right again. Along with those injured, a further twelve were arrested for brawling with police after AFA had departed. The landlord of The Princess Louise pub told the *Camden and St Pancras Chronicle*: "We got infested with National Front types or people who call themselves patriotic but they were just football hooligans. It got a bit out of hand when they started singing nazi songs."

2.12

THE HUMBLING OF BLOOD & HONOUR: HYDE PARK, MAY 1989

In the late 1970s, the National Front's White Noise Club was set up largely to counter the influence of Rock Against Racism and, in addition, to promote fascist bands. By the mid-80s 'financial mismanagement' saw the bands break away from the NF in order to set up the Blood & Honour organisation (B&H) that would be controlled entirely by the bands themselves. By 1988, they had established themselves in London's West End. Two shops, the Merc and Cutdown, just off Carnaby Street, stocked B&H merchandise, and a number of pubs local to this area were used as meeting venues.

Around this period the European situation was changing rapidly, with the Far Right arguments beginning to gain a staggering level of electoral support across a range of countries. On the continent and, to a lesser extent, in America, the skinhead scene played an integral part in selling the core nationalist message to working class youngsters. In what would soon be former Communist Europe, skinheads would also be used as shock troops in the political arena. Politically, as the skinheads were by far the most overt and visibly extreme, any toleration of their political existence made any more astute and politically ambitious right-wingers appear moderate by comparison.

It was this perceived role as a stalking horse that caused *Red Action* to describe the B&H phenomenon a shade colourfully as the "outer tentacles of the beast". Within the scene itself, in terms of pulling power and prestige, Skrewdriver's Ian Stuart Donaldson reigned supreme. Consequently, once Stuart had set up court in Carnaby Street, it was not long before delegations of fascists from Europe began to visit the area to pay homage.

Not unexpectedly, AFA felt that B&H should be confronted. A leaflet distributed at the time outlined the organisation's concerns: "The shops openly sell nazi propaganda and the pub is used as a meeting place for nazis from all over the world (we're not exaggerating). Nazis coming to this country know where they can rely on meeting their British counterparts in the Carnaby Street area, so it has become more than just a meeting place, more like a political headquarters where nazi campaigns can be planned. We are sick of people such as shopkeepers, pub landlords, and music promoters who, while claiming not to be nazi sympathisers, are happy to make money out of them. As far as we're concerned, you are either for or against them, and if you are against fascism then have nothing to do with them."

Politically, Carnaby Street was fast becoming the centre of a growing Blood & Honour network, both locally and internationally. One result was that Blood & Honour supporters, emboldened by the situation on the continent, began to launch a number of attacks on bands that they considered to be legitimate targets: the Pogues (Irish), Desmond Dekker (black) and the Upstarts (socialist). The last attack was captured on video and, as well as showing a sea of sieg-heils, it showed a small group of fascists, armed incredibly with an 20ft scaffold pole, trying to storm the stage.

Cleverly, AFA challenged the media to have a look for themselves, knowing that B&H propaganda would raise eyebrows even among the most hardened of hacks. They were not disappointed. This report in the *Morning Star* conveyed a real sense of astonishment: "Shops stock nazi paraphernalia including swastika flags, T-shirts, and armbands. They sell SS rings, far-right fanzines, and records and tapes of bands like Skrewdriver and Brutal Attack. One magazine called *14 Up* features race-hate cartoons showing a variety of ways to assault black people, and photographs of a woman being internally assaulted with a beer bottle" (*Morning Star*, 11th January 1989).

Evening Standard reporter, Keith Dovkants, was just as taken aback: "It was noisome stuff: cartoons depicting violence against blacks, records with songs extolling white power. Pictures of youngsters making sieg-heil salutes. Walking out of the shops with a copy of *Blood & Honour*, emblazoned with its swastika-variant emblem and bearing a picture of a skinhead joining hands with a 'Wizard' of the Ku Klux Klan, it was hard to believe that such ideas could take hold in a city that still bears the scars inflicted by the Third Reich. But the evidence suggests Ian Stuart is sowing his seeds in fertile ground." In the same article a senior member of the Board of Deputies of British Jews remarked: "He [Stuart] and his movement are turning London into a Mecca for neo-nazis and fascists from all over the world. It is extremely worrying" (April 1989).

One integral part of AFA's campaign against Blood & Honour was the setting up of Cable Street Beat (CSB) in October 1988. As White Noise was set up to counter Rock Against Racism, so CSB was set up to counter B&H. It was the militants in AFA who initiated CSB and, while the dispute with the liberal wing was yet to be resolved, CSB's first leaflet nailed its militant colours to the mast. The words of the 'Ghosts of Cable Street' by The Men They Couldn't Hang left little room for doubt as to the authors' political aims: "So we learn from history / Generations have to fight / And those who crave for mastery / Must be faced down on sight / And if that means by words, by fists / By stones or by the gun / Remember those who stood and fought / For their daughters and their sons / So listen to the sound of marching feet / And the voices of the ghosts of Cable Street / With fists and stones and batons and the gun / With courage we shall beat those Blackshirts down."

AFA tended to interpret the lyrics literally. On 4th October 1988, CSB held its first major gig to a sell out crowd celebrating the battle of Cable Street at the Electric Ballroom in Camden. Battle of Cable Street veteran, Solly Kaye, captivated the thousand-strong audience with a rousing speech. As a result of positive coverage in the national media, AFA was presented with the platform to highlight the Blood & Honour colonisation of parts of Central London.

With militant approval, the campaign was actually launched at a press conference in the House of Commons. After receiving a letter from AFA, Cllr. Miles Young, chairman of Westminster's Environment Committee, replied: "I share the concern about fascist activities in Carnaby Street and at the preponderance of fascist material on sale in the shops there. However, I am afraid that, as far as direct action to stop this is concerned, the City Council had no locus" (*Westminster Times*, 17th Janaury 1989). Listings magazine *Time Out* was equally pessimistic: "The success of the campaign will depend on whether the police and Westminster Council consider there is a case for prosecution. Similar approaches by the Board of Deputies of British Jews to the Director of Public Prosecutions and Scotland Yard three years ago were unsuccessful."

Shoulder shrugging of a very different kind came from the *Daily Star*, who warned that the campaign itself was "naïve and unnecessary". "To treat them [Blood & Honour] as a serious threat to society is just the kind of recognition these tin-pot trouble makers are looking for." Plainly the 'see no evil, hear no evil, ignore them and they will go away' solution will find a resonance whatever the conditions.* But if the local council, *Time Out*, or the *Daily Star* thought the AFA-generated publicity was pitched as a plea for the authorities to intervene, they did not know much about AFA. And if the Council felt it had no 'locus', the militants made sure there were points of reference aplenty. So, with the preliminary media/political propaganda beachhead established to their satisfaction, AFA immediately set about ameliorating the right-wing presence through the use of a wide variety of tactics.

A blizzard of pickets, petitions and meetings ensued involving locals, including students and nurses. One pub in particular, The Store, whose landlord made a small fortune each Saturday from his fascist clientele, was understandably reluctant to lose so lucrative a trade and, having indicated as much publicly, became a natural target. One evening a large number of fairly grim-faced customers, led by a be-suited black man, walked in. Seventeen halves of lager were ordered and paid for with a £20 note. The group then drank in complete silence and left without a word.

* In the same year that the BNP would see their first ever councillor elected, *Melody Maker* and otherwise trendy journalist, Simon Clark, wrote: "Fascism is the biggest invisible presence on Planet Rock 1993 ... so go on, AFA and ARA, end the phoney war ... terminate Britain's 200 or so nazi skins."

Terry: "It was designed as a bit of theatre. We wanted to convey a sense of menace without the necessity of actually making any threats. We also knew once we left we would automatically be the subject of conversation. The black man as leader of an otherwise all white crew gave it an added touch of the exotic, but the joke was that, while he was dressed like a city gent, crombie and that, the £20 quid note was a sort of prop, as he had been forced to borrow it from one of 'his minders' before we went in."

In the hubbub that ensued, two female undercover AFA operatives, dressed as if for a girly night out, were perfectly placed to gauge reaction to the stunt and, more importantly, accrue what would prove to be vital information. Their natural sympathy for the patrons encouraged the governor and his wife to reveal that he had been told to anticipate trouble. With the backing of his lodgers and the doormen of a night-club a few doors away, plus the fact that his brother managed another pub at the top of the street, he was confident he could see off any threats. If all else failed, there was also the recently installed panic button to the local police to fall back on. Armed with this information, AFA immediately decided to trigger his security.

One evening not long afterwards, the manager found his pub surrounded by over 20 pickets, busily informing would-be drinkers of the type of clientele who were entertained there at the weekends. Not surprisingly many decided another pub might be more 'relaxing'. Then others, either in sympathy with the leaflets being distributed, or just possibly intimidated by the rough looking protestors, began to walk out despite the manager's protestations. Immediately, the manager pressed the panic button. Within minutes three vans of police screeched to a halt and dozens of obviously hyped-up police jumped out. But, instead of the lines of militant enforcers they had been told were menacing customers and staff, to their surprise and visible disappointment, they found mainly female students from the local university. With them was a solicitor who happily discussed the finer points of picketing with the officer in charge, and after about twenty minutes the police departed, crestfallen. Within a minute of the vans departure, the AFA heavies reappeared. Realising he had been tricked, and now fearful of the consequences, the manager acceded to the militant demands to shut the pub that Saturday, and every Saturday thereafter. B&H had lost the first round.

Round two arrived on 21st January, when an AFA picket of the shops poured over 300 anti-fascists into a tiny side street off Carnaby Street. It had been called for 11am. At one minute to eleven, AFA stewards were nowhere to be seen and early-comers were getting nervous as bands of Far Right 'casuals' were loitering with intent. On the dot of 11am, heads swivelled as a body of men, ten wide, ten deep suddenly emerged from the mouth of a nearby alley. One female activist, a solicitor working as liaison with the media on the day, described the effect as like "a scene from the 1930s". The effect of the choreography would certainly not have been accidental, as the more muscular anti-fascism of previous generations clearly served as both a validation and inspiration.

As part of the strategy on the day, it had been decided that, in addition to the intimidating physical presence, a petition of the shops would be useful. The purpose was three-fold: One, because the nazi paraphernalia was proving so lucrative that many other shops, in addition to the skinhead shops, had also begun to stock it. Two, the picket would also have the effect of isolating B&H from other traders once the list was publicised. Three, it would serve as a warning to all of the kind of pressure that could be brought to bear should anyone be tempted to back-track.

Finally, the concern being expressed by Westminster Council was marshalled when a fairly self-effacing Labour councillor, Peter Bradley, who represented Millbank ward, was invited to front the petition. He set about the task with considerable enthusiasm, but early results were disappointing. He approached the chief steward a bit downcast. "People are refusing to sign it," he said. "Don't worry," came the reply, "I have a remedy to hand. What you need is a 'delegation' to accompany you." To the astonishment and delight of Councillor Bradley, the improvement in response was both instant and dramatic.

Joe: "How it worked was, along with another half-dozen picked for their appearance, 'Hefty' would enter the shop slightly after the councillor and stand there in watchful silence as the Labour councillor made his pitch. Once convinced the owner had 'got the message', they would slip out before the Councillor, unaware of their contribution, had finished his speech. It worked like a dream."

All but one (an Arab who regarded anti-fascism as being pro-Jewish) duly signed up. The councillor was overjoyed at the dramatic, almost Damascene, change in attitude. In order to ram home the message further, the same evening Cable Street Beat organised a gig featuring the Upstarts at a music venue called the George Robey in Finsbury Park. The area was firmly in the region of north London which, from the early 1980s, anti-fascists had controlled politically, and the pub itself was considered ideal to repulse a full-frontal assault. B&H had organised the attack on this band while on stage at the Astoria in May of the previous year, and confidently predicted the Upstarts "would never play in London again". No one could be in any doubt that this was a 'come-on' to the Far Right, but equally, from a militant standpoint, whatever happened it was designed as a 'win win' situation.

Inside the packed venue the atmosphere was electric. Outside in a darkened street with the windows of the pub boarded up and painted black for the occasion it was all fairly forbidding. Naturally, everyone entering was thoroughly frisked. To help emphasise AFA strength in depth, it was decided to allow in some known fascist sympathisers. One small group were spotted in the queue. Mensi, the Upstarts lead singer, greeted them. They responded uncertainly. A steward nearby happily clarified the situation for them. "Okay, boys, this is the score, you're welcome to come in, but any stiff-arm salutes and we'll rip the arm off and raffle it. Have a nice evening." In the event there was very little trouble. In part this may have been because of the example made of one suicidal 'sieg-heiler', who was torn from the body of the crowd by security stewards and launched head long into and through the fire exit door (which was shut at the time) and out into the street. He travelled about ten feet through the air, hit an opposite wall and crumpled. There were understandably no repetitions.

At one stage in the evening, the Red Action battle cry "We are the REDS!" rent the air. In the relatively small venue, the hundreds that joined in made it a deafening chorus. The six or so bone-heads 'on licence' first swung round in a panic, and then, with mounting horror, realised they were beginning to attract interest simply by standing still. With fixed death's-head grins, they joined in the clenched fist celebration. If B&H had ever regarded the Upstarts' gig as an opportunity to recover the considerable prestige lost earlier in the day, they clearly thought better of it and never showed. They had other plans.

The full scale of their ambition was revealed four months later. With the support of a Jewish businessman who also acted as a front man, Camden Town Hall was booked for 27th May by an outfit called 'International Music Exchange'. The request for an £800 down payment was handed over without demur. B&H could well afford it. At £10 a head up-front and with spin-offs from merchandise on the night, politics apart, it was a commercial venture with extremely lucrative potential. Seven bands from across Europe were advertised. Though there was a ban on overt publicity outside identifiable circles in Britain, AFA were tipped off six weeks earlier by a contact in Belgium.

Terry: "We knew the assembly point was Speakers' Corner in Hyde Park, so we had over a month to try and find the venue. We also knew that B&H, in an attempt to convince the punters that £10 up-front was a good investment, had a little recklessly promised them their money back if the gig was cancelled. Now, either they made good their promise or they defaulted. Either way, if we could get to the venue first, they would be faced with a choice of losing financial or political capital."

A wide sweep of what were considered suitable venues in the surrounding area began at once. Letters were sent to all London Boroughs' race relations units, union officers, council leaders and booking offices. To much surprise, there were more than twenty responses. So dogged and widespread was the trawl that eventually the branch secretary of Camden NALGO discovered a booking on the day by an organisation called the 'International Music Exchange'. "Was it possible one of London's politically trendiest councils was going to play host to 1,000 neo-nazis?" she wondered. She rang Searchlight for confirmation. Though still loosely involved in AFA at the time, Searchlight decided to conceal the information from what was still the security wing. Mainly because a sting type operation in co-operation with the police had been set up instead. With just 24 hours to go, a member of the Institute of Race Relations somehow got wind of it. She contacted Gerry Gable. He tried to convince her to leave the militants in the dark. She flatly refused and instantly informed a leading member of RA.

Even with the cat out of the bag and the possibility of extensive trouble, Searchlight and the covert police unit apparently continued to argue the gig should be allowed to go ahead. The local police commander in the King's Cross area was, however, having none of it. On police advice Camden Council banned the use of their premises on the day and, in gratitude for the political embarrassment saved, handed the £800 deposit to Searchlight, who duly pocketed it.

B&H supporters were instructed to meet at Speakers' Corner between 5 and 6pm to be given the name of the concert venue. The flaw in the planning was that the supporters would themselves have to prove sufficiently confident and numerous to stand their ground, in order to still be in place for the final instructions to be verbally delivered sometime around 6pm.

Called for 4pm at the fascists' redirection point, the AFA demo put anti-fascists in the vicinity of Hyde Park an hour before travellers from the continent were ordered to assemble. One DAM member recalls: "The date coincided with the three-day DAM National Conference in Wiltshire, but a mini-bus load of us came back to London for the day. It was another one of those occasions when most of us were convinced we were going to be massacred! Everyone knew that Blood & Honour could muster several hundred or even a thousand bodies. If it was left to me, I would probably have suggested that we all go home and have a nice cup of tea. But fortunately the 'movers and shakers' within AFA are more daring than me! Afterwards, we, Red Action, and various other anti-fascists headed down to Marble Arch about 100 strong, and considerably more confident. And what a success it turned out to be!" (*Bash the Fash, Anti-Fascist Recollections, 1984-93,* K. Bullstreet).

Even before the AFA security wing arrived, scattered confrontations had begun to take place. Once the AFA stewards took centre stage, running battles became the norm. A scene of utter lawlessness was enhanced by the coincidence of a huge Muslim demonstration against the author Salman Rushdie degenerating into a riot in Parliament Square at exactly the same time. With police overstretched, anti-fascists had an almost entirely free hand. All around the Marble Arch area, gangs of would be gig-goers, many of them German, were continually confronted. One group of about half a dozen were set upon in a side street outside Marble Arch tube station. Two were floored. As they had no identifiable insignia, the anti-fascists paused momentarily, awaiting further instructions. Perhaps not fully comprehending why they were being attacked, or possibly mistaking the hesitancy for apology, one member of the group began to berate the attackers in his own tongue: "They're Geerrmaans!" an indignant Scouse voice accused, and the anti-fascists returned to the attack with renewed vigour.

One event typified the day. A coach from Derby, packed with expectant skinheads, arrived at Speaker's Corner around 5 o'clock. The driver began slowing down with the intention of allowing the fifty-odd skins to disembark. But a section of the crowd let up a joyous roar of savage anticipation and charged towards them, effortlessly vaulting six-foot railings. The astonished driver accelerated away, just as a metal bin smashed through a rear window. The coach party almost had another run in with 'Reds' later in Oxford Street, and then, to their utter astonishment, three hours later, as they were making their weary way home, the skinheads again came under gratuitous attack from a group drinking outside a pub near Great Portland Street station. They could hardly be expected to know the attackers were part of the original AFA contingent from earlier in the day, now on standby for phase two of the B&H demolition to be set in motion.

Back at Hyde Park, right-wingers from practically every country in Europe were represented. They were hunted relentlessly for the two hours up to six o'clock when

A fascist gets taught a lesson at Speakers' Corner, Hyde Park, 27th May 1989.

police reinforcements arrived in numbers. Such was the fierceness displayed on this occasion that one Red Action member, a Joe Pesci character, personally intervened to bring to a halt a beating being dished out to one lone skinhead. To do otherwise, he felt, ran the risk of it ending in a fatality. Inevitably, given the chaos, it was hardly a surprise that many hundreds of B&H supporters failed to reach the rearranged venue in Kent.

It was a rout, but, for the more determined anti-fascists, the day was far from over. Once the inevitable heavy-duty police influx materialised, the AFA stewards, their job done, abandoned the area both to police and triumphant anti-fascists, and went hunting for fresh quarry. With one eye on internal affairs within AFA, the militant leadership wanted very much to maximise their advantage, as well as impressing on the foreign visitors that the days of London as the 'cultural Mecca' for the extreme Right were over.

Exiting from Oxford Circus, there was an immediate clash with a group of foreign skinheads. So swift and spectacular was the demolition that half a dozen young black girls watching from across the road burst into spontaneous applause. In contrast to what had gone before, within minutes, plain-clothes police were re-deployed, but this too had been catered for. A few minutes afterwards, to the wry amusement of the AFA organiser responsible, plain-clothes police were heard desperately asking for instructions from their controllers as, with only a cursory consultation, the 'stewards', still numbering about one hundred and fifty, abruptly splintered into four groups and headed off at pace in totally opposite directions. Surveillance had been anticipated and had now been dumped. Each group had a separate rendezvous. Notting Hill, Camden Town, etc. All the pubs selected were sited within yards of a tube station, both for convenience and to avoid attracting unnecessary attention while on the streets. It was a level of thoroughness never matched by the opposition and rarely by the police.

Later that evening, a B&H retail outlet in Riding House Street, off Oxford Street, which had already been forced to move once from Carnaby Street, was attacked. At 9pm exactly, locals emerged from a nearby pub to witness slack-jawed as a large and menacing group suddenly appeared and stood tensely silent at the corner of the street. Then, out of the crowd, emerged two men wearing balaclavas and carrying what, in the gathering dusk, to the more imaginative may have looked like firearms, but were in fact sledgehammers. Immediately, they set about demolishing the shop front. Initially, some of the onlookers thought to protest but apparently thought better of it. Once the windows went in, figures seemingly reckless of their own safety leapt through them. Much of the stock was then destroyed with acid.

Within a matter of weeks, B&H's essential vulnerability as a moneymaking enterprise was exposed to an international audience, and the last of their shops, which ironically had been rented from the family of one of the first British doctors to enter Bergen Belsen concentration camp after the war, was on the point of closure. As part of the campaign, the family decided to take legal action to get the neo-nazis out. Without question, the militant attack strengthened their hand and accelerated the B&H eviction considerably.

The *Sunday Telegraph* of 2nd July reported: "On May 27th Cutdown became a gathering point for dozens of skinheads and neo-nazis from all over the world heading for an international concert in Gravesend. That night the shop was attacked by anti-fascists with sledgehammers. After a second attack on June 10, Mr Coigly's insurance company said his cover would be revoked unless he installed a watchman at a cost of £100 a day" (*Sunday Telegraph*, 2nd July 1989).

2.13

SKREWDRIVER SCREWED, 1989

In an interview with the *Evening Standard*, Ian Stuart gave a clear indication of the effect AFA were having: "We have to advertise our gigs by word of mouth. If they (AFA) get to hear about it they want to turn it into a bloodbath." Apart from the serious political disappointment surrounding 27th May and the financial loss of the shops, he had pressing problems closer to home.

Stuart rented a room in a seedy hotel in Argyll Square in King's Cross, where he routinely received visitors and gave interviews to the press. King's Cross was in a part of a wider north London area Red Action had come to regard as its own since the early '80s when, as they saw it, it had been politically rinsed. Understandably, Stuart's high media profile was an affront to this sense of territory conquered. Stuart felt under siege, a reality he did not attempt to conceal in an interview with journalist Keith Dovkants for the *Evening Standard*'s *ES Magazine* in April 1989. "It [the King's Cross area] has now become difficult territory for Ian Stuart. The entrance to his tiny flat in a square near the station has been daubed with pink paint, and pickets have been organised by Anti-Fascist Action at pubs where he and his cronies drink. He is appalled by this: 'The Reds talk about civil liberties? I can't go to the shop round here because the communists have told the shopkeepers not to serve me. The only ones who will serve me anything are the Asians...'" Understandably obsessive with regard to his personal security, Stuart was by now patently aware that personal catastrophe was often just a footstep away.

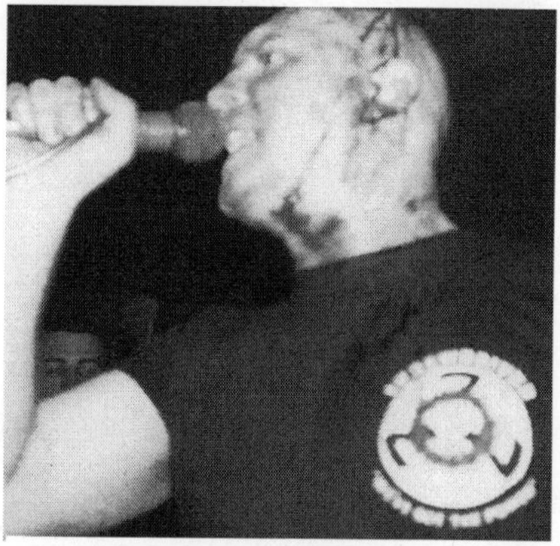

Ian Stuart on stage at the Swiss Cottage Skrewdriver gig.

In the preceding months he had been attacked and injured by an AFA scouting party while enjoying a pre-gig drink with minders in a pub in nearby Swiss Cottage. "They found out we were doing a gig near Swiss Cottage and I was having a quiet drink with my mates and about 15 of them came storming in. They had baseball bats. They tried to smash my elbows and knees with the bats. I got this cut on my head..." He was later photographed on stage blood pouring copiously from a head wound that he claimed "needed 26 stitches" (*ES Magazine*, April 1989).

His local in King's Cross, The Prince Albert in which he used to hold court, had been marched on and picketed. The police, invited by the management to offer assurances in the event of further coercion, declined to do so. Then, on returning from an early evening jog, Stuart was spotted at his front door by a passing RA member and coshed. Even more disquieting must have been the ambush of a group of visiting foreign skinheads, who were beaten and left lying unconscious, literally toe to toe, on the doorstep of his hotel in Argyll Square. In truth, this was a spontaneous retaliation for a near fatal race attack by skinheads at London Bridge on a Moroccan, who had lost a kidney as a result – events *British Nationalist* reported on with a sickening relish. In the search for suitable victims, the pubs around King's Cross were picked by Hefty who lived nearby, mainly out of convenience. But Stuart would have no reason not to regard it personally.

He had an extremely narrow escape when a private party in his honour in Hatfield in Hertfordshire was gate-crashed at about 2am by a thirty-strong force of anti-fascists who arrived just minutes after Stuart had left. As Stuart was the real target, those in the house got off relatively lightly, though the same could not be said for the house itself. Not long afterwards, open season was declared on his followers as well. Easily distinguished by the paramilitary style 'uniform' of head shaved bald, black flight jacket with black cargo pants and sixteen-hole Doc Martens, they came under attack without fanfare. Two were clubbed to the ground in broad daylight in Oxford Street. Some others, having been intimidated into leaving a Ska gig in Camden Town, were waylaid and beaten insensible outside. Around the same time, Dessie Clarke, Skrewdriver's drummer, was enjoying dinner with friends in a café in Parkway in Camden, when he was set upon by a group of AFA militants who had dropped in for a meal. Hit full in the face by a plate of spaghetti and gassed, Clarke fled the scene leaving his companions, one of whom was stabbed in the buttocks with a fork as he tried to jump through the serving hatch into the kitchen, to fend for themselves.

On another occasion, fellow band member Martin Cross, later to be convicted of murder, was dragged into an alley in Swiss Cottage and beaten bloody. Then, following a confrontation outside a gig in Hammersmith, Ken McLennan, lead singer of the band Brutal Attack, was bottled. Less notable scalps were even more numerous. Travelling on the Piccadilly Line, a day-dreaming B&H skin suddenly notices the person opposite reading a copy of *Red Action*. Alarmed, he carefully scans the carriage for 'Reds', fervently hoping against hope he hadn't been spotted. The journey continues without incident and he begins to visibly relax. As the train pulls into Holloway Road tube, two noticeably large men get up, but instead of stepping onto the platform merely hold the doors. An attempted intervention by a Guardian Angel, complete with beret, couldn't save the bonehead from a brutal beating.

A week or so afterwards, in the same area, an AFA scout car on other business spotted a Pizza delivery boy sporting a Skrewdriver T-shirt. With tyres screaming the car U-turned. Without further ado the pizza boy fled, dispensing with both pizza and crash helmet to aid his getaway. Desperately looking for sanctuary he gate-crashed a wedding reception in a nearby community centre and hid under a table. It is possible that in his panic he may not even have noticed that almost all of the guests were black. Shortly afterwards when AFA came calling, some initially offered him protection, but when the situation was fully explained he was physically ejected, with even the best man joining in the subsequent battering.

Early one winter evening, three members of north London Red Action dropped into a curry house in Theberton Street in Islington. Hardly had they sat down than they became aware the neighbouring table was occupied by a couple of B&H admirers. At the anti-fascist table a discussion began that centred on when, rather than if, the attack should be launched. The choice was either before or after they had eaten! Suddenly, though quite unaware of their fate, the fascists upped and left – without paying the bill. One walked quickly onto Upper Street expecting to be swallowed up in the rush hour crowd. But almost literally on his heels the anti-fascists immediately affected a citizen's arrest. He was frog-marched back to the restaurant. Only when he had paid up and made to apologise to the puzzled staff were his political affiliations challenged. A brawl ensued that spilled out on the street. After a suitable pounding he was let go on his way. His compatriot, wary, but not exactly sure what had occurred with his buddy, cautiously approached the restaurant from the other direction. Not suspecting for a moment that there might have been a political dimension to the altercation he had only half-witnessed, he offered to make financial reparations for his earlier error of judgement. Soothed by the reassurances of one the anti-fascists standing outside, he returned to the scene of crime. In an instant he was bludgeoned to the ground with a half brick taken from a skip, while the astonished restaurant workers, including waiters and kitchen staff, peered in wide-eyed wonder over the net curtain rail at the developments taking place on the pavement outside.

On many occasions the assaults were launched, as with the example above, without provocation, in that the right-wingers were not offering violence at the time. This allowed the neo-nazis to cast themselves in the unlikely role of victims. The writer of a feature on subcultures that appeared in the *Independent* at the height of the militant offensive in 1989 must have been sufficiently moved by the self-pitying stories to inform her readers that Blood & Honour was "opposed, even hounded, by a group called Red Action which has the opposite politics" (*Independent*, 23rd January 1989). The article did not expand on what 'opposite politics' might mean in practice.

Inevitably, given the scale of the offensive, not all of those challenged would have B&H, or even fascist, connections at all. The possibility of error was complicated by the fashion among some gays to ape skinhead culture up to the point of displaying nationalist badges and insignia. On one occasion, a number of skinheads were challenged near King's Cross station. So traumatised was one by the rudimentary but menacing inquiry, he collapsed with an epileptic fit. Ironically, they were on their way to The Prince Albert which, having changed hands, was now an exclusively gay nightspot. In Camden Town, a couple of skinheads bumped into an AFA patrol. Questioned as to the political significance of the St George's Cross pinned to his sleeve, the skin responded stoutly but unwisely that he was "a patriot – what of it?" He was head-butted and fell unconscious from the blow. It was later discovered he was a research assistant to a Labour MP.

That the militants were on a roll was proved by a bizarre encounter that could and should have been a major own-goal, but instead ended up being seen by the opposition as another propaganda coup for the 'Reds'. Drinking in the West End one afternoon, a small number of north London Red Action members began a high-spirited pub-crawl that drew back toward the Islington area. So, when they came across some decidedly dodgy looking skinheads sitting outside a pub in Russell Square, it was instinctively identified as a situation that could only add to the entertainment. An opportunity to mix business with pleasure was an opening certainly not to be missed.

Terry: "We were messing about as we went through the door and didn't pay the slightest heed to the other punters. We were at the bar when one of the lads comes up to me and muttered, 'Stuart's here!' It was only then that I took in that the pub was full of fash boneheads – about 40 of them, plus about a dozen more rockabillies. To make it worse, the pub seemed to have only one door and they were gathered around it. Now, we knew Stuart would have recognised us from countless clashes and, being the main man, the onus was on him to give a lead. Despite the bull-like build, Stuart, we knew, was not really a street leader. You could see he didn't really fancy it. But he had no option. That or lose face. Half-smiling, he sauntered across to one of the lads called 'Scouse'. Now Scouse was of slight build, probably never more than ten stone, but was hard as nails. 'Haven't I seen you around King's Cross?' Totally unfazed, Scouse takes his time before replying 'Not me… [pause] … It's all drunks and prozzies round there anyway, isn't it mate?' Whatever the response Stuart was expecting, that wasn't it. Looking uncertain he returned to his followers, who by now were all staring at us.

"We had been served by now, with everyone having taken a sudden fancy for a pint of light and bitter, and retreated into a suitable corner seat with our backs to the wall. Further stocking up with all the heavy ash-trays we could lay our hands on, and even refusing to let bar staff clear away the empties, we sat and waited.

There was no way out of the pub, mobile phones were a thing of the future, we were outnumbered ten-to-one, so, whatever happened it was going to be bad. Everyone was agreed that the first fascist to make a move was to be butchered – then, God help us. The tension was unbearable. But the evening wore on and nothing had happened. A small glimmer of hope began to appear. Then I noticed that the biggest lad with us appeared to have fallen asleep (he later joked that he simply fainted). I don't know what the opposition made of it, but at that moment I probably hit as low a point as I have ever experienced.

"Come closing time and the fascists walk out. The giant 6ft 7in skinhead barman insisted they'd gone. 'Oh, really?' We sat tight. No chance of a cab as the pay phone was broken. Eventually, there was nothing for it but to leave ourselves – with every bottle, ash-tray, and glass we could carry with us. The pub door was locked behind us. Outside was totally silent. We cautiously edged along the wall and peered round the corner. We fully expected an ambush of some sort. But the streets were very dark and more important – very empty. With the realisation that we might just have got away with it, the draining of tension was incredible. Looking back on it later, we realised that, had it been anyone other than Stuart in charge on the night – someone like Nicky Crane say – it would have been intensive care for all of us – or worse. This theory was confirmed by a chance encounter the following morning. Travelling to work, an RA supporter found herself sitting across from some fascists. 'Did you hear about the Red Action fuckers who came into Blitz last night. There was only five of them. Flash bastards.' They thought we had gone in there on purpose!"

Apparently unable to accept the encounter for what it was – namely a rare but serious blunder by the militants – B&H had, it seems, convinced themselves the incursion was motivated by simple bravado, or alternatively could all have been part of some elaborate trap just waiting to be sprung.

Stuart's personal breaking point came at 9am one morning, when he popped out to the local shops for the paper and a pint of milk. Two stocky men in their mid to late twenties, one black, one white, passed him heading in the opposite direction. As they did so, the white one reached into a litterbin, and with the next movement smashed a heavy wine bottle over Stuart's head. Within days, Stuart had relocated to Derby in the East Midlands. Understandably, he had had enough of King's Cross. However, he was not simply disenchanted with life in the capital. In an interview with journalist Nick Ryan, an associate called 'Sid' suggests Stuart was close to packing it all in. "Yeah, I got to know Ian fairly well, especially after he came back up here to Derby. You know he had his fingers fucked up by AFA. Yeah. With a hammer. He didn't want to go through that kind of thing anymore" (*Homeland: Into a World Of Hate* by Nick Ryan, page 86).

So generally awe-inspiring were such displays of militant ruthlessness that, when, a number of years later, Ian Stuart Donaldson was fatally injured in a car accident, at least one fascist fanzine speculated that AFA might have been responsible. In what is, one presumes, an example of projection, C18 went further, in claiming that "on the day of his funeral, his father had to make the painful decision to cremate his remains. This was because the Reds would definitely dig up his body and desecrate the grave if he had been given a normal burial. That is the sort of SCUM we are dealing with"(*Combat 18*, issue no 1).

By 1989, at street level, London AFA was only getting into its stride. The combative calibre of the many hundreds of anti-fascists who rallied to the AFA call on the 27th May (to Hyde Park Corner) was regarded by militants as bearing out their political analysis, with the scale of the response serving to underscore the AFA shortcomings they had already identified. Simply put, the top-down executive structure was not capable of democratically accommodating such recruits on a day-to-day basis. By the summer of 1989, with internal battle lines so firmly drawn, the two Red Action delegates were always outfought and always outgunned at committee level. It was not at all unusual for London AFA meetings to record the vote as 24-2 for or against. But after 27th May something simply had to give. And it did.

2.14

LONDON AFA RE-LAUNCH, SEPTEMBER 1989

"There were two opinions amongst the stewards: one, fuck 'em, we don't need this, we'd be better off going it alone, and two, fuck 'em, its our organisation as much as theirs, we'll fight for it even if we just end up with the banner and nothing else." Eventually the latter sentiment prevailed and the militants turned their attention to the task of reshaping the organisation, and reshaping what was up to now a largely reactive strategy. "The job for AFA is not to be content with merely confronting the organised fascist gangs, but to cut off their supply line of renegade recruits at source: on the terraces, at the gigs, in the working class communities. We must bring the war home to the fascists" (*Red Action*, issue 54).

Though unarguably an ambitious and indeed radical departure from what was considered a sensible custom and practice, it was no great surprise that the call for a new orientation had few sympathisers within the existing executive. But, for the incumbent members of the executive, their greatest political difficulty lay in establishing a rational and convincing resistance to the call for an accountable and democratic structure.

Additional pressure came when a rally organised by Searchlight at Friends House in Euston, on the 100th anniversary of Hitler's birth, 24th April 1989, saw the Red Action speaker use the occasion to make the demands for democratic reform within AFA public, with a reference to the resentment felt by delegates that proposals "could be outvoted or ignored by individuals or cliques of individuals who, at the end of the day, represented nobody but themselves." Among the more conservative members of the executive, there was fury and embarrassment (one speaker opened his briefcase and hid behind the lid for the duration of the speech) at what they considered to be an airing of dirty linen. But RA patience had run out. By this stage the Red Action proposals to revamp AFA were almost a year old and had not, as yet, been seriously discussed. Not discussing the document now was obviously no longer an option, and so the liberal wing finally put pen to paper on 11th July 1989. In doing so, they sought to fight on the ground of their choosing – race.

"The individual/clique argument is an insult which belittles the political differences between us and avoids constructive debate. The present crisis within London AFA should more correctly be described as one between black/anti-racist groups on the one hand, coming from a tradition of community politics and independent struggle outside the confines of the Left, (who all too often try to manipulate struggles against racism for their own ends), and Red Action on the other, operating as a party, and coming out of the tradition of revolutionary socialism ... The real debate is not the lack of democracy in AFA but what shape that democracy will take."

This was a fairly blatant attempt to reshape the debate on familiar 'black and white' territory. And yet they could not escape the reality that many of the key players in London AFA were by now members of Red Action, or identified with its basic politics, and yet Red Action's role in the decision-making process could, and indeed had, for the last year, been reduced to that of a bit player on the steering committee. While on the streets, RA influence and authority was indisputable. So glaring was the disparity, the Secretariat felt obliged to concede that "Red Action are one of the few groups on the Left who we cannot accuse of acting in an opportunistic manner and this is why we have respected Red Action and worked with you for so long."

But without an alternative strategy to accommodate new recruits, the executive was on the defensive. Addressing the need for new recruits, they asked: "Why have old members dropped out? One interpretation would no doubt be that these people were non-confrontational anti-fascists who could not take the heat of physical battle ... Red Action have to take responsibility for the fact that their delegates have adopted heavy-handed and intimidatory tactics to isolate individuals and make them feel that, because they don't 'run' with Red Action, they are wimps."

A more credible interpretation might be that some people were unhappy at being pulled up for shoddy work. Red Action also had members who might be classed as non-combatants, but, as an organisation, constantly emphasised that what passed for acceptable standards on the liberal Left were in fact poor standards. Clearly the fascists would not be beaten if the anti-fascist organisers were indifferent or, worse, incompetent. RA argued that it had, from the very beginning, been prepared to collaborate with others in the anti-fascist camp, but only on the basis that they were serious people who were prepared to make a serious commitment to the tasks at hand – which is to say, showed the same level of commitment and expertise RA demanded of themselves. Unable to compete on those terms, the moderates effectively prepared the grounds for their departure.

"In Red Action's document, reference is made to national and autonomous groups being given special privileges (automatically allowed two delegates on a council body). This causes us some concern. Why should these groups (we presume what is meant is orthodox Left groups) have special privileges when they have contributed not one iota to the struggle against racism. Quite frankly, we are not prepared to waste any more time debating with people who operate in a doctrinaire way, have not related to the struggles of the black working class in Britain, refuse to recognise that the working class is changing, and are locked in the idea that, unless you are a white male manual worker, you are not part of the white working class and, more likely than not, a middle class wanker."

By coincidence, while RA was still digesting the implications of this critique of their proposals, they received a letter asking for their help with 'stewarding' a lobby of Bexley Council on 19th July. This was in opposition to plans by the council to offer planning permission to the BNP to set up a shop in Welling. "At a previous meeting, a number of comrades were badly hurt in an ill-prepared meeting to protest." This was a reference to a meeting organised on the 28th June by the Labour Party, according to London's *Evening Standard*, who headlined the story: 'Blackshirts on rampage'. "An anti-fascist meeting organised by the Labour Party erupted into violence last night when black-shirted opponents raided the building and attacked the audience. Women dived for cover as more than 20 men stormed the meeting and smashed chairs and windows at the library building in Welling. Twelve people in the audience of 60 were taken to hospital ... As fighting broke out, some members tried to flee by smashing a window to a fire escape from an upstairs room. The public meeting, organised by Bexley Labour Movement Campaign against Fascism, was abandoned after police said that only one officer could be provided to cover the remainder of the meeting" (*Evening Standard*, 29th June 1989).

By pitching their appeal for help specifically to Red Action, anti-racists in Bexley seemed to be suggesting that AFA was not up to the job. Now, if even supporters of the Labour Party thought AFA too respectable, then the image re-vamp demanded by militants was long overdue. In truth, by the time the re-orientation was aired in public, AFA was on its knees, both in London and nationally. Apart from turning out on the day, not a single member of the executive lifted a finger in terms of organisation for 27th May (B&H, Hyde Park). All the prior political planning, research and propaganda had been conducted under the auspices of the 'security stewards'. And, inevitably, it was from here the new political leadership would emerge.

Red Action issued a document calling the meeting for 5th September 1989 and on the day representatives from about 15 groups and organisations attended. From the platform, militant representatives stressed their support for the original founding AFA statement, but also stressed that, as anti-fascists, they were not, and could not be seen to be, fighting fascism to maintain the political status quo. Therefore, any strategy committed to the long haul needed to be looked at through the prism of *class* rather than race. For them, this was the bottom line.

"In recognition that it is the white working class youth who provide the fascists' 'natural' recruits, it is with them in mind that AFA must aim its propaganda. Appealing to good reason or conscience will never defeat racist attitudes, especially in areas of grinding poverty. It is only by demonstrating through activity and propaganda, that blacks and Asians are being made scapegoats for the problems of the system, and that fascism/racism is not in the short or long term interests of the working class, will significant and lasting progress be made. It is essential, therefore, that when appropriate, AFA propaganda *must* contain a class message. One, to provide an answer to common prejudices; two, to avoid presenting all white people as the enemy; and most important to negate the efforts by the fascists to present AFA as a bunch of middle class *outsiders*, part and parcel of the establishment, working in the long term interests of the status quo."

As well as pointing to the "escalating rise in race attacks" as proof of a deteriorating situation, and the need for AFA to "put down roots in the community," RA speakers also called for the security wing to be afforded formal recognition within the national decision-making structure. To make sense of this accommodation it was argued a "standing stewards group" needed to be formed to which, ideally, all organisations would contribute. Apart from protecting AFA initiatives, to collate and centralise information, etc., it was argued it would also provide AFA with an alternative strategy to organise quickly to counter fascist initiatives, "where there isn't time for a more traditional protest, or where there isn't sufficient information to justify one. In addition it will provide effective propaganda by impressing people of our sincerity and ability to organise ourselves effectively, without fear of the fascists and without relying on the police for protection."

In the meeting, the Newham Monitoring Project (NMP) continued with the line of argument that a distinction between 'community/grassroots' groups and 'political' groups had to be recognised: 'grassroots good, political bad' was the mantra. This was the prerequisite and the only basis for valid anti-racist/fascist work, it argued. Of course, in real terms the NMP and their associates were no less 'political' than their adversaries; they simply represented a different type of politics. So, when a community activist from Broadwater Farm, introduced by the NMP to showcase their arguments, found himself in sympathy with the analysis being offered by his white working class counterparts, the battle for the soul of anti-fascism was as good as over, for the time being at least. It later emerged that the NMP and their political associates had secretly set up an organisation called the 'London Alliance Against Racism and Fascism' (LAARF) with the intention of rivalling or replacing AFA if the conference proved to be a success. But, like ARAFA before it, LAARF would never seriously get off the ground.

Meanwhile, armed with the new strategy and a constitution specifically designed and equipped to accommodate individual unaligned recruits, militant anti-fascism in the capital was further boosted by the formal return of the Direct Action Movement (DAM) to the fold. Another group, the orthodox Trotskyist 'Workers Power', also threw their weight behind the new strategy. This meant there were now three national organisations involved with AFA, each equipped with their own publications and with a network of branches around the country. As well as new members, AFA was now well equipped to publicise the need for an active anti-fascist resistance, and by so doing attract and influence wider left-wing opinion.

In London, AFA branches were set up to accommodate activists and a structure implemented that saw the organisation for the first time run from the bottom up: in other words, controlled by the activists. For the first time, AFA was being democratically run and working towards a mutually agreed strategic objective. All importantly, and possibly uniquely, the political and street leadership had been amalgamated. It meant that, as well as being confronted with finding practical solutions to day-to-day issues, there was another reason for scrupulous attention to detail. From now on, those doing the hatching would invariably implement any plan of action.

Joe: "The fact that the strategists were invariably 'first through the door' had a number of benefits. One obvious one was that no one was asked to do anything we wouldn't do ourselves. This obviously was extremely good for morale generally. Because of this, the leadership on the ground was trusted, which meant that on the day quite complicated manoeuvres could be implemented without the necessity of everyone being constantly informed at every turn. Which made for great operational flexibility. It also made the task of effective infiltration that much more difficult. Finally, because the political and technical were in tandem, even the most adventurist activity almost always had a wider political dividend in mind."

2.15

AFA BREAKS WITH LABOUR, 1989

Organised on the technical/political leadership paradigm, the London AFA model would eventually serve as the prototype for much of the rest of the country. To accompany the new structure, the next step would be to expand AFA's field of operations nationally. Although there were other 'AFA' groups around the country, the only contacts outside London that had a capacity to operate unilaterally on the street were all in Manchester. Whereas groups in Tyne and Wear and Leeds had local profiles, and though both identified with the AFA name, any common ground with the new leadership more or less ended there.

Besides, both these groups were politically directed by Searchlight, who, as events would later demonstrate, always had a precise agenda of their own. Where they were active it was generally for the purposes of gathering intelligence. And, while their newsletters were aimed at exposing individual local fascists to employers, neighbours and landlords, invariably when it came to confronting the Far Right, the local authorities and police were invited to take action. Furthermore in Newcastle, Tyne & Wear Anti-Fascist Association's (TWAFA) funding came directly from the local council. If this ever restricted the scope of the branch's activity, it was never a relationship they felt motivated to change.

And while the Far Left spent most of the '80s calling on the working class to 'kick out the Tories', it was, militants accepted, largely the Far Right that showed the potential to attract support among a disenfranchised working class. Thus the first step in trying to build any progressive working class movement was to remove the fascists from any areas, be it cultural (football or music) or geographical, where they might enjoy influence. As any form of co-existence was a non-starter, it was only with the space vacated the Left could attempt to 'fill the vacuum', militants would argue. By and large this was a doomsday analysis rejected by all the groups outside AFA who still saw anti-fascism as a distraction from the real struggle. Add to this a habitual reluctance on the part of others to take practical steps, even to defend initiatives of their own, and AFA in assuming overall responsibility had a busy schedule. For the new rank and file recruits it was a testing time. Involved as they were in violent and illegal confrontations with fascists on a habitual basis, a sense of camaraderie or *esprit de corps* developed quite naturally.

By contrast to the routine of branch meeting, paper sale, petition, familiar on the Left, the street activity pursued by AFA in this period often rested on a tightly disciplined outfit, where physical reliance on each other was paramount. Self-evidently, the consequences of people not turning up for activities when expected and a weakened outfit appearing on the streets were perfectly obvious to all. While not always literally a life or death situation, it was something that could not be totally discounted either, and thus proved a tough schooling for new members. Which meant that, while an increasingly hardened layer of activists developed, others would appear for a single activity never to be seen again.

Increasingly, too, AFA was aware it was conducting business to a background of neo-fascism growing in influence throughout Europe; something even by the mid-80s Red Action in particular was pointing to as a warning against complacency in Britain. In particular it took issue with an article in *Living Marxism*, an organ of the Revolutionary Communist Party, because of its explicit attack on anti-fascism. "The disturbing thing today is that no matter how obscure the fascists become many on the Left will waste time and energy chasing them ... [We] ought to let the miniscule Right rot and get on with the job of opposing the government which has rendered it impotent for a decade" (*Living Marxism*, No 7). Red Action countered with an argument that would be used repeatedly afterwards. "If groups like the NF or Blood & Honour are not confronted, how can they be beaten? If you cannot beat them when they are weak, how can you hope to defeat them when they are strong?" And "if the Left is not strong enough or determined enough to defeat them, how is it even possible to even talk of confronting the State?" (*Red Action*, issue 52).

Prior to AFA bursting on the scene the preferred anti-fascist strategy meant that, when confronted with an electoral challenge from the Far Right, a vigorous campaign in defence of the usual Labour incumbent was mounted. Sadly, those championed as 'anti-fascist' were often the very people who were responsible for working class alienation from the Left to begin with. Years of incompetence, indifference and pursuit of anti-working class policies had begun to fatally erode working class faith not only in Labour but also in socialism itself. By way of response, from the early 1990s AFA increasingly began to stress the importance of creating an independent working class alternative to both the BNP and, crucially, Labour. Although it would be some years before it would be fully articulated, its eventual materialisation was entirely consistent with the need to 'orientate to the working class' and does perhaps help summarise the often unspoken tensions and contradictions that existed in the 1985–89 period.

Too often it is assumed that the decisive difference between the liberal and militant factions revolved around the use of physical force. But for the militants the central issue revolved around what, and possibly who, AFA was fighting 'for'. Post-1989, the politics were presented more and more in terms of militant anti-fascism being a holding operation in expectation of a more favourable political moment, and with it a general working class renaissance.

2.16

INTERNAL AFFAIRS REVISITED – SEARCHLIGHT BREAKS RANKS

Within weeks of the re-launch in September, the nature of the mobilisation around Remembrance Day that November would serve to highlight the size of the strategical breach that now existed within the wider anti-fascist movement. Searchlight in particular was adamant the march to the Cenotaph should take place as planned. For some time Red Action had not been convinced a protest march was making the best use of resources, or that anti-fascism generally was getting the type of return commensurate with the level of investment demanded. In *Anti-Fascism in Britain*, Nigel Copsey records that the "internal disagreements became especially heated with unity within AFA collapsing," In point of fact, by this time London AFA was now totally unified on the issue, any public falling out having already occurred two months earlier with the re-launch in September.

"The militant wing insisted that the AFA Cenotaph march should not be repeated because marches in 1987 and 1988 had seen numbers of participants fall, had generated no useful publicity and had failed to stop fascists from marching. The only positive aspect to these marches, AFA's militants argued, was the mobilisation of AFA 'defence squads' which after the march would defend the anti-apartheid picket outside the South African embassy in Trafalgar Square from attack by fascists." Again Copsey rather presents the militant position in caricature. In fact what militants were actually arguing was that the activity should be judged primarily in regard to what actual effect it had on the NF mobilisation, and warned of a diminishing political return if it continued to descend into an annual parade.

With militants making it plain they favoured a return to a more direct approach, traditionalists led by Gerry Gable and Euro MEP Glyn Ford, along with the NUS, Union of Jewish Students, and Islington ARAFA, marched to the Cenotaph as usual. Afterwards Searchlight, more than a little optimistically, described the marchers as "delegates, representing millions of workers and students." In Copsey's estimate it had actually attracted between 150 and 300. Not happy with merely championing their own march, Searchlight also sought to undermine AFA generally by claiming with breathtaking revisionism that the "only regrettable feature" of AFA-led demonstrations in the previous years "has been the narrow and often sectarian nature of the event. This year Searchlight, in joining together with Islington ARAFA, has broken that mould".

Well if the mould had indeed been broken, the result could not be said to be entirely positive, so a considerable rewriting of recent history was required. In its original description of the 1987 march in which it had taken part, Searchlight had written: "Last year AFA decided it should mount its own parade and lay its own wreaths to remember those who fell fighting fascism and the victims of fascism and racism since World War Two. Over 2,000 people assembled for the march ... [O]ur march had been well disciplined and orderly and, despite an early attempt by the fascists to attack us, had shown restraint and dignity because of the nature of the occasion."

'Discipline, restraint, and dignity' was to be re-interpreted as 'sectarian' two years later. "Twisted logic," was the opinion of Rajiv M., representing LAARF who, in a letter to *Searchlight*, reminded them that it was their failure to "honour a previous agreement with AFA that the two demonstrations... would pass off with the full and comradely cooperation of the organisers of both events. Searchlight's refusal to cover the AFA event has unfortunately led to unnecessary and unproductive ill-feeling" (Letter to *Searchlight*, 16th November 1989). Indeed, so incensed were LAARF that both it and the Refugee Forum withdrew their sponsorship of the Searchlight initiative.

Of course, it was the knowledge that the NF would be fully engaged by the militants at Victoria that gave the political pretenders for the leadership of anti-fascism the confidence to march at all. In the following year, when they were unable to second-guess AFA intentions, Searchlight itself abandoned the Cenotaph counter-demo as too risky, and called instead on anti-fascists to travel to York to support a protest organised by the University of York Students Union, at the same time as AFA was planning to march through the fascist heartland of Bethnal Green.

That bright, crisp Remembrance Sunday morning in 1989 saw a fighting force that grew to in the region of 500 arrive in Victoria and take over the fascists' assembly point by 11am. When pubs in the vicinity opened they were effectively commandeered, thereby allowing AFA to control the surrounding streets from then onwards. In all the years the NF had been marching at Remembrance Day, there never had been an attempt to actually physically stop them forming up. In provocatively occupying Shakes pub, normally a rendezvous point for the Chelsea Headhunters, the presence in the area of a large number of AFA stewards led to a series of brief encounters with the assembling and understandably unnerved NF, delaying the start of their march for several hours.

Copsey admits the AFA tactic "so clearly rattled the fascist contingent there was no subsequent attack on the anti-apartheid picket." More than that, it proved to be a body blow to NF morale from which it never recovered. The figures tell the story of decline. Only three years previously in 1986, the NF assembled an impressive

2,000 marchers. But by 1990 the turnout had withered to nearer 200. With numbers like that, it was only possible to march with conspicuous police protection and everyone knew it: all the customary swagger was gone. Sometime later, Richard Edmonds justified the decision of the much smaller BNP not to take part in the annual right-wing get-together in Victoria with a pointed reference to the "area being full of Reds." By 1991, having dispensed with the NF as an unworthy opponent, AFA chose to mark Remembrance Day by marching through Bethnal Green in opposition to the emergence of support for the BNP in British fascism's historic heartland. Once again militants had stepped up to the plate and this time the entire Left, including the SWP, would be obliged to follow them.

If anything characterises militant thinking around this period, it is the marked absence of a blueprint. And, while this made AFA tactically flexible and unpredictable, it also meant every single mobilisation had a very specific, if not always strategic, purpose. By no means were all events physical in character, but militants were always working towards a precise goal. To the irritation of orthodox anti-racism, AFA never expected the state intervention to be benign. Moreover, in accepting that political responsibility for 'remedying the situation' had been left to them, there came with it an impatience with others who failed to appreciate the full gravity of the situation the Left in general had created for itself. Thus by 1990, with the focus switched to Bethnal Green, AFA was determined to make progress at street level, regardless of how this was perceived by the media or anyone else. And, while the liberal agenda called for protests against fascist violence, for more police involvement, and for the state to deal with the problem of an aggressive Far Right, the militants were intent on developing a strategy that would stop the fascists being able to operate openly within the white working class *per se*. What's more, rather than orientating to the victims of fascism, the militant strategy was increasingly directed at fascism's potential recruits.

SECTION 3

1990 ONWARDS

Previous page: The Met's finest prepare to confront anti-fascists at the entrance to the underpass on Theobald's Road, London, 1996.

3.1

1990, 'RIGHTS FOR WHITES' AND THE BNP COME TO THE FORE

In the Spring of 1990, within months of the AFA re-launch, the BNP initiated their Rights For Whites campaign in London's East End. When in January 1990 a gang of young Asians stabbed a 15-year-old schoolboy called John Stoner in a racist attack, they saw their opportunity. As far as the AFA leadership was concerned, the timing was also fortuitous. For one thing, the turnout by NF supporters for their Remembrance Day showpiece did genuinely reflect the low state of morale in the organisation as a whole nationally. And while B&H would re-surface at a later date, it was at this time still licking its wounds after the 27th May debacle in Hyde Park. All this meant AFA could turn full beam on the BNP in the East End, without the distraction of having to contain different organisations on other fronts.

In February the BNP, although keeping a relatively low profile at the request of organisers, took part in a 300-strong protest march against the attack on John Stoner. Amid considerable press and media coverage, the fascists, as might be expected, received a favourable response to their propaganda among the local white population. Then some young Asians stabbed another white man on the day of the march. Terry Swinney was actually returning from the Stoner march when his car was bricked. According to a report in the *Hackney Gazette*, Swinney had been surrounded by a group of about 20 Asians. "He was punched and kicked, beaten with iron bars, a tree branch and a baseball bat, and repeatedly stabbed" (*Hackney Gazette*, 30th November 1990). With one youth charged with attempted murder (by coincidence he was the brother of Mac who would later become the primary Asian contact for AFA in the East End) feelings were running high when the BNP organised a march under their own name on 11th March. In effect, this was the official launch of the BNP's 'Rights for Whites' campaign.

British Nationalist, April 1990, reported: "In response to requests from many East Enders, the British National Party decided to help launch the 'Rights for Whites' campaign, the purpose of which was to give the white community a real voice – after all the other supposed 'community' leaders had blatantly sided with the Asians. In order to channel the anger of the white community in a constructive direction, it was decided that a second march should take place. This march, however, would have a much more overt political flavour than the previous one, with the BNP not, as before, adopting a low profile..."

Press statements were released and thousands of special leaflets were delivered throughout the East End, with others going out in Bermondsey and Chingford, as well as at West Ham and Chelsea football grounds. "Our teams of leafletters were received like a liberation army in the beleaguered council estates of Bethnal Green, Stepney and Mile End. Gradually the media began to realise that the BNP was, without apology, heavily involved in the 'Rights for Whites' campaign..."

"The *East London Advertiser* had greeted the news of possible BNP involvement in the first march with the glaring headline 'Fascists bid to hi-jack march'. This time the paper, while still disapproving, was a little more polite towards us, and its pre-march coverage recognised the BNP as the legitimate champion of the white community. Sunday, 11th March came. Hundreds of East Enders turned out, including members of the families of the victims of recent Asian attacks, along with about 120 (mostly local) BNP members. Together we formed up and marched some 400-strong through the heart of Bethnal Green, with flags waving and banners aloft. As the column marched through the streets, passers-by cheered and clapped. A small crowd of reds congregated at Bethnal Green Town Hall, fresh from

Weavers Field, 1990 – a moment's calm before kick-off.

their rioting in Hackney and still clinging to their anti-poll tax placards, but they kept well out of our way!"

Soon the campaign was extended to other parts of the country, with specific focus on the conditions experienced by a white working class largely abandoned or sidelined by the mainstream parties. The BNP were now working in local areas, dealing with local issues, and by August 1990 they had won 25% of the white vote in a local by-election in the East End. What this revealed was not only the depth of BNP ambition but also their ability to quickly change strategy and tactics, something alien and incomprehensible to a thoroughly orthodox Left. Copsey remarks that AFA must have found the result "depressing" when in reality, faced with a Left stubbornly blind-sided to the BNP potential, it was actually AFA who first drew attention to the racial demographics in the ward. It was very much in the militants' interest to draw attention to the electoral ground the BNP was capable of making if allowed. By underscoring that one out of every two households in the ward was Asian, AFA effectively doubled the BNP percentage from the otherwise fairly unremarkable 12.5% officially recorded.

Alongside the electoral strategy, the fascists continued with the 'march and grow' line of attack, with confrontational rallies, marches, and meetings prominent, all self-consciously calculated to depict the BNP as a 'party of power'. Paradoxically, it was this very strategy that enabled AFA to wreak havoc among their activists on the ground. Before long the BNP hierarchy was admitting in private that the negative impact of the militants' interventions extended well beyond the physical damage caused to individual BNP activists. For when it came down to it, to remain credible in the eyes of their working class supporters, humiliation at street level had to be avoided at all costs. And for a relatively small organisation, attempting to provide such a guarantee inevitably put tremendous pressure on the BNP logistically. What's more, the scrupulous attention to security necessary did also run counter to BNP propaganda of every recruit being morally staunch and physically robust. Aware of the contradictions and the subsequent vulnerabilities, AFA would seek out the BNP whenever circumstances permitted. The first significant opportunity to test the premise came with the BNP announcement that it intended to contest a by-election in Bethnal Green in April 1990.

As part of the overall campaign, the BNP also gave warning it intended holding an election meeting at Weavers Field School in the heart of Bethnal Green. London AFA duly mobilised in order to make an intervention and early efforts were made to try and coordinate activity with other groups on the Left who intended to protest. To this end, the east London branch organised a semi-public meeting with the intention of explaining the likely AFA tactics on the day, but neither the SWP nor the Revolutionary Communist Party, who had been specifically invited, turned up. Unperturbed, the decision to physically confront the BNP on the day, 'to get into them' was agreed nonetheless. Some members of Workers Power later admitted their shock when what they had assumed was mere 'rhetoric' was interpreted so literally. The events around the Weavers Field School were an eye opener for others, too. It was a very public debut for the new AFA and, because of this, helped shape the nature of the campaign against the BNP up and down the country for the next four years.

3.2

WEAVERS FIELD, 1990

On 21st April 1990 at about 3pm, some sixty AFA stewards assembled at an intersection near the school, and were on hand as the second forty-strong BNP contingent, led by leading BNP-er Tony Lecomber, approached. For many militants it was their first serious look at the BNP close up. The street was narrow and, because the police presence was small, a decision on how to respond had to be made in an instant. Happily for the AFA chief steward, the police took the matter out of his hands.

Joe: "We had just arrived on the scene. To our left about 50 yards away, were an additional thirty BNP with banners and placards. Nearby, separated by a five-foot railing, were about 100 SWP/Labour types. The appearance of Lecomber's crew obviously posed a dilemma. For one thing, we knew this was a fraction of what was available, on the other hand it was a narrow street and they were walking right into us."

The apparent indifference of police to the potential for serious disorder was explained when the officer in charge approached what he obviously assumed were BNP fellow travellers and ordered them to join the BNP contingent! From an operational perspective he had seemingly decided he wanted what looked like all the 'bad eggs' in the same basket.

Joe: "By now the BNP were only yards away, and some of the lads, eager to take advantage of police confusion, had begun stepping into the road ready to get into the opposition. But I could also see the tactical advantage in obeying the law, at least for the time being, so on instruction AFA joined the back of the BNP contingent."

To any onlookers it must have appeared the BNP ranks had swelled from about forty to over a hundred. Not unnaturally the thirty-plus BNP supporters who had defied the anti-racists by gathering at the school gates earlier were overjoyed at the tables being turned and vented their rage on the SWP. In the verbal exchanges between the marchers and the anti-racist protestors it was noticeable that the AFA squad, having been mistakenly targeted for abuse, were happy to give back as good as they got.

Not all, however, were as convinced as the liberal Left of the *bone fides* of the new arrivals. One female rockabilly, with attendant blonde bouffant, sensing something was awry, asked her boyfriend: "What is it? Are they National Front, then?" "Just shut it and keep walking," came the terse reply from out of the corner of his mouth. Someone else who surely must have guessed the identity of his latest 'recruits' kept strangely silent. Even when the BNP and 'guests' reached the school gates, which were still locked, forcing everyone to stop and mingle, Tony Lecomber was still searching for the right words to explain the situation to his followers. For the anti-fascists it was a surreal moment, as well.

Joe: "I found myself positioned behind this big bloke in a council donkey jacket and wearing Ray Ban sunglasses who was pumping Lecomber's hand as if he had lifted the siege of Mafeking! Wearing a cut-throat smile, Denis, who had only recently moved to London from Manchester, sidled up: 'Well, are we going to do it, then?' I just nodded. A right hook from Den caught 'Ray Bans' behind the ear and he took a couple of more shots of similar quality before nose-diving into the floor."

Instinctively, the anti-fascist fighters had mostly stationed themselves on the periphery of the crowd, which added to the fascists' utter confusion as they appeared to be under attack from all sides. Lecomber was one of the first to go down, having been crowned by a heavy Grolsch bottle purchased especially for the occasion. In the midst of the hand-to-hand fighting, one burly character with cropped hair and wearing a three-quarter length mac approached a smallish group of BNP supporters who, up till then, had been largely involved in shouting encouragement from the sidelines. Despite everything they had witnessed, they nonetheless assumed he was 'one of us'. It took a powerful headbutt that knocked one instantly to the ground, with the other two collapsing under him, to disabuse them. Fighting would pause as if people had come to their senses and then start up again. Initially the only people more bewildered than the BNP were the police. Gradually, however, by concentrating on the aggressors, they began to noticeably thin AFA ranks. Simply to avoid arrest some were forced to flee the scene. One, an amateur rugby player, executed a hand-off in the face to a diving sergeant that was so technically exquisite it would have had his coach purring had it been employed in more conventional circumstances.

Andy: "When it kicked-off I was standing next to Lecomber. I immediately pulled out a large beer bottle and hit him over the head three, maybe four times before it broke. I'd chosen a Grolsch bottle because the glass was particularly thick and heavy and, by the time it smashed, Lecomber was not only bleeding from the head, but almost unconscious as well. Out of the corner of my eye I spotted a copper coming for me and I just managed to hand him off as I got up speed. I was then confronted by a large police sergeant who was trying to block my way. Instinctively I gave him a full 'straight-arm' and he flew backwards through the air. All that went through my mind was: 'Fuck, if I get nicked now, not only will it be affray and assault on a copper, but that sergeant is bound to arrange a right good kicking for me.'

"I legged it as fast as I could with a couple of constables in hot pursuit but luckily managed to outrun them. As soon as they gave up the chase, I stopped running and began walking as we'd all been taught to do, which was just as well because, straight after, a squad car appeared round the corner and, if I'd been less professional, I would have been nicked for certain. I decided to employ another principle from the textbook and get myself off the street. I ducked into this pub, which was your typical East End local boozer. They were still common back then, as the gentrification of the area hadn't started to kick-in yet. I went up to the bar and ordered a pint. I got a few sideways glances from the punters and the girl serving me looked a little bit out of sorts, but I just put it down to me not being a regular; you know how cliquey those places could be. Just then I spotted one of the DAM members lurking in the corner who I guessed must have had to do a runner as well. I acknowledged him, but he began frantically pointing to his forehead and indicating with his thumb that I should retire to the gents. When I looked in the mirror I could see the reason for his anxiety. My face was studded with tiny fragments of green glass and gently oozing claret. After tidying up, I safely made my way to a nearby British Rail station and out of the area.

"Later that year, however, I was arrested at nearby Brick Lane and charged with 'Affray and Violent Disorder'. I'd been wearing the same jacket that day and the coppers made a clear beeline for me. It made me wonder if that sergeant I had felled

Tony Lecomber taking second prize at Weavers Field, London, 1990.

was getting his own back. Who knows? Either way the result was I landed up in the dock alongside my old friend Mr Lecomber!"

Order was only finally restored when police hastily ushered the 70 or more BNP inside the school, leaving a depleted AFA, temporarily victorious, on the other side of the gate. By this time between 150 and 200 Left activists had assembled in the park and positioned themselves behind a 5ft metal railing separating them from both AFA and the BNP. Numerically weakened, with some of the most able arrested or literally 'on the run', the remaining militants, numbering by now around forty, were confronted by a second BNP outfit of similar size to the first. As they came around the corner hurling threats they made as if to charge. AFA stood firm and, in contrast to the snarling BNP, remained totally silent.

Terry: "Maybe this unnerved them because, when still about thirty yards away, they allowed themselves to be corralled by a lone policeman. Personally, I was delighted as they were all individually a large and ugly bunch – many later signed up for C18 – and it was sure to have been a bloody encounter."

Noticeably, even with the political identities no longer in doubt, with the notable exception of comedian Lee Hurst who scaled the fence, none of the hundreds of anti-racists present made any attempt to assist their fellow anti-fascists. The implications would not be lost on the AFA leadership.

Terry: "From that moment on, we knew that when it came down to it we were entirely on our own. This meant that for possibly the first time we were aware that whatever happened the political responsibility to shape events rested entirely on our shoulders. Not only did others not want to help us win, it later became perfectly obvious for a variety of self-serving reasons they would prefer to see us lose."

Even though the incident received widespread coverage on the ITN evening news, there were no arrests resulting from the footage and, to the delight of those already charged, the case was treated 'apolitically' by the magistrates with everyone getting off with a summary £50 fine. Being treated apolitically would not be the case for the militants for very much longer. With over 500 police at his disposal, Chief Superintendent Grieve was quoted in the Hackney Gazette as calling the operation "a triumph for democracy" (*Hackney Gazette*, 27.4.90) but the BNP were understandably less enthused. Not for the last time policing arrangements on the day were blamed for the physical damage caused by AFA's intervention.

"In negotiations with the police in the run-up to the East End rally on April 21st, BNP officials secured a firm commitment concerning the pre-rally assembly. This was that party supporters would be permitted to rendezvous by Bethnal Green Underground and then proceed in one single body to the rally location. This was for the purposes of security. Left-wing opposition was expected, and it was known that this would be violent if the leftists were given any opportunity to pick on BNP people in ones and twos or in small groups; on the other hand, if all BNP personnel stuck together in one solid phalanx, the leftists would not dare to attack them.

"However, when the final day came and it was time for BNP personnel to proceed from their rendezvous to the hall, the police officer in charge insisted that they do so in small groups some distance apart. This was a decision of the most monumental stupidity (or worse). In that event the Left would be presented with easy targets for attack – unless of course there was sufficient of a police presence all along the route to ensure that these small BNP groups would be protected. The latter proved not to be the case. Police numbers along the route were woefully inadequate, and at some points non-existent. The Left did exactly as anticipated: they made several attacks in sectors where they were able to pick on the BNP in tiny numbers. A number of BNP supporters suffered injuries, one of them an elderly pensioner. Another received a hairline fracture of the skull and had to be taken to hospital. And this was not all. In some cases where BNP men defended themselves vigorously against the left, despite being outnumbered, *they* [the BNP] were arrested for 'breaches of the peace'.

"After the rally had ended, the police, seeming to have recognised their folly of earlier in the day, allowed the BNP contingent to proceed as one solid mass from the hall to a place outside the area. This body looked formidable indeed, consisting of 100-200 people, many of them hefty young men well able to deal with trouble. The reds wouldn't have stood a hope if they had tried to rush this body. They contented themselves with hurling abuse from behind an iron fence and with plenty of police (who had been strangely absent earlier) to protect them" (*British Nationalist*, May/June 1990).

The inference that militant victory could only be secured when the BNP were hopelessly out-manned was a recurring theme that was worn like a comfort blanket for the duration of the campaign. In public at least, all inadequacies could be explained away by citing either police or anti-fascist treachery. The strategic importance of such self-deceptive propaganda was illustrated by another incident not long after, when a thirty-strong AFA group had clashed with the BNP outside a pub in the area. A local teacher later informed AFA that it had caused a buzz in the school for the rest of the week. *Red Action* used the incident to draw attention not just to the value of physical force generally on BNP supporters, but also to the negative impact it had on their support base.

"The correctness of this strategy was endorsed by a local teacher, who expressed his support for the tactic of confrontation, purely for the propaganda fall-out that resulted from a similar clash between the BNP and AFA three weeks earlier. On that occasion a group of about 30 fascists were challenged by AFA outside one of their pubs. The majority ran. The ones that stood their ground [including Tony Lecomber] got whacked. The effect on the young onlookers, some his own pupils, was electric. They talked, he said, of little else all week. The so-called 'hard men' had been run, effortlessly. They couldn't believe it. They had evidently never seen that happen before. In the battle for hearts and minds the first point was scored in the propaganda war" (*Red Action*, issue 56).

As well as defining its relationship with the BNP, events on this day also defined AFA's relationship to the Far Left. A number of groups, including the SWP and the RCP, had been approached in a fraternal manner prior to the event and again on the day itself. So, as far as AFA was concerned, every attempt had been made by them to maximise the effect of the anti-fascists' activity. And, although the day proved a success, it begged the question as to how much more could have been achieved had the Left forces combined their efforts? AFA concluded that with a modicum of co-ordination it would have been possible to stop the BNP meeting altogether. As always the militant outlook was essentially practical. This was in contrast to a Left who, when it came down to it, looked to its own immediate interests first, and would remain committed in the decade that followed to the tactic of bustling activity largely devoid of end product or wider strategic consideration. When, eventually, it was embarrassed into responding to the BNP challenge, those that could, the numerically bigger organisations like Militant, the SWP and to a

An AFA supporter arrested at Weavers Field in 1990.

lesser extent the Communist Party, each put their weight behind rival organisations who had one thing in common: a mutual loathing of the platform the militants espoused.

As damaging as such antics would be to the image of an already discredited Left, of greater concern to militants at the time was the emerging evidence which suggested that BNP progress among white working class communities was often assisted, albeit unintentionally, by the activities of local authorities. Tower Hamlets Council, in particular, seemed to have developed a knack for this. Time and again, the BNP were able to highlight ill thought-out policies or decisions that seemingly disenfranchised the white working class, while at the same time appeared to favour immigrant communities. Regardless of whether the local authority was guilty or not, perception in politics is everything, and the BNP were not slow to milk the opportunity.

Reporting on a by-election in Park ward, Bow, in July, *British Nationalist* (August/September 1990) commented: “Early on in the campaign we heard through the grapevine that the council was planning to cut off funding to an all-white nursery, while still giving money away to various Bangladeshi, Somali and Chinese youth groups. We knew that the white mothers were up in arms about this and were planning to picket the next meeting of the Education Department, which was responsible for the allocation of such funds. At short notice, we produced a special leaflet and also turned up at the Town Hall with a twenty-strong team carrying placards and flags.

“The mothers welcomed us and began chanting our ‘Rights for Whites’ slogan. Soon after, however, the nursery teachers arrived. They were obvious leftists, and they browbeat the mothers into moving away from our demonstration. Once everyone was inside the Town Hall, the mothers allowed a Liberal councillor to insult them by telling them to remove their children from the public gallery. When the council members announced the allocation of funds to various Bangladeshi groups, the meeting was interrupted by a chorus of disapproval from the BNP contingent and the council chamber was flooded with our leaflets. As we left the Town Hall, many of the mothers were waiting outside with their children. Out of the clutches of the leftist teachers, they gave us the thumbs up sign!”

Much of the material carried in the *British Nationalist* at this time was in the same vein: detailed reports of the fascists’ intervention at a local level and particularly in the East End of London. Articles also considered the local political terrain, including demographics, and the conditions experienced by the white working class constituency in which the BNP were busily making inroads. “Park ward has probably the smallest immigrant population of any ward in Tower Hamlets: around 10 percent. Therefore, amazingly as it might seem, many people did not feel threatened. The ward also has a good social infrastructure. Although it consists overwhelmingly of council estates, nearly every property has double-glazing and central heating. Most flats have security entry phones and new lifts. The area is adorned with gentrified lamp posts and litterbins, and it borders the pleasant tree-lined open spaces of Victoria Park. Some of the tower blocks have concierges: 24-hour porters, always black, who are supposed to look after the blocks. There is a high proportion of old people's homes in the ward, and the Labour Party has the votes in such places virtually sewn up."

Yet, despite a widespread belief among the Left that Labour had the whole area 'sewn up', this was exactly the type of political intelligence, followed by well planned activity, that eventually enabled the BNP to attract support amongst sections of the white working class community in Tower Hamlets. Compared to the Left, the relative sophistication, aligned to the clumsiness of the local authority, culminated in the shock breakthrough for the Far Right with the election of Derek Beackon in October 1993.

3.3

THE ENFIELD 'STING', 1990

If the BNP had cause to regard the militants with growing anxiety, behind the scenes the authorities had also begun to display signs of concern. As the driving force behind London AFA, Red Action was, as they say, already 'known to the police'. During negotiations for the first Remembrance Day march in 1986, when the AFA negotiators made it clear that they wanted to march and lay a wreath at the Cenotaph, the police commander was candid about his concerns: "What if, when we let you get there [the Cenotaph] you decide you want to stay there? What do we do then?"

The commander accepted sincere reassurances from the genuinely law-abiding elements on the AFA negotiating team that they would never conceive of doing anything so underhand, but then asked, "Can any of you speak for Red Action? It is, as I understand it, their sworn duty to try and rip the heads off their opponents whenever they see them?" No doubt what was in the mind of police strategists was a possible repeat of the riot at Red Lion Square in June 1974 when, unwisely, police had allowed a National Front and an anti-Vietnam war demonstration to converge, with fatal results for demonstrator Kevin Gately who was killed in the ideological collision. So, as far as police were concerned, both AFA and the NF assembling at the Cenotaph was out of the question. Moreover, to avoid any possible clash with the NF approaching from Victoria, AFA was forced to rally on the other side of the river as well. Any wreath laying could be carried out by a lone AFA representative, police insisted. However, when police implied AFA might also have to march behind the Peace Pledge Union at about 4pm, even though the call was to assemble at noon, the Red Action fundamentalist reputation was fully exploited, this time to the benefit of the AFA side. Now it was the anti-fascists turn to play hardball.

"If you [police] insist on being unreasonable, there is the possibility demonstrators might be re-directed or lured by militant elements (a.k.a. 'Red Action') away from Trafalgar Square to where the NF would be assembling in Victoria. If this was to happen the responsibility would rest with you." This was not so implausible a vista that the police could afford to ignore it. Indeed, this is more or less exactly what would happen three years later, anyway. So after a brief recess, police negotiators returned without demur to the business of properly accommodating AFA within the schedule.

This fundamentalist character attributed exclusively to RA in 1986 would, within a year of the 1989 re-launch, be extended to include London AFA as a whole. And, even while fully aware and accepting of the creeping surveillance that came with it, leading 'players' were nonetheless taken aback by the elaborate nature of the plot mounted against them prior to a planned NF march in Enfield, north London on 18th August 1990.

In the run up AFA, already conscious of NF plans but not too concerned, were contacted through an intermediary and invited to a planning meeting called by the local Labour Party. At the meeting the AFA representatives listened politely to what was being said. Throughout, the emphasis on there being 'no violence on the day' preceded or ended every single contribution by both Labour Party and SWP members. Wholly in line with this pacifist approach the SWP publicly declared their intention to assemble, not at the train station the NF were expected to exit from, but at another one, two miles down the line. At this, an AFA member pointed out that such a plan would concede the initiative entirely to the NF: "Tactically is it not far better, surely, to assemble the counter-demo an hour or more prior to the march at the station the NF are to exit from, if the intention is to disrupt the march?" There were no takers. As the atmosphere at the meeting was anything but cordial, the AFA representatives left, quite mystified as to why they had been invited in the first place. Notwithstanding the reception, militants decided to mobilise anyway, with The Silver Bullet pub, outside Finsbury Park station in north London, selected as the AFA re-direction point.

The pub being firmly within what AFA regarded as its domain (a mere 30-minute train ride from Enfield) and, given the short time limit between the decision to organise and the day itself, there was thought to be little risk of plans being leaked which might result in chance encounters with the opposition. But, despite this, the usual precautions were taken. As the militants began to assemble, reports began to trickle in from scouts of a certain amount of suspect characters being spotted in the vicinity. Within minutes it was evident to the organisers that something untoward was going on, but what? Before long the instinct of the AFA scouts was thoroughly vindicated.

Joe: "I was outside the pub making some final arrangements when someone brushed passed me. I thought he looked familiar but couldn't place him. As he came back out it suddenly dawned on me he had been at the meeting in Enfield. I first called out to him but he ignored me so I signalled to stewards to stop him. He was grabbed immediately. Someone else who appeared to be with him just kept walking as if nothing had happened. Obviously something was badly amiss. The other one now being held by the scruff of the neck and visibly nervous first tried to deny ever being at the Enfield meeting and generally tried to bluff his way out. Realising in mid-bluff, so to speak, he was digging himself deeper, he made a sudden a break for it, with such desperation he stepped clean out of his jacket one of the lads had been holding him up by. At that very moment the train pulled in, so we had a decision to make: either give chase, catch the train, or abort the operation. A little troubled, we got on the train."

On arrival in Enfield, AFA stayed well within the station confines waiting to see if others would show their hand. They did not have long to wait. Apart from the anti-fascists, the station was totally deserted when a blonde woman in her mid-thirties walked through the crowd as if to get to the platform.

Joe: "I watched her go and next thing I saw her re-emerge and walk towards the exit. She looked anxious and edgy. I did not discount the possibility she might just have been intimidated by the appearance of our lot hanging around. But I put a tail on her just in case. It was no great surprise when the report came back that she had disappeared into a nearby timber yard to be greeted there by a man, probably police, clearly waiting for her to return."

Shortly after, the first police vans arrived outside the station. AFA now knew the identity of the 'operatives' at The Silver Bullet. (This was confirmed later when a van that had taken on passengers at The Silver Bullet was stopped and searched on the motorway.) With the cover blown it was decided to abandon the station and head for the town. Eyebrows were further raised when along the way a contingent of BNP (including leading BNP activist Robert Jarvis) were spotted lurking in a pub doorway. Odder still, when AFA got to the town centre, it was noticed that the SWP counter-demo, in addition to mobilising more than a mile away, had also selected a cul-de-sac for their assembly point. For the militants this meant any advantage of mingling within a larger gathering to avoid drawing undue attention was out of the question. For, once in there, there was no way out. Looking, then, to set up a base of operations and get off the street at least temporarily, the anti-fascists moved to a pub, but were hardly inside the door before being informed the "pub was open to locals only." The same scenario was acted out in other pubs in the area. Evidently, a degree of forward planning had been mounted to keep AFA on the streets and visible. But to what end, activists wondered?

And, if The Silver Bullet had been 'busy', the area the militants now found themselves in was alive with intrigue. A camera mounted on a tripod was spotted through a second floor window of an auctioneer's office, while a middle-aged couple most people wouldn't normally take a second look at, him complete with sporting blazer and badge crest, were seen communicating by radio. Worse still, more obvious players in small groups, whether police or fascist sympathisers – and anti-fascists couldn't tell which – seemed to be everywhere. The more obvious had been confronted and even photographed by AFA intelligence officers. Their resulting nervousness made the militants all the more uneasy. Television crews were also in evidence. But what were they doing here when the NF march was assembling elsewhere, organisers wondered?

One cameraman blatantly filming AFA personnel was challenged. "Who are you working for mate?" "Metropolitan Police," he replied calmly. Then the chief steward was informed the crew from ITN had been overheard discussing the imminent possibility of 'trouble', at a time when AFA knew the NF had not even fully assembled, and were still more than a couple of miles away. All suddenly became clear when, under the noses of outwardly unconcerned police lounging in carriers, the small gang of BNP who had been spotted earlier suddenly reappeared and, led by Jarvis, brazenly marched down the middle of the road against the traffic and directly toward the much larger anti-fascist grouping. Immediately responding to the challenge some AFA stewards began to advance toward them.

Joe: "Suddenly the appearance of Jarvis and the BNP made sense. His role seemed to be to provide police with the pretext to wade in once battle was joined. Which meant everything would conveniently be captured on camera. To counter this I immediately ordered everyone to step back into the market square, right among the shoppers and stalls, which would provide us with some cover. At least if it kicked off in here it could not be recorded on video. And then, in the confusion, who could say with any accuracy what had happened? Sure enough, as soon as we pulled back, Jarvis, seeing our intent, halted."

Afterwards it emerged the NF had been directed by police to march in the opposite direction, and so to militants it was blindingly obvious the complex police undercover mobilisation in the town centre was nothing to do with 'law and order' and everything to do with entrapment. AFA were the target, the NF/BNP mere bait. How much collusion there had been between the organisers of the meeting to which AFA was invited and the police operation was also a concern. In addition to the initial incident, Jarvis was also overheard suggesting that "we can get into them now if you don't nick us" to a police officer, who laughed. The order was given for AFA to pull out. One activist described it later as "like stepping out from under a noose." Within minutes of the AFA withdrawal being confirmed, fascists attacked the remaining anti-racists including the SWP.

The Met had announced their arrival as the new kids on the block. From now on, as well as dealing with violent parties like the NF, BNP, and Blood & Honour, AFA had yet another adversary to deal with. The price for failing to deal adequately with the new arrivals became clear a month to the day of the failed sting in Enfield, as explained in the next chapter.

Returning to what was by now more familiar terrain, AFA again attacked the BNP during a by-election meeting in Weavers Field on Wednesday night, 22nd August. Though both the BNP and police were better prepared this time, AFA still made its presence felt, both before and after the meeting. The subsequent reports of disorder led Bow and Poplar MP, Mildred Gordon, to observe that BNP meetings could hardly be regarded as legitimate 'public' events, as "police have to escort them [BNP] to their private meetings" (*Dockland's Recorder*, 30th August 1990).

Local fascists were particularly appalled to discover militants loitering in the vicinity of Bethnal Green Road and casually drinking outside the nearest BNP pub, The Sun. Almost as put out were some local youngsters. "Wait until the BNP turn up," they threatened. "We're here," came the amused reply, "but where are they?"

3.4

THE AUTHORITIES SHOW THEIR HAND, 1990

Nicolas Vincenzio 'Nicky' Crane, a 6ft 2in heavily built and tattooed bonehead, began his career as a front-line fascist in the late 1970s as a member of the British Movement. He first came to prominence in 1978 when he led an attack by 200 skinheads on the Asian community around Brick Lane. In 1980 he was branded as "worse than an animal" by a judge at the Old Bailey when sentencing him to 12 months for an unprovoked attack with a bottle on a black family waiting at a bus stop. During the 1980s Crane served two further prison terms for politically motivated and violent offences. During one four-year sentence for organising an attack by up to one hundred skinheads on a largely black cinema queue in Woolwich, he lost any possibility of remission after he attacked and badly injured a number of prison officers with a metal tray. In between prison terms, he had served on the Leader Guard of the British Movement, was a key National Front activist, and later Ian Stuart's right-hand man as head of security for the B&H organisation. By appearance and reputation he was the epitome of right-wing idealism: fascist icon and poster boy.

So, not surprisingly, when he was spotted by some AFA members in the vicinity of the annual Bloody Sunday commemoration rally, an event routinely targeted by the Right, they automatically assumed he was up to no good. He was immediately confronted but, after a brief scuffle, managed to get away. That might have been that, but not long afterwards he was again spotted in the back of a black cab, and all importantly heading back into the area. It being a Saturday afternoon, aligned to the disruption caused by the marchers, traffic in Kilburn High Road, which was bad at the best of times, was near gridlock. Within seconds the cab was surrounded, and the driver was ordered to open the back doors. Despite putting up a fierce resistance, Crane was overwhelmed and dragged out. By the time police intervened he was already unconscious. Identified by a number of eyewitnesses, three AFA members were arrested at the scene. On Monday 18th September 1990, at Wood Green Crown Court, in spite of the admission of perjury by one police officer, they were jailed for a total of eleven years.

In her summing up, the judge, who incidentally was Jewish, put Crane's own record totally to one side, stating that, in her opinion, the actions of the defendants did most damage to the rule of law and as a consequence carried the greater potential threat to the status quo. "Though we might find the political attitudes of Mr Crane repellent, nevertheless it is your actions that will cause them to win, and then we have anarchy." The real gravity of the offence in the eyes of the judge, as she made clear, was not the physical damage inflicted on Crane, who had almost immediately discharged himself from hospital, but the political single-mindedness of the attackers, who attacked with such disregard for the law that the scenes, as damningly described by witnesses (which included an off duty soldier) carried the stamp of a latter-day lynching. Those jailed included a twenty-one year old Irish building worker with no previous convictions who got three years, while an unemployed twenty-two year old and a hospital porter aged twenty-four were both sentenced to serve four years each. As Red Action noted at the time, the anti-fascists collectively got five more years than the six-year sentence handed down in the same week to a pimp convicted of repeatedly beating a woman around the head with a hammer.

Tellingly, as with the convictions in Rochdale, the official AFA statement appealed not for clemency but for solidarity: "The prisoners made no apology for their actions then nor do they do so now. What they do need, and what we ask on their behalf, is for your support, political, moral, and financial. Financial support in cases of this kind is of course mandatory and something that at the end of the day we in AFA guarantee. All donations to help them or their family are gratefully received. What is perhaps even more important in the long run, with the fascists once again limbering up across Europe, is that they receive your political support, are seen to get it, and that you and your organisation are seen to be willing to give it."

An AFA Welfare Fund was immediately established to offer financial and moral support to the activists on the inside, with a 'welfare officer' appointed to fund-raise, coordinate visits and handle the prisoners' affairs on the outside, as required. A letter written from gaol by one of the AFA prisoners, Tony D., explained the importance of this work: "As a person currently serving a four-year prison sentence for anti-fascist activity, I would like to let people know the need and importance of an effective support group. People who suffer at the hands of the courts, whether in the form of a fine or imprisonment, must be supported with both moral and financial support. From personal experience, I can let people know how important this support is to those who find themselves imprisoned. Support comes in many forms, through the letters and cards sent in, through to the financial support which allows me prison luxuries such as radio, books, daily newspapers and toiletries. It may not sound like a lot to someone who has never served a prison sentence, but to a prisoner it makes life bearable. So I would like to thank those who have shown support for me in whatever form. I would also like to appeal to people to help the support group in whatever way they can. Not just for me, but for anybody who comes before the courts through anti-fascist activities." Immediately on his release, Tony got re-involved. He would later go on to become the organiser for the London area.

If it hadn't been obvious before, then it was certainly obvious now, that AFA could expect little sympathy from the Left. Although, within less than 18 months of the militants' conviction, the ANL would re-launch, and in the wake of that the entire Left would rally to the anti-fascist cause, it is remarkable that at the time not a single organisation, publicly or privately, offered political or financial support to the prisoners or their families. Indeed, when the matter was raised by an AFA sympathiser during a Troops Out Movement branch meeting in Kilburn, he was left stunned when what concerns were expressed focused on the recovery, and general well-being of Nicolas Crane!

There can be little doubt that the longest sentences handed down for anti-fascist activity were intended to serve as both warning and deterrent. The judge's rather extraordinary summing up did little to disguise the political element in the sentencing. This tacit declaration of hostilities, coupled with the experience in Enfield, was not likely to be something the militant leadership would, or could afford to, ignore. In truth, if sentences of this magnitude were now to be considered the norm, then far greater care would have to be taken a) to avoid arrest, b) to ensure each activist had drummed into them the importance of not co-operating in any fashion once arrested, and c) the management of the defence cases would need to be politically supervised, prior to them being placed in the hands of professional advocates.

This meant that following almost every arrest thereafter, a senior AFA member would be designated to supervise, politically, the running of the campaign for acquittal, unbeknown to legal teams, solicitors and barristers with whom the defendants were supposedly working in tandem. Among other things, this involved the establishment of the correct 'facts', the procuring of witnesses to support the appropriate order of events plus the coaching of said witnesses, sometimes prior to any statements being made to a defence solicitor. Even on a minor charge, in order to avoid a valued activist clocking up a series of convictions that might eventually lead to jail or impede the granting of bail, some form or other of the process would be implemented.

As it happens, the prototype for such a level of interference in judicial matters had been established two years earlier when a Blaggers gig in Telford in the West Midlands was infiltrated by a large number of Blood & Honour boneheads. Their leader, it was reported, was seen brandishing a knife. Already heavily outnumbered, the stewards decided to initiate the action while they still had the chance. As the leading skinhead re-entered the gig, a senior steward snatched the blade from his back pocket. In the mêlée that followed, the owner of the knife was stabbed a number of times in the face with his own weapon. His companion was also hurt.

Police descended on the gig and a large numbers of arrests followed. A staggering forty witness statements were collected. It also quickly became clear that, together with those supplied by members of the public and B&H supporters, a number of compromising statements by peripheral AFA supporters had been accumulated by the police, with one militant in particular being fingered for the stabbing.

Acutely alert to the consequences, the London AFA leadership promptly offered an amnesty to anyone who may have co-operated in any fashion with police to allow AFA officers access to identical evidence that they had provided to police. More than anything, what they wanted was to gauge how the case against the accused looked from a prosecution standpoint. To general astonishment, the most damaging statement by far was by the steward's own brother.

Joe: "From a prosecution viewpoint his statement would, we knew, be regarded as invaluable by the investigating officers in the Midlands, once they had a chance to assess the case. And they would also realise, if they could force him to make a statement, it was just as likely others could force him to retract it. So the chances were they would try and make the statement watertight or maybe even put him in some form of protective custody until the trial. So, on the Monday night, he was informed he would not be returning to his flat in north London, as alternative accommodation had been provided for him south of the river. Someone else would pick up his stuff, he was told. It proved to be a prescient manoeuvre. On Wednesday morning at 7am, at the request of their colleagues in the Midlands, the Met came calling, only to find the prosecution's principle witness had vanished. And, in spite of the huge number of other eyewitness accounts, so successfully thereafter did AFA muddy the waters, even when the suspect was actually arrested that October, the case against him and two others never made it to trial."

A subtle variation in the coaching of witnesses for the defence came in 1992, when AFA went further by supplying witnesses for the prosecution. In March 1992 the trial of the 'Brick Lane Four' collapsed on day one at Southwark Crown Court. Just a month later, one of the defendants, a prominent RA lieutenant, was charged with GBH with intent. The charges followed an incident in a pub in Hertfordshire rumoured to have been used by the BNP. 'A' was chatting with colleagues when he was subject to an unprovoked attack from behind by one of the bouncers working the door. The mêlée that followed cost the bouncer most of his teeth and a £5,000 bill for reconstructive dental surgery. Police were on the scene so quickly it was concluded they must have been on their way before the attack was launched. Immediate counter-measures were called for. Investigating detectives were delighted when a number of eyewitnesses stepped forward to offer an unusually articulate and lucid account of events. It was only when the CPS carefully studied the transcripts did problems emerge that proved impossible to ignore: the most persuasive and cohesive account thoroughly exonerated the two AFA members police had already charged. The case never made it to court and all charges were dropped in August 1992.

As such, the overall effectiveness of the AFA anti-criminalisation measures can be gauged by the high ratio of acquittals thereafter, more often than not as a result of the defence being better prepared than the prosecution. One AFA member in particular turned the tactic of perverting the course of justice almost into an art form. Well-built and handsome, of mixed race and a one-time (junior) member of the American Black Panther Party, he not only secured his own acquittals on numerous occasions but also lent his expertise to others. To those who knew him his appearance in the witness box, dressed maybe in a roll neck pullover under denim dungarees, looking for all the world, as one put it, "'like some presenter off of *Blue Peter*," could be cringe making. But like a good method actor, he adapted to each twist and turn in the trial entirely in character.

On one memorable occasion in Crown Court, this time on charges of allegedly bashing a bus inspector who had had the temerity to rip down an AFA poster, he became involved in a battle of wits with the prosecutor. The latter, knowing that a verdict was unlikely without his cracking the façade of open-eyed wonder, produced the lovingly handcrafted cosh: "Have you seen this before, Mr J?" "No, sir, I have not," came the reply. "Would you take it in your hand for a moment?" offering C. the weapon. Now the prosecutor would, no doubt, have been privy to his adversary being 'known to the police' and was striving to see this side of the defendant's character surface by creating the pretext for the jury to see the defendant armed with a cosh in hand. Instantly recognising the ploy but unable to refuse outright, C. took hold of the weapon as instructed, not by the handle as the prosecutor had anticipated, but by the base. It was akin to a building labourer picking up a shovel by the blade. "Genius, pure genius," someone chuckled in the public gallery. It resulted in yet another 'not guilty' to add to his already extensive curriculum vitae. When the law did catch up with him eventually in the late 1990s, the judge all but apologised to him for having to send him down, convinced as he was that he had 'been led astray' by others!

Perhaps, though, the ultimate illustration of militant ingenuity and ruthlessness in dealing with the authorities is the curious case of Dave Hann. Originally hailing from Bristol, and a one-time associate of the Bristol City football firm, he contacted Red Action soon after falling foul of the Chelsea Headhunters attack on the Remembrance Day march in 1987. A plasterer by profession, he was quickly christened 'Dave Cap', because of the perennial headgear, a vain attempt to conceal a thinning pate. Once he divested himself of the cap he was, with characteristic sensitivity, re-christened 'Baldy'. Generally he took the ribbing with good nature and slotted smoothly into the hard-drinking lifestyle of Red Action members in the north London area.

As a result of a romantic entanglement that began on the annual RA trip to Belfast, Hann moved up north. On one of his first outings he almost lost an eye in a gouging incident when, along with some other security stewards at a Manchester Martyrs social, he was sucked into an immense brawl involving an entire wedding party which was taking place downstairs at the same venue. This somewhat comical situation resulted from Matty, the combustible lead singer of The Blaggers, mistaking one event for the other. On his being refused entry he exchanged insults, then punches, with those working the door. Cue reinforcements from upstairs.

Along with Gerry M. and John H., Hann went on to form part of the triumvirate that ran RA in Manchester and was hugely influential within the AFA Northern Network.

A call one morning in early April 1995 set the alarm bells ringing for AFA intelligence. Dave Hann was on a charge of robbery and was expecting to go down. He had been arrested a year previously, but had concealed it from nearly everyone, and particularly from the *de facto* leadership in London. Only with time running out and implications of doing serious jail time to the forefront of his mind did he decide to come clean, confessing all to his Manchester co-organiser Gerry M. As Gerry told it: "You could see the fear in his eyes, he knew he was going to jail." Although D. had been operating in the South East from the early 1990s, for many, including the Far Right, he continued to be regarded as the city's foremost anti-fascist, and it was to him that Gerry turned to for advice. It was an alarming story. Not only had Hann been arrested and charged with street robbery, the actual trial was due shortly. A hefty sentence apart, what made the affair even more politically toxic was that the victim of the robbery was probably gay. Or, in other words, a member of a minority ordinarily targeted by bigots and fascists, the very people anti-fascism was ostensibly there to protect. Short of being accused of Jew-baiting, 'Paki-bashing' or wife-beating, this was about as bad as it could get.

Hann, Gerry believed, had belatedly come clean in the expectation that the information would be passed on to London, and that the 'dark arts' employed so successfully to get others off the hook would now be used to save his neck. Throwing himself at Red Action's mercy was a fairly desperate ploy, but as it happened Hann had the devil's own luck.

In the months prior to the Hann disclosure, a number of reports indicating a specific interest in the anti-fascist scene in Manchester had been picked up by AFA intelligence. Taken individually, each incident would have been regarded as a curiosity and nothing more. But when judged against the light of the most recent disclosure, a pattern began to reveal itself. First off, there was the letter to former AFA front-line fighter Liam Heffernan, then serving a 23-year sentence in Long Kesh for conspiracy to cause explosions, membership of the INLA and other offences. A Manchester-based journalist, Peter Walsh, fully aware of Heffernan's political lineage, was inviting him 'to tell his side of the story'. Not too surprising on the face of it. But what created the first tingle of suspicion was that Walsh's real interest, as he made plain, was not in exploring how an English working class lad had ended up in Long Kesh, sharing a wing in the high security prison with some of the most dangerous political prisoners in Europe, but rather the political journey that led to his involvement with them to begin with. Somewhat perversely from a journalistic point of view, it was the Manchester/London anti-fascist, rather than the Manchester/Long Kesh Republican angle, he expressed the greater interest in picking over. Instantly suspicious, Heffernan passed on the introductory letter to AFA, and within an hour of receiving it AFA intelligence was aware that Peter Walsh was widely regarded in police circles as an asset.

On the back of this nugget of information AFA intelligence then got a tip-off from independent researcher Larry O'Hara. A rumour was going around the BBC that *Panorama* were preparing to 'do a number' on Red Action. "Do you know anything about it?" O'Hara inquired. A week later, an Asian BBC researcher and long-time AFA sympathiser confirmed the existence of the rumour. Feeling humiliated and possibly betrayed by the high profile arrest of Pat Hayes, Gerry Gable had been heard to declare his ambition to 'get Red Action'. Following the call to D., all these apparently abstract bits of intelligence were now being pulled together.

There was something else that only now seemed to make sense. In November 1994, Dave Hann had conducted an interview with the BBC News outside Old Trafford football ground. His appearance was as a result of his involvement in a football/anti-fascist fanzine called *Red Attitude*, sponsored by AFA. However, among fellow anti-fascists, the interview raised eyebrows for a number of reasons. For any AFA activist to agree to a face-to-camera interview was inexplicable. It jeopardised any future street work in which he might be involved, not to mention running the possibility of being identified retrospectively for operations he might previously have been engaged in. In addition, the subject matter was regarded as pretty thin, and certainly not commensurate with the level of personal risk it involved. But thin story or not, Hann had apparently been convinced it was worthwhile and the commissioning editor seemingly had sufficient clout for the interview to feature on the BBC *Nine O'Clock News*.

An investigation into the chronology behind Hann's television debut was now ordered. Again within a matter of hours AFA knew the identity of the BBC contact. It turned out to be one of the original 'Squad', Steve Tilzey. Though once popular, he had over the years slithered down the food chain and was by now held in the same esteem as any other lowly Searchlight factotum.

After some further digging it emerged that in the initial arrangement with the BBC, Tilzey was to do the interview himself, but for some reason or other pulled out at the very last moment. And so, sporting a silly Russian fur hat complete with earflaps,

Hann, already on bail for robbery, was deputised by Tilzey in his stead. For people who had learned not to believe in coincidences, swift conclusions were drawn.

Instantly, AFA intelligence saw the November BBC interview as pivotal. This was because, as a result of it, Dave Hann had been elevated to the position of AFA national spokesperson. In the absence of other contenders, for all the obvious reasons, he was now effectively the organisation's public face. From there it would only be a short step and jump to introduce him as 'AFA leader'. (And by a curious coincidence 'leader' was a position Hann would award himself in his autobiography a decade later.*)

By now it was accepted that some sort of media attack on militant anti-fascism as a whole was looking likely. If so, the obvious damage limitation formula that might have been available to AFA – reducing Hann to the ranks retrospectively – had already been closed off. The Tilzey/BBC ploy had seen to that. Moreover, it very much looked like Hann, or to put it more accurately his anticipated conviction, was

---

* In a book called *No Retreat*, co-written with Steve Tilzey (and published in 2004), Hann deliberately glossed over when he actually joined RA and prevaricated about his reasons for leaving, implying his expulsion was based on his principled opposition to calls for AFA to adopt a new approach. In an interview to promote the book, he shamelessly allowed himself to be presented as an 'AFA founder member', accusing the real founders of being cowards who had 'betrayed the anti-fascist movement'. "I strongly believe that several senior RA members were no longer up for the physical side of things anymore, and as a result steered AFA in a less confrontational direction. Hence the formation of the IWCA [Independent Working Class Association]." (Interview www.fullfrontalrecordings.co.uk)

As might be expected, this self-serving alibi cum epitaph does not stand up to much scrutiny. As our chronology demonstrates, it was not AFA but the BNP that abandoned the fight for dominion of the streets in early 1994. As a result, by 1996 there was hardly anyone left to fight. IWCA pilot schemes meanwhile did not become operational until 1997. In Newtown in Birmingham, a nascent IWCA branch, spearheaded by front-line AFA fighters in the Midlands region, grabbed media headlines with the launch of an anti-mugging campaign, while in Hatfield in Hertfordshire a former AFA activist D.P. shook New Labour by snatching 1,100 votes (50% of their total), in a county council election. And it was not until 1998, a full four years after the BNP threw in the towel, that similar IWCA schemes were formed in London. However, it is certainly true that in the mid-1990s, when discussions about the need for militant anti-fascism to adopt a more holistic outlook were first mooted, speculation as to the real motivation of the sponsors was rife in some circles. AFA appeared to be on the crest of a wave at the time, and many could not accept the BNP had decisively changed strategy and, even if they had, that it would amount to much in terms of votes. Consequently, outside of the militant anti-fascist core, the forecast that they would swiftly become 'the radical alternative' was widely derided. But there are few serious commentators who doubt their potential to do so today.

to play the role of anchoring the media offensive. With Hann likely jailed, for 'mugging gays' no less, the street orientated *modus operandi* of AFA and Red Action could be cast in an altogether different light: not just politically extreme (Hayes, Heffernan) but criminally deviant (Hann, Noonan). Should they pull it off *Panorama* would have managed something *World in Action* had tried and failed to do two years earlier. Which is to say, sterilise AFA's growing influence and place the entire militant network in political quarantine.

Meanwhile, by concealing his arrest, from both RA and AFA, Hann would have known he had committed a sackable offence.

Any contact with the authorities, no matter how trivial, was to be passed on to a superior. The thinking behind the general order was an attempt to avoid precisely the situation Hann had put himself in: an activist leaving him or herself open to manipulation, and the entire organisation compromised as a result. Guilty as charged was the only possible reason to conceal so serious a risk to his liberty from comrades. Nor did it help Hann's case when it came to light that his co-accused, Mark, a shadowy figure on the AFA periphery, had seemingly developed a fondness for mugging students. Another rumour of a serious assault in a bar called The Salutation in which a student was stabbed in the neck with a broken bottle and lost part of an ear, and in which Hann was involved, was also looked at in a new light. One way or the other, Hann was finished politically, regardless of the outcome of the trial. The primary concern was to avoid having his undoubted guilt being hung around the neck of the entire anti-fascist movement. The question AFA intelligence was faced with was this: if his conviction is indeed what *Panorama* is relying on, would they still have a worthwhile story if he was acquitted?

On Wednesday 5th April 1995, within 48 hours of the phone call to D., three senior AFA members travelled to Manchester and before the journey was over the broad outlines of a solution had been agreed. In the car there was a constant buzz of questions being asked, ideas traded, and curses muttered as the worst suspicions were confirmed. But apart from letting off steam the venting was actually serving a purpose: the known facts were going through a process of being sifted. Out of the exchanges, a small and seemingly irrelevant detail suddenly came to light. From the information to hand it emerged that the victim, in making the complaint of robbery, omitted any mention whatsoever of the role his sexuality might have played in his selection by the robbers. But when the mugging took place it seems he was heading to or from, or at least in the vicinity of, a gay pub or club. If he was a red-blooded heterosexual was he not somewhat off the beaten track? Or did it mean he was in the closet? So far so good, they thought, but it was not nearly enough. Then out of nowhere came that intuitive sparkle wealthy clients, especially the guilty ones, hire top end lawyers to provide. The AFA members exchanged looks. There was an immediate sense they were onto something.

In the remaining hour of the journey all they had to do was pull the fragments together into a sufficiently plausible picture to prevent Searchlight/*Panorama* putting militant anti-fascism as a whole in the dock.

When they arrived in Manchester, no one bothered to brief Hann, already *persona non grata*, on the political backdrop that prevented his immediate suspension, though the body language of his interrogators spoke volumes. He was in trouble, and so, because of him, were they. During a tense question and answer session it emerged that his 'not guilty' plea had hitherto rested on a thoroughly imbecilic claim of mistaken identity. (Not only had he been arrested within a hundred yards of the scene on the basis of the descriptions given by the victim to a passing motorcycle cop, to top it off, some personal items belonging to the victim were actually found in Hann's possession.)

Originally, the prosecution had every reason to be optimistic. Could it have been more cut and dried? The victim had given a pinpoint description of the two robbers. Both had been arrested almost immediately in the vicinity from the precise descriptions he had given of them. When searched Hann was found to have a Manchester University library card belonging to the victim in his back pocket. The money was, however, not recovered. On top of all that, neither he nor his co-defendant had offered any explanation for what happened – until the trial.

Standing 6ft 2ins in the dock, with his guardsman's build, brush moustache and Hollywood leading man jaw-line, Mark had the look of an extra from Village People; that almost exaggerated masculinity that causes a certain type of woman or, more critically, a certain type of man to go weak at the knees. In short, the archetypical stud, or what the gay community would describe as 'rough trade'. When the lightly-built victim, a medical student, took the stand his account was straightforward. He had been accosted by the accused and identified Mark as the one that had shoved a broken bottle to his face and demanded money with menaces. He had then flagged down a motorcycle cop, provided their descriptions and the culprits were detained within minutes. Until the defence barrister stood up to cross-examine, guilty verdicts looked an absolute given. He began with a number of innocuous questions and then went for the jugular: 'Are you married?' 'Were you at the club?' And finally, 'Are you gay?' When the answer to two and three was in the affirmative the hook was in. It was then put to him that it was he who had propositioned Mark for sex. When Mark named his price and the money was produced, it was snatched and Mark and Hann simply took off. It was the perfect legal 'ambush' (which incidentally the law has since been amended to try and prevent) and the prosecution knew it. As anticipated by the architects, the alternative scenario had introduced the critical element of 'doubt' into what was an otherwise open and shut case. In a deal with the prosecution Mark agreed to plead guilty to a lesser charge, in return for a hefty fine, while Hann skated without a stain on his character, in the eyes of the law at least.* The planned *Panorama* 'exposé' was never made.

In the late 1990s two leading AFA members travelled to eastern Germany to address an anti-fascist seminar held in the grounds of the former concentration camp in Buchenwald. Over the weekend, the AFA representatives outlined the basic 'hit them whenever you see them' strategy to the audience. An extensive question and answer session followed. "Why are you not all in jail?" one sceptic inquired. As martyrdom held no appeal, the real skill, it was explained, lay not only in the ability to implement this or that plan, but also in getting away with it. This, in turn, was a matter of attention to detail as much as anything. By and large, at least as much

* Following a relatively minor disagreement over an article in *Red Attitude*, Hann suddenly volunteered his resignation from Red Action in the spring of 1996. But, protected as he saw it by his 'not guilty' verdict, he let it be known via the internal newsletter that he still expected a bright future for himself within AFA. As the whole affair still came under the banner of intelligence, everything had been conducted on a 'need to know' basis. Which meant that, outside of the half a dozen or so directly involved in the shaping of his defence, no one else in either Red Action or AFA even knew Hann had been to court. But where Hann badly overreached was when he then announced that he intended to privatise the *Red Attitude* fanzine. As Red Action and the fanzine shared a Post Office box address that he had opened in his own name, "Red Action," he told an intermediary, "had better get a new box number."

"Tell Baldy," came back the furious reply, "there will be a new box – and he will be fucking in it!" The implication was clear.

Though livid, the Red Action leadership knew it was a situation that still needed delicate handling. Manifestly, it was not acceptable that Hann be allowed to continue in AFA. The expectation had been that after the trial he would retire into private life. That was the *quid pro quo*. He was now reneging on that tacit agreement, yet the finger could not be publicly pointed without the whole story unravelling. A meeting under the auspices of AFA was called in Manchester to resolve the impasse, and Hann was summoned to explain himself. Attending were London AFA organiser, Tony D., 'Terry Mitchell', the editor of *Fighting Talk*, and Nadir, a highly respected anti-fascist in the city. From the outset it was made clear that there was going to be no compromise and Hann was to step down from his role within AFA forthwith. But, guessing correctly that the real story behind his acquittal would still not be used against him publicly, Hann was initially sullen and stubborn. "What's in it for me?" he demanded sulkily. "I felt like hitting him," Nadir commented later. Shortly after the meeting he was given a three-day deadline to hand over the fanzine intact. Having complied, he followed Mark out of Manchester, never to return. It is telling that, in spite of his book and countless sympathetic interviews in the fifteen years following the trial, Hann never once felt moved to shed light on why he was identified, arrested and charged with a street robbery, much less what happened in the alley or the critical role AFA intelligence played in securing his acquittal in court.

time and effort went into planning the getaway (which sometimes even included the construction of a thorough defence, should charges follow arrest) as went into any major operation. As a consequence of this more professional approach, the savage sentencing of the three London AFA members in 1990 proved to be a watermark. Thereafter, in spite of an escalation of the conflict and the increased attention of the authorities, no more than a handful of AFA activists anywhere in the country were incarcerated as a result of political activity.

3.5

THE BATTLE FOR BRICK LANE, 1990–1993

At 10am on Sunday morning 5th October 1990, the militants took everyone by surprise when a fifty-strong stewards group occupied the joint BNP/NF pitch at Brick Lane in the heart of the East End. The last time the fascist paper sale had been contested was by the ANL in late 1979.

Instinctively, the local police and fascists alike reacted indignantly to what they regarded as anti-fascist provocation. Shoppers and market traders were more bemused than resentful. One little old lady on taking a leaflet mistakenly congratulated the AFA contingent, "Well done boys, there's more of you here every week!" Asian passers-by were also taken aback to be politely handed leaflets by individuals they believed to be racial opponents. By contrast, a tough looking market trader who seemed to know exactly who AFA were, smiled, and drew his finger across his throat in eager anticipation of the arrival of the 'real' NF/BNP. Somewhat less gung-ho was the BNP's Derek Beackon, who jumped on a bus and headed back toward Bethnal Green station in order to alert his colleagues. Not realising he had already been spotted, he was taking his place on the upper deck when, to his evident fury, a choreographed wave from the militant line-up mocked him as he passed.

To the chief steward, the arrival of a van-load of police served as a warning of an imminent attack. Suddenly, the two small groups of AFA members on the opposite corners of the road looked vulnerable. His fear was that they would be attacked: first blood to the enemy. Worse, the obligation to come to their aid would put the larger group, forced to cross heavy traffic, at a serious disadvantage. Shouted instructions to outlying AFA members ordered them to cross over. Not a moment too soon either. Within seconds, a joint force of forty BNP and NF fighters materialised on the opposite side of the street. In command, Richard Edmonds tried for a Churchillian-type pose. Arms aloft, he shouted, "Right, gentlemen!" This served to steady the attackers, allowing them to form into ranks before the mass charge through the traffic. Just as they reached the white line the anti-fascists, who had been deliberately held back, exploded out of the blocks and tore into them. If the watching police thought it would be a walkover, they were bitterly disappointed. Within a matter of seconds it was evident who was gaining the upper hand, but it was only when the attackers were effectively repulsed that the police decided to intervene, making a number of arrests on both sides. Approaching the AFA chief steward, the sergeant shouted: "Right! Now, you lot. Fuck off!"

In drawing up their plans, militant strategists had anticipated that, in the event AFA emerged victorious in the confrontation they felt was inevitable, the police would more likely than not respond in such a fashion. It also being accepted there was no way AFA could be seen to then walk away without everyone assuming they had been intimidated, it was agreed that a 'mass arrest' was preferable to apparent mass surrender. Literally nose-to-nose, the bull-like sergeant and AFA chief steward squared up. "You lot are just here for trouble. You heard me! Fuck off – or the lot of you are nicked!" "Go on, then!" came the snarled reply. "You sat there and saw what happened – we're going fucking nowhere!" After a pause he followed up with, "You *fuck off*!" Genuinely flabbergasted, but faced with odds of at least four to one, Sergeant Daly may have felt they had little option but to withdraw, along with the equally chastened right-wingers. Just as stunned were local bystanders, in particular the market trader who had been making gestures earlier

The NF join the BNP to attack AFA on Brick Lane.

and was now hurriedly piling his stock of umbrellas into boxes. "What are you doin', mate? Running a closing down sale?" an anti-fascist heckled. Guffaws all round.

Now, it may well have been the case that the BNP leadership realised that this was just AFA putting down a marker which said: 'Bethnal Green is now a contested area' – but they couldn't be sure. What they couldn't do was ignore it – the very last thing they wanted was for Brick Lane to develop into a second Chapel Market. And so, by 9am the following Sunday morning, between sixty and eighty BNP/NF hard-liners were already in position to defend the pitch. Of course, AFA never showed. And never had any intention of doing so. The strategy was to put the BNP under pressure without the necessity of even getting out of bed. All the BNP could manage by way of reply was to throw a crude homemade device over the wall of the Davenent Centre in Whitechapel as AFA was holding a public meeting there a month later. It exploded at the back of the building and there were no injuries. Elsewhere, in the same month, BNP leader John Tyndall narrowly escaped a DAM ambush in Norwich.

Joe: "Every week AFA would scout the area, partly as an aid to intelligence-gathering in general, but also to assess the BNP mindset specifically. The body language was particularly interesting. All the time they were constantly on the look out for signs of a hit. Even when leaving the paper sale en route to the pub they would be constantly checking over the shoulder for something untoward or unpleasant. On one occasion, I was in an AFA car trailing a large group and, rather than be forced to pass them, we decided to pull in to the kerb to allow a greater distance to develop. It took a moment before we realised the car we had pulled in behind was also shadowing the BNP but – on their behalf! Having spotted us first, but thinking they were about to get done, they went literally rigid with anxiety. Of course, as we were outnumbered anyway, the very moment a gap appeared in the traffic we were more than happy to slip past. Though a small incident, it reinforced my belief that we were getting to them psychologically as well as logistically. This meant that, to maintain their level of expectancy, it was actually beneficial every now and again to let them know they were under surveillance."

On Sunday 17th March 1991, AFA returned to Brick Lane, the intention to do so being publicly advertised in advance. Over three hundred anti-fascists responded to the call. With the police knowing that AFA was coming, they too flooded the area. Nonetheless, though not as definitive as the first encounter, the numbers and publicity generated helped keep the BNP firmly on the back foot. How on the defensive the BNP leadership really were was demonstrated by the public call to 'Defend Brick Lane!' in *British Nationalist*, in answer to the announcement of yet another AFA picket on 20th October. By accident or design, the anti-fascist demonstration was timed for the day after the BNP AGM, so hundreds of supporters on both sides ("about 300 each" according to the *Independent*, 21st October 1991), plus equal numbers of police, descended on the market area.

From an AFA perspective, the show of strength from the BNP was almost as important as the numbers they mobilised themselves, as their underlying message was, as always, to try and draw attention to the level of threat they believed the BNP represented. This is not to admit to some form of symbiotic relationship between the two, but rather a resentment at the still stubborn refusal by the wider Left to even acknowledge a problem. On the day itself, the anti-fascists used the mobilisation to good effect when it placed The Sun pub, which AFA intelligence indicated was probably the primary BNP operational base in east London, under the media and anti-fascist spotlight.

The Sun was particularly important to the BNP, sited as it was less than a minute's walk from the nearest tube and thus easily found. Another advantage, though unadvertised, was that it was in spitting distance of the local police station, which made any type of full-frontal assault by opponents, in terms of arrests and so forth an obvious non-starter. So, as well as inflicting the loss of prestige that would result from losing 'their' pub, AFA was keen to separate the BNP from the proximity of the police station and the protection this afforded to the coming and going of their activists.

Joe: "Operationally, what we really wanted was them off Bethnal Green Road altogether. For our purposes, them being tucked away in an obscure back street would be ideal. So the idea was to sort of gradually bounce them off the main strip altogether. This, in addition to having to defend the paper sale, would pile further pressure on their rank and file in what, remember, was the heartland of the Far Right nationally."

Further anguish for the BNP leadership came later that Sunday when National Organiser Richard Edmonds, already out on bail on charges of affray and possession of a machete, was ambushed by an AFA contingent at King's Cross in north London as he was dropping colleagues off at the station. Notwithstanding the immediate medical attention that he received from "a passing doctor," according to the *Jewish Chronicle*, it was recommended both he and his female colleague seek further treatment at a hospital. But when police who attended the scene searched the van they discovered two cut-throat razors on the floor. This led Edmonds, along with the eight other occupants in it, to be arrested.

And if the governor of The Sun thought he had seen the last of the militants, just four days later they were back when a 'flash picket' of about forty stewards surrounded the entrance to the pub. Two AFA stewards, one black, one white, entered and openly but politely confronted the bar staff as to the true nature of their customers. A photo of leading BNP member Tony Lecomber was produced and placed on the bar. "This is one of your regulars. Are you aware he has a conviction for bomb-making?" Momentarily taken aback the middle-aged woman in charge nonetheless responded defiantly: "What's that to me?" "You don't mind if race attackers use your pub then?" the AFA members asked. "Speaking for myself – no." After a pause, the white steward replied, "Good. That's all we wanted to know," and with a wink, turned away from the bar and walked out. For the next half hour, all her regulars were regaled with the story of the exchange with the 6ft-plus strangers. That is until, as the young couple sitting unobtrusively at the bar reported later, she got a most unwelcome rejoinder. Having politely listened to the story, 'John' the regular replied deadpan: "Oh, that will be the Reds," and pointedly walking to a far corner of the bar, he added, without turning his head, "You're in trouble now." Jaw visibly agape, the bar lady stared after him. And, as with pub-owners before, her defiance proved short-lived. When the BNP sellers turned up the following Sunday morning, they were politely but firmly, and maybe a little apologetically, informed they were no longer welcome. As if instinctively aware of the AFA aim, rather than find another pub of comparative size elsewhere, as would have been logical, they opted for two smaller pubs instead, one directly beside the police station, the other one more or less directly opposite it.

The AFA picket was a prelude to what turned out to be one of the biggest anti-fascist demonstrations since the 1970s, and right through Bethnal Green, to boot. It says everything about the wearing down of BNP morale that on that day the 'party of power' was nowhere to be seen. For the BNP it was a growing paradox.

The BNP mobilise to defend paper sale in Brick Lane, March 1991.

Just as there were signs of gaining ground in electoral terms, they were losing ground on the street. This was troubling for, according to Mosleyite edict, controlling the streets was prerequisite to controlling the local council. Indeed, preferable to it. Almost exactly two years to the day, the BNP's resolve to hold on to the pitch finally cracked when, following the election of the BNP's first councillor, an impromptu protest by anti-fascist forces descended on the Brick Lane area. Initially, there was a stand off, until "a small group of young men came walking down the street singing the national anthem and 'Rule Britannia'. Assuming they were right-wingers, the police allowed the baseball cap-wearing group behind the barriers and towards an increasingly nervous BNP contingent. By the time everyone realised they were anti-fascists, it was too late; the police were trapped behind the barricades while the BNP contingent felt the full weight of bottles and punches. The Anti-Nazi League, massed on the other side of the road, cheered as the BNP ran in every direction" (*White Riot*, page 52).

The *Daily Star* was not nearly so impressed. "Cops couldn't tell the difference between Lefties and Fascists slugging it out in a street battle yesterday. Yobbos on both sides looked identical in torn jeans and tattered bomber jackets. Police had to rely on tasteless tattoos and barmy badges to decide who was who. At first it was easy. On one side of the Brick Lane, in London's east end, stood howling anti-fascists. On the other screamed British National Party supporters. Then the two sides went for each other and to police it was one grunting mass of confused thuggery. A bemused PC said later: "Nobody could tell the difference between a nazi or a militant* but it made no difference, we nicked them as necessary" (*Daily Star*, 20th September 1993).

Sky TV, no doubt alerted by the ANL, beamed the fracas on live TV, a fact that no doubt led to the BNP leadership finally abandoning the historic Brick Lane pitch for good. Though perhaps the more salient reason behind the retreat was that elements in the BNP leadership were already set on a decidedly different approach.

* The reference to 'militant' was probably not accidental as it was by and large recognised as a 'Militant Tendency' group rather than an AFA operation.

3.6
TURF WARS

As much as the fight against the NF/B&H/BNP was ideological, it was also very much geographical. For, more than anyone, the AFA leadership knew how difficult it was to operate effectively in any area once it was politically contested. Once again the experience in Islington in the early 1980s was proving an invaluable lesson. And from the understanding gained through the crushing of the NF a decade earlier, militants were absolutely resolute in denying the Far Right even the tiniest foothold in any previously conquered territory. With such a mindset, it was perhaps predictable the two possibly bloodiest encounters in the entire campaign would incur in the AFA heartland of Islington. The first occurred in the summer of 1986 when a mob of skinheads confronted a pool player in a pub on Upper Street. His crime was wearing a Celtic shirt, which they regarded as evidence of IRA sympathies. Funnily enough, though no doubt prompted by bigotry, their targeting was spot on, as the football fan in question was indeed a card-carrying Red Action stalwart. With the situation in the pub getting ugly, word quickly reached the nearby White Horse pub, packed with Saturday night revellers from both RA and also from DAM. On receiving the news, about forty instantly volunteered to affect a rescue.

So ferocious was the resulting tear up involving both fascist skinheads and some local youngsters, it triggered an 'all Metropolitan police alert'. In the minutes it took police to arrive, many of the skinheads had been seriously hurt, and others suffered from just cuts and head wounds. A pub they had fled into for sanctuary had had a metal table thrown through the window. (The pub closed on the night never to re-open. Marking, ironically, the beginning of the gentrification of Upper Street.) A couple of Red Action members were also badly beaten. One had his nose, cheekbone and hand broken as well as losing some teeth and received twenty stitches in a head wound. The damage had not been inflicted by fascists but by police. So ferocious and lengthy was the assault that horrified police officers later testified to blood spraying from the back of the van on to the windscreen of the van a WPC was driving, eventually forcing it to stop.

Terry: "I was in the Upper Street police station foyer waiting to be processed. This character was brought in drenched in blood. His hair was matted with the stuff and I couldn't see his features. I assumed it was an old tramp that had been battered by another wino or something. It was only when he winked at me that I realised it was Mickey."

After some lengthy persuasion by the officers from the internal affairs division of the Met, who appeared to genuinely believe the officer involved was psychopathic and desperately wanted him off the streets, Mick O'Farrell pressed charges: "I don't want him to be able to do it to anyone else." To say there was a healthy scepticism within militant ranks at the wisdom of the move was putting it mildly. For one, the primary civilian eyewitness to testify for the prosecution was not only a leading RA member but, to top it off, he had just finished a six-month sentence for breaking a police constable's nose! This, plus O'Farrell's hooligan background and political leanings, turned the trial into the farce many in RA had suspected it would be.

From the very outset, it was not the defendant but the witnesses for the prosecution that were on trial. Basically, the strategy of the defence was to question them on everything bar the events on the night in question, while the actual prosecutor, whose heart clearly was not in it, twiddled his thumbs and looked at his desk. If O'Farrell's own considerable CV was not enough to blacken his character, the defence lawyer introduced a long time acquaintance called Billy Lacey who, he duly informed the jury, was "a well known brigand"! Then the police officer took the stand and sought to explain why, although he had been off-duty at the time, he was nonetheless armed with a baton. A far from convincing witness, he almost made some on the jury gag when he explained that "the only other time he had cause to draw his baton was to put a cat out of its misery after it had been hit by a car." Even with the damning evidence of other serving police officers against him, predictably enough he was acquitted.

Smaller, but more savage, was an AFA ambush in Holloway Road tube station in August 1990, following an Irish Freedom Movement march through the district. This was a particularly daring anti-fascist attack mounted in broad daylight almost literally under the noses of hundreds of police primed to prevent just such an outbreak. In anticipation of trouble, militants had arranged for two carloads of weapons to be parked at opposite ends of a mile long stretch of road where the trouble had generally occurred in the past. On this occasion the victims were a rough looking crew thought to be from south London, who had confidently travelled into the Islington area specifically with the intention of 'getting the IRA'. Not realising they were already under surveillance, their final act before heading home was to attack an Irish youngster with a Celtic top unlucky enough to cross their path. He was left bloodied and shaken as they swaggered towards the train station.

Joe: "As our cars passed on the other side of the road, some of them were lounging on the railings oblivious. Sharp instructions were issued not even to look at them. We wanted this to be a surprise. We pulled into a side road about 30 yards away. It so happened the second car (police had rumbled the first one) containing the tools had been parked just yards from Holloway tube. The gym bag was opened and people began to rummage in it for their weapon of choice. That usually meant something they would be happy to use, rather than what looked the most 'medieval'. Armed, we turned into the main drag and sprinted back toward the tube. The main concern was that a train might arrive before we did. With weapons concealed beneath jackets this, if anything, might have made us look more menacing but it couldn't be helped. The visibly alarmed shoppers standing at the bus stop might have thought we were armed, or that we were police, or it was all a scene for a movie. Either way, we entered the station and thundered down the emergency stairs. It must have sounded like a troop of heavy cavalry crossing a metal bridge. Hearing the racket, one of the gang popped his head around the corner just in time to catch an axe handle on the napper."

Moments after entering Holloway Road tube, most the rest of the gang were dispatched in a similarly brutal manner. With hammers and pickaxe handles being employed, some right-wingers preferred the risk of being electrocuted or worse by running into the tunnel. One anti-fascist ended up on the wrong platform. "Where is everybody else," he thought. He took four or five punches to the face from a fascist lurking there before backhanding the attacker across the forehead with a club. On the adjacent platform a pensioner sitting on a seat on the platform calmly watched without moving as another right-winger suffered a beating next to him. Even when a wristwatch on the fascist's arm shattered near his face, he merely commented; "You'll kill him, you know." Even though the numbers had started about even, the attrition rate meant that within a very short period the anti-fascists were doubling or tripling up on their opponents. The last man standing had backed almost to the tunnel wall before defiantly adopting a boxer stance, tattooed arms up, chin tucked in. Though the anti-fascists admired his pluck he was shown no mercy, losing consciousness within seconds under a hail of blows. The arrival of a train brought the attack to an end. Horn blaring it screeched to a halt halfway down the platform, with the final victim almost gratefully slumping against it rather than tumbling to his probable death on the track.

Andy: "They were hit with everything, bars, hammers, baseball bats. Yes, it was savage enough, I suppose, but not gratuitous. We were taking the opportunity to send them all a message. The thing was, we knew that if they ever felt comfortable in north London, if they began to do to us what we were doing to them in Bethnal Green, then the game was up. Remember, by and large, though we concealed it fairly well, we were heavily outnumbered. Politically, too, we were totally on our own and already way out on a limb."

So with the isolation came resolve, and with the resolve came an inevitable callousness. Sirens were already screaming hysterically as the anti-fascists rapidly exited the tube. Weapons were abandoned and jackets switched in cursory exchange as the attackers made their getaway. Aware that the police would be on the scene in massive numbers within a matter of seconds, the instruction was to split up, but only to get as far away from the scene as possible so as to avoid being fingered by any eye-witness in the immediate vicinity, then immediately to go to ground. This was a simple enough tactic, but one that made it near impossible for police to affect the all-important scene-of-the-crime arrests. As ambulances and police sirens vied with each other for attention all the perpetrators had to do was hold their nerve and hope for the absence of resolute eyewitnesses. One group, in a fairly typical 'so far, so good' mode, had sought sanctuary in a pub, but stiffened perceptibly on realising the neighbouring tables were occupied by garrulous and drunken members of the National Front.

In the investigation conducted by the Transport Police in the weeks afterwards, a number of likely suspects seem to have been provided by an unusually helpful security service. This led to a number of promising early arrests with, on at least one occasion, a door literally being kicked in, but sufficient evidence was never amassed to bring any charges, chiefly because the individuals targeted were never involved. To a man, all were either extremely peripheral or ex-members of AFA or RA. It leads to the suspicion that the investigation was deliberately given a bum steer by spooks that would perhaps not have taken the Transport Police too seriously and were in any case notorious for hoarding information and sources.

It is a theory supported by the curious arrest of two young brothers who, coincidentally, shared the surname of an AFA stalwart whose file was produced during the interrogation of others and who had in fact been present. These two unfortunates were in the hat simply because, though they had travelled over separately with Troops Out, they had later been seen in the company of the RA delegation in Belfast the previous August. This emphasises the level of scrutiny the militants were under as a matter of routine and, of course, the incongruity of the individuals fingered by the SB/MI5 as being the architects of what was a most expertly executed hit. The brothers hardly helped themselves when they readily admitted to having being in the vicinity, to having inexplicably walked off the march around the time of the incident, which meant they could not have been in any police video footage of the marchers thereafter, and that they did so within fifty yards of where the attack took place. And, having put this circumstantial noose around their necks, they topped it all off with the kind of meaningless alibi often found in cases of miscarriages of justice: they had 'gone drinking in Camden where they met two blondes' whose names or addresses or descriptions they could not for the life of them remember! Thoroughly chastened no doubt by the consequences of their flirtation with the rougher end of the political market, they were eventually released without charge and were never heard of again.

3.7

HERTS, 1991

What was deemed neutral territory or 'non-fascist' territory was watched over with only marginally less zeal. In April 1991, when AFA activists in Hatfield responded to a call for assistance from local anti-fascists in Hemel Hempstead, leading London AFA activists responded energetically as well. As they saw it, here was another opportunity to put their unmistakeable 'not welcome' stamp on yet another part of London and surrounding area.

On Saturday 13th April a local primary school was selected as the venue for an NF pre-election rally. As expected, the local SWP mounted a thoroughly ineffective picket at the school gates, lollipops and copies of *Socialist Worker* prominent. By contrast, leading elements within London AFA, with Herts members as guides, had been out prowling the area and had already encountered the local NF leadership en route to the meeting. A member of the NF entourage was Paul Nash, who had been badly beaten at Kingsbury a decade earlier. In the style widely copied but patented by RA, it was reported as follows: "A pre-election meeting with the NF candidate John McCauley was requested, and much to his surprise granted ... The would-be councillor ended face down in the road along with two other well known NF faces and was in no condition to continue. One of his minders ended up in a hedge and refused to come out!" (*Red Action*, issue 59).

In good heart the anti-fascists made their way to the school, verbally chastising a couple of young NF recruits en route. On arriving at the school gates the thirty- to forty-strong group was greeted by police and a very vocal SWP picket, both of whom decided the approaching anti-fascists, if appearances were anything to go by, simply had to be NF reinforcements. With the screeches 'Nazis Out!' ringing in their ears, police on duty obligingly opened the gates and AFA swept in.

Andy: "At once we recognised familiar faces from the NF leadership, including Anderson, and Whicker with a video recorder. Mick O'Farrell, who had been charged with assaulting Anderson in Chapel Market ten years earlier, hailed him: 'Ian, long time no see.' Anderson, relying on the judgment of both pickets and police that the late arrivals were indeed 'fellow travellers', stepped forward, hand outstretched, and offered a very polite 'How very nice to see you again' greeting. A right hook planted Anderson in the geraniums."

Alerted, the NF inside, mostly youngsters, rushed out to get the 'Lefties'. Possibly encouraged by the fact that some of the Militant members at the back fled, the young NF confidently joined battle and took a bit of a pasting. Afterwards there were further scuffles as the meeting broke up. "The London NF contingent, including the 'leaders' needless to say, crammed into their team coach and were driven away under heavy police escort. This left the locals and those who had thoughtlessly parked their cars outside the pub to fend for themselves. And believe you me, they didn't look too happy about it," was how the local Herts AFA bulletin reported the NF departure.

In relative terms, what was a rather minor incident, which was treated almost as 'friendly' by veterans, showed how malign militant activity could be to right-wing fortunes. Here we had what would have proved a run of the mill encounter played out between NF, police, and SWP being dramatically transformed by the militant tactic of violence as a first resort. And, but for this intervention by the militants, it is undoubtedly the NF who would have been physically dominant, with the Left taking the casualties and withdrawing under police protection instead. What's more, the seemingly graceful nature of the triumph successfully encouraged local Left activists into play. Off the back of the activity, Herts Anti-Fascist Committee, with contacts in St Albans, Hertford, Bishop Stortford, Hitchin, and Stevenage, came into being.

Under the headline 'Front See Off Labour Thugs', the NF told an unrecognisably different tale. "There were smiles and waves from the people of Hemel Hempstead as the NF loudspeaker van cruised through the town on Saturday 13th April. The van was bedecked with Union Jack Flags and election posters with the public address system playing patriotic music ... At 3.30pm the election meeting was held at Chaulden Junior School and, despite a picket of 30 Labour Party supporters, attracted the interest of a dozen or so members of the public who came in to see what the NF had to say. With the meeting well under way, 25 Labour thugs tried to disrupt it but were competently dealt with by the NF stewards on duty ... The day was a great victory for freedom of speech, with the National Front standing firm in defence of its democratic rights and refusing to be intimidated by blatant Labour Party thuggery."

But as it turned out there could be no real pretence of two enemy camps meeting in a violent clash; the fascists had been intimidated and outclassed. One Militant member, more than a little over-awed, nevertheless found himself inquiring if the motivation of the working class street-fighters could be considered to be "really political?" Though a throwaway comment, it does go some way to exposing the mammoth gulf that existed between AFA and the orthodox Left even as late as 1991. What retaliation did come from the Front came in the form of anonymous calls to the homes of those arrested. These included death threats made to children. This evidence of ruthless degeneracy aside, the NF lacked the courage to contest the General Election in the area in 1992, and when they did finally return to support NF candidates contesting the county council elections in 1993, despite the talk of 'Labour thugs being competently dealt with', Chairman Ian Anderson formally requested that riot police actually steward the NF meeting to allow it to take place at all.

3.8

THE MURDER OF ROLAN ADAMS, THAMESMEAD, 1991

Already heavily committed in and around Bethnal Green, following the racist murder of a black youngster, AFA opened a new theatre of operations in south east London. For a multitude of reasons this proved very difficult terrain. Geography, and long stretches of suburban sprawl, proved very different from the inner city landscape where militant hit and run tactics had been honed. Additionally, what is known as 'white flight' meant a latent fascist sentiment existed amongst sections of the local population that made the possibility of unobtrusively mingling for the purposes of intelligence practically impossible: rather bizarrely, de facto colour bars, for instance, still existed in some pubs and Trades and Labour clubs. Taken together with the usual hostility from what were ostensibly anti-fascist allies (the only consistent contact AFA had in the area was a council funded monitoring group in Greenwich) and the sheer physical distance from inner London, this meant that militants were forced to mount incursions into what was by any definition alien territory. Inevitably results were mixed. And AFA had to dig deep.

In early 1991 a racist attack in Thamesmead, south east London, led to the murder of a 16-year old black youth called Rolan Adams. Almost immediately the nascent BNP 'Rights For Whites' campaign sought to cash in on the tensions that resulted. In order to try and ratchet up existing divisions, the BNP applied for a march through Thamesmead. With calculated callousness, they demanded the right to rally directly outside the Hawksmoor Youth Centre where Rolan Adams had come from on the evening he was murdered. It was patently provocative but agreed to by the authorities, nonetheless.

Talk of the need for a counter-rally among a number of anti-racist groups began at once. AFA were invited by local anti-racist campaigners to send representatives to the planning meetings prior to the march. At the final meeting on the Wednesday before the march, a wide cross-spectrum of ethnic and political interests were in attendance, including black MP Bernie Grant* at the request of the Adams family. As can easily be imagined, opinion was harshly divided on what those present

* Following the Broadwater Farm riots in the mid-eighties, in which PC Blakelock was cut down by a mob, Bernie Grant became a controversial figure when he publicly defended the rioters and claimed that "police got a bloody good hiding."

considered would be the most appropriate response. In accord with the situation, the AFA advice was to keep it simple. "The rally should assemble outside the youth centre. If it is ever considered necessary to move at all, it should only ever move in the direction of the BNP." After hours of haggling and shadow-boxing, a consensus was finally reached, with this tactically undemanding strategy of a static counter-demonstration adopted for the day. What helped clinch the argument in the militants' favour was when a black nationalist, who had originally been openly hostile on the grounds that all bar one in the AFA delegation were white, finally agreed the plan was the most sensible. He further recommended that it should be supported by the meeting, and, moreover, AFA stewards should be given "a free hand on the day." Adding, to some nervous laughter, "I don't even want to know what they're up to!" Visibly uneasy from the outset, Bernie Grant stood up at this point, and without a word, abruptly left the meeting.

By midday an impressive 2,000 anti-racists had already assembled. However, the basic plan, hammered out and agreed after hours of argument to keep the counter-demo static, was immediately cast aside. Not by the usual sinister outsiders beloved of the tabloids, but by self-appointed community leader, Lee Jasper,* former race adviser to London Mayor Ken Livingstone who, with fulsome police backing, imposed a diktat of his own. As might be expected the police/Jasper solution was the polar opposite of the AFA recommendation. Put simply, the anti-racists were to vacate the area to make way for the BNP. By the time the militants arrived at the scene, partly as a result of being delayed by an exceptionally violent clash with some fascists near Abbey Wood station, the dye was cast.

Already alerted to the way the wind was blowing and sensing duplicity, AFA stewards took the precaution of placing a physical distance between themselves and the main contingent. By not mingling with the main body of protestors, although it denied them the opportunity to influence others, they gambled it would help them retain sufficient forces to move to Plan B. News of the AFA arrival coincided with a myriad of rumours of supposed BNP plans and sightings that came swirling around the easily identifiable militant contingent.

Joe: "It was very strange. As soon as we arrived we were bombarded with all sorts of 'helpful' information. Even local kids on bikes seemed to know who we were. Interestingly, all of the information necessitated us moving somewhere other than where we were. Nothing could be verified. So we sat tight. To top it all an ITN news team complete with camera turned up for – an interview!" Repeatedly warned off, the camera crew eventually retreated after being subject to a hail of stones. Later in

* Lee Jasper was forced to resign from his position following an investigation by London's *Evening Standard* in relation to a sum of £3 million in grants to friends and associates for which there was no audit trail.

the day, with tempers short, another cameraman, having ignored requests to stop filming, was head-butted and his camera thrown in the river. Much of the counter-rally, now a march, was already out of sight when the first BNP flags were sighted on the horizon. The tail end of the march, judged by the militants to be retreating, guiltily trudged past, seemingly indifferent to the abuse hurled in their direction.

Joe: "Most just kept their heads down. Others looked entirely uncomprehending. One strode over to confront me. He pushed his face into mine and shouted, 'How did you know where the fascists are?' Of course I didn't know. But what I said was: 'Look, if this lot are heading that way, it's a fair bet the BNP are heading this way!' With that a roar went up and we both looked up to see the first ranks of Union Jacks appear over the trees. He stared at me in astonishment. It was a pure Hollywood moment. Then he just turned on his heel and rejoined the march."

More in hope than expectation, AFA messengers were dispatched to inform the front of the march of the BNP arrival. In the meantime, with just the back up of some local kids from the estate willing to lend a hand, AFA decided to confront the BNP anyway. In order to do so, they had to evade the riot police first. By staying off the main roads and crossing some waste ground some militants got near enough to bombard the march with a volley of rocks. It was an unexpected show of

In Thamesmead, south east London, the BNP attempt to walk by the spot where Rolan Adams was murdered in a racist attack.

resistance sufficient to convince the police officer in charge, Superindent Mellish, later described by *British Nationalist* (June 1991) as a "quivering jellyfish", to order the BNP to turn back.

Militant disgust at what it described uncompromisingly as 'betrayal' was hardly mollified, particularly when the marchers who had ducked confrontation with the BNP later got drawn into a straightforward brawl with police. The BNP meanwhile were jubilant. "Saturday, May 25th witnessed the biggest nationalist march in south London for more than a decade. Millions of viewers watching all 3 TV channels saw a forest of Union Jacks – a solid phalanx of marchers on national TV news, marching for rights for whites" (*British Nationalist*, June 1991).

In turn a document presented to the Rolan Adams Family Campaign outlined the AFA criticisms. "From the time that the BNP march was rumoured to be taking place, through when it was known to be taking place, to the actual march itself, AFA made every attempt to be kept in touch with plans, both through GCARA (Greenwich Campaign Against Racist Attacks) and through the Rolan Adams Family Campaign. However, it was only through our own perseverance that we discovered the time and venue of the series of meetings prior to the 25th May, this despite the fact that AFA is an affiliated organisation to the campaign.

"During the week prior to the demonstration there was a meeting every night. These meetings were only significant insofar as they underlined and highlighted the infighting and the cynical manipulation of groups allegedly keen to oppose the fascist march. These meetings ranged from the sublime to the ridiculous; from instances where it was suggested that white anti-racists be excluded and Asian anti-racists be restricted in representation, through to meetings where the main agenda item was how the meeting itself could have been more effectively built – and this in the week of the proposed mass mobilisation.

"The planning meeting, which occurred on Thursday 23rd May, was an unmitigated failure. The meeting seemed to be open to anyone who cared to attend, regardless of his or her experience and regardless of what they had to offer. This meeting should have been the last opportunity to tie down and confirm details for stewarding, security, and legal cover. In fact it was a brainstorming session where it became apparent that few, if any, people – other than the AFA delegates – had put any thought into what the objectives were for the day, what the plans for the day were to be, what strategies and tactics were to be employed.

"No sooner was the anti-fascist march out of sight than the BNP march was spotted. Who organised the anti-fascist march? Was it the police, or was it cynical political manipulators attempting to gain recruits or brownie points from their high profile on the day? Whoever took the decision was responsible for the fascists' success. Whoever was responsible should be in the dock facing charges, not those who were arrested whilst actually opposing fascism, or those whose anger and frustration, deliberately built up by the organisers' pre-demo hype and rhetoric, was vented uselessly on the forces of the state. It seems probable that it was intended that the BNP would march through the estate and finish at the Hawksmoor Youth Club. Not only had the hijackers of the anti-fascists abandoned all attempts at principled opposition, not only had they betrayed the trust of the militant protestors, but they had also abandoned their rallying point, their vehicles, their sound system and their credibility to the fascists.

"The speeches from the truck provide the final denunciation of the anti-fascist demonstration and illustrate the Toytown mentality of those involved. It was declared that the fascists had been defeated on the day. It was declared that the anti-fascist rally had been a success. It was declared that the fascists and racists had been shown they were unwelcome in Thamesmead. When were the fascists defeated? How can a large number of anti-fascists marching away from a march celebrating white supremacy and rejoicing in racist murder and racist attacks be considered a success? Who has shown that the fascists are unwelcome in Thamesmead?

AFA suggest that none of these targets were reached. The next weeks and months will only too vividly show that the fascists and racists have been strengthened by the events of the afternoon of the 25th May."

It was no surprise, however, that AFA's hard-edged criticism received a frosty reception at the post mortem. Lee Jasper, who had been the architect of what AFA referred to bluntly as a "betrayal", blatantly sought to deflect attention from himself by playing the race card: accusing AFA reps of being motivated by racism, at which an already tense meeting threatened to slip into actual fisticuffs. However, the AFA delegates – who were responsible for tactically linking the murder of Rolan Adams to the BNP HQ in nearby Welling in the first place (resulting in the first of a number of large protest marches against the premises) – already decided prior to the meeting that further attempts to rescue the campaign were likely to be futile. Had they not, violence would more than likely have erupted at some stage.

As it was, when the black female chair asked the head of the AFA delegation if he thought he or his "organisation might possibly benefit from watching a race awareness video," he responded by beginning to gather together his papers. Replying as he did so, "For what it's worth, I think the suggestion is a disgrace, you're a disgrace for asking it, and the conduct of this meeting as a whole is a disgrace." At this he and the rest of AFA delegation walked out to a backdrop of complete silence. Within weeks, as AFA had forecast, Lee Jasper moved the Rolan Adams meetings from Thamesmead to his Brixton stronghold, and that effectively was the last anyone ever heard of the Rolan Adams Campaign. That, however, was not the last of the BNP or racist murders in the area.

In April 1991, following another anti-racist march against the BNP HQ, an article in *Red Action* made a chillingly prescient warning. "A protest march once a year," it argued, "will not cause the shop [BNP HQ] to close. If the entire anti-fascist movement accepts the challenge, we must be seen to finish the job this time. If we fail again, the price will be high. For if the fascist influence in south east London is confronted but not crushed, it will as a result be strengthened. Their morale will be strengthened. The race attacks will multiply. Next year or the year after, there will be other marches because there will be other funerals. This is how the road runs" (*Red Action*, issue 59, June/July 1991).

Twelve months later, in July 1992, Rohit Duggal was stabbed to death in an unprovoked racist attack. Another year on and Steven Lawrence would meet his death in a near identical incident in the same area. More marches did follow as a result of more murders. The RA forecast was being played out.

A commemorative march on 7th November 1992 by the Rohit Duggal Family Campaign drew attention to the interconnection between the rise in racist attacks and the resulting brazenness of the Far Right activists in the south London area. Because the Duggal family were not prepared to allow the march to be hijacked by the likes of the Anti-Racist Alliance or the SWP, as they had seen happen with the Rolan Adams Campaign, these groups sent only nominal representation. Unfortunately, the hands-off approach by the family also extended to an extent to AFA, even though relations between AFA representatives and family members were perfectly cordial. Accordingly, it was only when the six hundred anti-racist marchers turned into Eltham High Street that the dangers in keeping it a family affair hit home. Waiting there for the marchers was an exceptionally volatile and ugly crowd, comprising 300 fascist street fighters and local thugs, with a sprinkling of C18 faces very much to the fore.

Terry: "Unlike the recent clashes in other parts of London you could tell their confidence was high. The Duggal family were subjected to vicious and sustained abuse. AFA activists were pointed out as we passed. As we got to the park for the rally, police were struggling to hold back the mob. At the rally the AFA speaker abandoned his prepared speech. This was not the time for rousing speeches. An event called to remember a young life taken by racists and to be a show of strength against them was already a nightmare. The priority now was that as many marchers as possible would leave the area in one piece."

While it was not impossible that there would still be an attack on the rally, the real potential for serious if not fatal injury was after the rally when smaller groups made their way to the train station. AFA stewards assumed control, ordering the coaches, mini-buses and cars to take extra passengers out of the immediate area. When some coach drivers objected to people sitting in the aisle, stressing they would be breaking the law, which was technically correct, the police commander who saw what was happening, and could also see the alternative scenario, briskly ordered the drivers to allow the marchers on board. Around half a dozen AFA stewards remained to the last. Despite relations with Searchlight being frosty at the time, Gerry Gable came to the rescue, piling the remaining militants into his own car before leaving the area at speed.

Terry: "All the marchers who followed our instructions got out safely. Others, of course, knew better. Some members of ARA and the SWP insisted on walking back to the station on foot. They were met by a fascist ambush. A number were hospitalised, some with fairly serious injuries. These are the people who like to call the fascists 'stupid' by the way. The soft targets had boosted fascist confidence and their activities continued well into the evening, attacking a local left-wing pub, taking out someone's eye in the process, proving once again that the groups that only play at anti-fascism often have serious consequences for others than themselves."

The lessons of the homicidal cycle were not lost on everyone. Rolan's father, Richard Adams, would later reflect on how AFA projections had been treated. In July 1993 he travelled to Birmingham to make an appearance on the BBC series *Nation*, hosted at the time by Trevor Phillips. The item under discussion was the continuing escalation in racial violence. Afterwards in the lobby Adams bumped into AFA representative Gary O'Shea. Brushing aside some fawning attendant anti-racist careerists, he gripped the offer of an outstretched hand firmly, commenting: "You boys were right all along."

But Richard Adams was very much in the minority. Differences over tactics withstanding, Lee Jasper's deep loathing of AFA came in part from his personal belief that whites, and working class whites in particular, were inherently and hopelessly racist. "The white Left has recently been viewed with a high degree of cynicism by some black people but this was not always the case. During the 40s, 50s and 60s, black people joined the Labour movement and Communist Party in large numbers, where they spent more time educating their comrades out of their racism than addressing real issues. But black people realised they had to rely on themselves when the white Left stated that the white working class were our natural allies – although the white working class were in the main perpetrators of the racism and violence unleashed toward black people." Drawing on the memory of the AFA walkout from the meeting in Thamesmead he went on to inform readers of the leading black community paper, *The Voice*, that anti-black feeling was ingrained within militant anti-fascism. "London members of Anti-Fascist Action (AFA) reportedly attended a 'race awareness' course recently run by AFA's one black member" he crowed (*The Voice*, 27th October 1992).

This insidiously debilitating idea that racism was in "white peoples' genes", according to a National Black Caucus speaker (*Black Flag*, issue 203, autumn 1993), gained influence in the 1980s when it formed the basis for 'racial awareness training' (RAT) mainly used in the public sector. RAT was theoretically underpinned by the writings of an American academic, Judith Katz. She believed racism is "a psychological disorder … deeply embedded in white people from a very early age, on both a conscious and unconscious level" and that "being white … implies being racist" ('Racism Myths and Realities', *International Socialism* 95, summer 2002).

From that perspective even the slightest hint of resistance served only to confirm the original prognosis. For liberals who subscribed to the Katz theory, members of the working class needed to prostrate themselves completely simply in order to be tolerated. In this world-view, the highest honour any white working class activist could expect would be to qualify, after serving a considerable time on probation, as a sort of 'racist anti-racist'. Not too surprisingly, militant body language was never going to be sufficiently humble to pass muster. Nor was Jasper's attitude so uncommon. Another *Voice* columnist, Tony Sewell, also took AFA to task for being "predominately white and male." Clearly it never crossed his mind to consider what effect the common or garden prejudices regularly displayed by him and his fellow columnist may have had in discouraging black youth from doing their bit, thus ensuring groups like AFA remained predominately 'white man's business'. Instead of any real insight, he offered up some cod psychology. "Their [AFA] desire to meet violence with violence on behalf of oppressed black people is only an excuse for white men to have a good ruck. This type of rivalry has become a kind of war game, where racism is the red rag for men to test their masculinity" (*The Voice,* 28th February 1995).

Of course, in one way he was right. Because, for the vast majority of militants, the idea of AFA fighting "on behalf of oppressed black people" would certainly have been regarded as utter nonsense. And while the casual racist comments in the presence of any AFA activist at the time rarely went unchecked, with physical retribution not being an uncommon response, as an organisation AFA was at pains to make clear the underpinning for their 'war', as they saw, it had very little to do with race, and absolutely everything to do with class.

3.9

KENSINGTON LIBRARY, 1991

Even allowing for the underlying tensions identified, the overall militant analysis, demeanour, and 'can-do' attitude served to make a favourable impression on Richard Adams, and also other elements involved in the Rolan Adams Campaign who, for a variety of reasons, would normally have been wary of the 'white Left'. A number of informal discussions took place as to how best they might help tilt the balance against the BNP in south east London. The counter-demo against the BNP, on Thamesmead on 25th May 1991, promised to be an ideal backdrop against which to gauge how co-operation might work in practice.

It was agreed to meet in The Abbey Arms, adjacent to Abbey Wood station, at 1pm on the day. AFA organisers expected a 30-strong, mainly black local firm, led by a cousin of Rolan Adams, to meet them there. At 12.40pm AFA alighted from the train and headed towards the pub. Though it was thought likely the BNP would be using other stations, as an added insurance, AFA scouts had been sent ahead by car to verify the supposition to be correct. On arrival at Abbey Wood railway station, there was some slight unease that the scouts were not on hand to report as arranged. But the bored middle-aged police manning the exit helped reassure AFA everything was as it should be. This was not an unreasonable assumption in the circumstances. But it was also very wrong.

The Abbey Arms was a large, old-fashioned boozer, all red carpet and dark mahogany. Because of its proximity to the railway station, it had been used a number of times before by AFA delegates travelling to and from mid-week meetings in Thamesemead. The main entrance was through a single door at the side of the pub, rather than through the front. Inside the single door was a frosted glass partition to screen drinkers from any casual survey, meaning it would be necessary to actually be in the pub, before you could take stock of the occupants.

Joe: "We were only feet inside the door, when we spotted a group near the back of the pub sporting English rugby tops. There were about a dozen or so, all in their early thirties, none of them known to us, but all the antennae pointed to them being players, and members of the opposition. And even though we did not know any of them, their tense reaction suggested they had probably guessed who we were too. We paused. Now we had the numbers. No problem there. But if we kicked it off we would have to abandon the rendezvous, as police were already posted outside the pub. 'There's only a dozen of them, let them sweat,' we thought and I headed for the middle of the long bar. The others had begun to funnel through the narrow doorway behind me.

"I had just ordered when Russell, one of the lads, came walking back toward me, wearing a wry grin. Knowing his demeanour, I knew that what he would have to reveal was going to be interesting to say the least. 'It's mobbed,' he said. 'The pub is a dog-leg. There's about another forty of them around the back.' It emerged afterwards that some fascists had actually tried to escape via the beer garden but found the door was locked. There was no chance to relay the news, as the opposition suddenly seized the initiative. The main man snatched up one of those heavy wood tables with wrought iron legs and, with the help from a couple of others led a screaming charge headlong into the anti-fascists near the door.

"I had just ordered a pint when suddenly the roar went up and the barmaid fled. I quickly leant over and grabbed two pint-pots from the shelf underneath the counter. I launched the first, the base of it catching an 18 stone bruiser high on the forehead. It bounced off. He kept coming. The second, thrown from a distance of only about six to eight feet, smashed on the upper chest of the one next to him and exploded. Then they were into us."

Using the heavy table as a battering ram the fascists slammed into the small number of AFA grouped just inside the door. Immediately a number went down. Vicious hand-to-hand fighting broke out in the confined space. Customers fled in panic. One of the attackers took a beer bottle flush in the face. Another had an arm broken. An ill-aimed projectile sent shards from the plate glass window tumbling into the street outside. Caught up in the mêlée, a wheel chair was over-turned, tossing its screaming occupant onto the floor. From entering the pub to 'kick-off', the dozen or so militants had had no opportunity to move away from the door. Because they were heavily out-numbered, they were now being driven back, blocking any outside from getting in through the narrow doorway.

Joe: "Because I was standing at the bar, the initial charge toward the door swept past me. I had recovered another glass. A heavy-set bloke with a close-cropped ginger beard came at me in a kind of crouch. I now had my back to the bar, and wiggled the glass in my right hand and winked at him by way of invitation. I had been maybe ten feet in advance of our lot when it kicked off. So I hadn't had time to assess the situation from kick-off, but assumed from the racket that we were at least holding our own. But stealing a quick glance, all I could see now were three or four rows of them, between a dozen and fifteen, and all between the narrow exit and me. Luckily for me the 'beard' hadn't twigged my dilemma. Basically, if I moved too early he would be able to grab me from behind as I passed. If I waited too long to make my move, the others at the door would turn and see me. Whether or not he saw or sensed some change in my demeanour, he suddenly lunged in, clawing for a hold, with me swerving back to avoid him. Like a boxer on the ropes I leant back over the counter, managing to evade him for a second time. Knowing it was now or never I swung with my right hand, down and across in an arc. The tumbler must have connected satisfactorily enough to matter, but by then I was already on my way, in too much of a dash for the door to worry about it. Most of the 'fash' were still facing the other way or just on the point of turning when I came smashing into them. There were shouts of alarm and curses. I could feel hands grabbing at me. Then a beer bottle shattered against my temple. Just as suddenly I was through the door and out. I was bleeding from a head-wound but that didn't bother me in the least at the time. It had been a close shave all round and we all knew it."

Among the less experienced anti-fascists grouped outside, the sight of experienced AFA stewards being driven back was unknown territory and the beginnings of panic were fully evident. Had the attackers been more courageous in seeking to capitalise on the initial charge, they could have made a serious name for themselves. But, by the time they had mustered sufficient pluck to venture out, a couple of senior stewards, armed with bottles and one bleeding, had posted

The Abbey Arms in south east London.

themselves immediately outside the narrow door. Their snarled defiance proved just enough to discourage further adventures. Making her getaway, a middle-aged Asian female, who had travelled with Islington ARAFA and who, entirely by accident, had alighted from the same train as AFA, drew wry smiles as she sniffed, "Isn't it terrible, you can't even come to a march without something like this happening!" – seeming to forget that a spiteful murder of a child was the reason she was there in the first place.

Composure recovered, AFA were more determined than ever to keep to the original rendezvous and so moved the main body to a pub less than 100 yards away and in the same street to allow them to keep an eye on developments. (Ironically the appointment would not be kept, as the promise of support from the black community failed to materialise.) The large police presence that had been so conspicuous by its absence earlier promptly swung into action and ordered that pub closed. AFA were then instructed to get on buses out of the area – or face immediate mass arrest. Curiously, though militants were being threatened with arrest for resisting police orders, with regard to what by any standards had been an extremely violent brawl moments earlier, basic police inquiries were not even forthcoming. Particularly as, according to the officer in charge, there were "six people seriously injured in The Abbey Arms."

"Well, that's something, I suppose," an AFA member acknowledged conversationally. There was something else that bothered leading stewards. AFA had been instructed to get on buses out of the area but this meant heading back towards The Abbey Arms where the fascists had re-grouped.

Joe: "The whole thing smelled to high heaven. For instance, even though police posted outside must have known fascists were in the pub they did nothing to stop us going in. Then we are kicked out of 'our' pub but the BNP are allowed to stay in theirs. Worse, police then forced us under pain of arrest to march back past the scene of the original clash. As we retraced our steps back toward The Abbey Arms we could see the mob outside. Another smaller outfit was gathering outside the bookies and on our side of the road. I was puzzled as to how police were going to handle it when the answer was provided. The police were not going to handle it. Abruptly, the police escort was withdrawn. We were on our own."

Feeling that even the smallest sign of hesitation could prove fatal, senior militants realised there was nothing for it but to 'front it out'.

Joe: "Twenty yards from the bookies the little mob gathered there suddenly vanished as if they had been 'hoovered' inside. Immediately, I shouted to our boys to step off the pavement into the road, fully intent on crossing toward the pub. Though we numbered about sixty, many were untried and, as well as that, the opposition had the advantage of an unlimited supply of bottles, glasses, pool cues, etc., while we were unarmed. Everyone looked extremely tense. Not only for the fact that 'round two' was likely to be rougher than round one, the police were allowing it to happen, with all the obvious implications. With less than forty yards separating us I could see some movement by the pub door. "Fuck!" I thought "There's more of them coming out." We kept going, anyway. Then it seemed to me the crowd was actually thinning. By now I could pick the monster I had tagged with the pint pot: still bleeding and, encouragingly, looking pretty apprehensive. Then, suddenly he was gone and the rest deserted the doorway just as quickly. Even allowing for what happened, we must have made a bigger impression on them than they had on us."

British Nationalist later praised the occupants of The Abbey Arms for being a "particularly tough bunch of patriots". This suggests the occupants were likely to have been members of the British Movement, known to have a base in the area. It later emerged that a gangster with the unlikely name of Johnny Starbuck owned The Abbey Arms. He was said to be less than pleased with the day's events.

One of the BNP casualties on the day was afterwards identified to AFA intelligence. It turned out he was a highly vocal BNP supporter in his local pub in Charlton, but had returned there with a broken arm after the fracas at The Abbey Arms. Eighteen months later, when fully recovered and thus back on 'active service', he suffered a head wound requiring twenty stitches at 'The Battle of Waterloo'. The thoroughly negative impression on potential recruits in his periphery can easily be imagined. When you consider that not dissimilar scenarios were likely to have been repeated hundreds of times up and down the country throughout the ten year campaign, it bears testimony to the competence of the militant strategy in thinning out and wearing down the opposition.

That afternoon, having breached police lines to confront the BNP march, forcing it to turn back, AFA immediately regrouped and set off at a brisk pace across London to Kensington. A League of St George symposium, involving a wide spectrum of the Far Right, was to take place at 7pm that evening. Jeffrey Hamm, Oswald Mosley's secretary, was down as guest speaker. Searchlight had put plans in place to have a team take over the hall prior to the arrival of the fascist security. They would, however, need considerable AFA back up to be in place by 6pm at the latest if the operation was to succeed. AFA was determined to make the deadline.

Coinciding with the arrival of London AFA, a small but physically formidable looking, mainly Jewish outfit led by Searchlight's Steve Tilzey appeared. One blond, crop-haired and tattooed Manchester martial arts expert, looking every inch the neo-nazi, was appointed, along with a great bear of a man wearing tinted glasses, to take their place (the original stewards having been bundled unceremoniously inside) at the main entrance. So thoroughly relaxed was their performance that a raw rookie cop, oblivious to what was happening downstairs, chattered excitedly to them like a teenager on a first date.

Meanwhile, the symposium organisers sat grimly at the front of the hall in the company of the main body of anti-fascists, while unsuspecting fascists, many elderly, continued to trickle in. Once inside, they were ordered to sit at the front and keep their eyes on the stage. All complied without much fuss. Their mood was not helped when some of the crowd broke into a rendition of 'Always look on the bright side of life…' Despite the fairly jovial atmosphere, it began to dawn on militants that this would not prove a protracted affair. Unavoidably, on entering the downstairs foyer, one group of fascists accompanying Jeffrey Hamm did sense something amiss. Peering into the hall the sight of his compatriots occupying the front rows only and sitting unnaturally stiff and silent caused him to trigger the alarm. "It's a trap. Get out! Get out!" he screamed and turned to flee. He was bludgeoned to the ground. Though otherwise unharmed in the mêlée that ensued, Hamm lost his spectacles. A search to find them was ordered. Bleeding profusely, some others were meanwhile locked in the projection room. The rest were ordered to behave and sit with their increasingly grim-faced colleagues. Clearly, with more and more fascists arriving there was the recognition that the anti-fascists' ability to retain control of the crowd would diminish.

Nor was it entirely apparent to AFA organisers what the endgame was to be. Terrified by the possibilities unfolding, some young Class War student supporters from Leeds, near to tears, demanded they be allowed to leave. Walt Whitman once said that every life needed "one brief hour of madness and joy." Evidently the students had just experienced their hour of madness and now wanted out. Not too long afterwards following a brief consultation AFA too decided to pull the plug. But as the main body of AFA exited, they clashed with another group of fascists at the top of the stairs. Finally alerted, the lone policeman tried to intervene and make arrests but was shoved aside. The anti-fascists now poured through the doors. A group of skinheads were left in an unconscious heap in the stampede. But, despite reaching Kensington High Street in a matter of seconds, the anti-fascists found the immediate area flooded by police. Although the vast majority made good their escape in the confusion, a total of seventeen were arrested at the scene. None made statements and eventually all were released on police bail, pending further inquiries. The *Kensington News* led with a front-page headline: 'Mayhem At Right Wing Meeting'. The article quoted police who referred to victims with "severe head wounds" being taken to Charing Cross Hospital. Police also reported "a search of the building revealed a bag full of concrete blocks and metal pipes," though it was not made clear who they thought they belonged to.

All told, the political fall-out from the day's events would be far-reaching for all concerned. Within AFA, Workers Power, who had up until then retained the hope that the wider Left would be brought on board, began to revise their opinion following the events both before and after the Thamesmead march. For AFA strategists, the rather bizarre behaviour of the police at Abbey Wood, together with their suspiciously prompt arrival at Kensington, was a serious cause for concern. It appeared to them that police at a fairly senior level were working to a political agenda that had little to do with the maintenance of law and order pure and simple. The question taxing all involved was, to what specific end?

When it emerged later, during a subsequent criminal trial at Southwark Crown Court, that the call that triggered the massive police response at Kensington had not come from the young officer on duty at Kensington library, as was originally claimed by the prosecution, it begged the question: if there was no phone call, who alerted the police? The belief in AFA leadership circles was that shadowy forces were at work. So, notwithstanding the quiet satisfaction afforded by the not insignificant disruption to the fascists at opposite ends of London in one day, there was pause for much personal reflection, as the isolation of militants could hardly have been less ambiguous.

Never a fee-paying party, AFA always attracted a 'fly-by-night' periphery motivated mainly by the sense of excitement and adventure. Very much an outer layer, they never took part in branch meetings but would be expected to turn out only at activities publicly announced well in advance. At best camp followers, they nonetheless helped make up the numbers, but no one was in any doubt that their loyalty to AFA rested entirely on the ability of those who took the primary responsibility to deliver victory. Generally, while the AFA rank and file proper had shown itself to be of far superior pedigree, one former Militant member, Mick H. from Canning Town, later confessed he himself had often advertised the benefits of joining AFA to a colleague on the grounds that "It's easy. All you do is wait for the big boys to put them down and you kick them when they're on the floor."

Now with the full political implications of the encounters at Abbey Wood, Thamesmead and Kensington sinking in, many ordinary members, including rather extraordinarily the entire AFA membership from Hackney, were beginning to display the first signs of uncertainty. Even with the militants still winning, there was a creeping feeling of vulnerability, with the realisation of just how politically cut off AFA actually was. Hackney AFA in particular seemed to have been hit by a collective loss of nerve. "Unless things changed," a senior RA member Peter C. was informed by Mark M., "many in Hackney would leave." But if he had imagined the off the record threat of resignation would lead to a reappraisal of the tungsten-tipped attitude, it was a serious misreading of the motivations of a hard-line leadership.

Senior members of RA in particular had already been at the coal-face for a decade, even discounting time served in the ANL. It was hardly likely they would swerve away from the goal of driving the fascists from the streets just when the possibility of it actually happening was beginning to take tangible form, and on a national basis. Moreover, their analysis from the beginning was based on the understanding that it was a case of either/or: either socialism or barbarism. (Of course, what socialism would come to represent was also moot, as the model of obsessive party building adhered to by the post-war Leninist formations had already been thoroughly exposed in their eyes as not being fit for purpose.) Because it was an analysis that left little room for manoeuvre, there was an acceptance that personal risk was, and had to be, part and parcel of the struggle. In their eyes, it followed that democratic structures would only work if the principle of this acceptance of risk applied to everyone directly involved. Thus any caterwauling in the ranks was a signal of a retreat from the principle that made physical force anti-fascism dynamic and, therefore, invariably regarded as the thin end of the wedge. Or as one RA member put it when hearing of the Hackney ultimatum: "If that's the attitude when we're winning, imagine what they'd be like if we were losing!"

Tellingly, it was evidently a time for reappraisal on the Far Right as well. Immediately after 25th May, the preliminary discussions around the need for some form of a 'super stewards' group would take place. Combat 18 was about to enter the arena.

3.10

AFA IN SCOTLAND, JUNE 1991–1992

By the summer of 1991 AFA was spreading the message up country. The AFA Northern Network had come into being in the previous eighteen months and was involved in engaging the BNP head-on in the satellite towns surrounding Manchester: Rochdale, Oldham, Burnley, Preston and so on. At the same time as the anti-poll tax movement was growing in working class communities in Scotland, another smaller, but probably no less significant, political development was also taking place, largely unnoticed by most on the Left. This was the growth and development of the BNP. AFA's campaign in Scotland was launched at a public meeting held on Friday 21st June in 1991 as a direct response to this development. And their impact on the emerging BNP in Scotland would prove both instantaneous and long lasting. Indeed, to the present day it could be argued that north of border the BNP have never properly recovered at all.

Initially, the BNP focused their efforts almost exclusively on young Glasgow Rangers fans with paper sales at Ibrox, home ground of Rangers, through identifying themselves as supporters of Ulster Loyalism.

Having developed out of the remnants of the old NF, the early leadership of the BNP in Scotland was made up of those who had previously been seen as the best of the NF's youth wing. People like Eric Brand and Gus McLeod had been Loyalist-leaning recruits to the NF who had gone to university and emerged as educated young leaders of a burgeoning BNP. Younger men like Stephen Cartwright, Scott McLean and Ian McMillan had also joined the BNP, liking the rhetoric of BNP paper sellers outside Ibrox. Cartwright and McMillan were making names for themselves with the local media, constantly seeking publicity for themselves and the BNP. This culminated in a front-page story detailing the party's growth in Scotland and featured photographs of the Glasgow organiser, Cartwright, and the Scottish Youth Organiser, McMillan. The latter lived in Dennistoun and was associated with the Rangers hooligan firm, the ICF.

Stevie: "The first time that we came across the BNP in our own area was as members of our local anti-poll tax union in the east end of Glasgow. Leafleting in Duke Street would often be interrupted by some of the younger fascists from the area coming past calling us 'IRA bastards' and generally making threats against us. We were then passed information that local Loyalists and fascists were seriously discussing the possibility of violence against some of our activists. Very quickly we moved from the need to be informally aware of what the BNP were planning to the need to be politically and physically prepared to defend ourselves against them.

"At an anti-poll tax demo in Glasgow, the BNP's three main organisers in Scotland, Cartwright, McLean and McMillan, were spotted around its edges. Members of our local group from Dennistoun, along with a few members of anti-poll tax groups from Sighthill, Possil and Pollockshields were prepared to confront them physically but were dissuaded from doing so by the chief steward and other Militant members who felt that to confront them physically would be a distraction from the real purpose of the demonstration against the local council's collusion in the implementation of the poll tax. We agreed to this as long as the stewards made it clear to the fascists that if they tried to join the march or even follow it they would be confronted."

The annual St Andrew's Day March against Racism and Fascism through Glasgow had become a regular pilgrimage for the fascists. They would turn up at the march, sometimes at its starting point, freely mixing with and abusing the marchers. Later, as the march made its way through the streets, they would arrive at a point in the city centre singing Rule Britannia and making nazi salutes. As they dispersed, supporters of the march would be picked off. Recognising that the weakness of the Left was both physical and political, the fascists felt confident enough to turn up each year and behave in this manner without fear of reprisals, even when vastly outnumbered.

This increasing confidence inevitably resulted in attacks on other Left events. After a meeting in Dennistoun supporting striking ambulance workers, local BNP members led by Ian McMillan attacked one of those who had attended with CS gas spray and batons as he was leaving. The intended targets had been SWP members. The fascists did not bank on attacking a working class activist who had links to those who were to form Glasgow AFA. Less than two weeks after this attack, Glasgow and Edinburgh BNP members combined to attack an SWP public meeting as it dispersed.

Stevie: "Two SWP members were hospitalised, as was Eric Brand, the BNP's Scottish organiser at the time, who was allegedly stabbed up the arse by one of his own over-enthusiastic gang."

The SWP relied completely upon the police to take action against their assailants. Even when fascists intimidated witnesses and their families, the SWP were more concerned with defusing any violent reaction from the militants, than in protecting and defending their own members. Four BNP members subsequently received twelve-month prison sentences for their role in the attacks. One of them was the youth organiser, Ian 'Crazy' McMillan.

In addition to the 'let sleeping dogs lie' attitude of the SWP leadership, physical force anti-fascism also had to contend with the attitude of Militant itself. Formally, Militant simply did not regard the fascists as in any way threatening politically.

Indeed, so confident were they that they could deal with the fascists purely from a political point of view that, at one point, through Tommy Sheridan, one time member of the Scottish parliament, they actually offered the BNP 'a platform' to promote debate in Pollock. This obviously ran counter to their widely stated position of 'No Platform', but the BNP in any case refused the offer. Afterwards, Militant argued that this was in fact all part of a cunning plan to lull the BNP back into the area and for them to be physically dealt with. Needless to say, this explanation did not entirely convince AFA in Glasgow.

Some months later, Militant got their comeuppance when all those present at a meeting they had organised in support of their council candidate for Penilee, Tommy Sheridan, were forced to negotiate a way out of the area after the BNP mobilised the local youth against them. The BNP leaders, Cartwright and McLean, were not only allowed into that meeting, complete with entourage, but were allowed to participate in the debate with the people who had felt so confident in Pollock but who appeared very meek when the BNP turned the tables on them in Penilee.

Quite clearly, Militant had underestimated the strength of the BNP in this area and had also seriously overestimated the ability of their own forces to physically stand up to a fascist group that had been blooding its members on the streets and in football hooligan gangs for some time. Besides, the lads that Militant brought over from Pollock were effectively seen as members of a rival gang from another scheme and, as a result, the BNP were able to mobilise on a parochial as well as a political basis in order to oppose them. After the show of strength, the BNP was firmed up as a significant political force to be reckoned with in the area, to the extent that many years later, in 1997, an AFA leafleting team came under attack from tooled-up fascists when leafleting in Penilee.

While the BNP was moving on from just selling papers at Ibrox to building links with young people in the Loyalist flute bands, by 1991 they also began to show an ambition to break out of their self-imposed recruitment ghetto of Loyalist-supporting Rangers fans. As a consequence the militant strategy was initially one of containment: to keep them confined to traditional strongholds, repel their increasingly violent attacks on the Left, and to take the fight to them where possible. RA activists then set out, as had previously been done in London, to build alliances with others on the Left who understood the dangers posed to all progressive working class activists by the fascists. Not unnaturally, given the history of co-operation south of the border, the DAM was the first port of call. Indeed it was the DAM that initiated the contact.

Stevie: "Initially, this organisation was called Glasgow Anti-Fascists [GAF] and was constituted much along the lines of an AFA branch. However, increasingly, the anarchists seemed more intent upon using GAF to promote their brand of anarchism, rather than promoting anti-fascism as an activity borne out of political necessity rather than political ideology. In one discussion between a rank-and-file GAF member and a member of the DAM, the DAM member described GAF as essentially being a branch of AFA, to which the member then argued that if "we were effectively an AFA branch anyway, why weren't we calling ourselves Anti-Fascist Action and applying to affiliate to the national body?" This idea was rejected by the DAM in favour of 'building our own local identity first and then later deciding which national bodies if any we would participate in.'"

Increasingly impatient with such subtleties, RA broke away from GAF, effectively rendering it politically useless, and set out to form AFA proper in Glasgow. Initially, the Glasgow branch of AFA found support from Red Action, Class War, the Direct Action Movement, Workers Party Scotland, Scottish Anti-Racist Movement and the Republican Bands Alliance. Sixty people attended Glasgow AFA's first public meeting at Dennistoun in June of 1991. This is an area with a large Loyalist presence and as such was being targeted by the BNP for recruitment at this time. On the night of the AFA launch Ian 'Crazy' McMillan proved to be anything but. Confronted by a large body of anti-fascists armed with a variety of weapons, "he made a fast exit from the area and persuaded the 25 boneheads and other assortments of the master race who had been mobilised to 'smash the reds', that the only smashing that night would have been their own heads on the pavement. About 25 new contacts for AFA signed up on the night" (*Red Action*, issue 60).

Outside of the immediate sponsors, the response from others on the Left was predictably somewhat less than enthusiastic. For example, when an SWP paper sale in the city centre on the same weekend became the target for the fascists who took photos of the paper sellers and gave out leaflets without response, the SWP sought to place the blame on AFA and Red Action 'squadists' for whipping up the fascists in an area where, according to their local comrades, "there is no significant fascist activity!" This followed an allegation that AFA had deliberately left fascist graffiti in order to perpetuate 'a myth of a BNP presence' which was a step away from simply accusing AFA outright of being responsible for the graffiti. In truth, in Glasgow as elsewhere, the SWP had no real interest in orientating their largely student membership to militant anti-fascist activity. Unremarkably, Militant also ignored the public meeting despite having been involved in recent mobilisations against fascists in Glasgow and Dundee.

"Groups like Militant and the SWP, at leadership level, had long settled down to the task of building the vanguard revolutionary party. Anything that interrupted that process, a cold dose of reality for example, was just simply annoying. Indeed, a distraction from the tasks faced by the leading cadres of the international proletarian revolution. Fascism could be so distracting that it was probably best not to mention it at all, even when it walked right up and kicked you, or more accurately your rank and file member, in the head. Rather than admit that their members basically aren't up to it, they construct a cock-and-bull story that there are hardly any fascists anyway! The result for them last February was that the BNP attacked one of their public meetings and hospitalised one of their members. Not one single word about this attack ever appeared in any of the SWP's publications, even after four BNP members were jailed for the attack!" (*Fighting Talk*, issue 1, 1991).

Meanwhile, within Glasgow AFA tactics were discussed in order to find a strategy that would allow the militants to cause damage to BNP morale, and also expose the lack of integrity of the liberal Left. By this time Glasgow city centre was visibly dominated by the BNP. As well as attacks on Left paper sellers, boneheads in full paramilitary regalia would parade with impunity on Saturday afternoons. Together with the targeting of left-wing meetings and individual anti-poll tax activists, BNP gangs had ensured fascism was feared as a physical force. Not unrelated, and in parallel with this aggression, there emerged the additionally growing problem of racism and racist attacks across Glasgow.

Faced with this multi-faceted problem the instinct of the militants was to simplify matters by taking the fight to the fascists. What this meant in practice was that a policy of 'zero tolerance' would be implemented against them, starting with the clear-out of the city centre. As one AFA member at the time explained: "It's time that the BNP were forced to start looking over their shoulders. Let's see how they like it when it's them and not the Asians who don't know where the next attack is coming from!"

This policy took the form of small squads of AFA members touring the city centre on the look out for fascists in the vicinity of well-known haunts. On being positively identified the fascists would, without any provocation on their part or even any warning, be physically attacked. Totally unused to such tactics the intensity of anti-fascist commitment caused evident disarray within BNP ranks in a matter of months.

Many well-known 'faces' who themselves had previously instilled fear were now themselves being intimidated from stepping into parts of the city centre. Leading 'street' elements like Ian 'Crazy' McMillan, who had earned the nickname after distinguishing himself in a particularly vicious brawl in a UVF pub, became a particular AFA target. On one occasion, after he became the main suspect for the spray painting of an anti-fascist's flat, masked men visited his house and he was forced to barricade his door to prevent them getting in. On leaving the close they spotted his motorbike. It was kicked over in order to spill petrol from the tank. Then as local urchins stood and gaped, they set fire to it before strolling off into the Glasgow night.

Already utterly paranoid and beginning to suspect he was possibly out of his depth, his morale could not have improved when a rumour surfaced in fascist/Loyalist circles that the infirmity of the one-eyed Glasgow AFA organiser was the result of him surviving a shotgun blast to the face. Though it did indeed have the effect of lending an otherwise even-featured face a rather menacing appearance, it was in actual fact the result of an accident at work that occurred while he was serving an apprenticeship as an engineer. But for 'Crazy' this unfounded rumour may possibly have been a tipping point. In any event not long afterwards the BNP youth organiser for Scotland announced his retirement from all political activity at the ripe old age of 22. Another prominent BNP member, Cumbernauld organiser, Stuart McLean, was beaten with hammers in an apparently disproportionately violent attack after he and BNP National Directorate member, Richard Fawcus, had growled at a couple of 'hip-hop boys' in Central Station. The 'hip-hop boys' in question were, in fact, key AFA activists D. and C. who were involved in the business of conducting their own tour of duty around the train stations. The specific purpose of this was to intercept BNP members coming back from their annual St Andrew's Day outing.

By now, whenever the fascists attempted to rally they were, and expected to be, met with large mobilisations and firm resistance from AFA. In Edinburgh, Dundee and Glasgow their activities were severely disrupted in violent demonstrations against them. Of these encounters, the largest and possibly most devastating came in the run-up to Christmas on 1st December 1991 when an AFA mobilisation completely closed down the BNP's annual Scottish rally. John Tyndall and other BNP leaders in attendance were witness to a rout in what, up till then, thay had hailed as their "most important area outside of London".

AFA Edinburgh sticker.

On the day the militant operation surpassed all expectations. A benefit gig held just the night before was used to organise a substantial turnout for the next morning's event. Other elements from the Left were approached for support but only Militant and the anarchists responded. One SWP full timer who did show up seemed content to play the role of liaising with the police and was reported to have been advising demonstrators not to get involved in the 'madness'. And to many witnesses madness it must have appeared to be. Organised fighting squads repeatedly confronted small groups of fascists on the way to the meeting. Along with this, a large and noisy Left presence hemmed in those already at the initial fascist meeting point, which included BNP leader, John Tyndall, who, with about twenty others, was holed up in a pub in Argyle Street. Plainly, both police and the fascists had been taken completely unawares by the size and complexity of the AFA operation.

Having being forced to reassemble at another pub near Central Station, the BNP found that this pub was also surrounded. The *Daily Record* gave the scenes a true tabloid flavour: "Women shoppers screamed in terror as an angry mob of about 130 anti-fascists – some with their faces covered – laid siege to the Gallery Bar at Central Station ... [A]s the chanting youths barricaded the two entrances to the pub fighting broke out ... Startled shoppers and tiny children were pushed aside as the angry mob spilled onto the busy road and others tried to force their way into the bar. Around 50 police officers ... with drawn batons ... intervened but were attacked as they tried to bundle youths into police vans."

Straining to put a positive spin on events, the BNP's low-key response failed to conceal the pervading sense of gloom. Having been driven there in "police vans", *British Nationalist* explained, one "BNP contingent waited in another pub while attempts were made to find an alternative meeting room nearby and to locate the other groups of party supporters in the city with whom contact had been lost. In fact neither proved possible. In the end a short rally was held in a nearby park in the gathering dusk" (*British Nationalist*, December 1991). In an interview with the *Daily Record* Tyndall remained defiant but the 'backs to the wall'-style language betrayed a profound dismay. "Our recruitment campaign in Scotland will continue. We will not give in. Scotland is our best recruitment ground. We have a better proportion of our members in Scotland than anywhere else in the UK." That Tyndall needed to be escorted down "to the pub cellar and a tunnel to safety" underscored the scale of the disaster. Aware of the political symbolism, *Red Action* opted to describe the 'tunnel' as a 'sewer'.

Up to 1st December 1991, if Scotland had genuinely been held to be the best recruitment ground for the Far Right generally, that certainly would not have been the case afterwards. Though the clashes continued unabated, it was conducted from then on with militant anti-fascism as the primary aggressor. And in seeking to maintain the loyalty of the hardcore hooligan element, the BNP profile as a political party was largely abandoned. In fact, in many ways, this stripped-down approach was following the AFA model, for it was in Scotland, arguably more than anywhere else, that militants had reduced anti-fascism to physical terror, pure and simple. It was a form of confrontation that in theory ought to have been meat and drink to BNP recruits, but in fact they struggled to cope and the entire BNP political operation was driven underground as a result. To date, if compared to other regions, they have not as yet visibly recovered.

"The Scottish branch of fascism has been under extreme pressure from militant anti-fascists for the last three years and is now unable to guarantee the safety of visiting dignitaries from south of the border. The BNP's isolation in Scotland was epitomised by the fact that they brought their 1992 rally forward by three months and moved the venue to a remote outpost in Lanarkshire. The main reason for the change of date and move away from rallying either in Edinburgh or Glasgow was not because 'the police disrupted last year's rally', as they claimed in *British Nationalist*, but was, in fact, due to the fact that their 1991 Scottish rally was physically smashed by a militant anti-fascist mobilisation organised by Glasgow AFA.

"In addition, several incidents during 1992 served notice that the BNP were literally 'under the cosh'. Fascists have found that even their safest watering holes are not immune from attack. Two BNP members were ambushed while out stickering and pursued into their pub, where further meaningful 'debate' took place. Such was the terror created by this incident that other fascists in the pub sat quietly watching one of their mates taking a beating, whilst the barman vaulted the bar and fled up the street never to be seen again. In another incident in Glasgow city centre, six fascists had to barricade themselves in a pub when they came under attack from three anti-fascists! In other incidents, boneheads from the sticks, out for the day in the big city, have been advised to dress more carefully as a result of meeting irate members of the public, keen to display their hatred of nazis. The biggest public humiliation for the fascists in Scotland came at the end of 1992 when anti-fascists clashed with BNP members before, during and after the annual march against racism and fascism in Glasgow. In all, seven BNP members required hospital treatment – the most notable being Richard Fawcus, one of the BNP's English leadership, and Stuart McLean, a local BNP organiser. The political equivalent of shooting grouse out of season?" (*Red Action*, 1994).

The militant operations were far from confined to Glasgow. Edinburgh AFA too began as it meant to go on.

Euan: "AFA had just got off the ground in Edinburgh and I suppose we were eager to get into the action, so to speak. Our debut came after a long-standing member of Militant who had attended some of the initial AFA meetings and had been turned over by the local BNP asked us for some back up on the day of the trial, in case the BNP turned up mob-handed. So at about 9am we met in Hunter Square, just off the High Street. With us was a lad from a conventional anti-racist group from the north of the city. I think he was expecting to take part in a traditional left-wing demo with placards, but about a minute after we moved off, to our surprise and delight, who did we walk into but the BNP branch organiser, G.R., and a colleague. One of the boys went up to him and said: 'You know who we are, eh?' Both of them took off, with us in pursuit. One of them tripped right in front of me, so I immediately put the boot in. Another who had spotted the trouble and come back to help, put me on the floor. He had hold of my hair all the time some of the AFA lads were beating him senseless. Eventually I got to my feet, the groups parted, they going one way, we the other. Then one of the fascists shouted 'You Red bastards!' We all started laughing as the three of them looked in a really bad way."

Indeed, when the BNP got to the court the SWP picket were reportedly so shocked at their battered appearance, they stopped chanting. It later emerged one of the BNP defendants was nursing a broken arm. To complete their misery the Sheriff hinted that if they ever appeared in front of him as shabbily dressed he would have them done for contempt of court!

3.11

BERMONDSEY, AUGUST 1991

Three months after the tactical debacle that was the anti-racist counter-demonstration at Thamesmead, elements of the National Black Caucus, led by Lee Jasper, unilaterally announced it was holding a march through Bermondsey in order to prove 'racism existed in the area'. Only a few miles from Thamesmead, Bermondsey enjoyed a lively reputation. Millwall was the local team and, after the fashion of the archetypal amateur, the march was called on the day of a home match, Saturday 24th August. On top of this, no attempt was made to conduct any research on the ground. The primary function of the endeavour was not to win 'hearts and minds', but had far more to do with securing a financial grant through proving 'racism existed'. It follows that such casualness was not entirely inconsistent with the objective. Immediately sensing the glaring weaknesses surrounding the motivation and planning, the BNP, in the weeks leading up to the day, were busy knocking on doors, cleverly calling on locals to resist the planned 'invasion of Bermondsey'.

But by midday on 24th August no more than 300 marchers assembled at Oval Station for the 'invasion'. The calculated rumours of mass support from the black community in the surrounding areas had predictably come to nothing. AFA, who anticipated trouble, decided to attend the march, anyway, as the only way to witness first hand the shambles it expected would unfold. As the march progressed it was accompanied by the constant buzz of sightings of BNP and racists waiting on the Old Kent Road. However, on turning into the estates it was instantly apparent the level of opposition had been grossly underestimated. The streets were alive, with numerous groupings of as many as sixty voicing an extremely belligerent opposition to the march. On reaching Southwark Park, the march was confronted by almost the entire population of the surrounding estates leaning from balconies and lining the streets, complete with Union Jack flags, shouting abuse at the 'invaders'.

Fighting Talk: "As we started to enter the park, further progress was prevented by a wave of some 300 racists storming across the park towards us. This was bad, but worse was to come, as two further waves of about the same numbers also charged across to join their compatriots. Fortunately they did not attack ... however there is no doubt that the vast majority ... were willing and able to physically oppose the demonstration. Equally ... the vast majority of the demonstrators were both unwilling and unable to defend themselves. As the threat became more apparent, the march stewards formed up holding hands, with their backs to the racists, and faced the demonstrators – see no evil and there is no evil! The organisers began demanding that the racists be removed from the park, claiming that the police had reneged on their promises. How can they seriously expect those that they purport to oppose to either make promises in good faith or to honour those promises once things begin to go wrong – particularly given that the most consistent chant on the march was 'Who are the racists? – the police are the racists!'"

Another eyewitness account from *Socialist Organiser* confirms the AFA account was no exaggeration. "Suddenly there was a huge roar from the park. I saw a large crowd of fascists running across the park to attack the march. It was very frightening: we were outnumbered two to one by the fascists, and in danger of being crushed against the park railings. The police drove back the mob in the park but the lull was soon broken. In the middle of a group of SWP placards, someone started to burn the Union Jack – an act of great stupidity in the circumstances. The BNP redoubled their efforts to get at us..." Meanwhile, two leading AFA security stewards on serious charges from previous encounters, though wary of joining the march, were nonetheless keen to assess the situation on the ground for themselves.

Joe: "We had been dropped off by a car at the other end of the park from where it was expected the march would be confronted. From where we were we could see many hundreds of BNP supporters near the gate, clearly determined to prevent the marchers entering. One old boy was walking his dog and stopped near us. 'What's that about?' I asked. 'They're out to get the wogs,' he replied amiably. A moment later we became aware of a growing hubbub behind us. We swung round in time to see a huge number of BNP, hundreds of them, with the lanky Richard Edmonds prominent, sweep into the park. If we could recognise him from that distance, it struck me instantly, he could recognise us. Just then the shout went up: 'There they are!' followed by a blood-curdling roar as three hundred fascists charged. Instinctively, I stepped behind a hedge and beckoned Andy to me so that we were at least concealed before making a break for it. In some situations adrenalin can actually work against you. Within seconds of taking off I could hear my feet slap against the tarmac like a couple of wet dishcloths.

"We swung right and away from them and then right again along a pathway fringing a small pond. Though concealed by some small trees and bushes we were running parallel to them but also back toward the gate they were still charging through. We both knew that if anyone of them spotted us, or the old boy informed on us, they only had to stand their ground to cut us off. If so, the chances of getting out of this situation in any reasonable shape were about slim to zero. Every one of them would want to get in at least one good kick."

As the BNP poured into the park along one path, the AFA scouts could see them through the trees. It was also obvious the BNP were still coming through the exit they were heading for. Panting, they stopped, trapped.

Andy: "Only then did we realise to our unimaginable relief that the 'they' they were after was not us but the 300-strong mob of their supporters occupying the park who the BNP had charged thinking they were marchers! Later as we left the area by car, knots of BNP 20-strong seemed to be on every corner. Travelling in the car at about 40mph we were still pointed out at least twice. I can remember one scene where Jarvis was addressing a mixed group. Standing at the back were a young boy and an old man. The placards they were carrying read 'Tomorrow belongs to us'. We certainly were in no position to argue."

Racist rioting lasted several hours after the marchers had escaped from the neighbourhood. The BNP had been gifted an opportunity for a show of force the like of which had been unknown since the heyday of the 1970s, and they grabbed it. Race relations were probably set back a decade. Lecomber would later claim that in the region of 800 had responded to the BNP call, but to militants present on the day this tally was if anything a little on the conservative side. By contrast, a leaflet put out by the SWP at the time rather bizarrely refers to the BNP operation, the biggest show of strength by any Far Right party since the heyday of the NF, as a "minor victory" for the BNP, while conversely the counter-demo in Thamesmead was pronounced a success, on the basis that nazi attempts to mobilise had been "thwarted". This, despite the fact that within just three months, the odds of ten to one in the anti-fascists favour at Thamesmead had been resoundingly reversed in Bermondsey. Naturally, neither could be presented with any sense of objectivity because, as far as the SWP leadership was concerned, fascism was not an issue. But

Bermondsey 1991, one of only two occasions when the BNP could be said to have 'controlled the streets'.

this may merely have been the public face. For behind the scenes the same SWP leadership was already toying with the idea of re-launching the ANL.

Searchlight may well have had the Bermondsey adventure in mind when its *Community Handbook,* containing information and advice on how best to respond to fascism and racism at a grass-roots community level, was published in 1995. Contemporary anti-fascism simply had to be rooted in the community, it pronounced. With national anti-fascist organisations, such as the ANL and presumably AFA, the handbook concludes, the principle problem is their inability to put down local roots. "All too often they are seen by local people as 'parachuting' into areas with serious problems of racial violence, gaining some publicity and moving on again." In support of the proposition, Copsey quotes anti-racist legend A. Sivanandan who denounces what he describes as 'floating' anti-fascism, whose "actions tend to be reactive and follow a pre-set formula, organising around a specific eventuality or threat. But such floating anti-fascism renders local communities mere venues for disconnected actions and prey to the fascist backlash once the marchers have gone."

In the first place, it should be pointed out this criticism of 'parachuting' was hardly original or uncommon, certainly not by 1995. Such arguments were often employed by conservative anti-racist organisations in order to undermine support for any type of direct action of which they did not approve, particularly actions that might involve or invite violence. But differences over tactics aside the Searchlight/ Copsey/Sivanandan evaluation contains three fundamental theoretical blunders.

Of these the most glaring is the criticism of anti-fascism being 'reactive' rather than proactive. By definition anti-fascism is reactive. It is at heart a counter-measure and it can do no other than organise against some "specific eventuality or threat". Indeed, directing forces against some 'specific threat' is essentially what anti-fascism is designed to do. It does not and has never contained within itself, as some mistakenly believe, the basis for a political solution *per se*. It is a wholly defensive formation: a consequence of progressive forces having already blundered and lost some fairly basic arguments along the way.

Which directs us to another principle flaw in the Searchlight/Copsey/Sivanandan remedy: the notion that racial justice could ever take root in predominately white working class areas, without being 'connected' to the wider question of social justice is delusional. And if, quite properly, the anti-racist element is indeed tied into the wider question of social justice, then surely sooner or later the remedy it proposes would be obliged to take electoral form. A scenario that would immediately pose a contradiction for council-funded bodies like the NMP or TWAFA for whom Copsey repeatedly expresses admiration, as the onus would be on them to support, tacitly or otherwise, the candidates of the party that pay their wages – most likely the very people who carry the responsibility for the growth of the Far Right to begin with.

Thirdly, there is the proposition that any anti-fascist intervention almost automatically "renders" the host community "prey to a fascist backlash once the marchers have gone." Quite apart from it being a guideline that if followed would lead to utter passivity, it is fatally blind to the vital question of who emerges victorious from the encounter.

Joe: " Crucially, in the event it kicks off, what decides matters is – who wins. It is necessary to understand the fascist psyche. The 'backlash' becomes a possibility only when, as in Bermondsey, they win. A resounding defeat means they will be more concerned with licking their wounds and working out how to avoid a replay to have time to bother anyone else. That has always been our experience."

Tellingly, the BNP never made the political inroads it might have expected to in Bermondsey. At the time the candidate, Steve Tyler, an articulate local organiser, was considered a leading light in the BNP. Part of his skill in organising leafleting and canvassing was to have his troops assemble outside Surrey Quays tube station. One Saturday morning the canvassing team was attacked in broad daylight. Tyler and White (from the BNP HQ) were singled out, knocked to the ground and beaten unconscious. Tim Hepple, Searchlight mole within the BNP would later attribute this "bad beating" to "unknown assailants", while Searchlight itself hinted it might have been down to rivalry with the NF. Such head scratching was, to say the least, disingenuous, as the militant *modus operandi* had by 1991 been in vogue for well over a decade. Though Tyler did recover physically, he left the BNP for good shortly afterwards, and the BNP operation in the Bermondsey locality would never recover politically. Here then, considering the 'floating anti-racism' that preceded it, was a model of 'parachuting' in no genuine anti-fascist could honestly condemn.

3.12

THE LIBERAL 'LEFT'

From early in 1991 the intensity of fascist and anti-fascist activity was increasing, and not just in London. The BNP, who had now completely overtaken the NF as the dominant fascist party, were active from Edinburgh to Southampton. Together with their itinerary of meetings, marches and paper sales were added attacks on left-wing activities, especially SWP paper sales. As a visibly soft target, the SWP suffered badly at the hands of fascist hit squads. At first the SWP leadership adopted a policy of denial, with no mention of these activities in *Socialist Worker*, but the damaging effect that these attacks were having on the morale of the rank and file meant that this censorship could not hope to be sustained indefinitely.

Together with these difficulties, the rising level of race attacks, as well as the heightened media profile of the Far Right at home and abroad, not to mention the increasing numbers being drawn toward AFA, meant that anti-fascism, if only for reasons of good business, could not afford to be ignored for too much longer.

The militants were fully aware of a possible U-turn but were unclear as to exactly how it would come about, or the best way to deal with it when it happened. Their primary concern was that AFA structures could be swamped by organisations such as the SWP, or possibly Militant, politically encouraging their members to join the existing branches *en masse*. Alternatively, they could set up new branches, even possibly create entirely new regions. Under the democratic structure that existed, the implications were ominous. And having made the mistake of allowing the militants to be outmanoeuvred and excluded from decision-making in their own organisation between 1985 and 1989, they were determined on only one thing: it would not happen again.

These reservations aside, AFA also felt compelled, whenever the opportunity afforded itself, to approach the Left with a view to cooperation. With the wider numbers available to these groups, by working to an agreed plan, militants could put the fascists under further pressure, and, less selflessly, the involvement of greater numbers would also provide cover for leading 'players' against being targeted and picked off by the authorities. However, in the time honoured fashion, the AFA olive branch was generally rejected out of hand. Yet by the autumn of 1991 the militants were by now utterly convinced by their own analysis, and had an increasing faith in their own ability to deliver. With or without the support of the wider Left, this inner confidence led AFA to mount its most ambitious campaign in the east end of London which was now also officially a national priority for the BNP.

On 8th September that year, AFA had surprised everyone by organising the biggest anti-fascist event for over a decade, drawing 10,000 people to the Unity Carnival on Hackney Downs. Supported by a wide range of organisations, from the Hackney Joint Shop Stewards Committee to the Fire Brigades Union, the Carnival programme again drew attention to rising levels of race attacks and urged people to become pro-active. "We have organised today's event to draw attention to the growing number of racist attacks, especially in east London. The fact that some sections of the community virtually live under siege is unacceptable and we hope you are prepared to do more than just come to this symbolic show of unity. Support the activities on the back of this programme to get organised and do something to *stop* the racist attacks."

Originally, it had been intended that the event should be held in Bethnal Green, but permission from Tower Hamlets Council had been withheld on security grounds. But even in neighbouring Hackney, AFA knew that in organising such a large event, it was nonetheless very much putting itself on offer. Accordingly, security was very tight with eighty security stewards, armed with a variety of coshes, bars and baseball bats, on duty and in position from 8am that morning. It is perhaps instructive, given the chaos AFA had shown itself capable of causing to opposition set pieces, that the marshalling and discipline was so commanding throughout the day there was not one single arrest. One St John's ambulance worker commented afterwards that it was the "best organised event he had ever attended." While demonstrating an increasing wariness of the militants, the BNP did continue to vent their frustration on the wider Left, with an attack on a Class War conference in Stoke Newington, for instance, on 28th September.

Two weeks later on 12th October, AFA staged a rally in Whitechapel dedicated to "the lessons of Cable Street" and, less than a fortnight later, led a 300-strong demonstration against the fascist paper sale at Brick Lane. Immediately following the carnival, their focus turned to putting the final touches to a major national demonstration against racist attacks on Remembrance Sunday, 10th November. Not down Whitehall this time but instead through Bethnal Green, the very locale British fascism considered its historic heartland. Against a backdrop of a photo of the battle of Cable Street, posters advertising the event read: 'Beating the Fascists: a great East End tradition.' Though this was in part a deliberate provocation, the demonstration had a more serious message: to draw attention to the connection between the political potential of the BNP and a rising level of race attacks which had for so long crystallised militant concerns.

"We have chosen the East End because of the high incidence of racist attacks in that area. But increasingly the fascists and racists are active all over the country, and a national march will be an important demonstration of working class opposition to them. The increase in racist violence has been widely reported. Nationwide, it is estimated that there is an attack every 26 minutes, and east London has the highest level of attacks in the country. The fascist British National Party (BNP) have made their work in east London a national priority. They held three marches and stood five candidates in local elections in 1990. In the St Peter's ward election (Bethnal Green, August 1990), the BNP's one-in-eight vote represented, in a ward evenly divided along racial lines, some 25% of the disillusioned white working class vote" (AFA leaflet).

Up to that point, AFA apart, the Left was united in denying there was a problem. But by any standards an anti-fascist march mobilising in the region of 4,000 people and attracting widespread media coverage nationally simply had to leave an imprint. And it did. Just as instructive, the unswerving work AFA had put in over the previous twelve months caused both the BNP and NF to duck the calculated militant challenge on the day. As it was almost unheard of for any major left-wing initiative not to attract fascist opposition, for AFA here was proof that militant anti-fascism could 'neutralise' any area, even one as notorious as Bethnal Green. Indeed, so daunting was the AFA reputation, that not only had the organised Right abandoned Bethnal Green, the local working class population on whom the BNP and NF relied on for support appeared to be just as intimidated.

Tracey: "As we went down Bethnal Green Road there was practically no one on the streets. Even the area outside pubs where the BNP were known to drink was deserted. You could see people standing on seats inside watching the march go by, but in total silence. It was almost eerie. Throughout the march the sole gesture of defiance was restricted to two doddery old men, and someone waving a white hanky from a balcony. But when we got into Whitechapel, Asian kids greeted us like a liberating army. The contrast with the near nightmare in Bermondsey could not be more marked."

Flyer advertising the AFA national demonstration on 10th November 1991.

Another notable sign of progress was the appearance on the back of the march of several hundred SWP. After a decade of studiously maintaining the 'fascists were tiny', the SWP were not only heavily represented on the march, but with routine duplicity had even claimed in a radio interview that it was, in fact, an SWP rather than an AFA initiative. Thus, when denied speaking rights at the pre-march rally on the grounds that the SWP had not publicly sponsored the march, SWP full-timer Julie Waterston responded by heckling the female Red Action speaker. "Let's hear what shite you're gonna come out with!" Her screeching was halted when, without ceremony, she was taken by the throat by a senior AFA steward and lifted kicking and screeching out of earshot, with an outraged but ineffectual SWP train in tow. It was a small incident, but one that amply illustrates the level of scorn felt in AFA ranks for the Left as a whole, and the SWP leadership in particular. And while it was still some weeks before the impact of the AFA initiative on the Left's position became fully apparent, AFA ended 1991 buoyant and self-confident.

A further indication of AFA's political development had been the launch of the magazine *Fighting Talk* in September 1991. Previously, anti-fascists had relied on *Searchlight* for information as well as publicity for activities, but over the years this relationship had, to say the least, become strained. Searchlight's willingness to collaborate with everyone and anyone, and their ever-changing attitude to AFA – sometimes for, sometimes against – made the AFA decision to publish its own magazine a necessity. For the first time militant anti-fascists had their own voice. It can surely have been one of the very few left-wing publications of its size to uniformly turn a profit.

Central to AFA's strategy in the East End at this time was to try and encourage the involvement and support of groups and individuals from within the black and Asian communities who were under attack. As always, tactical advantage intertwined with what might otherwise only have sounded like high-sounding principle. Exactly what AFA had in mind was laid out at a public meeting in Whitechapel.

"Tower Hamlets has the highest ratio of race attacks in a country where it is estimated an attack occurs every 26 and a half minutes. It is only in this area of London that the BNP/NF are allowed to operate openly. It is not a coincidence … at the moment many areas of Tower Hamlets are divided along racial lines. To transform this situation and isolate the BNP, we must first destroy the conditions and climate in which they prosper, by polarising the entire community on political lines. Therefore our first job is not to unite people but to divide them … between fascist and anti-fascist, racist and non-racist, militant and moderate, the passive and the active. It is our intention to smash the existing [racial] status quo, so it is not to coalitions we look but to co-insurgents" (*Red Action*, issue 58, spring 1991).

Overtures to the local Asian youth began promisingly enough, particularly when contact was established with one individual, Mac M., whose family had been involved in a conscious fight against the racists and fascists for over a decade. A photo of his brother, who had been slashed by racists from the nape of his neck to his lower back often featured on anti-racist leaflets. Mac, having already sampled what the Left had to offer in the shape of Workers Against Racism, a propaganda offshoot of the Revolutionary Communist Party, judged the militant *modus operandi* the more realistic and down to earth. In turn, in Mac the AFA leadership saw a potentially invaluable conduit and ambassador between themselves and local Asian youth. He had already demonstrated his influence when his prompt intercession served to prevent a misunderstanding between a large group of young Asians and some AFA members, who had been mistaken for BNP interlopers, from turning ugly. But if the militants could see the vast potential, they were not the only ones involved who were alert to the possible political fall-out.

After a number of meetings with leading AFA members, Mac agreed to publicly come out as an AFA supporter. But just before he did so, events took a sinister turn, when Special Branch officers called at his home and, without mincing words, calmly stated that unless all contact with the militants ceased with immediate effect, they would "fit him up".

Joe: "Obviously both SB and ourselves knew how valuable to us he would be. Here was a leader of local Asian youth in Bethnal Green who was prepared to publicly throw in his lot with militant anti-fascism. As dynamic as this would be in tipping the balance locally, the repercussions would be felt outside of Bethnal

AFA march in the East End, 1991.

Green and, of course, might not be restricted to the single issue of anti-fascism, either. Because of all that we knew, a fit-up was far from inconceivable, and when he said he was going to have to drop out, hand on heart, we had no convincing arguments to persuade him otherwise."

Strangely, despite securing his acquiescence, Special Branch seemingly decided to make good their threat anyway. For at 9am on Christmas morning in 1991, a seriously hung-over Joe Reilly was woken by a call from a hysterical and, to him, almost unintelligible Asian woman. It turned out to be Mac's mother. Mac had given her his number. She was phoning from the police station. Her entire family, including children as young as nine, had been arrested in the night and were at that time still held in custody. Police claimed "a shotgun had been found on the roof." Reilly somehow found a sympathetic solicitor and the family were released within a matter of hours, pending further inquires.

At the Whitechapel meeting Mac was to address, the chair, a Workers Power member, so over-indulged the SWP present it degenerated into a polemic between the SWP and members of the audience. To the disgust of Red Action, the young Asians present were allowed to drift out and away. Thereafter, the AFA strategy lost momentum. Special Branch apart, political elements, including individuals associated with the NMP, were working hard behind the scenes to turn young Asians away from AFA. Considerably less discreet was Tower Hamlets councillor, Jalal Uddin, who told the *Docklands Recorder* that; "Asians could stand up to racists and didn't need any help from people like Anti-Fascist Action" (*Docklands Recorder*, 22nd November 1990).

Given the level of opposition, it is hardly a surprise that the AFA hard-liners never managed to overcome the loss of impetus resulting from Special Branch intimidation. Today, when considering the state of 'separate development', officially labelled the 'promotion of diversity' in which a separatist BNP thrives, the opportunity lost in 1991 was arguably not just a set-back for anti-fascist militancy but for the cause of anti-racism/anti-fascism as a whole.

3.13

THE NORTHERN NETWORK, 1991

From about the mid-1980s fascist activity in the north-west of England had been largely confined to the mill towns surrounding the city of Manchester. Places such as Rochdale, Bolton, Wigan, Blackburn, Burnley and Oldham. Having been literally kicked off the streets of Manchester by the 'squadists', the NF had not made a determined or sustained attempt to operate politically within the city boundaries for a decade. For the BNP, too, every attempt to put down sustainable roots in the city ended in near catastrophe. The first issue of *Fighting Talk* that appeared in September 1991 analysed the state of play:

"Manchester BNP has suffered several set-backs over the past year. Firstly, their attempt to organise a rally in Blackburn ended in disaster when they found they couldn't attract sufficient local support, and had to cancel the event. The few unwitting fascists who did turn up found themselves unwillingly involved in some impromptu 'street theatre' and received an escort out of town by the local constabulary.

"The prestigious 'Friends of Oswald Mosley' meeting, which was organised by the local branch, and for which they were to provide stewards, was cancelled when the true nature of the event was revealed to the owners of the hotel in which the meeting was to be held. This was followed a couple of weeks later by another 'secret' meeting ending in chaos, when the management of Parker's Hotel in the city refused entry to John Tyndall and his handful of followers. This led to the Fuehrer addressing the masses on a patch of waste ground behind a railway station. Unfortunately for the dedicated few, some of the wasteland ended up on them!

"In November 1990, a clash between anti-fascists and fascists outside Mother Mac's, a pub in the city centre, left two fascists needing hospital treatment. The pub had been used by the BNP for branch meetings and had been under surveillance for some time. The irony was that on several occasions they could be heard boasting that the 'Reds' would never suspect them to be holding meetings in a pub managed by an Irish landlord."

Perhaps the most dramatic illustration of the undimmed resolve of Manchester anti-fascists had occurred the previous year following the annual Manchester Martyrs Commemoration march through the city. Traditionally, this event had been violently opposed by fascists and Loyalists. Of the latter, by far the largest and most militant contingent travelled in coaches from Liverpool, organised by the Independent Loyal Orange Lodge (ILOL), a militant break-away from the mainstream Orange Order, which liked to boast of a direct connection to the UVF death-squads. On average at least two fifty-seater coaches, plus cars would travel from Liverpool and then join up by pre-arrangement with local Loyalists and NF supporters somewhere on the route about twelve noon. As usual, by the time the march rallied in a local Pakistani centre at about 4pm, it was nearly dark, and so, aware of the danger of loitering in the vicinity, the counter-demonstrators who had harried the march throughout the day liked to make tracks.

For some time the level of support coming from Liverpool had been a concern to the organisers and to anti-fascists. Not only did the additional numbers of fighters considerably embolden the NF, but perhaps more than that, the Manchester police were publicly beginning to tinker with the idea of employing the spectre of 'Loyalist' violence in order to justify banning the march altogether. Chief Constable James Anderton had publicly said as much. Needless to say, any such ban would be greeted by the NF not just as a major moral victory in itself, but would also be presented as a vindication of fascist tactics of intimidation generally. After toying with some ideas, including staging a breakdown of a van on the motorway decorated with Tricolours and other paraphernalia as an enticement to the returning Loyalists to stop their coaches, it was finally agreed something requiring considerably less personnel would have to suffice.

On the morning of the march, stewards travelled into Longsight to take control of the market and the surrounding access roads. Four vanloads emptied onto the market, while the police made the short hop from Longsight police station to take up their positions. Suddenly, a different mob of about forty casuals appeared at the top of Dickinson Road, and instead of heading for the parade of shops where the Loyalists and fascists, who had yet to appear, would normally congregate, they began to drift toward the assembly point. Rumours had reached the organisers that the Chelsea Headhunters were mobilising to supplement the counter-demonstrators. Was this them?

Denis: "We pulled eight lads together and slipped away from the market. On the way Dessie goes to Nadir, 'You'd better stay back otherwise they'll suss us.' 'That's discrimination,' Nadir replies and ignores him as we cross over Dickinson Road and walk right into the back of them. Two mounted police are on either side of this group as we begin to mingle. A couple of our lads speaking in soft low tones introduce themselves and explain the level of violence they could expect as the day wore on. The wolves were in the herd and they knew it. Unsure what was going to happen or what to do, they tried to edge away but as we were in the middle of them it made it difficult for them to pull away and re-group. The tension and unease emanating from them transmitted itself to the horses who began twitching, neighing and backing up, announcing to their riders that something was awry. The police responded by urging their horses into the middle of the group forcing an opening. We stood our ground but our friends moved almost as a flock to place themselves on the other side of the horses, away from us. They then pulled further back to Stockport Road and headed back into town. They were not seen again that day."

A day that began badly for the Loyalist supporters was destined to end disastrously. As night drew in, with the meeting just starting, a packed van, noticeably low on it axles, edged slowly out of the car park adjacent to the hall. Police probably assumed it contained marchers innocently heading for home. But inside were anti-fascist heavies – in more ways than one. Bar the driver, almost everyone was either 6ft or over, and built accordingly. A name check of the occupants would have revealed some of the most hard-line anti-fascists in the country. Accompanying 'the London lot' were forceful 'Mancs'*, some of whom worked the doors in the burgeoning club scene in the city at the time. Their target was not just any old right-wing stragglers, but what anti-fascist intelligence had identified as the main ILOL 'string-pullers'. Quite unaware they had been under surveillance from the moment they arrived by car in Manchester that morning, the Loyalists nevertheless walked briskly in a tight group to the cars they had parked in Rusholme. It was a cold wintry Sunday evening about 5.30pm. It had rained earlier and the streets were quiet with very little activity.

Had the Loyalists been armed with a little more street savvy the sight of a van cruising past, only to return moments later heading in the opposite direction, would have been enough to send hackles rising. But no such collective instinct seemingly existed. These were not street-fighting men but more white-collar middle management.

Suddenly the van swerved into the kerb and pulled up sharply alongside them, causing the sliding doors to crash back so suddenly one of the bulky occupants who had been crouching near the door was catapulted onto the pavement. Quickly he scrambled on to all fours but rather than lose the element of surprise the others used his broad 16-stone frame as a springboard for the assault. "Go! Go! Go!" Identifiable boot-prints were found on his light-coloured bomber jacket afterwards.

Joe: "There were no weapons, but none were needed. The attack was so swift, not one of them got away. One, I remember, was whacked so hard he travelled three or four feet through the air before hitting a fence post and crumpling. Another trying to fight off a black lad from London soon resembled a rag-doll. Within less than a minute half a dozen bodies were prone and unmoving. The unluckiest was the one who had mingled with a bus queue and so avoided the first wave, only to be caught in the backwash as everyone put in at least one boot as they headed back toward the

* One of the passengers, Belfast-born Paddy Logan, would be shot dead by unidentified assassins at his home years later. To date, no one has ever been charged.

van. As the first Loyalist went down, two middle-aged women complete with Union Jack umbrellas instinctively sought to raise the alarm, but, possibly recognising in the demeanour of the attackers a risk to themselves, walked off into the night, not once daring to look back. As had rightly been anticipated, the 'Rusholme massacre' ended for good Loyalist ambitions with regard to Manchester."

To outsiders it may well have looked as if the city was sewn up, but privately those occupying the top table were fully aware of how hard-earned was their supremacy and correspondingly, now the bar was raised to such a ruthless standard, any small lapse in concentration on their side would invite calamity to come calling.

It was early in 1989 when the idea of doing a gig in Manchester was floated with a view to building on the public bond that had developed between the Angelic Upstarts and AFA in London; Dave Hann volunteered to check for a venue, arrange publicity, security, and so on. Whether it was down to inexperience, whether he wanted the plaudits or possibly he genuinely believed the fascists wouldn't dare try anything in Manchester, outside of a small circle, senior anti-fascists in the city were never fully tied into the plan.

Unbeknown to Hann, in some of the mill towns surrounding Manchester, the news of the much-hated Mensi's pending arrival created a tremendous buzz of excitement, especially among the neo-nazi skinhead element who immediately began to make preparations. Such was the intensity that, in the weeks running up to it, one prominent anti-fascist in the city, Nadir, picked up rumours from sympathetic barrow boys in the local market of plans by Rochdale skins to turn over a gig in Manchester. Knowing little of the politics of that particular subculture and their obsession with Mensi, widely regarded by them as a renegade, he was more puzzled than alarmed, as he had no reason to connect the rumour with the AFA fundraiser. Come the night in question and The Swinging Sporran, slap bang in the middle of Manchester, is rammed with neo-nazi boneheads "like fucking beans on toast," as one awed gig-goer put it later.

Denis: "I turned up with Hefty, Gerry and Nads. We had catered for enough to man the door and a bit of chucking out, if required. Instantly, from the numbers we could see something else was going to be needed. Not exactly panicking we decide to look round to try and take proper stock of the situation. When we reconvene, Nadir offers the opinion that 'It isn't too bad, I counted about thirty or so.' 'There's far more than that,' Hefty replies. After a brief exchange it becomes apparent that, whereas Hefty's total was based entirely on the venue area upstairs, Nad's count was restricted solely to the downstairs bar! Around eighty all told. A quick assessment of the situation indicated that as long as we didn't allow any more upstairs, which was the gig venue, we could buy ourselves time to get proper backup up in place. The view was that the skins weren't likely to properly kick off until the gig was well under way and they were nicely liquored. We began to draw up a shortlist, and me, Hefty and Nads set off to round them up. Dave was to stay behind. Before departing it was fully understood that on no account was anyone to be let into the gig area until we returned with the necessary security to control the door."

Less than an hour, later an impressive unit of a dozen plus, suitably armed with claw hammers and similar implements of destruction, assembled outside The Sporran, the plan being to first take control of the door, prevent any more coming in, and then begin weeding out the undesirables. However, upon entering the downstairs bar it was immediately apparent there would need to be a change of plan, as 30 or so neo-nazis who had previously been downstairs had, in the meantime, joined the 50 or so already upstairs. "Who the fuck let them in?" an irate Dessie Noonan inquires. "It was that or the manager said he would pull the gig," Hann explains. "What does the manager think is going to happen now?" Nadir asks, all innocence.

At 6ft 4ins and weighing in at around 18 stone, the knife-scarred visage of Noonan automatically became the focus for the suddenly apprehensive skins as he surveyed the venue. He beckons Hann to him: "Get on stage and tell them they will have to leave." Over the mike the challenge is laid down. "This is an anti-fascist benefit, any right-wingers should be advised to leave now… or… they're getting it." By now the rest of the team are spread around the room, primed to respond to the slightest hint of resistance. But there is little reaction with each and every skin individually mulling over the proposition. Each of them wondering, 'Do they mean me?' In the absence of a natural leader coming to the fore, the collective response is to keep the head down, avoid eye contact and hope not to be noticed. As one fascist attempts to roll down his shirtsleeves in order to conceal some compromising tattoos, Hefty makes his move, grabbing the right-winger and hustling him toward the stairs. In seconds the bar begins to clear as others eagerly join the exodus. No heroes here. In as little as three minutes the neo-nazis have been herded down the narrow stairs, through the bar and into the night. Apart from a brief scuffle at the door and a few small stones thrown at the windows, the prospect of violence of potentially medieval proportions being unleashed had caused the neo-nazi strike to fold without a real punch being thrown.

It was from this unforgiving template that Manchester AFA would formally be re-launched in November 1991. With John P. having been blacklisted and eventually dropping out of activity in the late '80s, and Denis C. moving to London in 1990, a political vacuum now existed in Manchester. It was quickly filled by a triumvirate, made up of Gerry M., a recently arrived Glaswegian, Carol W., a well-respected ten-year veteran of activity in the city, and Dave Hann.

Previously the centre of activity for AFA in the North had centred on Leeds. There, Gordon Lunn, a bluff trades council activist who attended meetings in a sports jacket and cardigan, pulled the strings and largely set the political tone for anti-fascism in the north-west region as well. From the outset, along with Geoff Robinson from Bradford, he was a political foe and vocal opponent of the militant delegates, particularly from London. At one AFA Secretariat meeting, he described a *Guardian* photograph that depicted a female AFA member being physically assaulted by a police officer in a clash outside South Africa House on Remembrance Day as counter-productive. On another occasion, he insisted, "Nazis in Leeds were harder than nazis in London." Privately, the London leadership regarded him and his cronies with derision, describing them as 'Lunnites'. With the formal integration of Manchester into the new AFA regional structures complementing the signing up of a particularly muscular DAM branch in Liverpool to the Northern Network, the centre of political influence shifted from Leeds westward. With Manchester-born former Militant full-timer, John H. joining Red Action not long afterwards, the new centre of AFA operations in the North West was consolidated.

Unable to organise in Manchester proper, by the early 1990s the BNP focused on the satellite towns in the surrounding hills – Oldham, Burnley, Rochdale, Blackburn and Pendle. So rather than sit back and await the inevitable 'invasion' of Manchester, it was decided AFA should confront this embryonic growth at source. While it proved a critical decision strategically over the longer term, on the very first outing of the 'new' AFA absolute catastrophe was only narrowly avoided. Just.

Jon: "From the very start AFA in the north-west knew it was up against it. The fascists always had fighters there, they had always had connections and unfortunately they always had a certain electoral base. The first day out for the newly relaunched Manchester branch was in Rochdale and showed how things were going to be. The BNP had a fair few likely lads, maybe about forty plus, and had never been up against AFA before. On the other hand the AFA stewards' group was only a few days old, and with the exception of Red Action, had no real experience. With about even numbers the BNP came charging at us. It was make or break time. People looked at each other uncertain on how it was going to go – fight or flight? Then the two leading RA people stepped forward and broke bottles off the wall. Instantly people rallied, the fascists slowed, then stopped, uncertainly. Next thing we were into them. For many, that day set the tone for the five-year campaign that followed. Had it gone the other way, who knows?"

Before long, Tyndall, aware of the damage being inflicted on what was otherwise resonant terrain, decided to shore up morale by encouraging members from other areas, including London, to stiffen BNP resolve in the region. This influx now posed a problem for AFA who faced the prospect of being seriously outnumbered for the first time. Gerry made an approach to a senior member of Red Action pointing out that, as the BNP were sending coaches up, shouldn't London AFA do likewise? "No way!" was the unequivocal response. "If we tried to match them man for man, AFA would be bankrupt in a month. In any case, if they are demanding national mobilisations – this is only proof you are doing your job, isn't it?" he said smiling and went to walk off. "Well, what about a carload of 'advisers' then?" Gerry pleaded. "Not necessary either," came the reply. "Just make sure you pick a position on the day where you feel you cannot lose and if conditions permit, build on it." Though the briefest of exchanges, it does reveal not only the hit-and-run nature of the operation but the essentially guerrilla mindset that came with it.

Denis: "How it would work is that, say the BNP mobilise two hundred and we only have forty – knowing where they are likely to mob up, the very first thing is to mobilise your own outfit a sufficient distance from them to avoid crossing swords with them early on in the day where their superior numbers could be decisive. Then by assessing intelligence from scouts you begin to edge nearer as the day progresses. Essentially what you are looking at all the time is intelligence to allow you to second guess them, but also for any apparent loss of concentration whereby a section of theirs is left behind, breaks away or, for whatever reason, momentarily hands the superiority in numbers to us. Five to one was a favoured ratio because, apart from taking any element of contest out of the clash, it also meant maximum damage could be done in seconds so that by the time police arrived we were long gone, without any prospect of arrests and with morale high, looking for fresh quarry. Two or three hits like that over a day would give a far healthier return in terms of disruption, damage to morale, and general loss of face than any one big set-piece confrontation requiring at the very least five times the numbers. This is one reason we always punched far above our weight."

On the eve of what was likely to be a major clash with the BNP in Rochdale in the run-up to the General Election on 4th April 1992, Gerry and Dave were arrested in Rochdale. Red Action stickers were found in their possession. Following their arrests, police also obtained warrants allowing a search of their homes. They were kept in overnight, probably in the hope the AFA

BNP founder John Tyndall.

demonstration might be called off or disrupted. However, such contingencies had long been catered for with plans for the day carried out by able deputies. Later, both activists were released without charge. By this stage the authorities, having worked to a plan of targeting key players across the AFA network, had begun to realise it was not working effectively, largely due to an inability to secure convictions when charges could be laid. So the strategy was largely abandoned in favour of setting out to 'criminalise' the organisation as a whole.

In accordance with the Tyndall edict, and as two firm devotees of the BNP as a 'party of power' anyway, leading BNP figures like Richard Edmonds from London and John Peacock from Leicester routinely made their way to Rochdale in order to beef up the campaign of their candidate, ex-squaddie and ex-Tory, Ken Henderson. The Northern Network rose to the challenge.

"AFA mobilised over 200 people to oppose the BNP rally. We even successfully managed to persuade the ANL to join a demonstration at the fascists' redirection point, rather than simply give out leaflets miles away from them ... Having occupied their first redirection point and driven away a number of BNP thugs who were being bussed in for the rally, AFA learnt that the main fascist force had moved to another pub. Immediately, we argued that the demonstration should follow them" (*Fighting Talk*, issue 3).

AFA made their way to the pub and immediately fighting broke out. The BNP were driven back. *Fighting Talk* continues: "We left them cowering inside, awaiting police protection. When the bulk of the other counter-demonstrators arrived we simply surrounded the pub, withstood police attempts to clear us off and kept the fascists pinned down for almost three hours. Finally, instead of a rally, the fascists were escorted out of town by the police."

Three weeks later on 25th April, 120 anti-fascist fighters from "all over the north" were mobilised to confront a BNP leafleting operation in Rochdale. Again AFA were successful in spoiling the fascist activity.

"A third attempt to rally by the BNP a couple of weeks later was cancelled at the last moment when a suitable venue could not be found. AFA still mobilised, anyway. We had no sooner started to leaflet one of the areas they were standing in when word reached us that the fascists had been spotted in a pub on the other side of town. A flying column of anti-fascists was despatched to the pub in which the BNP members had hidden themselves. No sooner had the anti-fascists arrived than the pub doors were locked and bolted. At this moment the BNP's minibus was spotted at the rear of the pub. It was set on with glee, and hundreds of pounds worth of damage was done to the van while the master race cowered inside the pub. One anti-fascist who returned incognito to the pub in the evening was told that the landlord, fearing for the safety of his pub, had considered throwing the fascists out into the baying mob, until two of the boneheads burst into tears, and another disgraced himself in a somewhat smellier manner" (*Red Action*, issue 63).

A week later the BNP did manage to hold a rally on the steps of the Town Hall. The success of this operation was entirely down to a last minute change of plans, and, of course, a considerable police presence. A BNP rally in Dewsbury on 29th June saw further clashes with three AFA members arrested. At the beginning of 1993 news of a threat to the AFA band The Blaggers saw a large mobilisation of over one hundred stewards travel to Blackpool to secure the venue and vicinity. A large numbers of fascists were spotted lurking along the motorway services, "too frightened to enter the venue," according to *Melody Maker* (27th January 1993).

The next notable rendezvous between AFA and the BNP in the North West came in the tiny town of Colne in June when the latter put up a candidate in a council by-election there. An election meeting was arranged for the final Saturday before polling day, but rather than contest the town centre, the venue selected by BNP organisers was a community centre in the middle of a park, on the edge of town. If they had thought such a display of self-effacement might see militants downgrade their own response they were wrong. Bright and early, an 80-strong militant task force arrived to occupy the entrance to the hall. Not for the first time the police convinced themselves they were BNP and when about 30 genuine BNP, complete with flags, appeared on the other side of the park, police duly herded the not unwilling militants in their direction. Entering into the spirit of things "AFA members cheered and 'Sieg-Heiled', hoping to entice the fascists into the park" (*Manchester Red Action*, Bulletin No 6).

Despite, or because of, this encouragement the right-wingers began to edge nervously back toward the park perimeter, and so AFA charged. Only the intervention of police dog handlers prevented a total rout. Having re-grouped, the BNP organisers were more than happy in the circumstances to settle for a meeting in a corner of a field. But it was an arrangement that did some late and befuddled BNP arrivals few favours when they "ended up on the wrong side of police lines and paid heavily for it." Meanwhile, the Anti-Nazi League who had inevitably opted for a leafleting session in Colne town centre, "were in a quandary". They were unsure if they should condemn AFA's actions or claim credit for them. In the end they ignored the contradiction and tried to do both. "They condemned AFA to the press, and claimed the credit for stopping the BNP to their own supporters" (*Manchester Red Action*, Bulletin No 6). "We have the same aims as the Anti-Fascist Alliance [sic] but don't necessarily approve of their more direct methods," an ANL spokesman told the local press.

A by-election in Todmorden later the same month meant it witnessed an action replay. Once again the ANL played it safe by leafleting in direct support of the Labour candidate, Carole Gilbraith, while AFA sought out the BNP by direct methods.

"Anti-fascist militants stormed a pub where British National Party members were gathering. About 20 men burst into The Hare and Hounds in Burnley Road, Todmorden, smashing windows and over turning tables." The BNP present, who were preparing for a leafleting campaign, "threw chairs at the attackers and fled out of the back of the pub to safety. The attackers wrecked their Ford van before making their getaway." Later that day some 100 BNP members travelled to the Stoops area of Burnley where once again with depressing inevitability AFA was waiting for them.

"The Stoops estate gained nationwide notoriety last year when it erupted in a wave of anti-police riots. The candidate on this occasion, baby-faced Scott O'Sullivan, obviously wary of local opinion and the estate's reputation, attempted to play down the 'law and order' aspect of BNP policy. This tactic failed when, prior to a mass leafleting of the estate, the BNP were ambushed at their re-direction point. This forced the BNP to invite the police to accompany them onto an estate with a long-standing hatred of the forces of law and order. For the rest of the afternoon, the BNP provided the police with an ideal opportunity to mount a show of strength on the estate. This lack of respect for local feelings and the fact that the police were visibly protecting the BNP from the anti-fascists no doubt contributed to their feeble showing in the polls. A miserable 53 votes provided a clear thumbs down for the forces of law and order" (*Fighting Talk*, issue 6).

If the voters were not impressed by the party of law and order the local press was increasingly condemnatory of anti-fascism. Although often critical of the BNP, this editorial in the *Lancashire Evening Telegraph* was hardly any more sympathetic to the activities of the militants: "Let us be frank. The British National Party is a noxious organisation, peddling racism under the cloak of patriotism. But it has an undeniable right to do so – within the confines of the law. So when its members, gathering in a pub before a leafleting campaign in support of their candidate in next Thursday's county by-election at Burnley, are set upon by a gang of anti-fascist militants, smashing windows and overturning tables, what cause is promoted? Certainly, it is not that of anti-fascism. Indeed, the BNP may even benefit if its opponents are perceived as lawless thugs. And, even if this is not the case, those who seek to defeat the BNP with violence will be seen as being no better than the BNP. Remembering the outrageous, unlawful violence used by BNP members to attack an anti-apartheid meeting in Blackburn in March, it is obvious that the party has standards, as well as policies, that decent people are happy to condemn. But they prefer their condemnation to be confined within the scope of law and order and the ballot box. And that is what these anti-fascist thugs must learn or be tarred with the same brush. It is a mad policy that sets out to smash the opposition and ends up being likened to it. We don't want these punch-up merchants. The real muscle in British politics lies not in pub fights between extremist hooligans, but with the electorate, which is quite capable of seeing off the repellent, hate-inspired organisations which crop up – be they far-Right or far-Left. And if in the interim, they break the law, they must be caught and punished."

As the tone of the *Telegraph* editorial indicates, the activities of the Northern Network was capable of upsetting more than the BNP. And while nationally AFA had by now begun to physically dismantle the BNP operation across the country, the 620 votes accrued by Henderson in a parliamentary seat in Rochdale gave activists in the North West pause for reflection. A considerable amount of work had been done by the Manchester branch in Rochdale but following the election result, though moderate by today's standards, the Northern Network priority thereafter was to try and build a home grown anti-fascist presence in the town of Rochdale itself. Coincidence or otherwise, not too long afterwards Ken Henderson announced his retirement from political activity altogether.

In spite of what was indisputably a series of reverses, the BNP with impressive stamina opened up with a new front in east Lancashire. There, in the months between May and September they contested four by-elections, three attempted rallies, and reported new units in Colne, Nelson, Burnley and Blackburn.

Dogged determination aside, the ceaseless AFA harrying could not fail to draw attention to the irreducible contradiction in the BNP strategy at this time. For although as a party the BNP was street orientated and had at least the ambition, if not always the means, to challenge for control of the streets, by degrees AFA had begun to force the BNP to focus their efforts on avoiding contact with the anti-fascist opposition at almost any cost. As well as this, the fascists also desired electoral respectability, but not only were they forced to devise elaborate logistical arrangements for any public activity including re-direction points, the 'party of power' was patently obviously reliant on police for security. Such elementary contradictions could not fail to impact negatively on the public, and consequently on membership self-esteem. Events in Burnley two months later were illustrative of the general demoralisation that had developed in the BNP ranks as a result of the militant campaign. An article in *Fighting Talk* summed up the state of play as follows:

"Clearly unable to take a hint, the BNP announced that they would be standing a further two candidates in Burnley during local elections in September. They also announced plans for a major march and rally in the town on Saturday 28th August. Despite being forewarned of possible trouble, the police seemed determined to allow the march to go ahead. This decision seems even more remarkable considering that Burnley FC was playing at home that day. On the morning of the 28th, 150 AFA activists arrived at Burnley Central Station. Although we were unable to avoid detection by the police surveillance operation, we were at least in the area in which the BNP intended to march. This in itself represented an achievement, considering the manner in which the police had kept us off the Stoops in June.

"The presence of this large group also attracted the attention of a small section of Burnley fans, who having been wound up by five or six local BNP members, attempted to attack the AFA contingent. This attack failed, and the assailants were chased off. AFA has no quarrel with fans of any football club, and had at first ignored attempts by these fans to start trouble. However, when this bunch started throwing bottles at anti-fascists, then the course of action was never in doubt … AFA members later met 'spokesmen' from the main Burnley firm, who declared themselves impartial, and announced that they would attack whoever was in town after the game, although they were not too pleased at the way the BNP had tried to manipulate Burnley fans.

"If it was the intention of the BNP to use Burnley fans against AFA, then the plan back-fired, because the police refused to allow the BNP to leave their re-direction point, due to 'serious public disorder' in Burnley. This sparked a furious row between local activists and party leader John Tyndall, who meekly complied with police orders not to travel into Burnley. A few locals defied the police and ventured into town anyway, where irate Burnley fans slapped them around.

"Their plans thwarted, the BNP turned on each other. One of the candidates, David McNee, withdrew from the election declaring that he was 'totally disillusioned with the BNP.' Others started fighting amongst themselves, while most just bemoaned Tyndall's lack of bottle. In the end the BNP mustered a pitiful 32 votes for the candidate who withdrew, and a magnificent nine votes for the candidate who stayed the course. In attempting to sell a tough streetwise image to white working class youth, while still attempting to win over respectable voters, the BNP have managed to do neither."

As a result of the setbacks Burnley BNP split with the dissidents operating under the title of the 'Anti-Marxist League'. In a leaflet produced by the group it was argued that: "the patriotic cause in this area was given a blow on at least two occasions this year. This was courtesy of their egoist, media-seeking Tory regional leadership. The breaking point for many patriots in this area with the BNP came when this organisation failed to organise a simple rally – let alone a march – in Burnley on 23rd August 1993 in support of two candidates … They totally ignored them and were content to hold the rally in a public house well outside of Burnley. By doing so… they had allowed the reds to rule the roost."

Notwithstanding these victories and the dismal showing of the BNP in the polls, the AFA Northern Network leadership warned against complacency, insisting that these setbacks were likely to prove only temporary. As proof, attention was drawn to the announcement of new BNP units in Bury, Bolton, Broughton and Tameside.

So by September 1993 the puzzle for AFA was that as soon as they put down the BNP in one area they sprang up in another. Coupled to the BNP success in the by-election in Millwall in east London, some militants for the first time began to look at influences other than the political efforts of the BNP itself, for its enduring political appeal among sections of working class youth. Before the end of the decade AFA would be among the first to denounce the 'my tribe, first or only'* ethos espoused by official multiculturalism which for some in the leadership was one the key reasons behind the BNP resonance and resilience.

And if there were any illusions with regard to BNP ambition in the region, these were thoroughly dispelled by the announcement in *British Nationalist* of a new contact point in south Manchester itself, considered by Manchester AFA to be its heartland. Within a day AFA intelligence had traced the PO Box to two previously unknown and evidently new BNP recruits called 'Nolan' and 'Red'. In attempting to avoid detection they had used a false address, which simply allowed AFA personnel to obtain a duplicate card allowing access to contacts writing to the PO Box. Thereafter began an assessment of the competence of the BNP men who had unwittingly placed themselves in the firing line.

Jon: "Straight off we realised 'Red' was a real 'no-mark' who we would have been more than happy to have left in charge, confident they could never develop and with an eye to gaining an insight into the wider BNP operation in the North West. 'Nolan' was different. As well as appearing a fairly normal sort – his wife was a teacher, I think – he himself already had lots of contacts through his job as a taxi driver. Besides, he was operating from south Manchester, the heart of the AFA manor, so apart from anything else an example would have to be made."

'Red', who lived with his parents, was the first to realise he had been rumbled when the house was hit late one night. A follow up call left his parents in no doubts as to the determination of the callers. Nolan was next. First the house, then his livelihood, the taxi, was damaged to the cost of thousands of pounds. Moreover,

* A decade before mainstream party leaders like Tony Blair and David Cameron began to mouth carefully calibrated reservations at the evident consequences of multicultural excesses, militants had begun to publicly argue that the underlying thesis behind multiculturalism was not merely fatally flawed but wrongheaded, reactionary and anti-working class.

"What is clear throughout is that by failing to address the factor of class the anti-racist initiatives, whether well-intentioned or cynical, inevitably leaves race as the prime motivator. The implied obligation for black and white alike is that you identify with people of your own race first. Or only. One consequence of the strategy is that individuals are encouraged or forced to think along nationalist lines politically. What do *we* get out of it? Meaning my tribe rather than my class. Alternatively, if you identify along racial lines from the standpoint of a race or culture other than your own, see it from the other point of view, from an anti-racist perspective, such a sentiment immediately registers as mealy-mouthed, weak or ambiguous. To actually act on such a principle means thereafter to be regarded as a renegade whose views will always be suspect" ('Cruel Britannia', *Fighting Talk*, issue 20, August 1998).

neighbours puzzled by the motivation of those behind the campaign, began to wonder if he had "raped someone".

Jon: "Eventually, we came for him personally. There was a comical scene when one of our most experienced operators, instead of cutting the phone line, mistakenly snipped the wire for the doorbell! But realising he had had a narrow escape Nolan then immediately made contact with AFA."

A meeting was set up in a bar in Oxford Road. Suspicions were instantly raised when neither Nolan nor Tilzey, who as intelligence officer for AFA had been acting as liaison, turned up at the meeting. A cursory investigation drew the conclusion that Tilzey, a Searchlight operative, was probably trying to hi-jack the AFA operation. With a direct contact between Nolan and himself established he was now attempting to sever any link between Nolan and AFA. This proved hugely embarrassing to the organisers in the city, not least Dave Hann, who had personally championed Tilzey's re-instatement within AFA.* As far as AFA was concerned, Tilzey was really finished this time but the Nolan situation itself remained unresolved. Gerry turned to Denis C., now living in Hatfield, for advice on how to recover the situation. The conversation went as follows. "What did you do to bring Nolan to the table?" "Pressure," comes the reply. "Is Nolan still under pressure?" "No." "There's your answer."

Immediately, the campaign against Nolan resumed. In the meantime, Denis rings Tilzey asking him what he is playing at. Tilzey admits he pulled the meeting, but on the grounds that he was not convinced the AFA people could handle the situation; "clumsy questioning," he felt, might cause Nolan to clam up, and if that happened, "violence could result." He was told to re-schedule the meeting for the following Saturday and that Denis would be in attendance. In the meantime, Gerry had Dessie Noonan and a couple of lads tour the pubs in Chorlton, letting it be known they were looking for Mike Nolan. By coincidence, a mate of Dessie's worked for the same taxi firm as Nolan. He in turn relayed a story to Nolan of picking up three blokes of Middle Eastern appearance who were also asking serious questions about him?

* Having separated from his partner, Tilzey came to suspect she was having an affair. He just didn't know who it was. Meanwhile his 'ex' reported receiving threatening phone calls from fascists at home. But even when the authorities in the school where she worked were notified that she was a 'supporter of the IRA', Tilzey was strangely relaxed. Smelling a rat, a leading anti-fascist directed a colleague to phone her at home when he knew Tilzey would also be present. On hearing the blood curdling threats a panicky Tilzey immediately contacted the same anti-fascist demanding 'something be done'. The ruse had worked. The Tilzey phone call had confirmed AFA suspicions that Tilzey himself had been behind the initial calls. Within days Searchlight was duly notified by the Manchester Martyrs Committee that 'his [Tilzey's] safety could not be guaranteed' should he appear at the campaign events.

On the morning of the planned meet, Tilzey rings Hann with some bad news: "Nolan has pulled the meeting and there's nothing I can do about it… I feel as let down as you do" are his closing comments. Denis gets Nolan's number and rings him direct. "Mike, I understand you have pulled out of the meeting with us." "No, I have arranged no meeting with anyone." Pause. "Who are you?" "This is AFA, I believe you have been speaking to Tilzey?" "Yes." "And you're still having problems?" "Yes." "Looks like you're talking to the wrong people." "Yes, I realise that." "When can we meet?" "In an hour?" "Where?" "In The Whalley." Up to this time Nolan may have thought he was actually dealing with AFA, or if not, that Searchlight were either the senior partner or a surrogate. He began to suspect otherwise when, despite the assurances from Steve Tilzey, his house continued to come under attack. Almost as a last resort, Nolan even turned to the BNP for advice, spelling out the seriousness of his predicament. "Given the circumstances I'm surprised you're still alive," was the regional organiser's reported reply, before putting down the phone.

Jon: "At the meeting, which at his insistence was held in a public place, Nolan proved very helpful, not disguising his out and out anger at the way his now former comrades operating from the relative safety of the mill towns had dropped him in it. At the same time, he was only going to reveal as much as he had to out of concern of retaliation by them. Attempting to further increase his bargaining position, in hushed tones he informed us that one of the fellas in the bar has "just recently been acquitted of murder … I've heard he wants to speak to me, too". "Actually he's with us," Gerry responds nonchalantly. Dessie then walks over to the table informing Nolan in a voice loud enough to be heard in the public bar and beyond to co-operate fully with the AFA de-briefing or he would regret it. Dessie returns to the bar, leaving the pub ten minutes later. A three-hour question and answer session ended with Nolan posing us a question, "Is he still here?"

Partly to find out how far Tilzey/Searchlight were prepared to go in upsetting AFA, and partly out of mischief, Denis insisted that pressure be kept on Tilzey to deliver on the promise of the meeting between AFA and Nolan. Eventually Nolan possibly tired of playing 'piggy in the middle', extracted himself

Manchester AFA sticker.

from the situation, by stubbornly refusing to pay some minor fines and was imprisoned.

Tyndall who had doggedly put great store in 'set-pieces' (where nationalism, through sheer physical power would chasten all opposition), was facing a moment of truth. While few would deny the 'set-piece' scenario as described was working, it was the Northern Network not the BNP which was repeatedly shown to be masters at seizing the moment. For BNP organisers this was a harsh reality. Seeing a branch thriving for six months or more, steadily building up support and membership until the day dawned for them to fly the flag in public, only to witness the painstaking months of morale building effectively vaporise on contact with a more experienced and ruthless enemy. Little wonder that, as early as 1992, some senior BNP strategists like Butler and Lecomber were beginning to question what nationalism might achieve without the advertised 'come and have a go if you think you're hard enough' routine demanded by the Tyndall hubris.

3.14

1992, ANL RE-LAUNCH

At face value 1992 began with a major strategic victory for AFA. Since 1985 a large slice of AFA propaganda had been taken up in warning the Left of the latent appeal of the Far Right. As a consequence, the announcement on 15th January 1992 of the re-launch of the Anti-Nazi League by Peter Hain MP, Ernie Roberts, a former Labour MP, and Paul Holborow of the Socialist Workers Party, who had all been party to the original launch fifteen years earlier, was the most public confirmation of their analysis militants could have wished for.

There would, of course, be no admission of the AFA role in 'holding the line' in what *Searchlight* described as "the increasingly violent years of the last decade"; instead, in what was seen by many as a calculated snub, Paul Holborow stated that the ANL Mark 2 was "not interested in the politics of the punch up." "AFA won't like that," Lee Jasper whispered to a crony. But with Glenys Kinnock and Harold Walker, deputy speaker of the Commons, three union leaders, and the Scottish National Party leader Alex Salmond, plus scores of MPs, sports and media personalities all offering the ANL their support, Holborow could hardly afford to say anything else.

Despite the enormous left-of-centre establishment backing, arch rivals to the SWP, Militant, retaliated immediately by setting up Youth Against Racism in Europe (YRE) as a direct rival. Just two months previously in November 1991 the Anti-Racist Alliance, with support from MPs Ken Livingstone and Diane Abbot, had also thrown its hat into the ring. Chair Mark Wadsworth declared the ARA remit to be limited to "community action and legal remedies." A number of years later Ken Livingstone made the rather absurd claim that the "only reason the ANL reformed was because of ARA's success."

However *Fighting Talk*, other than to pointedly ask "Why now?", responded in a low key fashion to the various announcements of what were, in effect, meant to be rivals. *Searchlight*, which had not been consulted, much less invited to sponsor any of the new groupings reacted to the repeated snubs with fury, declaring that "Over the last couple of months the anti-racist and anti-fascist movement has made an ass of itself." In another acid attack it described the SWP and the "politics of deceit being practised [by it] as beyond the pale" and further blistered it for "closing down the original ANL in the early 80s and the mass expulsions of anti-fascist activists at around the same time." By March the editorial tone had hardly softened, with *Searchlight* claiming it had "stripped bare the lies of the Socialist Workers

Party," causing "many people who had got involved with the ANL to think again."

"The ANL's mass leafleting of Rochdale in late February," it fulminated, "demonstrates its overall weakness: only Asian estates were leafleted; do Asians really need to be told about the BNP? The ANL totally avoided the white estates that were often hotbeds of racism and the BNP's main recruiting ground." By contrast, it argued AFA was "growing daily into a much more nationally based organisation and many different groups and communities are looking for it to give a lead. It must take up this challenge and give activists against racism and fascism a decent organisation to work with ... Last year AFA had 10,000 people at its carnival and 4,000 marchers in east London on Remembrance Sunday. Now is the time to lead the movement by example and Searchlight will be marching right along side" (*Searchlight*, March 1992).

By now thoroughly familiar with Searchlight's opportunism, the AFA leadership took the endorsement lightly: lessons had indeed been learned and the type of top down, cross-class, state-friendly, 'decent organisation' Searchlight craved was never likely to materialise if they had anything to do with it.

Of greater concern was the effect the ANL re-launch had on political differences within AFA itself. For Workers Power, in particular, the ANL re-launch was seen as a lifeline, a chance for AFA to come in from the cold, and with honour. So they were eager to seize the opportunity as, in other ways too, it suited their own agenda to do so. Having sprung from the SWP more or less fully formed in the early 1970s, Workers Power had since then maintained a parasitic relationship with the parent body. In a transparent attempt to mimic that set-up, it began to argue AFA should either join the ANL outright or, failing that, to be sensitive to the ANL agenda. While the advantage of being less exposed to the authorities through the involvement of greater numbers on a day-to-day basis might have had some appeal to the streetfighters, in terms of 'realpolitik' it was always an improbable confection. Particularly as, in gauging the sincerity of the SWP, which until the final few months of 1991 continued to insist the fight against fascism was a 'distraction from the real struggle', influential figures within militant anti-fascism had become even more jaundiced as to the positives, publicity apart, the ANL could possibly bring to the struggle.

Besides, from 1982 onwards they had been allowed to shoulder total political responsibility for the conduct of the struggle; now, as was clear to everyone, the ANL was re-forming to displace, not buttress, the militants. And even supposing the ANL was not regarded as a threat in that way, there was a legitimate concern the political body language of the ANL might undo much of the work AFA had by now completed, in the East End in particular.

Given the scale of the misgivings, the ANL's first outing in Bethnal Green did little to set militant minds at rest. In planning an extensive leaflet drop around the

Whitechapel area, the ANL mobilised in Altab Ali Park. But so lax was security that, when two leading AFA members wandered over to study the route map for the day's events, they went unchallenged. The media present immediately assumed they were BNP, even asking them for a quote. Exchanging looks, they decided to identify themselves to the main ANL organiser. "A large force of BNP were in the Blue Anchor pub less than fifty yards away," they told him. Without offering any thanks, the ANL organiser haughtily turned his back on them, instructing the hundred or so ANL to "stick together in groups of ten." Disgusted, the AFA members strolled off without another word.

Given the fighting calibre of the opposing groups, in reality two groups of fifty might not have prevented the ANL taking a beating. As it was, tidy 'groups of ten' were an added convenience for the armed and lurking fascists. Literally within five minutes of setting out the ANL groups were ambushed. Tim Hepple, a Searchlight mole within the BNP, later recorded: "We trailed them at a discreet distance, but once they were on the estate we ran them. There was no shouting or threats; a whole gang of nazi skins just swept over them, kicking, punching, and, as if prearranged, driving them in the direction of two narrow exits from the flats. For those who managed to escape the first wave of skinheads, another group was waiting nearby.

A demonstration after the racist murder of Altab Ali in May 1978. The park in Whitechapel where he was randomly attacked is now known as Altab Ali Park.

The only available exits for the Anti-Nazi League supporters were concrete subways connecting the estate to the nearby roads. Here, hidden in the shadows, were dozens of other nazis, this time not skinheads or bootboys but older, more hardened extremists. As the left-wing activists fled in terror they were met with baseball bats, iron bars, heavy spanners and bottles" (*White Riot*, page 14). A good number were hospitalised, with at least two suffering from knife wounds. Three BNP members were later charged with grievously bodily harm.

Andy: "It may seem harsh but the preparation was so amateur and complacent – and deliberately so – that as far as I could see they only got what they deserved. Truth be told, we were rather pleased. We felt vindicated. Just prior to the leafleting, this middle class woman was overheard exclaiming her 'shock' at the news of an attack the previous day on an SWP paper sale in Ealing. "In broad daylight! I didn't think they would be so brazen." The ANL approach was more like amateur dramatics than anything else. We didn't know whether to laugh or cry. But their feigned disinterest in security, all the shoulder-shrugging and eyeball-rolling, to us, trivialised the struggle. So there was little sympathy from militants. Frankly from that very first day they were regarded as an embarrassment – at best."

Somewhat more generously, Copsey puts the "ill-preparedness" demonstrated down to the fact of an SWP not having "seriously monitored fascism for many years." But if ignorance or ring-rustiness was really the reason, one might have expected a significantly altered attitude thereafter. But no change of plan was ever forthcoming: fast-forward seven months to August 1992 and Brick Lane Market. "They didn't seem so bothered at first," remembers reformed NF member Matthew Collins, who was out with C18 on the day. "They seemed to think they were dealing with the usual shouting and slanging match there is sometimes between us…then it just went. We ploughed into them. We used bottles, bricks, we hit them with everything we could. Turned their stalls over. Kicked them senseless, really. One particular bloke took it really bad in the head."

The victim, local school-teacher Paul Williams, later admitted to *World in Action* that the SWP failure to anticipate such an occurrence was because: "It was a very busy day so we didn't realise straight away that they [C18] would come and attack us." Not long after being approached and threatened in his local school, he left the ANL and crossed over to East London AFA. Despite a rash of such attacks on their members all over the country for the next two years, the SWP refused to be 'provoked'. They could do little else, for even if the will existed, the 'street-fighters', as they had been forced to admit a decade earlier, did not. So they did nothing. To admit their concern was to admit to their inadequacy. If it carried any report at all, *Socialist Worker* would use the catch-all term 'socialists' to refer to the victims. On occasion, if news leaked out, the SWP leadership would do its best to play down the level of personal injury, where it could.

The 'see no evil' edict was no accident. For example, at the beginning of 1990 an eyewitness report of an attack on the SWP in Glasgow was carried in *Red Action*. A group of about sixty SWP members were attacked leaving a meeting. A letter from a reader was sent to a left-wing regional publication, the *Somerset Clarion*, expressing disquiet at the implications. Immediately the SWP denounced the entire story as a Red Action invention.

Leading SWP member Eddie Provost wrote: "I have checked with my comrades in Scotland and on the Central Committee and no one has ever heard of the incident." To the intense embarrassment of both Provost and the SWP, Red Action responded by producing a copy of the *Glasgow Evening Times* that had run the subsequent jailing of the attackers on its front page under the screaming headline, 'Neo-Nazis Jailed: Sheriff slams thugs who attack rivals'. One of the SWP victims, "Mr Brown, a welder, was taken to hospital where 13 stitches were put in his head wounds. One of his fingers was broken" (*Evening Times*, 24th October 1990). Replying for the SWP, Andrew Newman simply denounced the *Somerset Clarion* as a "sectarian gossip sheet." In truth it was not only the leadership that was in denial. One Saturday lunchtime, as an internal AFA meeting in Oxford House in Bethnal Green was breaking for lunch, an SWP paper sale came under violent attack from a number of youths. Witnessing what proved to be the back end of a brief but vicious assault, the militants raced to the rescue.

Terry: "Initially the SWP thought we were a second wave, and apart from one loud middle class woman, all visibly cowered. After identifying ourselves, we asked where they had gone, what they looked like, and so forth, but co-operation was not forthcoming. 'It's alright, it's alright,' this other woman kept insisting, while a few feet away her colleague was stretched out unconscious on the pavement. This was not the politics of the Lenin they always went on about: this was the politics of Gandhi. We just shook our heads and walked away."

On a wider political level the contradiction was even more pronounced. Here was an organisation that employed Holocaust iconography to demonise its opponents, routinely called for the BNP to be 'smashed', and yet still expressed incredulity when its members were assaulted. At the same time, even the tiniest nod toward the need for some form of self-defence was likely to be dismissed as unwarranted, or denounced as militarism.

It is, of course, possible the largely academic SWP leadership may have believed an image of near total passivity by their party would soothe fascist rage, but if so they didn't know their enemy. In truth, the more inert the SWP body language, the greater the fury of their opponents, and the greater the number and intensity of the attacks. On one celebrated occasion, a former British Army squaddie, Dave Ha***nd, who at the time ran a tidy little operation (against 'the baddies' as he called them) in south east London bumped into a female SWP full-timer he knew:

"To my knowledge you [SWP] have been attacked six times in the last month without reply. When are you going to do something about it?" "Oh," came the reply "You mean Barnet?" "Well that's seven, then!" he said, laughing.

Outside of London things were little better. One of the areas of most concerted violence was in West Yorkshire. A snapshot of what everyday life was like for the SWP/ANL rank and file in the early 1990s is provided in *White Riot*: "Two weeks after anti-fascists prevented a BNP election meeting in mid-March 1994, a group of Leeds-based nazis attacked a Socialist Workers Party paper sale in the city centre. A week later the SWP were attacked again. In protest against the growing right-wing violence, an ANL-organised demonstration was held a fortnight later. This, too, was attacked, with one nazi brandishing a machete. Two more C18 attacks on the SWP came that summer" (*White Riot*, page 137).

Even to the leadership, the inadequacies of the party for street confrontation may have appeared unsustainable, and in his book, *Fascism: Theory and Practice*, Dave Renton, a member of the SWP, attempts to measure real anti-fascism, not by what disruption it is capable of inflicting, but more by what it is prepared to endure. "For anti-fascists," Renton writes, "violence is not part of their world view, they do not seek to create a society where violence is natural or commonplace, violence is not something which anti-fascists can glorify. For these reasons physical confrontation against fascism has to involve large numbers, must be primarily non-violent and should involve layers greater than any professional anti-fascists in order to build a truly mass opposition." This, note, was the same theory expounded by the SWP leadership with regard to the NF in a particular period in the early 1980s, but Renton's argument is that it has a universal application.

AFA sticker.

Leaving aside the reality that anti-fascism as a negative cannot be in the business of 'creating' anything, if ever there was any concern among the SWP hierarchy that revisionism of this calibre sailed close to what their mentor, Trotsky, had condemned over half a century previously as "flabby pacifism that arouses only disgust and loathing," it was not forthcoming. And if, as a consequence, the SWP/ANL had become fascism's 'unconscious helpers', as militants accused, then as the 1990s wore on, many of the SWP rank and file were unconscious in more ways than one.

Joe: "To be honest I always thought it was only going to be a matter of time before one of them was killed. What was increasingly happening was that AFA was getting stuck into the BNP, and the BNP in return were getting stuck into the SWP. Had the BNP retaliation been visited on innocent members of the ethnic communities there would have been sympathy from militants but most likely the response would have been to hit the BNP even harder. As it was, politically the ANL was seen to be very much part of the problem. Looked at from a wider ethical angle, the attitude of the leadership toward its own membership was frankly immoral."

At the beginning of 1992, one *Fighting Talk* editorial openly inquired if the SWP/ANL tactics were cynically designed to create "a new martyr in the anti-racist cause for the 1990s?" (*Fighting Talk*, spring 1992). As committed advocates of the Roosevelt doctrine: "Talk quietly and carry a big stick", the safety of recruits always had primacy within AFA. Moreover, for all the gung-ho reputation, AFA rarely if ever subscribed to the principle of taking a punch to land one. Liberal critics might sneer that the militant stance on security was close to 'obsessive' but from early on, first RA, and then AFA, recognised the powerful paramilitary cachet attached to its near omnipotent reputation on the street, and so risks, when taken, were invariably calculated. Moreover for the AFA activists who were in it for the long haul, there was the recognition that it might well end either with a lengthy sentence or with the decks awash and guns blazing. This made them determined to approach every operation with practised caution, and a sometime fastidious attention to detail, which they hoped and had reason to expect would put off the day of reckoning for as long as possible.

Andy: "Right from when I got involved the first lesson I was taught was that anti-fascism was only about 'winning'. To seek to engage the enemy and then lose was seen as criminal stupidity. To avoid this there was almost always a Plan B and usually a Plan C. As little as possible was left to chance. Sometimes operations were so carefully plotted out to the extent that how the initial approach might play with a jury at a later date would even be factored in. If things weren't felt to be right, though it didn't happen too often, the operation would be cancelled."

Joe: "People might imagine that giving the go-ahead for an operation with untold consequences for all involved (jail, serious injury and so on) was difficult, but in fact cancelling one with everyone primed was always the more troubling. This was because you had to balance the circumstances against how you might be feeling yourself, your personal instinct, against what appeared to be objective reality to others, and often weigh this up in a split second."

Given the safety-first mindset, quite mundane events such as leafleting sessions were loaded with logistical difficulties. For example, in February 1992 when AFA mounted a mass leafleting campaign in the Bethnal Green area involving tens of thousands of leaflets being delivered door to door, it was – unlike with the ANL, say – no simple matter of getting enough people to do the leafleting. Of paramount importance was that those doing the leafleting were adequately protected while carrying it out. This emphasis meant that on more than one occasion the numbers involved in security would heavily outnumber, sometimes up to five to one (the apparent imbalance came from the recognition that when leafleting tower blocks, for instance, it was often the unit on the ground that was the more vulnerable), the membership proactively involved in promoting the political message. Against this, AFA felt that being visibly able to distribute on predominately white estates without challenge was a propaganda victory in itself. And what's more, with security always at a premium, an almost military discipline was demanded from the membership in order for AFA to be able to maintain an unbeaten record. All told, as one activist's diary from that period illustrates, the volume of activity and the subsequent level of commitment demanded was intense. (The diary actually belonged to one of the Brick Lane Four.)

Jan 25 – Bloody Sunday demonstration: 'stewarding'.
Jan 29 – 'Defend the Brick Lane 4' meeting, 7.30, Hackney.
Jan 31 – AFA public fundraising benefit, Stoke Newington Town Hall.
Feb 3 – Leafleting Bethnal Green, 6.30.
Feb 4 – North London AFA branch meeting.
Feb 5 – Leafleting Bethnal Green, 6.30.
Feb 10 – Leafleting Bethnal Green, 6.30.
Feb 13. – AFA public meeting, 8.00, Davenant Centre (Whitechapel).
Feb 22 – South London demo.
Feb 23 – 10am picket of BNP paper sale at Brick Lane.
March 2 – First day of Brick Lane 4 trial at Southwark Crown Court.

As if confronting the BNP was not enough, by now AFA was addressing the differing problems posed by both police and political rivals on the Left. In February a meeting called to discuss anti-fascist strategy was inevitably boycotted by the ANL.

The following month an AFA contingent on an anti-racist march through Camden was targeted by police with a selected number of 'faces' forced off the march. By coincidence, it would be in Camden five years later that the policy of criminalisation would come to full maturity, with the public banning of an international conference to be hosted by AFA, on the instructions of that by-word for equal opportunities, Labour-run Camden Council. Camden Irish Centre, which had hosted previous AFA events and who receive a grant from the council, claimed their funding was threatened if they complied with the AFA booking. A *Mail on Sunday* article on 28th September 1997, entitled: 'IRA link militants plan London recruiting rally', had triggered the backlash. Interestingly, many years later, in March 2005, the journalist responsible, Daniel Foggo, would be referred to by Nick Griffin on the BNP website as an "alleged MI5 linkman."

Initially, Camden Council "vigorously denied" any involvement. AFA then produced a copy of a fax from Camden Council Voluntary Sector to the Irish Centre, that featured a copy of the original AFA press release with specific words or sections circled and commented on by the sender. It had been sent exactly five minutes before the management of the Irish Centre rang AFA to say the booking had been pulled. Ironically, the principal theme of the conference, scheduled to take place in the first week of October, was to address the 'growing criminalisation' of anti-fascism in Europe.

In a letter to AFA, Labour leader Richard Arthur, while continuing to deny any interference by the Council, stated: "The Camden Irish Centre appear to be well within its rights in refusing your organisation to hold meetings at the centre." He received the backing of a gleeful BNP who publicly praised the council on its website. Comment in the Irish press was mixed. In one letter a prominent supporter of the 'Irish in Britain Representation Group' compared the sensationalist coverage in the *Irish World* to the worst of the British tabloids. "Nor does the group [AFA] deserve the felon-setting in which Damien Gafney [*Irish World* editor] indulged himself, with references to the arrests and conviction by the British police and judiciary. If that is the basis on which we're to condemn people, then we'd have to condemn most of our leaders in history, as well as many others, such as the Birmingham Six, the Guildford Four and Frank Johnson. Fascists and fascism have to be fought at every level and more power to AFA for striving to do that" (*Irish World*, 10th October 1997).

It was many months afterwards that AFA decided to take the Irish Centre to court. Even then it had as much to do with the future as the past. As 'Joe Reilly' told *Time Out*: "We are concerned that Camden banning our meetings could have a snowball effect and other councils could ban us too. This is part of a whole drift to the right. It wouldn't have happened ten years ago." Even while in strictly financial terms the matter was concluded to AFA's satisfaction, with a four figure out of court settlement, in political terms AFA had never been more isolated, with majority liberal opinion comfortable with the implications of the ban and the quasi-legal parity militants now shared with the BNP. While support was forthcoming from the Jewish Socialist Group, neither Searchlight nor the ANL saw cause for even comment.

In a final irony it emerged that the assistant manager of the Irish Centre, Ian Wakefield, had had a previous connection with AFA. In 1991 he had been the landlord of The Sun pub in Bethnal Green that at the time AFA had regarded as the centre of operations for the BNP across east London.

3.15

'LEGAL VERSUS ILLEGAL' REVISITED

On 26th April 1992 the first formal national AFA AGM since the re-launch almost three years earlier was held in London. In the interim AFA had branches in all of the major metropolitan centres across the country. As in London, AFA nationally was run on regional lines, whereby the affiliated groups and individuals collaborated on geographical rather than on a 'party' diktat basis. Thus, as well as serving as a general appraisal of strengths and weaknesses, the purpose of the meeting was also to test if a basis existed for the development and linking of these regional structures nationally.

But coming as it did just three months after the ANL launch, together with plans for the stepping up of the pace, Workers Power (WP) chose to introduce a line of argument that within six months would see them denounce militant anti-fascism as an "obstacle" to effective anti-fascism. Their journey began with a call for AFA to begin to re-orientate back towards the Left. This was followed by a demand for a centralised organisation, with a nationally elected leadership that would begin the process of unifying anti-fascist forces, presumably under their political guidance. Rather than debate the efficacy of existing militant strategies, Workers Power made it clear their preference was for a discussion on the issues of political leadership and what that entailed, with specific reference to what they regarded as the 'wrong leadership'. And so what Copsey refers to as the "overarching historical divide between militant and constitutional anti-fascism" was again revisited.

What the WP leadership seemed to be after more than anything was the dismantling of the 'technical/political' working class leadership that had served to make AFA uniquely democratic and refreshingly forceful. To return to a more conventional, which is to say, failed, formula was never going to earn an easy acceptance, especially when delegates from RA and DAM did little to conceal their antipathy to the Workers Power recipe. One RA member put it bluntly: "Whether or not the time is right to attack a 'fash' pub in Burnley will not be decided by some fuckin' pencil-neck in London."

Bearing in mind the intensity of the street battles taking place around the country at this time, RA argued the unity of the militants was absolutely crucial if AFA were to continue to be anti-fascism's cutting edge. Furthermore, with the militants coming from a number of different political backgrounds, the quickest way to destroy this precious unity at street level would be the imposition of a top down national leadership. When it came to a vote, delegates overwhelmingly voted in favour of a national co-ordinating committee, which was entirely consistent with existing structures at branch and regional level.

Later RA spelled out its trenchant opposition to the WP blueprint: "AFA is about effective, militant anti-fascism on the ground. It is about making a difference. The activists are in local areas who meet in local branches, the local branches co-ordinate their actions in regions to do this; the regions meet nationally at the national co-ordinating committee: in other words from the bottom up. If we haven't got the strength on the ground, it is totally irrelevant what some national leadership might say or demand. Workers Power's idea of this national leadership was rejected because it is nonsense."

Although some WP rank and file understood the importance of maintaining AFA's organisational and political independence, their leadership was tired of this 'radical experiment'. Rather than continue to look outwards and to draw in new forces to the anti-fascist movement, the Left presented a more inviting and safer option for them. Moreover, earlier attempts to draw smaller Trotskyite groups into London AFA in particular, in a transparent attempt to again provide them with a stronger Trotskyite bloc against what they saw at the time as an RA/DAM axis, had been openly ridiculed. The tactic of improving Trotskyite voting power was finally abandoned when a leading member of the DAM, Mick P. threw a delegate from the RIL (Revolutionary Internationalist League) bodily out of a branch meeting in north London.

From its inception in the mid-1970s, Workers Power had orientated to the SWP. It was understandable therefore that the appearance of the ANL made the leadership a bit giddy. Here was a remedy for years of humiliation, if only AFA could be made to mimic the relationship with the ANL that WP 'enjoyed' with the SWP. After the Remembrance Day march in Bethnal Green in 1991, a leading WP member Mark H. confessed that perhaps the greatest satisfaction he had ever had in politics was "instructing the SWP to assemble at the back of the march, knowing that the muscle was there to force them to do so." There was another reason as well. For a time, while revelling in the prestige of running with the 'hard men' the strain on individual activists had begun to tell. Even by mid-1991 when it was decided AFA would march through Bethnal Green, WP had begun to shed its responsibilities. A leading WP member had been selected to do some preliminary organisation for the event. At the following meeting over a month later, when asked to supply a progress report he replied, "March, what march?"

By October 1992, just six months after the national meeting, WP was visibly looking for a door marked 'Exit'. Their effective resignation was contained within the set of proposals to the annual London conference they must have known would be rejected. One Workers Power motion called for an "orientation to the workers movement", which might have sounded radical to an untrained ear, but was in reality an appeal to essentially white-collar trade unions where the orthodox Left and specifically the SWP coagulated. Further, in the interests of 'unity' AFA would be required to address "the militants mobilised by the ANL, ARA and other self-proclaimed anti-fascist organisations, intervening in them to defeat their pacifist and cross-class orientation and overcoming their organisational sectarianism. This means: (1) For every event it initiates, London AFA will formally propose a joint mobilisation with the ANL, ARA, etc. (2) AFA will attempt to mobilise for every anti-fascist event, regardless of who organised it. Our aim in mobilising for ANL/ARA-called events is to turn passive demonstrations into active attempts to 'No Platform the Fascists' [sic]."

Once again the idea that the average ANL or ARA supporter was straining at the leash but being held back by a pacifist and sectarian leadership was far from convincing. By now there were very few in those circles that did not know what AFA stood for. In lining up behind organisations that loudly proclaimed the need to follow a non-confrontational constitutional path it is reasonable to assume individuals were doing so not through any lack of awareness but through choice.

More telling is that these proposals were submitted to the conference less than one month after the Battle of Waterloo, an indisputably pivotal moment in the history of anti-fascism. To all intents and purposes, this was boycotted by the very forces the WP leadership now demanded AFA should court with the specific aim of setting up 'joint defence squads'. Waterloo aside, AFA had made numerous attempts to work with the other Left groups, none of which had borne fruit. If militants were a little dubious, to say the least, as to the value of collaboration with the Left, it was only to be expected. And of course, what was being proposed here was that AFA should surrender operational and political independence to join up with what was, in militant eyes, at best a union of shirkers, dilettantes and incompetents. If nothing else, timing alone made the WP proposal a complete non-starter.

Terry: "There was another yawning credibility gap in the proposals. If these organisations – the SWP, Militant and so on – were the answer, what was the question? In reality the type of anti-fascism the ARA/YRE/ANL represented was mostly a compound of all the tactical blunders that had got the Left into trouble to begin with. Furthermore by this time we had come to realise that the rise of the Far Right, not just here but across Europe, was the consequence not the cause of the Left's failure. The fact that there was something fundamentally wrong with the Left was the rock Workers Power dare not turn over."

It seems fairly certain that the WP sponsors realised they had very little prospect of any of their ideas being accepted by AFA, much less by the ANL, YRE or ARA who, while loathing AFA, were equally dismissive of each other. More galling for Workers Power, now that the Left had been alerted to the potential of the extreme Right and had organised in a myriad of organisations, such as the ANL, YRE, ARA, and CAFE

[Campaign against Fascism in Europe], militants on a national basis increasingly looked towards unilateral and militarist solutions. Thus, in November 1992, Workers Power publicly denounced AFA for operating "a separate party-like organisation of those committed to physical force alone" which they proclaimed was "an obstacle to the construction of the united front" (*Workers Power*, November 1992).

When Workers Power joined AFA in 1989, the group had made a positive contribution to raising the profile of anti-fascism in general, and militant anti-fascism in particular, within sections of the orthodox Trotskyist Left RA or DAM could not hope to reach. Yet, almost from day one they appeared reluctant to take on any real responsibility within the organisation, seeing it as a temporary measure required to bring pressure to bear on the forces they were really interested in. Copsey offers the suggestion that the WP desertion was one of the reasons "AFA lost its grip in east London during 1992-3," but this is not supported by any evidence and in truth, by the time WP defected, their departure was hardly noticed.

On 18th May 1992 the BBC2's *Open Space* slot screened a programme called 'Fighting Talk', which had been largely written, produced and directed by two leading AFA members. It proved fairly controversial, particularly for a slot that more often than not ran programmes on radical gardening. So incensed was the *Daily Mail* it demanded the BBC grant the BNP 'a right of reply'. "A most serious error of judgement appears to have been made last night by the BBC in offering air time to a group which unashamedly advocates the use of political violence ... The people who spoke last night for a group called Anti-Fascist Action astonishingly were allowed to put the case for physically opposing their right-wing opponents ... How can it now with equity resist demand from the BNP for the right to reply?" In *The Sun*, columnist Gary Bushell who, during the early 1980s had nothing but nice things to say about RA but later swung right, insisted the BBC slot "had been given over to ugly Red thugs who glory in violence."

In its review *Republican News* called the programme "refreshing" and noted that by organising "street carnivals, public meetings, lectures, concerts, etc." AFA effectively belied "the thuggish image some of its opponents would attempt to give it" (*Republican News*, 21st May 1992). While the endorsement was no doubt warmly welcomed by some, in truth, with the entire Left now thoroughly engaged, the 'carnivals, meetings, lectures, concerts and marches' policy, which had been employed to force the Left to re-orientate, had served its purpose. By the spring of 1992 the Left was as engaged as much as it was ever going to be. So, with the exception of a hugely successful 10,000-strong Unity Carnival in Newcastle that same year, this area of propaganda was effectively abandoned. A further irony was, with the larger Left organisations crowding into the arena, it was the physical force image that so decisively distinguished AFA from the competition. And under the cover of liberal calls for fascism to be smashed, AFA was by now looking almost entirely to a militarist solution.

3.16

OPERATION BLACKSHIRT

In July 1992 the trial of Gary O'Shea of AFA, and Gerry Gable, editor of *Searchlight*, opened at Southwark Crown Court. The charges had followed the disruption of the Far Right symposium in Kensington library in November 1991. Initially, even though seventeen anti-fascists were arrested in the vicinity, only O'Shea was charged. Rather bizarrely, in addition to theft and charges of assaulting a police officer, he alone was also charged with 'conspiracy' to cause grievous bodily harm. Attempts by police to coerce those arrested into making statements, by implying that one fascist was on 'life support' and another had 'lost an eye', proved futile. All opted, as the investigating DCI remarked more than a little bitterly, for the 'professional no comment'. Though not arrested at the scene, and indeed not charged with 'incitement to violence' until ten weeks after the incident, Gable nevertheless appeared in court as O'Shea's co-defendant.

Why only O'Shea faced conspiracy charges with 'persons unknown', when sharing the dock with Gable, who had not been charged with conspiracy, left many a prosecutor fumbling for an explanation in pre-trial hearings in magistrates courts. At one of the hearings, it was explained to the puzzled magistrate that O'Shea and Gable enjoyed a relationship analogous to "a General and his Field Commander". "I felt like saluting," Gable later joked. Eventually, the state would resolve this contradiction between the alleged plot and the formal charges by dropping the charge of conspiracy against O'Shea and that of incitement to violence against Gable. Instead, both men were charged with a variety of complementary charges. This did little to diminish the seriousness for the defendants if found guilty, for lengthy periods of incarceration were predicted – up to seven years in relation to O'Shea.

However, from start to finish the trial left a trail of unanswered questions and, as events would show, traces of security service interference were in evidence throughout. Certainly, afterwards Gable would go on record in claiming as much. In addition, the judgment of the Crown Prosecution Service in regard to the selection of prosecution witnesses, in tandem with the behaviour of some police officers during the trial, left the objectivity of the proceedings very much open to question. In ordinary criminal cases, the Crown Prosecution Service normally gives the go-ahead to proceed with a case only where it is considered a 51 per cent chance exists of a conviction. All the more remarkable, then, that Gable was acquitted without even the necessity of taking the stand throughout the four days, and the case collapsed without O'Shea's name once being mentioned.

A rather memorable eyewitness account of the farcical opening day was carried in the next issue of *Red Action*. “On the opening day of the trial at Southwark Crown Court, the by now familiar blend of malice and laughable incompetence which had dogged the proceedings throughout was given tangible form. It first materialised in the shape of Mr James Keogh, a chief prosecution witness. A large man, over six feet tall, in his late 40s, he had a military air about him as he bustled purposefully outside the court.

“He attracted curious glances as a result of wearing a white ‘Casablanca’ type mac, several sizes too small. In addition, it was so tightly belted natural movement was restricted. The impression created was of some type of foundation garment, or corset, being worn over a suit. At 10.15am he made his move. He threw open the door of the court and declared to the clerk that he was ‘Counsel for O’Shea’! When it was pointed out to him that the defendant already had a barrister, he protested until he was led away by an usher who conversed with him in low and reassuring tones. The behaviour of Mark Taha, another prosecution witness, was only slightly less bizarre. Particularly seedy, he haunted the corridors of the court trailing a plastic bag or gibbered incessantly to himself in the canteen. On one occasion he caught the eye of some tough-looking customers sitting at an adjoining table. ‘Look at the fucking nonce!’ one snarled almost in disbelief.

“The principle witness for the prosecution was Keith Thompson. It was he who had organised what he described as a ‘symposium’ on 25th May. In all, he spent – served might be more accurate – more than eight hours in the witness box, seven of those under cross-examination. By the end of his testimony, both his and the integrity of the prosecution’s case were in tatters. Even the relatively simple matter of swearing on oath landed him in trouble. He swore on the bible but was forced to admit that he had once been an Odinist. He insisted that this was no longer the case. The defence responded with the inquiry: ‘Tell us, Mr. Thompson, when did Valhalla cease to play an important part in your life?’ The court erupted.

“To the visible astonishment of the jury, he admitted that he would have been, if he had been unemployed in Germany in the 1930s, a National Socialist. He denied the existence of the Holocaust and the gas chambers; insisted that the murder of millions was simply a matter of philosophy; maintained that he was not of the hard right, but preferred to think of himself as ‘hard centre’. Thompson while doing everything to ingratiate himself with Judge Eugene Coltran (a light skinned black man originally from the Cayman Islands), suddenly realised he was deep in Holocaust denial mode. Asked to explain how those who perished in the camps died Thompson insisted it was not deliberate Nazi policy, but resulted from ‘starvation and diseases such as typhoid’. At which Judge Coltran inquired dryly: ‘Was that better, then?’

“By 4.20pm on Tuesday, having been the object of the most gruelling cross-examination for over seven hours, he stumbled from the witness box looking physically and emotionally exhausted. Just before he stepped down, he was challenged to explain yet another contradiction in his evidence. He attempted to acknowledge the error but instead stuttered, 'It was a mistake' – a confession for which there appeared to be only unanimous agreement" (*Red Action*, issue 64).

The calibre of prosecution witnesses did not improve as the trial progressed. The credibility of one witness was all but destroyed before uttering a single word. Introducing himself to the court he gave his name, age and profession as chef. Leaning over, the judge who was taking notes inquired: "Did you say chef?" "Yes, your Honour," the witness replied, bobbing his head. "Oh," remarked the Judge dryly, "I thought you said 'Chief'!" Both the jury and public gallery chuckled appreciatively. Stephen Vallance, who was in charge of security on the day and probably felt he had something to prove, wasn't going to be intimidated. He ad-libbed outrageously, with little regard for his previous statement to police, the latter just about on a nodding acquaintance with reality.

Gable's barrister, who had clearly enjoyed himself up to this, seemed to slaver in anticipation. The expected opportunity to cross-examine, however, was to be denied. For Vallance, perhaps sensing the need to make up for ground lost by other witnesses, committed a fatal blunder. In his statement to police 14 months earlier he had told them that, after Gable's speech, another man addressed the crowd. According to his statement, this individual had said, "On behalf of 'Red...' – another word I didn't hear – thank you all for taking part. We will be leaving shortly." In court he affixed the word 'Action' to the word 'Red'. It was to prove to be an ad-lib too far. Up to that point, the prosecution had maintained that Gable was singularly responsible for everything that happened, that he, in the words of Thompson, was "running the show".

Judge Coltran pounced. "If what you say is true, then this man represented a source of authority other than Gable. If so, could it not have been the case that Gable led the journalists in first, and perhaps Red Action led the mob in later?"

It was at this juncture that the charge against Gable was thrown out. When the court resumed, the prosecutor also announced that the charges of violent disorder, police assault and theft were being dropped against O'Shea. With regard to the alleged assault, he conceded that the PC had reported no injury at the time. The theft of the flag, which O'Shea also denied, was in any case, the judge decided, "only a technical matter ... akin to winning the enemy colours and had only been used to tie him into the case." It was on this remarkably candid admission that the case for the prosecution ended in anti-climax. Both defendants were acquitted and awarded costs.

If AFA activists had been under any illusion that their activities were regarded either benignly or with indifference, this case would have disabused them. As it happens, the conduct of the trial was seen by the militant leadership as part of an escalating and organised response from the state to criminalise militant anti-fascism not simply as an organisation, but as a political entity. A range of incidents involving AFA members occurred during this period. In some cases activists were arrested and charged, only for the subsequent trial to be abandoned by Crown prosecutors, or for charges to be dropped without explanation. Homes were burgled and key activists were subject to overt surveillance when involved in all street level activity. In the most serious of these developments, three AFA members were tried and sentenced to a total of eleven years in prison after being involved in a confrontation with infamous fascist street fighter, Nicky Crane.

However, 'Operation Blackshirt' differed from most others, not just in terms of possible sentences, but also more particularly in terms of security service involvement. For one thing, O'Shea had been arrested at the scene on the basis of an alleged complaint from a police officer. Yet, though all such calls are recorded, no transcript of the description that led to O'Shea's arrest was presented as prosecution evidence, nor indeed was it made available to the defence when asked for. It, therefore, seems safe to conclude that no such call was ever made. Yet an order over the police radio was heard by a number of AFA activists "to hold him [O'Shea] on suspicion of police assault," indicating that someone other than the alleged victim had provided a precise description. Perhaps as ominous was the confirmation of 'spook' involvement during and after the trial.

Tracy: "One morning on the way to the trial, my eye was attracted to a woman in her mid to late 20s standing near the exit from London Bridge station. It was about 9.15 rush hour but I couldn't help admiring an expensive looking polka dot number she was wearing. It was a 'woman thing'. Eight hours later as we were exiting the tube on the other side of London, who was in the same queue for the lift but 'polka dot' – instinct alone told me she was at it."

Further scrutiny of her extraordinary activity that evening left no one in any doubt that the defendants were under surveillance by 'persons unknown'. Followed from the station, 'polka dot' entered Upper Street and met a muscular man there clearly by prior arrangement. They chatted briefly and then she returned past the pub where the anti-fascists were enjoying refreshments. She sat at a nearby bus stop. She got up and joined the queue as the bus arrived. But never got on it. This was replayed at least once more. Finally a motorbike pulled up. She jumped on the back as it accelerated at speed into the rush hour traffic. The guess was the police or some branch of the security services was looking for evidence of the defendants briefing witnesses.

Even more bizarre was the experience of a partner of another AFA activist. Months after the trial, she was travelling along Finchley Road in north London when she was flagged down by a uniformed traffic cop. During routine questioning he claimed that, according to the register at Swansea, her car was not registered in her name at all, but in the name of her partner, Peter C., a leading member of RA. Now a car, similar to the one he was registered as owning, had been mentioned in a succession of prosecution witness statements. Had 'his' car been linked to the anti-fascist operation the charge of 'conspiracy' would have been strengthened considerably. Had someone altered the registration to improve the link? But Peter C. had the perfect alibi in any case. By the time the clashes took place in Kensington he was already in custody, having been arrested during clashes in south east London. On searching the car, the police officer came across some copies of *Red Action* in the boot. He asked for one. But passed when told he would have to pay for it.

A couple of weeks after the trial, six masked men, led (AFA later discovered) by an Australian right-winger going by the name Gary Johnson, arrived at the address in Wembley O'Shea had given in court as his place of residence. Hesitation among the attackers allowed the athletic young woman, a fitness instructor, who initially answered the door to slam it in their faces. Because she was of Turkish descent, a disgruntled C18 later referred to her as "a Mud". As was customary in political cases, the Wembley address had been withheld from being broadcast in open court, so there was a suspicion that it may have been passed on by a senior detective, who was judged to be unduly sympathetic to the prosecution witnesses during the trial.

On what proved to be the last day, in an extraordinary professional lapse, the DCI had publicly exhorted police witnesses to finish the job, within earshot of an AFA supporter, who, rather than go the canteen with everyone else, was sitting outside the court, reading. Ruefully admitting that Gable had probably slipped the net, the detective told the assembled police witnesses during a break for lunch that if "you do your job we can still nail O'Shea." Due to the disastrous contribution of Vallance, the prosecution case was already in serious trouble. Had it not been, the DCI's outburst would surely have seen what remained of the case thrown out.

Many activists would have been in accord with the conclusion drawn in *Red Action*. "While there were never any grounds to show that the accused conspired together with persons unknown, it is not implausible to suggest they might have been conspired against by persons unknown." Gerry Gable told the *Guardian* that the case should never have been brought claiming he was being victimised for investigating the security services. "If somebody out there has got such an elitist view of this world they think they can silence the work of *Searchlight* by removing its editor, they are wrong" (*Guardian*, 24th July 1992).

Consistent with his demeanour throughout, O'Shea slipped away without comment. Later, some, including independent researcher Larry O'Hara, maintained that Gable was part of some plot to entrap militants. But as one leading RA member put it afterwards, "If his [Gable's] tears on acquittal were not genuine, then Gerry is indeed a great loss to the theatre."

UNSCREW SKREWDRIVER!

Assemble:

Saturday 12th September 1992 at 4.30pm

Waterloo BR

(Bring a Travelcard)

Anti-Fascist Action
BM Box 1734
London WC1N 3XX

The leaflet that launched a thousand anti-fascists detemined to cause the maximum disruption.

3.17

THE BATTLE OF WATERLOO

Across the country the level of militant activity continued during the rest of 1992 with numerous clashes up and down the country. Overwhelmingly, AFA was emerging victorious in confrontations that were increasingly as much psychological as physical. A fairly typical example of militant one-upmanship came when the BNP, buoyant after a successful meeting in the prestigious York Hall in Bethnal Green despite an ANL counter-demo, emerged only to discover a 70-strong AFA stewards group using their pub. Initially with only a dozen or so AFA visible outside, a hundred or so BNP charged down the gradient toward The Weaver's Arms. A large number of riot police, ready and primed for action, quickly blockaded the road. But they did so by lining up about thirty yards to the right of the pub when over a hundred BNP were mounting an attack on it from the left. Bar joining in the attack, there was little the police could have done to make their partiality more noticeable.

But, the nearer the BNP mob got, the larger the numbers of militants ready to greet them grew. And with familiar 'faces' in command, any prospect of a walkover faded away. Eventually, a visibly deflated BNP filed past on the opposite side of the road in almost total silence. A number of anti-fascists were lifted for possession of offensive weapons on leaving the area. That night on Radio Five Live the pub governor went out of his way to make clear to listeners that it was the "Anti-Fascist League [sic] who were the ones looking for trouble." When they "left my pub it was stripped of everything they could throw: glasses, bottles, pool balls, even darts," he alleged. "The BNP regularly used his pub and caused no trouble at all," he added naïvely. The next day every single window in his pub crashed in.

On 12th September 1992, central London witnessed the largest and most bloody head-to-head battle between the Far Right and anti-fascists since Kevin Gateley was killed in Red Lion Square in 1974. In what was dubbed the 'Battle of Waterloo', AFA took on a revamped Blood & Honour in a public showdown that, at the height of the fighting, caused traffic chaos. It also caused the closure of both Charing Cross and Waterloo BR stations, plus half a dozen tube stations on either side of the Thames. According to police estimates about 2,000 people were involved in the clashes that began at around 3.30pm and did not abate until around 7pm.

With B&H and the BNP working fairly closely at the time, a successful gig, publicly advertised and secured by a large mobilisation of fascists would, they hoped, enable B&H to operate more openly thereafter. Three years earlier, in an interview with the *Evening Standard*'s *ES Magazine* (April 1989), Stuart had claimed that he "could fill the Albert Hall with supporters if we were able to hold a concert without interference from the 'commies'." This theory was now to be put to the test.

Joe: "Rumour had it that a prominent music promoter, John Kurt, was interested in looking at the whole B&H scene from a purely commercial angle as a result of witnessing Skrewdriver's pulling power in Europe, where audiences of 3,000-plus for underground gigs in former East Germany were not uncommon. Waterloo appeared to be designed as a kind of showdown. A way of estimating what level of public support the band could expect from wide-scale publicity, including national press which they had always avoided for security reasons, and, as importantly, what level of support the 'Reds' would draw."

Terry: "In the run-up we were extremely sceptical. Bogus gigs had been called before. And even prior to the 'Main Event' in '89, the main concern of Blood & Honour at all times had been to keep everything word of mouth, and hush-hush. For the 'Main Event' it had been ticket only with applications to be made by post. Twelve hundred tickets had been sold throughout Europe in advance and a promise was made by B&H: 'Money back if not delighted'. We didn't know at the time about attempts to make things 'legit', so initially it was treated with caution."

With only a couple of weeks to go and with Waterloo station being selected as the re-direction point, it began to dawn on AFA that B&H were going for it. News of

Some members of the BNP on their way to York Hall, Bethnal Green, in August 1992 (Charlie Sargent of Combat 18 is seen in the foreground).

posters advertising the event were phoned in from as far away as Newcastle and Edinburgh. Besides the possibility of an elaborate hoax, another reason for AFA caution was that, if indeed the Far Right were after a showdown, AFA knew from experience not to count on support, fraternal or otherwise, from rival anti-fascists. So in making their calculations the AFA leadership knew that on the day it was likely they would be on their own – which, in effect, meant running the risk of being heavily outnumbered.

There was, however, an ace up the militant sleeve. The second AFA Unity Carnival was due to take place on 6th September, the Sunday before, which meant AFA would have direct access to many thousands of militant sympathisers. Regional organisers were canvassed around the country and AFA decided to go for it. 15,000 leaflets were printed. On the morning of the carnival it began to rain and rained steadily throughout the day. Despite this, the thousands attending were alerted to the importance of opposing the event. To further maximise the sense of occasion, AFA breached its own protocol by advertising the face-off with a press release two days before.

"We will be attempting to cause as much disruption as possible to the Blood & Honour gig on Saturday. We hope to be able to do this peacefully, if we are allowed to, but we are undaunted at the prospect of a physical confrontation, and in the end it may well be like the Battle of Waterloo."

Immediately the ANL announced in the *South London Press* that it hoped "to mobilise a large enough presence to stop them [B&H] giving venue details" and "do it peacefully" (*South London Press*, 11th September 1992). But in reality the ANL had no intention of being there at all. For as soon as the militants picked up the gauntlet, the SWP ordered the ANL to mobilise in support of a march in Thornton Heath on the extreme outskirts of south London. Afterwards, to the mocking laughter of much of the Left, the SWP would lay claim to Waterloo as an ANL victory.

Meanwhile, with Blood & Honour organiser Neil Parish publicly boasting he would be "available for interviews on the concourse" from 4.30pm, the AFA counter-demo was scheduled for the Waterloo concourse at 4pm. Sky News teams were on full alert and the possibility of serious trouble surfaced in red top tabloids like the *Daily Star*. Even *The Scotsman* sent a reporter. Boldly approaching a rough looking crew standing in the middle of the forecourt, he inquired as to the whereabouts of Neil Parish and was visibly taken aback when informed he was addressing members of the opposition.

If the media were expectant, the police seemed unduly relaxed, if not downright complacent. Normally, an attempt to gauge the scale of what was being planned would be assessed via tapped phones and general intelligence, but on this occasion phone traffic between key AFA players was proving minimal to non-existent.

Possibly this led Special Branch to conclude it would, despite all the publicity, prove low-key. An alternative scenario is that, with British Transport Police rather than the Met being formally in charge, relevant information may deliberately not have been passed on. For intelligence to be intentionally withheld from a security service rival is hardly unknown. Certainly when Chief Inspector Davison from the British Transport Police at Waterloo told the press that, "It's difficult to say exactly what our tactics will be on the day itself but we intend to isolate those responsible for the concert and keep the two sides apart," he obviously had little idea of who he was dealing with. If the police weren't sure of their tactics the AFA leadership knew exactly what was required of them: create as much chaos as possible. (This deliberate abandonment of orthodox forms of demonstrations, with stewards in bibs issuing megaphone directions and so on, would later be attacked by left-wing adversaries as 'criminal stupidity'!)

On the morning of the carnival, over 100 key security personnel were summoned to the stewards tent and informed of the time and the re-direction point and what was expected of them on the day. All were instructed to keep the information to themselves. It is this face-to-face meeting that explains the absence of phone play. A large Irish pub in Kilburn had been selected as the rendezvous. First, because it allowed direct access to Waterloo via the Bakerloo Line, but also partly because, due to its location (at a busy junction with a row of single story shops opposite), it was thought it would prove problematic for police to properly observe it without being spotted. The AFA leadership had very good reasons to keep a close watch on their own assembly point.

Tracey: "By this stage leading 'players' were being directly targeted by police. For the type of event planned, given the pre-publicity, we needed to know if conspiracy charges would follow. Key to this was to find out whether or not the timing and re-direction point had 'leaked'. If it had, plans would be adapted accordingly. So I was directed to handpick a team of six to put our own re-direction point under surveillance at 12pm, two hours before the main outfit was expected to be in position at 2pm. I'd been in the game for a number of years now and I was confident that if anything untoward was going on in the area, I would pick it up."

Publicly, AFA was scheduled to arrive at Waterloo at 4.30 pm, with the bulk of B&H expected at around 5pm. At 3.20pm, over an hour ahead of schedule, when an advance party of about 150 AFA security stewards materialised on the concourse at Waterloo, it took everyone by surprise.

Joe: "From scouts in the area we were aware that a large contingent of early B&H arrivals were drinking in a bar on the station. It was our intention on the day to deny them access to the concourse. To do that, we had to hold the station. That meant that the boneheads in the station had to be cleared out. Now, attacking a pub, even with superior numbers, is not to be recommended, particularly in an area that is 'camera-ed' up. One plan hatched en route was to drive them from the pub interior by bombarding them with a mixture of crow-scarers and smoke bombs. The noise would have been deafening and the smoke would have caused confusion and provided cover from the cameras. That was the plan, anyway!"

Within seconds of hitting the concourse it was learned the skinheads had already been moved on. For the chief steward, this was potentially disastrous. He was counting on the boneheads providing an immediate focus. A quick victory would set the tone for the day. The last thing he wanted was for the stewards to mill around aimlessly. Just then news came through that another smaller group had been spotted in another pub on the station. 'They'll do,' he thought. Within seconds AFA had stormed the pub. Dismayed skinheads fled as if for their lives. One jumped over the bar, holding off his assailants by chucking glasses and even full bottles of spirits, then ducking back under the bar as the anti-fascists replied in kind. This show of defiance ended abruptly when one steward assembled a dozen heavy dinner plates from the counter, took careful aim, and dropped them directly on to his head. At 3.25pm two ambulances, which had been on standby, drove onto the concourse to collect their first customers of the day, three 'boneheads', one of them rumoured to be a plain-clothes police officer, having been 'glassed'. So much for British Transport Police assurances of "keeping the sides apart". AFA had arrived. And the Battle of Waterloo had begun.

In an attempt to restore order, police immediately began making huge sweeps across the station with lines of police, arms linked, herding militants, elderly passengers, foreign tourists, and inevitably fascists towards the exits. Once outside, the B&H supporters were instantly attacked. This forced police to leave the station to intervene, thus leaving gaps in the 'thin blue line' that were artfully negotiated by anti-fascists who, time and again returned to mass on the concourse. As importantly, as every minute passed they were being reinforced by dozens of anti-fascists coming to Waterloo by bus and tube.

By 4pm the AFA objective of occupying the station had been secured. The tricky part now was being able to continue to do so. So long as AFA 'held' the station it would be the natural rallying point for the anti-fascist forces, while automatically rendering it useless as a redirection point for the opposition. Consistent with the strategic importance of holding the station, a decision had been taken not to try and impose any order on the wilder anarchist elements. For one, they were reckoned to be largely uncontrollable, and AFA strategists actually saw the benefit in allowing the 'crusties' to run wild. Siren calls from others in the station, including one individual waving a black flag, to 'ignore the stewards' and join the mêlée outside were silenced, following a few well-chosen words from leading AFA stewards.

So by 5pm, instead of being dispersed, there were anything up to a 1,000 anti-fascists on the station concourse. Brawls broke out, peaked and subsided all over the station area, inside and out. Pretty clearly police were not in control. Sky TV, meanwhile, was relaying events 'live'. A small group of black youngsters repeatedly missed their train rather than miss the action. Quoted in the *News of the World* afterwards, a police officer described the scene as like "Custer's last stand". One British Rail official said: "I saw a giant of a man grab two policemen and smash their heads together. It took another six policemen to hold him down. It was dreadful" (*News of the World*, 13th September 1992). Shortly after 5pm, Waterloo was shut down at the request of the station manager. Police Superintendent Mike Joyce explained that the decision "to evacuate" was "to keep the two groups apart" (*Mail on Sunday*, 13th September 1992). It would in fact produce exactly the opposite result.

Freed from political responsibility, and any inhibitions the existence of security cameras on the station may have had on their behaviour, large groups of anti-fascists, 100-strong, rampaged gleefully through the side streets, blending and splintering as the situation demanded. One 50-strong group of mainly right-wing casuals was trapped beneath a footbridge. Surrounded by dozens of police, they were nonetheless faced with a full-frontal assault. As bricks and bottles rained down on them from the advancing attackers, some fascists at the back tried to make a break for it. A policeman screamed a warning: "If you run, we're fucking running with you!"

Andy: "A group of us were driven out of the station and we immediately became concerned that we were going to get corralled-in by the police so we exited the area. As it was, the attention we were receiving simply meant that others were able to by-pass the boys in blue and filter back into the station. Using a familiar AFA tactic we went to ground, sipping orange juices in the Charlie Chaplin, Elephant & Castle, for a brief period before re-emerging ready to engage targets whenever and wherever we could.

"As we approached Waterloo again, we could see a large group in front of us who had spotted us at the same time. It turned out that they were anti-fascists and our ranks swelled considerably. At the rear of the station there was a large procession of vehicles backed-up all the way into the road. In the middle were two boneheads sitting calmly in the traffic, presumably oblivious to the mayhem occurring just yards away.

They gave the distinct impression of having borrowed daddy's car for their big day out, fingers drumming the steering wheel, impatient for the fun to start. And start it did. Immediately, concrete slabs were launched through the front and rear windscreens, followed by anything else people could get their hands on. The boneheads sat bolt upright, staring straight ahead as missiles came flying through the glass and I can only guess that they'd gone into shock. I moved to the side of the car with the intention of putting my arm through one of the broken windows and pulling up the locks so we could get the doors open and drag them out.

Just then another lump of concrete was launched into the car, showering me with glass. It made me stop and think. There were quite a few undisciplined elements with us now and all of a sudden I had visions of the infamous 'two corporals'* incident being replayed in south London. I changed my mind and instead we got people to turn their attentions towards the numerous battles taking place all around the station."

On the perimeters of the station, individuals and smaller groups of fascists, some on foot, some mobile, were being picked off expeditiously. One right-winger, having been thwarted from leaving the immediate area by roaming anti-fascists, sought to make himself less conspicuous by joining a bus queue. It was his considerable misfortune that he stood in front of a prominent militant who was having a little time out after being involved in a recent altercation. A half-brick to the head settled the matter. By this time, four other stations in the immediate vicinity had been "closed", according to a chalked notice board "due to riots".

Another large number of boneheads arrived on foot via the footbridge and swelled the fascists' numbers by another 150. But by now, everywhere you looked there was pandemonium. Hooligan elements, from Arsenal, QPR, Chelsea and Millwall, many wearing team shirts, supplemented one side or the other according to their political convictions. To prevent even more flooding into the area, police ordered Charing Cross BR station to close as well.

A couple of anti-fascists, Gerry and Russell, who had actually been involved with the NF and BM as teenagers, infiltrated the opposition, mingled cheerfully and 'sieg-heiled' with gusto. Skirmishes were frequent, bottles and bricks were lobbed into the fascist/police crowd with customary disregard. The police were visibly perturbed. They wanted desperately to be rid of their 'escorts', but the stations were all closed and the fascists themselves had no idea where the venue was. It transpired later that the actual organisers, including C18, had prudently arranged an alternative redirection point for themselves in Victoria.

By now, the entrapped fascists were demanding they either be rescued – or entrusted with details. Both requests were repeatedly denied, the standard reply being: "Rather than us come to Waterloo, you should come to Victoria." But with the station now closed and traffic jammed, the only option was to try to cross the river on foot. But instead of bringing them over the bridge, the police tried to smuggle them out via the arches at the rear of the South Bank complex, down Concert Hall Approach. This particular retreat from Waterloo was cut off by the arrival of 400 anti-fascists at the junction of Belvedere Road. First the

* In 1988 during the funeral of IRA member Caoimhin MacBradaigh, two undercover soldiers Corporals Wood and Howes, were mistaken for Loyalist assassins, dragged from their car by mourners and executed by the IRA.

police/fascists stopped dead and simply stared as the anti-fascists slowly advanced in almost complete silence. Suddenly a black youngster, a recent recruit to the security stewards, appeared in the mouth of a tunnel adjacent to where the opposition had grouped, and without a moment's hesitation began trading blows with those nearest to him. The fascists recoiled, horrified. Seizing the moment, the anti-fascists charged.

A large chunk of pavement slab flew through the air as a skip was plundered. Right-wingers, as well as policemen and their dogs, fled in all directions. Jack Shamash for the *Weekly Journal* reported: "Within seconds the scene was mayhem. I saw police hitting out in blind confusion with truncheons, sometimes hitting each other by mistake. Protestors from both sides spat at police. A rain of bottles and broken masonry fell down, the bottles shattering and sending splinters everywhere. At one point I saw police and protestors recoiling from a canister, which split open to release clouds of noxious gas. As I ran trying to avoid being hit, two people behind me were struck by flying glass. People had blood streaming down their faces. And I saw a policeman being led away, holding his face which appeared to have been struck by a missile" (*Weekly Journal*, 17th September 1992).

Another reporter from *Select* magazine, who had been directed by his editor to join the fascists to satisfy his readers' prurience, unexpectedly found himself among those doing the 'running', and duly wrote from that perspective: "Each time," he wrote, "there was always one or two psychos shouting 'Stand, stand,' but no one takes any notice." Famously, during these exchanges one of the Millwall 'psychos', called 'Tags', actually collapsed with a heart attack.

"They run, some with jackets over their heads to protect them from the barrage, down back streets and through startled traffic. You quickly learn that the best way to run is looking backwards at the sky. Once, I duck and jerk my arms over my head to protect it from a brick, only to discover it's just a frightened pigeon. Looking up, I find a young Tim Roth look-alike next to me has done the same. We grin at each other sheepishly. It's a weird moment. Several of the skins are injured by now. One, a sharp-faced boy, has blood streaming down his face from a head wound … Someone else, holding a dazed demonstrator by the arm wanders past, shouting 'Ambulance, ambulance'. It was a vile scene." (*Select* magazine)

The still able-bodied, mostly skinheads, had come to an indecisive halt at the base of Waterloo Bridge. For a time riot police formed a protective barrier, but after five minutes and without any warning they suddenly seemed to vanish. In panic, hundreds of fascists bolted down the ramp parallel to Waterloo station. Halfway down, they shuddered to a halt and then reversed at speed when they met 300 'Reds' on the way up. Exploding back onto the pavement, they ran into scattered groups of anti-fascists who had optimistically given chase when they fled, and now found themselves outnumbered by ten to one. For the briefest of moments the tables had been turned. True to form, it was the footage of fascists apparently in the ascendancy that was selected by BBC editors as the most politically appropriate metaphor to illustrate events on the day. This was no accident, as it was designed to prove that, despite the evidence, it was the fascists who were the more violently aggressive. Political camouflage such as this was hardly new.*

Large numbers of fascists had by now been shepherded onto Waterloo Bridge, stopping both lanes of traffic, while hundreds of anti-fascists in groups of 50 and 60 were corralled by police beneath it.

Joe: "For me the abiding memory of the day, one that summed up police befuddlement throughout, was the sight of fifty police with batons and shields wearily trudging up the hill in Indian file, heads down, oblivious or by now possibly indifferent to, similar numbers of 'Anarchos' and 'Reds' filing past them in the opposite direction, conspicuously in hot pursuit of further prey. Contact was made almost instantly. A small group of bones wandered into their path. They were devoured. One particular unfortunate disappeared under a scrum. It looked like he was being torn limb from limb. Then something flew into the air. For a crazy moment it looked like an arm. But was just the sleeve of his flight jacket. It was like a Bugs Bunny cartoon."

Eventually, under cover of darkness, the police escorted the crestfallen fascists to Temple tube where a train was commandeered. Less than 500 Blood & Honour made it to the Yorkshire Grey in Eltham, south east London. Not wishing to be seen to lick their wounds in public, the previously publicity hungry B&H organisers excluded the press. The *Mail on Sunday* reported "at least 44 arrests" with, according to the *Guardian*, "seven policemen" injured, although B&H supporters bore the brunt of the hospital casualties overall. For AFA it was a crushing victory, with no possible ambiguity about the outcome: a near-fatal blow to Blood & Honour in Britain, and the sheer scale of it sending tremors through the Far Right. One fascist fanzine, called *The Raven*, claimed it as "a moral victory" on the grounds that headlines did not read 'Nazis killed at Waterloo' the following day.

* "The British Union of Fascists' use of force in the 1930s always appeared to be more calculated, visible, more obviously organised than that of its opponents. In fact, the communists organised just as thoroughly with as much military precision, as did the fascists. But their use of force was largely concealed: they were the guerrilla army; the fascists the traditional army … [A]t the time these things were shrouded in darkness, a darkness partly induced by such left-wing bodies as the Council for Civil Liberties. 'It is fashionable to allege that we were starry-eyed idealists, but we certainly knew where to put the razor blades in the potato when it came to a fight,' says the veteran of many battles, Claud Cockburn" (*Oswald Mosley*, by Robert Skidelsky, Chapter 18, 'The politics of confrontation')

On the Left, alongside those like the ANL who tried to claim the credit for it, there were others who deliberately poured cold water on the victory in order to allow them to ignore the political implications for themselves. *The Leninist* described Waterloo as only a "relative success" (mimicking the 'moderate success' of the BNP in Bermondsey according to the SWP), while complaining that though "there was a divide on the day between fighters and non-fighters, it was difficult to tell who was who." Which was of course precisely the point. If they couldn't do so, neither could the police. The Revolutionary Internationalist League went considerably further. While forced to concede that "this mobilisation was radically different from anything we have seen in Britain for many years ... Waterloo showed us the militancy and potential of anti-fascist forces who turned up in great number on the one hand, and the utter incompetence, stupidity and criminal neglect of the anti-fascist organisation leaders. At Waterloo, AFA offered no leadership or organisation to the masses of anti-fascists who turned up to stop the nazis. Clearly it was necessary to have (identified or unidentified) stewards who were communicating with the crowds directing them in the most effective direction." According to the RIL, this "lack of organisation" meant the anti-fascists were effectively paralysed by much fewer but better organised police." Not a conclusion British Rail management, police strategists, or indeed B&H organisers were likely

Abandoned fash looking a bit lost around Waterloo, 1992.

to have much sympathy with. Oddball sectarianism apart, the RIL were plainly unnerved by the AFA 'chaos theory' and hankered after the safety of more orthodox formations with placards, megaphones, and friends and foe instantly identifiable.

Small wonder that the AFA press release was directed not at the vanquished Right but at the liberal Left: "The tactics favoured by the Anti-Nazi League and other liberal anti-racist groups have been eclipsed by yesterday's victory. Unlike them we don't believe in token demonstrations or in calling for state bans ... If the anti-fascist movement in Europe had implemented a policy of No Platform For Fascists with the same commitment as we did yesterday, Rostock would still be just a little town in Germany."

The Copsey verdict on the AFA performance was altogether more generous. But, in conceding it was "a major victory", he adopts a different line of attack. Stressing that it was "Blood & Honour and not the BNP that got smashed." The BNP taking 20% in a by-election on the Isle of Dogs a month later, he offered as the reason for a certain reserve. In his view AFA had allowed itself to be "diverted from concentrating efforts on Millwall" by the B&H attempts to "re-establish itself in London." Once again this charge of a misallocation of resources by militants does not hold up for an instant. For one thing, Waterloo, though spectacular, amounted to little more than a couple of weeks' work from start to finish. As for the Copsey juxtaposition of the B&H versus BNP, they were in reality known to be working more or less in tandem at the time. Indeed, such was the extent of the collaboration, had this fairly outrageous push by B&H to go legit been even partially successful there was the strong possibility it would have opened up a by no means insubstantial funding for the BNP. Even with the setback in Britain, B&H in Europe would go on to become a multi-million pound industry. Which probably explains why even mainstream music promoters considered it so potentially lucrative.

Finally, of course, had AFA not dealt with B&H, there was no one else on the Left equipped to do so. And had B&H ambitions not been crushed, considering a BNP election breakthrough was already being flagged by AFA, this would have resulted in militants fighting on at least two fronts: confronting a 'respectable' BNP euro-nationalism on the one hand and the commercialisation of neo-nazism on the other. While Copsey is seemingly ignorant of the implications of anti-fascism not winning, he does concede Waterloo represented a victory for AFA for another reason: "it finally established AFA's claim to the radical anti-fascist tradition." Truth be told, save for the scale and unprecedented advance publicity, Waterloo, in terms of intensity was probably indistinguishable from countless encounters stretching back for over ten years.

How critical the Unity Carnival had been to the numbers mobilised for Waterloo was proved to good effect just six weeks later when, on 26th October, AFA called a counter-demonstration in response to the BNP publicising a re-direction point at Euston Station for their AGM. Pre-warned by Waterloo, the Met dominated throughout, and even though AFA could not physically damage the BNP too much on the day, the simple threat of militants mobilising was enough to see numbers for the BNP AGM halve – from the previous year – the precise opposite of BNP expectations who had hoped to double numbers attending through the advance publicity.

Once again the militant call was boycotted by the ANL, ARA, and YRE, but whereas at Waterloo, where the sheer size of the turnout camouflaged their duplicity, there was no disguising it this time. To working class elements in organisations like Militant, increasingly restive at the party's hands-off approach, the leadership would caution: "You can't work with AFA, they're psychopaths." And while the Copsey allegation that AFA had allowed itself to be 'diverted' is easily refuted, nevertheless the corollary of the BNP being able to go 'about their business unhindered' in Millwall would make headlines across the world within twelve months.

3.18

THE WEST MIDLANDS, 1992

Even though AFA had been in nominal existence in the West Midlands since late 1991, following a 200-strong launch meeting held at Carr's Lane Centre in south Birmingham, it arguably only became properly 'operational' in militant terms in early 1993. For unlike AFA in the North West and Scotland where the structures and leadership reflected the priorities originally set out by London, similar elements in the West Midlands had yet to come to the fore. As neither Red Action nor DAM had any branches in the vicinity, this meant that as late as Spring 1993 the Midlands was widely regarded as a safe haven for white nationalists. To the extent that an organisation like the NF, which otherwise hardly dare put its head over the parapet elsewhere in the country, still had a power base in the area. Up until then, the orthodox Trotskyite Workers Power had the whip-hand organisationally within AFA there, but, partly inspired by Waterloo, in October 1992 younger working class militants now made it their business to reshape the organisation in the West Midlands from within.

Martin: "After Waterloo, Workers Power were eclipsed by youngsters, who had cut their teeth in clashes from London to Manchester, and wanted to apply the techniques learned in our own backyard. As far as we could see, all the old school in the Arran Isle jumpers and rusting 'Coal not Dole' buttons seemed to want to do was talk about standing around braziers picketing Saltley gates in 1972."

Paul: "We didn't initially set out for a coup, bloodless or otherwise. Some of us had been working alongside Workers Power for some time. People were sent to talk with them about 'stepping it up'. But, while some tried to appear diplomatic, the main man from Workers Power refused to recognise the delegation. It was an offer that wasn't going to be made twice."

Aware of the emerging threat, Workers Power sought to try and control events bureaucratically. Rather than encourage open political discussion to decide on priorities as was the norm elsewhere, Workers Power in Birmingham sought to cede power to an executive style 'committee' to which only those who had their political approval were allowed access. Such a formal hierarchical structure was anathema to the likes of the DAM and RA, ironically that it was an attempt to maintain their status and fend off the young Turks that would prove WP's undoing. On finding out from WP colleagues in London that an operation mounted by the newly formed Wolverhampton AFA had gone awry, and as a consequence had attracted the attention of the London leadership, WP in the Midlands sought to capitalise on some tactical errors made on the day by arranging for a disciplinary meeting with reps from London in attendance, wherein Wolverhampton AFA would be formally called to account. By putting manners on these upstarts with London's blessing, WP would, they believed, be in position to politically control the development of AFA across the West Midlands – and moreover do so entirely from Birmingham. It was to prove a spectacular misreading of both the extant situation and of the instincts of the London leadership. In fact, by the end of the meeting, West Midlands AFA had an entirely new leadership itself.

Originally stung into action by tales of alleged anarchist and hunt saboteur incompetence, a delegation from London AFA did travel up to Birmingham determined to knock heads. However, almost as an afterthought they decided to take a sounding from a tough young Red Action supporter in the city, Damian, who though having only recently signed up was highly regarded, not least by Patrick Hayes, the London AFA organiser.

Joe: " Not really knowing what was going on up there, we decided to pay him a visit. His insight into the real motives for the meeting and personalities involved threw a totally different light on events. It was an almost chance encounter but one that would seal the fate not only of WP in AFA but the Far Right in the Midlands. What really put the tin hat on it for many of us was when before the meeting he was brusquely informed that it was 'an executive only meeting and he would have to wait in the bar'. The looks on the faces of my colleagues said it all. Having been treated by many a martinet like this themselves, over the years, no way were they going to tolerate working class recruits being treated like this in their own organisation."

So, after confidently outlining the situation as they saw it, the collective jaw of the Workers Power delegation dropped, when the wrath they had so artfully cultivated was turned away from the sole female representative from Wolverhampton and – onto them. A statement from the deposed WP faction, formerly the 'executive', now calling itself Anti-Fascist Alliance, summed up in an unwittingly comic manner the differing priorities of the rivals thereafter.

"It is okay to get militants to take on the fascists in a few spectacular events like the 'Battle of Waterloo', but though such events are correct they are not enough. That means, unfortunately for some, getting their hands dirty and *arguing* [our emphasis] with reformist workers and other anti-fascist groups" (*Birmingham Anti-Fascist Alliance Bulletin*, 12th July 1994).

Martin: "What quickly emerged was that like attracted like. Our support came from the football and Irish clubs and those who had walked out or been expelled from the lefty cults; we figured if the Left didn't want them, they were probably sound! So, in the time the former 'executive committee' took to come up with a draft statement to condemn whatever, our people had been involved in attacking fascists in the streets, and most importantly building a database of active fascists from scratch."

As with other areas of the country, many of the AFA militants had been through the mill politically, were disillusioned with the Left but, unlike many on the Left, were solidly working class and all too aware of the dangers posed by middle class intrusion.

Martin: " For many of us, it was a case of AFA being seen as the last port before the storm. Disillusionment with an increasingly marginalised Left was a common experience, so from the outset our M.O. [*modus operandi*] was as much a case of knowing what not to do, as knowing what to do. For example, a rigorous vetting procedure was introduced to insure the basic character of Midlands AFA would remain a working class one. This was a deliberate move to protect AFA from opportunism and any dilution of its working class character. All our success up to this was because of a tight-knit but democratic approach to organising. Regular branch meetings and much protracted discussion within the group ironed out the overall formula."

In the early 1990s there was plenty of fascism to contend with in the West Midlands, both from the BNP and the NF. The BNP at this time were attempting to gain a foothold in the Kingstanding and Oscott areas of north Birmingham, while the NF were active in the Black Country, where they had consistently pursued an electoral strategy, largely unopposed, since the 1970s. In addition, B&H and C18 were also present and active.

Immediately the issue of leadership was clarified, AFA took the physical component of the struggle to the fascists with vigour. On 12th February 1993, a packed gig at Mansfield Labour Club announced the change of management. "In the week previous to the gig, the organiser had a burning cross planted in his garden and the BNP announced that they would not allow the gig to go ahead. On the night itself, the BNP very wisely kept their distance as more than 100 stewards waited patiently for the 'inevitable' fascist offensive. The single scout who did venture too near ... was last seen driving recklessly through two sets of red lights with his rear windscreen missing" (*Fighting Talk*, issue 4).

Thereafter, street activity varied from small-scale

opportunistic attacks through to larger scale, high profile mobilisations. Such set pieces were required to match similarly high profile opposition events, where 'controlling the streets' was regarded as quintessential to the fascist strategy. In such cases, AFA's aim was to reverse the equation and to be perceived by both observers and fascists as being clever and 'bad enough' to be able to turn the tables.

Systematic and intensive intelligence gathering was one of the key things that gave AFA the upper hand regionally. From a standing start AFA quickly became very familiar with the enemy. Individual activists, street activities and branch meetings were all monitored routinely. The latest in technical gadgetry was used to stay ahead of the game – two way AM radios, CBs and scanners to pick up on the police and listen out for mobiles, cameras and traces. In many ways the 'know your enemy' dictum was being taken to a higher level. Everything was collated with a view to future reference and research. From a simple car registration militants could quickly find out someone's name, date of birth, job and work address, plus details of relatives. Lone fascists were picked off in the street, sometimes merely to display ruthlessness, on other occasions the motive might be the appropriation of sensitive paperwork. 'Outing' posters were put up in areas where the fascists lived.

The fascist response was one of bewilderment and impotence. After the home of one fascist was repeatedly targeted by way of retaliation, threats were even made against the SWP paper selling pitches in Birmingham city centre and delivered to the militants via Searchlight! Understandably, anonymity was highly prized by militants. Unknown to the fascists, two key AFA members had actually appeared in a copy of *Redwatch* but were mistakenly identified as belonging to un-associated groups. A later issue of *Redwatch* hardly helped matters when it claimed a left-wing café, called 'Café/Resource Centre' in east Birmingham, was the nerve centre for militants in the West Midlands. A portion of chips bought from there, was more often than not, it was alleged, "wrapped in [a copy of] *Red Action*," they informed their readership. Militants just laughed.

On Sunday 12th September 1993, militants in the Midlands were involved in a public showdown with the NF who had called their AGM in Birmingham. The lobby of New Street station was picked as a re-direction point. AFA deployed around fifty security stewards in and around the station area. An early casualty was the leader of the NF, Andy Carmichael, who was beaten to the floor until rescued by British Transport police. Afterwards, he confessed to the *Evening Mail* that the re-direction points and the booking of the hotel under the name 'Heritage Foundation' were necessary, because otherwise "there would have been the same kind of scenes at Coleshill as there were at New Street" (*Evening Mail*, 13th September 1993). Four years later, Carmichael went to the press with a confession of a rather different sort. Announcing in the *Sunday Times* (27th July 1997) that he had for a considerable time been working directly under MI5 instruction.

Though encouraged by the rate of their success in pinning the fascists down, the relative failure of an AFA attack just a month later in October 1993 on the Thatched House Tavern, in what was regarded as the right-wing stronghold of Bloxwich, caused an overall review, and led to a decisive upping of the ante in the West Midlands. By now AFA were expert in operating in relatively small teams, but if the right-wingers were to be killed off politically it would require the routine deployment of large numbers of stewards onto the streets. When the discussion reached a national level, instead of continuing to chip away, Midlands AFA got the green light to begin to think in terms of an endgame.

One key player on the Far Right at this time, called Duane 'Eddie' Marlowe, headed up B&H/C18 activity in the Bloxwich area of the City. Marlowe had taken a bad beating in Digbeth in Birmingham in 1993, when he accidentally crossed paths with a leading AFA player. But perhaps the critical point in his political demise came on 12th November 1994, when a fascist counter-mobilisation led by him against a Trades Council march through Bloxwich was routed by a large group of AFA stewards. The BNP gathered to oppose this march on a regular basis in what they had come to consider their territory. AFA seized the initiative by forcibly moving in on two fascist pubs, The Chimneys, and The Crown and Sceptre. On the day, over fifty militant anti-fascists gathered in the centre of Bloxwich in the morning, with the aim of the day being to prove to the wider community, the Left and, most importantly, the fascists, that when confronted by militant anti-fascists these Aryan Warriors are not all they're cracked up to be.

"The AFA contingent set about visiting watering-holes that Duane Eddie and his Merry Men are known to frequent. The first pub we hit (forgive the pun) was one of Marlowe's locals. The landlord greeted us warmly and asked us if we were there to meet Duane, assuming we were fascists! Our intelligence then led us to the infamous Chimneys public house, as seen on TV picketed by the ANL on a number of occasions, and reputed to have hosted monthly fascist meetings. The AFA crew clashed with fascists just outside the pub, enabling those inside to do a runner and jump the fence to safety, indifferent to their comrades' fate. We soon discovered on entering the pub that Marlowe had made a phone call to the police saying, 'There's a large number of NF (!) in The Chimneys, tooled up with knives, iron bars and CS gas!' Presumably Marlowe's paranoia led him to believe that the police would be more likely to react to a fascist gang than to an AFA one.

"After one or two further altercations, AFA regrouped in The Queen's Head, near the rally. Word got to the police that the NF were steadily arriving there – and we were soon joined by a Branch man who told us in no uncertain terms that seeing as we were there to meet Duane it was 'no problem', for if we were all like Duane we were as good as gold! He had no qualms about our mock nazi salutes, and agreed with our mock patriotic overtones! Despite seeing our black and Asian comrades, this clever chap never cottoned on. Only after trotting off to talk to Duane did he realise the true identity of the fifty or so 'skinhead types' waiting in a nearby pub. Less friendly on his return, he greeted us with, 'You lying fat Reds!'

"Next we turned our attentions to The Crown and Sceptre, as scouts had earlier reported a gathering of fascists there, drinking safely out of the way. Local fash, Big Nige, was last seen clambering over the bar and through the back fence. His mates, sporting a variety of Rangers and Loyalist regalia, made an equally mad dash through the front. The fascists were visibly shaken, Marlowe was last seen re-emerging on the High Street, hood up, head down, scurrying like a rat. On this crucial day for the fascists, AFA controlled the area, which rendered their previously complacent strategy inoperable" (*Red Acton*, issue 70).

Mark: "It had taken twelve months and one day exactly to snuff the Blood & Honour operation in the Black Country. Twelve months meticulous research, followed by one day's shrewd manoeuvring of a solid group of disciplined and committed anti-fascists and that was that."

1994 was the turning point for the West Midlands campaign. At this time, small, medium and large-scale fascist activities were being regularly confronted by well organised, disciplined, intelligence-led stewarding. An early morning phone call on St Georges Day in April had sent three AFA scouts to Kingstanding, north Birmingham, to investigate reports of a BNP election team leafleting and canvassing the area.

John : "When we got there, about half a dozen BNP were parading behind a flag of St George with a load of near hysterical lefties in tow. It was embarrassing. Even though there were only three of us, as they came around the corner we decided to get stuck into them anyway. The flag bearer suddenly found himself being soundly beaten across the head with his own pole. Then one of our boys, a former champion kick boxer, was floored by two BNP. When he regained his footing there was carnage with one of them appearing to be left with not just one, but both legs broken."

If even by the standards of the time this was pretty savage, not long afterwards AFA would be collectively reminded of the high price they might all pay if arrested. One AFA operation in New Street station against Blood & Honour became entangled in a fatal stabbing when police linked the AFA presence to the murder.

John: "One Saturday we were forced to abort an attack on a group of Blood & Honour who were waiting to get picked up by coach to go to a large gig in the East Midlands. On our way out of the station a couple of the lads, a little frustrated maybe, began to beat the living daylights out of a B&H scout who had been clocking us for an hour. This was all happening right in the middle of a crowd of shoppers. Two old dears made an attempt to save him, then one of the chaps says, "Look ... He's a nazi!" they go, "Oh?" and sniff a bit, as if to say, 'Well you should have said,' and walked off. We all returned safely to base only to find out another B&H member had been stabbed to death just a couple of hundred yards from the attack on the scout. In their appeal for info, the police, perhaps understandably, were quick to publicly link the attacks. Even though we knew none of us had done it, we all instantly felt ripe for a fit up."

If things were being made rough for the BNP and Blood & Honour, the NF were not faring any better. In late October, having previously surveyed the situation, AFA dispatched a squad to deal with what was fast becoming a regular NF paper sale in Stourbridge.

Mark: "I think the NF thought of Stourbridge as a sleepy backwater where they'd be safe from AFA marauders. We ran them all over the place – one unwittingly triggered the security shutters in a bank such was his furious haste to get behind the counter. Another couple jumped the counter at McDonalds, while another sprinted straight for the cop shop. A passer-by went to intervene as a screaming 'NFer' was dragged down an alley by a couple of AFA stewards. 'Don't worry about him – it's his stag do!' came the reassuring reply."

The NF knew better than to return. Then, on December 15th, during an election count in Brierly Hill in Birmingham, unsubstantiated sightings of an AFA crew making their way to the count were enough for the NF candidate and entourage to flee though the back door. Such a reaction was by now perfectly understandable, as the respective leaderships of the NF, BNP and Blood & Honour had all learned the price of not treating this 'new Left' with sufficient respect.

Damian: "By the end of 1994 you could really see the difference. AFA turned their perception of the Left from a laughing stock into a serious and somewhat sinister inevitability."

As well as what might be described as routine militant activities, that Midlands AFA sanctioned a 'hit' on at least one prominent BNP organiser, Keith Axon, at his home was a sign of growing confidence. Overall, the level of activity in what was considered a type of reserve for British Nationalists up until then, would prove to have a very profound effect on how the BNP would operate nationally in the future.

3.19

'COUNCILLOR BEACKON'

Back in London, the annual Troops Out Movement march on 30th January 1993 drew the biggest fascist/Loyalist counter-demonstration seen since the 1970s. Such was the police alarm at the numbers mobilised, it was only considered safe for the march to go ahead after the mass arrest of some 400 hardcore anti-republicans. This was the first time Loyalists had confidently operated with mainland fascists since the debacle at Conway Hall in November 1988, and the potential in the partnership was visible for all to see.

On Tuesday 2nd March, the photo of London AFA organiser Patrick Hayes was broadcast on the midday news in connection with IRA activities in the capital. The Left was stunned. That evening, after leaving an AFA branch meeting, two RA members were forced to the ground and had guns put to their heads by armed police on the platform of Camden Road station before arrest. Another was picked up later. Further arrests of RA members were made in Dublin. Hayes, a Red Action member, had become involved in AFA after the Main Event in Hyde Park in 1989. His organising abilities quickly saw him take on the role of organiser for the London area. As well as acting as a liaison between AFA, the ANL, and Searchlight, he had also sat down for 'tea and biscuits' with senior police officers in his role as chief steward for the successful AFA march though Bethnal Green.

This undoubted crisis was accentuated by the arrest in Bristol two months earlier of a previously prominent London AFA member, Liam Heffernan, and his resulting charge of a conspiracy to cause explosions, and membership of the INLA. According to *The Sun*, MI5 informer Patrick Daly (who was responsible for Heffernan's arrest), was given a "£400,000 new start" for his undercover work. Feeling hugely vindicated, the BNP, among others, called for AFA to be proscribed.

While not going quite that far, Searchlight was nonetheless extremely keen to put distance between itself and Red Action. At the next meeting of the Northern Network, Paul B., a delegate from Leeds AFA acting as a Searchlight surrogate, recommended a 'cosmetic split' between AFA and RA might be prudent. It was the Bolton delegates who were first to react, condemning the suggestion in the strongest of terms. The proposal illustrated Searchlight's extreme apprehension and acute embarrassment, but the angry rejection by non-RA elements at this clumsy manoeuvre meant it was promptly dropped. However, the on/off relationship between AFA and Searchlight never recovered. Searchlight, which at the time advertised all AFA branch addresses on the back of the magazine, at once began to weed out those they believed had overt RA connections – London, Manchester, Birmingham and Glasgow, who formed the militant spine, were airbrushed out without delay. The purge continued unabated until, quite ludicrously, just seven AFA branches deemed to be untainted remained. Eventually, any reference to AFA was entirely deleted.

Meanwhile, the anarchist DAM, who RA had worked closely with years prior to the AFA launch in 1985, took it particularly badly. Some argued that AFA security had been compromised, making the rather ludicrous claim in the circumstances that the arrests had caused AFA "records and addresses" to fall into the "hands of the police". It probably didn't help that leading RA members appeared insouciant rather than either fearful or contrite. For example, some DAM members in Bristol appeared totally gob-smacked when, just four days after Hayes' arrest, two leading RA members known to be friends and associates of Hayes turned up as delegates at the Southern Region AFA meeting in Bristol, a meeting Hayes himself would normally have attended, and presented a very much 'business as usual' attitude. While the driving force behind AFA, Red Action, held their nerve in public throughout, the inescapable reality was that, if militant anti-fascism had been regarded with increasing concern by the authorities prior to the arrests, the hard-boiled activities of the organisation indeed cast it in an even more sinister light.

If that was a point in need of emphasis, the summary arrest of thirty RA supporters within minutes of their arrival in Edinburgh at 9.30am illustrated the authorities' intent. Red Action had travelled to Edinburgh to support a James Connolly march that had been banned by the local Labour Council. The objective was straightforward: to defy the authorities and break the ban. Forewarned, the police intended to intercept the coach en route but were thwarted when, anticipating a roadblock of some sort, the militants abandoned their coach at Falkirk and travelled the rest of the journey by train. Initially out-thought, the police swooped when a member of the James Connolly Society excitedly announced the RA arrival to a colleague by mobile phone that had been tapped by police.

A politically more sophisticated attempt to isolate AFA came not long afterwards, with sections of the media, including a *World in Action* documentary, pointing the finger at militants for what it is now widely accepted was a police-planned riot in Welling in south east London in October 1993. Notwithstanding the furore, AFA continued to mount operations with extraordinary single-mindedness and, with the scent of victory in their nostrils, actually began to step up the pace.

On 24th April AFA seriously disrupted an NF meeting in Hemel Hempstead. Riot police and dogs had foiled an attempted ambush by AFA of the NF en route but, after regrouping, AFA headed directly for the venue, Mountbatten School. In 'Groundhog Day' mode, the SWP/ANL picket greeted the arrival of the eighty militants exactly as they had done in 1990 with shrill cries of "Nazi Scum! Nazi

Scum!" But if they were still confused, neither the police nor NF was to be taken in this time. However, custom and practice is that police do not enter any political meeting, almost regardless of what might be happening inside, unless invited by the organisers to do so. But as the AFA team slowly began to filter into the hall, NF leader Ian Anderson lost his nerve entirely, with the result that the meeting began with riot police lining the walls, effectively stewarding the meeting on behalf of the NF.

As the Herts AFA Bulletin put it: "After the shortest speech of his life, Anderson attempted to rouse his edgy troops in a chorus of the National Anthem. It was cut short by a volley of chairs from the back of the hall as scuffles broke out. The meeting was routed. Regrettably, two arrests were made. Pushed out by the police, the anti-fascists covered both exits from the school. Almost two hours passed. Riot vans were called in and the fascists, huddled inside, were driven away to safety."

Not everyone was so lucky. An article in the *Watford Observer* carried a curious story: "A 26 year-old man from South Oxhey was viciously attacked while on a shopping trip for being in the wrong place with the wrong shirt. Police claim the man was attacked by anti-racist protestors who were in the town centre to demonstrate against the National Front rally there. They think the man was assaulted because he was wearing a Springboks rugby shirt and may have appeared to support the South African regime of apartheid." The victim was taken to hospital where, it was reported, "he received about a dozen stitches." The 'wrong place, wrong shirt' theme received widespread coverage in the local papers.

However, in the following month *Fighting Talk* (issue 5) named the 'innocent victim' as a prominent member of South Oxhey BNP. Interestingly, in the trial that followed the fracas with the NF, *Fighting Talk* deputy editor Mick P. was jailed. This illustrates that, four years after its introduction, the continuing attachment within AFA to the importance of maintaining a 'technical/political' leadership, despite the evidence of targeting by police and other security services, was as strong as ever.

Afterwards, National Front organiser Michael Stoneman explained how the NF were able to differentiate between AFA and ANL activists: "The ANL, you see, they're all teachers and mad professors – you know, social worker types. We weren't worried about them, they're entitled to their opinion, the same as we're entitled to ours." But AFA, "we know who they are, they don't wave lollipops – they throw chairs."

This was a rare admission. For even by 1993 a public confession by a leading fascist that some distinct social and physical delineation existed between the average AFA and ANL member was regarded as almost treasonable within right-wing circles. Not least because physical prowess had always been highly prized by National Socialism: 'healthy body, healthy mind' being the maxim. In the interests of political symmetry, fascism preferred its opponents to adhere to some opposite physical stereotype. Much store was invested in proving this to be case. Here is a pretty standard offering from *British Nationalist* following the AFA versus BNP clash at Weavers Field in April 1990:

"Looking at the two sides, one was struck, as often in the past, by the vividly contrasting calibre of the types present: among the nationalists an abundance of fit, hefty and powerful looking young men well able to cope with trouble; on the opposition side a collection of mainly weedy students and social drop-outs, some obviously on drugs."

Eddy Butler, a first class political thinker credited with being the architect behind the BNP victory on the Isle of Dogs, was not averse to public display of the same phobia. However, in writing under his pen name Jack Truman, in *Patriot*, five years later, Butler would allow himself to be far more candid with regard to AFA's capability.

"For the most part the AFA people are all talk. All they can ever do is attack nationalists when the latter are on their own and can be heavily outnumbered. When more than a handful of nationalists are together, the brave 'men' of AFA always keep their distance. AFA's addiction to violence is only an expression of its people's wimpishness and cowardice. They could not resist using their programme to puff out their puny chests and brag over what they fantasise about doing" (*Spearhead*, June 1992).

Predictably the question every one on the Far Right chose to avoid was why some 'über-nazi' outfit was ever needed to thwart opponents described as 'wimps'? It

BNP supporters celebrate Derek Beackon's local election victory on the Isle of Dogs.

would never be honestly addressed and, for reasons we will go into later, C18 tended to go to even greater pathological extremes in dealing with the core contradiction.

"Most people who have been involved in the struggle for a few years will be aware of this tiny group of mugs, misfits and cowards who call themselves Red Action. We at C18 who have monitored this bunch of no good fucking queers just regard them as one big joke, which gets funnier every time we hear it. The image they try and put over is that of a mob who've had enough and just want it with the fascists at every opportunity. In reality they are a bunch of 40–50 wankers who would never make it in any football firm in this country. Their claim to fame is that they have beaten up a few skinheads, pensioners and women on their way to right-wing events ... they wouldn't dare venture near our mob and stand."

This, needless to say, was not a description the mainstream media or the militants' many detractors on the Left would be in accord with. "Big boys who are going to come around and crack a few heads," according to *Blitz* magazine. "Burly Bill and Joe," who look like "conspicuously large football casuals with a physical presence that goes beyond mere self-assurance" was the view of a reporter for the *Independent on Sunday*. "Grant Mitchell look-a-likes" was *Green Anarchist*'s preferred stereotype.

While C18 tended to present the conflict as a rivalry between gangs, and militants for the most part saw it as a clash between philosophies, it hardly needs pointing out that reedy philosophy students were rather thin on the ground. And, of course, the neurosis behind this consistent need to portray the enemy as 'weedy, wimpish, puny-chested queers', makes it fairly easy to imagine the deep trauma in the ranks should so inadequate a foe ever dare 'stand'.

Joe: "We actually loved all the bluff and bluster and their chest-thumping. It made our job that much easier. Imagine being recruited on that basis, and the shock on being confronted with the reality for the first time. Almost as bad as the panic is the sense of betrayal from having been lied to that comes with it. For the more experienced the problem was the opposite. Fully aware that AFA always did its homework and rarely left things to chance, whenever we came into view, even when they were mobbed-up, you would almost always see the doubt, with them thinking: 'Is there something I don't know? Is there something I missed?' In the latter stages they were often beaten before the first punch was thrown. Personally this suited me fine. I had no problem with the use of political violence; it was the fighting I didn't like."

Now black propaganda, it is generally agreed, 'is fair in love and war'. But there comes a point when it can rebound on the purveyor. This is when he either comes to believe it himself, or having convinced others that it is so, feels compelled to act as if he did. By 1993 this was precisely the debilitating quandary in which British fascism found itself. Unable to seriously move forward because of the enemy, neither could they back down from 'a no-good bunch of fucking misfits'. Worse, for the thinking fascist like Lecomber, was the recognition that such vainglorious posturing was not even sustainable, as by now, with the upping of the ante in the Midlands, the BNP were struggling to hold their own anywhere in the country. Something dramatic would be needed to break the pattern. A spectacular change in fortunes would be required to allow for a strategic withdrawal by the BNP with honour (or an approximate of it) intact. When it came, it took almost everyone by surprise – including the BNP.

At 10.30pm on Thursday 16th September 1993, BNP stalwart Derek Beackon was elected to public office in east London, taking the Millwall seat situated on the Isle of Dogs from the Labour Party by a mere seven votes. Now, not since 1976 had the Far Right come anywhere near being elected, and among liberals generally there was palpable shock. The front page of the *Daily Mirror* ran a caption, along with a photo of Beackon that read: "Sieg Heil... and now he's a British councillor". "Votes, fists and boots for the BNP" was the complementary headline in London's *Evening Standard.*

Yet for AFA, who had warned of the potential of the Far Right since 1985, there was no panic, more a sense of 'told you so' satisfaction. "Most of the Left see the BNP as an army of racist thugs, skinheads with mis-spelled Skrewdriver tattoos. Refusing to take the ideas of the Far Right seriously allows the Left to escape the responsibility of having to challenge those ideas ideologically, or head on ...The BNP have succeeded in presenting themselves as a radical alternative to the ills of capitalist society. The failure of the Left, constituted almost entirely from outside the class, has left the radicalism of the Right unchallenged by an equivalent political force on the Far Left" (*Red Action*, issue 67, spring 1994). Interestingly, as far as we can discover, this is the first public reference to the need for physical force anti-fascism to be married to a viable political alternative.

Not all would see it that way then, or since. For example, rather than accept the BNP success for what it was, Copsey, rather perversely, sought instead to place the blame on militant tactics for failing to remedy the problem it alone had identified. And while conceding the militants had indeed been first to flag the political latency of the BNP, particularly in east London, he stubbornly maintains, "despite opposing the BNP's 'Rights For Whites' campaign from the very beginning, anti-fascist militants had not removed BNP influence from the area. In truth, quite the reverse happened: in September 1992, a BNP candidate polled 20 percent of the vote in a local election in Millwall, and it was in Millwall the following year that the BNP won its first ever council seat."

Rather strangely, Copsey never thinks to ask, why Millwall? Or for that matter, why not in the whole of Tower Hamlets, only ever Millwall? Instead, he compounds the original error by gliding over the compelling reasons that explained why

Millwall was the exception to the general rule. "Writing in September 1991, AFA believed that through its application the British National Party had been denied a foothold in Tower Hamlets and was hopeful that the "fascists' slow retreat in London" could be turned "into a national rout." In the spring of 1992, AFA remained confident that it had recorded an impressive number of successes, particularly in east London. As it turned out, however, AFA had got it entirely wrong." For while militants "can undoubtedly disable the street operations of fascist groups, a problem obviously arises when adversaries change tactics and adopt campaigning methods that avoid the possibility of confrontation ... [T]he potential weakness of militant anti-fascism clearly emerged from the experience of Millwall."

But had "AFA," as Copsey charges "got it entirely wrong"? Patently, if a party previously committed to controlling the streets suddenly sets out to avoid all confrontation, there would inevitably need to be some readjustments by their physical force opponents. If AFA had got it so 'wrong', why was the BNP at this juncture 'retreating' from the tactic of 'confrontation'? And why were the wider implications of the enforced 'change of tactics' only ever taken on board by the militant strategists whose analysis he scorns? More damning, in stressing the limitations of physical force anti-fascism, Copsey seems blind to the reality of this 'weakness' applying to anti-fascism *per se*.

A further unwillingness to differentiate between the BNP as an organisation and the extant political situation on the ground causes the Copsey study to further blur cause and effect. This encourages him to conclude that AFA alone was culpable in not preventing the Far Right being seen as the radical and acceptable alternative by a large section of the working class in what was historically a Labour ward. But on looking back, the real message from Millwall was just how intoxicating radical nationalism could be, once the AFA sanction had been lifted. This was certainly a conclusion the BNP would come to.

Not Copsey, though. In ignoring the evidence he does not pause to consider why the electoral advance on the Isle of Dogs dovetailed with the tucking in of horns by the BNP in the rest of east London as well as the rest of the country. No, because for Copsey, BNP influence was the primary cause of racist division on the Isle of Dogs, when in fact it was a symptom of the underlying tensions, provoked in part by the council's own policy of 'equal opportunity'. Now, it is not denied that the existence of a pronounced racial divide on the Isle of Dogs attracted BNP attention to begin with. As a racist party, it was only natural they wished to both widen and make political capital from it. But, at bottom, the BNP was not the root cause of the tension. Here, as elsewhere, the attitudes and polices adopted by what can loosely be defined as the liberal Left proved to be of great benefit to radical nationalism.

In the early 1990s Tower Hamlets was, and still is, among the very poorest and run down inner city areas in the country. A strategy to marry equal opportunities to resources saw the local authority fall into the trap of allocating these resources along racial lines and, fatally, being perceived to do so. "It takes some doing to be suspected of being anti-Bengali by the Bengalis and anti-white by the whites, but the council seems to have managed it. No doubt it will claim that it is the councillors' attempts to be even-handed that have led to the criticisms from both sides, but the form of the complaints suggests this is more a matter of bias, or worse, in one direction or another" (*Evening Standard* editorial, following publication of an independent inquiry into the running of Tower Hamlets council, 7th November 1998). Both inside and outside the Labour Party the Left worked to a strategy that saw the need for the white working class to be subdued for socialism and anti-racism to take root. A mindset that saw the white working class as the enemy, a tendency AFA consistently and bitterly warned against, would reluctantly be identified as the major factor behind the more substantial BNP breakthrough in the North West a decade later.

In February 1994 the *New Statesman* published an article that provides a peek at the contradictions dominating political discourse within the local Labour Party at the time, which inevitably had reverberations in the public domain. Two local working class women, Sandra Ireland and Kathy McTasney, who had respectively been Chair and Secretary of the Labour Party in Millwall up to the beginning of 1994, resigned, due to what they considered the disproportionate role that race played in housing priorities and provision. As one of them explained to the *New Statesman*, it was the struggle for dominance between the local working class and the 'new London Left' within the Labour Party that formed the background to the women's departure.

"When Kathy and I seek to press for a better deal for local people, we are immediately accused, without a shred of evidence, of being 'racists and gangsters'." She hit out particularly at Yve Amor, the still-sitting councillor (whose husband was a full-timer for Militant, incidentally), and two hard-Left councillors from neighbouring Blackwall, Christine Shawcroft and Dave Lawrence. "We have told you, as we have told the debrief committee, that at a meeting when Kathy and I attempted to press for a proper deal for the 'homeless at home', Christine Shawcroft said that neither she, nor Amor, nor Lawrence would house the homeless at home 'because they were predominately white'." Certainly when challenged by a *World in Action* reporter, Councillor Shawcroft did little to conceal her distaste for her white working class constituents. When the interviewer put it to her that "Islanders believed Labour councillors like her just didn't listen," she replied, "Listening was all very well…" but what she actually took notice of depended "… on what they're saying." "If they're saying we voted BNP because we don't like black people living here…" "I know what the BNP are saying – they're telling lies. We have consultation meetings regularly with local people. I have faced more public meetings full of baying racists than you've had hot dinners. You can't intimidate me!"

Bad enough, you might think, for such racial fault-lines to emerge within an ostensibly socialist Labour branch, but the perceptions of bias in favour of Asians extended far wider than local whites. In *Learning from the Conflict*, local vicar Nicholas Holtham, who was prominent in the campaign against the BNP, vouches for the highly racialised atmosphere, exacerbated by council policy, and perceptions of it.

"On the day after the by-election, journalists were around from 6.30am to 9pm. An interviewer for *Newsnight* in Millwall Park saw me with a mixed race child whose black mother had just told me privately that she voted for the BNP because she 'couldn't stand the Pakis!' (*Learning from the Conflict*, page 11).

This evidence of inter-ethnic antipathy,* never admitted by the Left, goes some way to explaining the otherwise inexplicable sight of a Somali-looking youngster whooping it up with BNP supporters following the announcement of Beackon's election. Against this background, all that was tactically required of the BNP was to appropriate the arguments of the 'new London Left' – and reverse them. It follows that the case for 'Rights for Whites' was being made, not by the BNP but by their self-styled 'hard-Left' opponents.

The dislocation between Left Labour and the working class was not by any means restricted to the Isle of Dogs. As one local resident put it rather memorably, the 'new London Left' generally knew more about "Cuba than Cuba Street" – a well-known street on the Isle of Dogs. Labour was not the only party at odds with itself. On 17th December 1993, the *Guardian* reported that in Tower Hamlets an internal inquiry into racism by the Lib Dems (who BNP activists had described as 'London's secret racist party'), "voted yesterday to recommend that three members, including former mayor Jeremy Shaw, be expelled from the local party … local party members claimed that up to 10 councillors could resign in protest at the report, form an independent party and deprive the Liberal Democrats of control of the council" (*Guardian*, 17th December 1993).

* An original and authoritative study, *The New East End: Kinship, Race and Conflict*, published by the Runnymeade Trust in 2006, underwrote the conclusions the AFA leadership had arrived at more than a decade earlier. In elections in May of that year George Galloway's party, Respect, with a dominant Muslim influence and orientation, compounded the growing Balkanisation of the area by becoming the official opposition in Tower Hamlets Council. The first to congratulate the party was the BNP, for in their eyes the success of Respect legitimised their own stance in promoting the exclusive interests of the indigenous white population.

It was against this background that AFA had set out to physically neutralise the BNP threat in 1990. By late 1991, they believed they had gone a long way to achieving that goal. Without question, due to the work put in between 1990–91 the East End had certainly been re-established as the 'contested area' it was in the 1970s. The absence of any BNP/NF opposition, or indeed any opposition of consequence, to both the Unity Carnival and the AFA demonstration through Bethnal Green, strongly supports the AFA contention that the BNP was indeed in 'slow retreat'. The unanswered question is, if indeed the militant formula was proving so successful elsewhere, why had it failed on the Isle of Dogs? Happily the answer is a simple one. For reasons we will go into, the physical force remedy was never applied there at all. Given that AFA had made east London a priority, and could not have been unaware of BNP ambitions, how is the aberration explained?

Joe: "The fact is, as well as having a close-knit community, the Isle of Dogs was almost an island in that there was just one or two ways on or off. This meant that the arrival of a large body could never hope to be a surprise. Not unimportant. As significant as there being one or two ways on, it was the same one or two ways off. So, say there was a serious incident, which is to say we had achieved what we had set out to do, all the police would need to do in turn was man the exits and wait for the perpetrators to be ratted out by a working class almost totally alienated by Labour's running of the town hall. Worse, in the eighteen months of the BNP campaign, AFA could never find a legitimate reason to be on there, which would have left us open to summary arrest."

Unfavourable circumstances notwithstanding, it is still a little startling to discover that from October 1992 to May 1994, AFA did not put out a single leaflet on the 'Island'. Even if unaware of this, the Copsey analysis opts to lay the blame on the one organisation that, because of its absence, must be considered blameless. All told, whether it was by accident or design, the BNP could not have selected a better location to experiment with the new strategy. Because what the Isle of Dogs represented for the BNP was a haven of calm: the one area in the country, even with AFA aware of their activity, where they could go about their business unchecked. Not that they took any chances. Canvassing teams normally amounting to no more than a dozen often turned out over 100-strong. None of this is to say that the wider 'change of tactics' did not play a significant part in the BNP victory, but in the short term the physical landscape was arguably as important in acting as a counterbalance.

For if, say, the BNP had secured 20% in any other part of the country, there is little doubt that their canvassers would have been just as vulnerable to AFA squads as their meetings, pubs, and paper sales had been shown to be elsewhere, if not more so. Whatever their new-found electoral sophistication, it would have offered scant protection against the abiding appetite for street warfare of their opponents.

But for all that, militants were the very first to acknowledge the political dangers Millwall represented. More than anybody they knew how immobilising to conventional BNP operations and ambition AFA had been up to then. And even if AFA, for the reasons relayed, was seriously inhibited on the Isle of Dogs, they at least knew the BNP was active there, even if they couldn't quite get to them.

Notwithstanding the brouhaha generated by the likes of Searchlight and the ANL, often the most reliable information on BNP intentions came from a distillation of what the BNP themselves were saying of their own plans. So for tactical reasons, should they ever avoid forecasting, as happened in nearby Newham not long after when the BNP came within 30 votes of taking another Labour seat, AFA was denied its most verifiable source of intelligence. And if the BNP were active without AFA knowing, what value the hands-on approach then?

Joe: "What was beginning to nag was if the BNP continued with this publicity-free, low-key, non-confrontational method outside of the 'Island', the likelihood was we would never really know how well or badly they were doing in this or that street, estate or ward until after the vote came in. Even worse, from our point of view, though the ANL and Searchlight, taking their lead from the national media, continued to portray the BNP as a 'criminal conspiracy', we knew by then they were beginning to operate as a conventional political party, with all the dangers that invoked."

And if that political message needed ramming home, AFA activists in east London had begun to report being increasingly asked, "Okay, so you're against the BNP, but what are you for?" Invariably they were stuck for an immediate reply, since to be true to itself as a political negative, anti-fascism could hope to be nothing more than 'against'. If the AFA leadership puzzled over how best to respond, the ANL as representatives of legal anti-fascism decided from the outset the ideal solution was a Labour victory, so there was no conundrum. The revamped 'Islanders Against the Nazis' proceeded to work for the Labour vote in the forthcoming local elections due in May 1994. But rather than consider challenging the BNP for the disaffected working class vote, liberal anti-fascism instinctively backed the status quo.

As a result, no attempt was ever made to address the political issues that the BNP were exploiting, or to get involved in the day-to-day problems experienced by working class people on the Island. Worse, the moment it was deemed decent, the ANL Steering Committee, in reality the Central Committee of the SWP, shifted the focus away from the Isle of Dogs, away from the root of the problem and declared the 'Unity march' on the BNP's HQ in Welling, south east London, to be the "best response possible" to the BNP's election success on the other side of the river. The Welling march and what followed merely confirmed for militants just how far the state was prepared to go to shape the battle for the streets in its own political interests.

3.20

WELLING RIOT: 'ROUND UP THE USUAL SUSPECTS'

On 16th October 1993, a month to the day after the electoral breakthrough by the BNP, the ANL, with the physical backing of the entire Left, mobilised an estimated 60,000 to march on the BNP HQ situated in Welling. As an event it served to bring to the fore the enormous gulf between the competing anti-fascist strategies and, more importantly, which of them the political establishment regarded as the more threatening. Hardly had the ANL march been announced than the Anti-Racist Alliance (ARA), publicly supported by the *Guardian* newspaper, called a rival march in central London for the same day. And while the Youth against Racism in Europe (YRE) weighed in behind the ANL, AFA refused to sponsor either event on the grounds that immensely difficult issues, such as the increasing level of race attacks, could not hope to be solved by yet another march on the BNP HQ. As well as 27 lobbies of the local council, there had already been over half a dozen marches designed to close down the HQ, all to no avail.

Furthermore, AFA argued that the BNP profile locally had grown, not as a consequence of the BNP bookshop, "but from an ability of their activists to exist anonymously and operate with impunity" within the local community. Thus, while regarding the ANL initiative as pure theatre, the opportunity that the mobilisation would afford militant anti-fascism to promote its own analysis was not scorned. A glossy gatefold leaflet was distributed from early in the day, announcing a public meeting to discuss the role of the BNP in the escalating number of race attacks in the area. And that might have been that, except there was another party who also wished to exploit the opportunities the mobilisation afforded – the state.

Terry: "Considering what was to happen afterwards, the reality is we had no political interest in the march as such. And once reports came through of C18 activity at Abbey Wood, our primary intention was to confront them there, as they had obviously gathered to pick off lefties making their way home afterwards. So we sat tight. However, long after the crowd had passed to join the march, plain-clothes police were still loitering in the vicinity of the pub we were in. Eventually, when we decided to leave, uniformed police stopped us from using Plumstead station, which would have taken us out of the area, and more or less frogmarched us onto the back of the march instead."

Why they wanted AFA there only became apparent later. Along with the closing off of the local railway stations to anyone who might want to leave, all the side streets off the route of the march were guarded by riot police. Except, that is, for the street that led directly to the BNP HQ which, pointedly, was manned by one "line of police officers in everyday uniform," including one WPC. It looked like an invitation for trouble, and it was. The night before, on *South-East News*, a police commander had actually predicted this precise spot as the 'flash point'. As the *Evening Standard* remarked later, "Rarely can a riot have been so perfectly forecast; both sides knew exactly what was going to happen, precisely where it would happen, and give or take ten minutes, at what time" (*Evening Standard*, 18th October 1993). When trouble began in the tightly packed street it was almost impossible to escape.

Andy: "At this stage an AFA contingent of over 100 security stewards was to the middle or back of the march. You could hardly move forward or back. After a quick consultation we reverted to Plan A: that is, to engage C18 at Abbey Wood. With the streets blocked off the only outlet was over a high wall and through a park. After about twenty minutes we found ourselves back on the road and headed off at a brisk pace towards Abbey Wood. As we came over the brow of a steep hill, we could actually see them in the beer garden about half a mile away. Given the distance and what was occurring elsewhere, they had no difficulty recognising us, either! We could see them pointing, running into the pub and running back out again like headless chickens. I think we were all quite looking forward to it."

Tony: "I was in position as back-marker, which is to say, making sure the end of the column stayed in tune with the head of the column. Look out for strays and generally manage the back of the AFA contingent in the same way as the chief steward in the front. Anyway, most of the boys had already left – there was still about twenty of us waiting to get over the wall when we were approached by typical looking lefties. "Quick, quick, the fascists are at the front of the march!" Some took the bait but I managed to head them off. However, in the confusion some of the 'out of towners' broke ranks. The next time I next saw one of the lads from Leicester he was in *The Sun* with a price on his head!"

Apparently the police had not been so preoccupied that the AFA departure passed them unnoticed. Literally within yards of the pub, AFA found themselves being intercepted by riot police who immediately cordoned it off. Apart from lobbing a few beer bottles over the wall, C18, for all their fearsome media reputation, made no attempt to come out. Instead a veritable 6ft 7in giant called 'Jacko' successfully wedged himself in the doorway to prevent police getting into the pub. So apart from some heckling directed at one C18 member who, in the previous week, had been gassed after unwisely stopping off for a pint in The Agricultural in Islington, there was little more to be done.

That night the Anti-Nazi League riot dominated the news. But by Sunday morning there was a subtle adjustment with regard to whom exactly the authorities deemed to be responsible. Whereas it was the ANL getting the blame in the Sunday papers printed on Saturday night, by Sunday morning, in an interview on Radio Five Live, anti-terrorist expert Professor Paul Wilkinson had effectively exonerated the ANL, and by inference the police, by pointing the finger at Red Action instead. In his opinion Red Action were to blame. And how had the eminent professor arrived at such a contrary deduction in so short a space of time? Well, we'll never know, because in spite of it being a fairly rudimentary question, it was never asked. But the Wilkinson rewrite proved a foretaste of what was to come. To begin with, the greatest contrast was drawn, as *The Times* put it, between ARA who had followed the tradition of the "Jarrow march rather than the Gordon riots," and the ANL. Writing for *New Statesman and Society*, Steve Platt, who had a thumb broken by a police riot shield, identified why the holding of two separate demonstrations, one confrontational and one peaceful, allowed for the "demonisation of those who chose to go to Welling rather than Trafalgar Square; and this, as much as anything, was what sowed the seeds for such a disastrous and brutal policing operation."

By the Monday the 'demonisation' became even more targeted when the London *Evening Standard*, a regional stable mate of the right-wing *Daily Mail*, confidently predicted arrests within hours. "Police are today planning a series of swoops on the homes of ringleaders of the militant groups behind the worst violence on the streets of London since the Poll Tax riots … [T]he most significant arrests are to come in the next few days including a hard core of extremists involved in two militant organisations, Panther UK, and Red Action" (*Evening Standard*, 18th September 1993)

For the ANL leadership, with the sensitivities of a large numbers of MPs to assuage, there must have been some relief at finding itself off the hook. Among militants there was some amusement but mostly puzzlement at the fingering of Panther UK, a little known group with an exclusively black membership but absolutely no track record to speak of. All would become clear quickly enough.

For just as C18, with Searchlight connivance, was being built up in the media as a fully-fledged paramilitary group with, it must be said, the co-operation of the C18 leadership who gloried in the infamy, a fairly determined attempt was being mounted by the same 'team' to prepare for AFA's proscription on identical grounds. That Monday an editorial in *The Times* actually called for the banning of the right to assembly by anti-fascist militants by drawing a very direct equivalence. Citing the arrest of a gang of C18 intent on attacking an ANL demo at Brick Lane, it argued: "Last month the police arrested 57 suspected BNP members believed to be planning the disruption of a demonstration. Equally firm pre-emptive action is clearly needed to stop the militant troublemakers hi-jacking future protests, even if this means restricting the rights of free assembly in a handful of cases."

Everyone, not least the militants themselves, knew just who the 'handful' being referred to were. By Wednesday it was being argued that, as well as hijacking the march, Red Action had hi-jacked AFA. "Formed as a legitimate protest group in 1985 by Unmesh Desai of the Newham Monitoring Project (NMP) to oppose far-Right groups," AFA, under RA direction, had adopted such violent "methods even the SWP did not want to know them." Needless to say, the "new style AFA has appalled NMP," which had condemned its "intensely paranoid, almost paramilitary tactics" (*Evening Standard*, 20th September 1993). Following the jailing of Liam Heffernan for 23 years for conspiracy to commit explosions, *The Sun* reported Heffernan as "a dedicated terrorist who belonged to the Red Action extreme Left-wing group" (*The Sun*, 17th December 1993). By now it was as if 'terrorist' and 'Red Action' had become almost indivisible, to the extent that further expansion or clarification was deemed unnecessary. An article on Red Action in the *Independent on Sunday* was entitled "The New Red Brigades". While a *News of the World* follow-up dispensed with both caveats and metaphors, with leading reporter Gary Jones referring to Red Action as a "London-based paramilitary group… blamed for two bombings on the London Underground" (*News of the World*, 30th January 1994).

The Sun had in the meantime popped up with an offer of £1,000 to anyone providing information on the rioters. While a similar process of offering money for information was followed after the Poll Tax riot, in this instance it is worth remembering the official hue and cry was being mounted against a political group

Clashes during the march in Welling, 1993.

who had played no part in the violence whatsoever. How this was managed, and the direct contribution of Wilkinson in instigating it, does all point to some spook involvement at a more rarefied level. Normally introduced at the time as an eminent 'Professor of International Relations' who worked as a 'consultant' to ITN, Wilkinson was, in truth, more a Cold War warrior for hire. A former RAF officer, he worked on a sub-contract basis for a variety of agencies and causes. For example, he became embroiled in what undoubtedly was a state-inspired disinformation campaign surrounding whistleblower Colin Wallace, who had made allegations of government involvement with Loyalist death squads in the north of Ireland, and was later convicted of murder in highly controversial circumstances, before subsequently having the conviction quashed.

With Wallace's eventual release and acquittal, and with state security possibly wary of further revelations, he became the subject of further smearing. A particularly successful part of the operation, according to investigative journalist Paul Foot, was the labelling of Wallace by sections of the media as a "Walter Mitty character" (*Guardian*, 2nd October 2002). Apparently up to his neck in this particular intrigue, Wilkinson was seriously compromised when a letter from him containing bogus information found its way to Wallace who complained to Aberdeen University, where Wilkinson was employed, and Wilkinson had to apologise. Subsequently, he lost his job as 'consultant' to ITN as a result. Worse was to follow when on 10th November 1996 the *Mail on Sunday* ran a piece headlined "Terrorist expert in college cash riddle". Wilkinson, the story went, had been forced to stand down as head of St Andrew's University School of History and International Relations "amid allegations of financial losses". It appears the School had run up a deficit "close to £180,000". Wilkinson, it added, was "believed to work for the British security services and the CIA" (*Mail on Sunday*, 10th November 1996).

Given Wilkinson's background, it seems safe to assume his invitation to appear on Radio Five Live the morning after the Welling riot was not down to chance, and that he went there armed with the singular brief to finger Red Action. In this same conspiratorial context the framing of Panther UK by the *Evening Standard* can also be explained. Anecdotal evidence from the day suggests the trigger for the trouble at the site, designated by the police commanders as the likely 'flash-point', was a group of about half a dozen black men. An obvious advantage in using people of colour is two-fold: one, they will not readily be suspected of being police; and second, there is the awe in which they would likely be held by the average left-winger who would thus be unlikely to interfere with them in any way, regardless of any suspicions as to their motivation. Now it may have been felt their involvement could not credibly be attributed to involvement with RA, notoriously, as we have seen, almost all white, so Panther UK was wheeled out instead. If this is considered a little too elaborate, it should be remembered that the *Evening Standard* article had boasted of the "undercover work carried out by MI5 and Special Branch" on the day, in what it stated "was the biggest intelligence operation ever carried out for a demo." So, all in all, it seems to point to a higher level of secret service subterfuge and sophistication than militant anti-fascists of previous generations might possibly have had to put up with.

At the time, if there was any lingering scepticism among anti-fascists of the existence of enemies in high places, a *World in Action* (*WIA*) 'exposé', commissioned to extend the blame for the violence to AFA, left few doubters. The intervention of *WIA* is especially interesting because, despite the extensive 'body mapping' of AFA members prior to the march, and 50 hours of video footage shot by police on the day, not one single AFA member had even been arrested, much less successfully prosecuted by the time the programme went out, a gaping hole in the construct, one would have thought. Nevertheless, in the *WIA* documentary, AFA was labelled "sinister" and accused of operating "cell structures".

While Copsey is prepared to concede to the existence of a political agenda to isolate AFA, he does admit to puzzlement over the involvement of *WIA*, because of a previous distinguished service record in the cause of anti-fascism. Yet, he admits "despite a record of anti-fascist investigative reporting, which had been revisited earlier in the year when Combat 18, a shady neo-nazi group, had been exposed, *World in Action* gave further credence to the line that a hard core of extremists had manipulated the Welling demonstration. In a subsequent documentary it turned on anti-fascist militancy, presented AFA as a paramilitary conspiracy and screened footage of violence at the Bethnal Green march to imply that AFA had deliberately planned disorder. The underlying message from the programme was that the anti-fascist movement and especially AFA should be avoided."

What Copsey does not consider is that the information supplied to *WIA* for the 'exposé' of C18 came almost entirely from Searchlight. So far as the AFA leadership was concerned it is not a coincidence the same *WIA* 'team' was now employed to tar 'extremists' at the opposite end of the spectrum. From where they stood it was patently obvious someone, somewhere, wanted to repackage RA/AFA and C18/BNP as terrorist 'twins'. The Copsey reference to the violence at the AFA Remembrance Day march through Bethnal Green is also of interest. Again there was, indeed, evidence of 'planned disorder', and again not by the organisers but by police. Trouble began when a lone pensioner visually heckled the march by waving a white handkerchief from his balcony on the sixth floor of a tower block. As if responding to a signal, some erupted in the section where the most visible anarchists were grouped. Just as quickly and seemingly over the heads of the officer in charge on the ground, vanloads of TSG were deployed. Seeing the danger, Patrick Hayes countered by directing AFA stewards toward the trouble spot, but crucially lined them up to face the police. As a result when police arrived, instead of the rabble they expected, they found they were faced by double-banked rows of disciplined stewards. The police looked at each other – 'What now?' Aware of the television cameras and robbed of their excuse, a visibly puzzled TSG, after some momentary hesitation, were forced to withdraw. Afterwards, an ebullient Commander Crooks offered his hand to the AFA chief steward by way of congratulations. "Not a bad day. Only five arrested. Three of yours, and two of ours." Noting the droll expression that greeted his unguarded admission he looked rueful, adding; "Perhaps I shouldn't have said that" (*Red Action*, issue 61).

If indeed the security services had used provocateurs to justify the TSG intervention at the AFA march, then later employed that footage to hang the blame on AFA for what happened at Welling, it is not hard to imagine someone, somewhere, getting a huge kick out of being able to make such economic use of the material. But then by 1993 cynicism was very much in vogue. For example, in the twelve months from October 1992–93, in addition to the considerable opprobrium heaped on it by its traditional foes on Left and Right and in the media, AFA had been denounced by former confederates Workers Power as an "obstacle" to anti-fascism, plotted against by Searchlight, and been denounced as "paramilitary" by the NMP. All too typically, when AFA called a public meeting on 6th November in Woolwich to outline a strategy to combat the dramatic rise in race attacks in the area, the support of the Greenwich Campaign Against Racist Attacks (GCARA) and public backing from the Indian Workers Association did not prevent it being boycotted by every other anti-racist grouping, bar none. Not only did the SWP, ANL, Militant, YRE, ARA, Workers Power, NMP or Searchlight not support it in any official capacity, militants noted wryly, they did not even send the usual paper sellers. Rarely can a group with such a high media profile at the same time have been so utterly isolated.

In such circumstances, if the strain had begun to show, it might have been understandable. But then again, for the leadership, isolation was nothing new. Nor would it have been unexpected. Six months earlier, when Red Action made national headlines following the arrest of Patrick Hayes in relation to a bomb left outside Harrods, what public solidarity there was came from an obscure orthodox Trot group called Workers Press who, in the process of offering support, did so in such a back-handed manner as to be classically comic. "Last Sunday's so-called quality press launched a crude witch-hunt against the involvement of Trotskyists in the recent bombing by the IRA ... Red Action is charged with being 'an extremist Trotskyist organisation'. In fact, Red Action have never claimed to be Trotskyists" (*Workers Press*, 3rd March 1993).

What caused many to clamber for distance was ironically also what allowed Red Action to endure. For ten years Red Action had been running trips to Belfast. The attractions were many. Like anti-fascism, that the Irish struggle had long ceased to be fashionable among the liberal Left only added to its appeal. In the British establishment there was also of course a common enemy. But possibly the enduring appeal was that in places like Belfast they found revolutionaries aplenty, and working class ones at that. If they hadn't previously realised, these exchanges helped confirm a number of things. In confronting state interests, vilification and worse was the name of the game. And a genuine adherence to revolutionary principle was dangerous. Over the years RA members had taken part in many illegal demonstrations and saw first hand how the British state really looks with the gloves off. Leading players were standing literally yards from an unarmed Sean Downes when he was shot dead at point blank range after the RUC opened fire with plastic bullets on a Sinn Fein rally. The authorities blandly denied responsibility until a Canadian media unit released footage of the murder.

In 1987–88 RA took political sides in a feud inside the Irish Republican Socialist Movement, which left thirteen dead. One individual regarded as a friend and political ally, at the time deputy president of the Irish Republican Socialist Party, Kevin 'Bap' McQuillan, escaped assassination literally by inches, when gunmen broke into his home. Though only yards from an army barracks it was hours before troops arrived to investigate. It was through this harsh prism that they largely regarded the world, themselves and others – a frame of reference definitely more Irish Republican than British Labour movement. And if it was this adherence to a template that for a variety of reasons was responsible for their notoriety, it also meant more often than not they were tactically at least one step ahead of their opponents: in their eyes, a satisfactory trade off. It also explains why, following the jailing of Patrick Hayes and Liam Heffernan for a total of 53 years, papers like *The Times* would refer to them as having "graduated from being weekend revolutionaries" (*The Times*, 14th May 1994). While Red Action representatives, when interviewed by the *Independent on Sunday*, insisted no such "quantum leap" had actually been required (*Independent on Sunday*, 25th January 1995).

Joe: "As we saw it we were in what we described as a 'three corner fight'. There was the 'fash', there was 'us', and there was the 'state'. By this stage nothing would have surprised us. Certainly Searchlight's behaviour did not raise any eyebrows, while the ANL, both in relation to Labour and their constant calls endorsing the state against the Right, many saw not as a mistaken tactic but as out-and-out collaboration. Also, as much out of self-respect as anything, given the propensity for infiltration, information was released on a 'need to know' basis. None of us wanted to be made to look like mugs."

'Not wanting to look like mugs' naturally resulted in constant tactical adjustments. For instance, within AFA, while the political structures remained open and transparent, by now the parallel structures responsible for security matters were, and had been for some time, directed entirely from the top down. For the leading security stewards one and one no longer made two, it meant eleven. Consequently, in operational terms, 'Who, what, why, where, and when,' was for the most part an entirely closed shop. It also meant activists who were considered vulnerable to security service manipulation for reasons of personality, drink or drug issues were summarily stood down. All this helped minimise security leaks but could not eradicate the possibility of deliberate infiltration.

Notwithstanding the continued AFA success, this increasing lack of operational transparency did inevitably create tension and dissent at a rank-and-file level. It created scope for elements who may have disagreed with aspects of strategy, who resented the Red Action authority, who might have preferred AFA to seek out calmer waters, or who may have deliberately infiltrated AFA on orders of the state or Searchlight, not forgetting the Far Right, with the express intention of making political mischief. Given that a covert Searchlight operation within AFA was uncovered in Leeds in 1997, and a former member of AFA in Hackney called Laurence Rustem actually stood as a candidate for the BNP in 2000, 2004 and 2005, it is not entirely improbable that AFA was penetrated by other agencies as well. In 2006 Rustem was finally elected as one of a dozen BNP councillors in Barking and Dagenham. Rustem, who was half-Turkish, had joined AFA in 1991.

At the time of his application, he stated that he had thrice written to Red Action, but had never received a reply. When this information was relayed it was discovered that on each occasion he had failed to supply a return address. Slight in stature, he proved an unexceptional recruit. Later when he appeared as a candidate for the BNP there was astonishment in the east London branch where he had been a member. Checks revealed him to be fairly immature and not in the least inquisitive. In 2004 when challenged by an undercover reporter working for the *Evening Standard* as to "how he could represent a party that rejects half of him," Rustem's reply was enigmatic: "Let's just say my entry into the party was unique" and refused to discuss it further (*Evening Standard*, 6th October 2004).

It is a reply that points to him joining the BNP as a result of some disenchantment with AFA, rather than someone having been in the BNP and sent to infiltrate from the outset. Moreover, there never once was the kind of suspicious security leak prior to 1994 to justify internal security mounting a witch-hunt inside the organisation. That is not to say that the militant leadership was not open to the possibility of infiltration but rather than allow activities to be restricted by undue paranoia, the thinking was that, as long as AFA kept winning, their room for political manoeuvre would prove marginal, at worst. And AFA was winning.

As even Copsey admits, the public outcry caused no lasting damage to the AFA reputation. "The point made in the [*WIA*] programme was that racist violence could be effectively managed by both legislation and the police; thus anti-fascism was not necessary. And since violent anti-fascism did nothing to stop racist violence, anti-fascism was also said to be counter-productive. But if the aim of the programme was to expose the 'sinister' side of anti-fascism and thereby discredit the anti-fascist movement, it failed dismally … [T]he militant wing of the anti-fascist movement did not suffer from *World in Action*'s treatment – AFA expanded to over 30 branches in 1994, rising to over 40 in 1995." Impressed by both the militants' defiance and analysis, working class elements from other parties and from no parties were throwing their weight behind what, for the orthodox Left, had become near untouchables. But far from mending their ways, AFA was going for the political kill. Just three months after Welling, it took a significant scalp, causing such a loss of face for the hard men on the Far Right that the repercussions are arguably still being felt at the highest level of government more than a decade and a half later.

3.21

THE END OF THE ROAD FOR COMBAT 18, JANUARY 1994

Early in 1994, when word filtered through that Blood & Honour were planning a comeback, militant ears went up into little tufted points. Here, some sensed, was an opportunity to deliver the *coup de grâce* to an already tottering C18. Notwithstanding the mutual loathing that existed between AFA and the ANL, an ever-pragmatic militant leadership offered both the ANL and YRE an olive branch. Despite the constant calls for 'unity', it says much that this was the first and only time representatives of the three organisations had ever sat down together to discuss business since AFA was launched almost ten years previously. Even though AFA had arranged the meeting, the ANL representatives nonetheless acted in what was considered to be a snotty, high-handed manner, evidently bristling at the notion of being considered subordinates. Despite a palpable lack of goodwill, business was concluded to the satisfaction of the militants.

Saturday 15th January was the date, and Old Street tube station was to be the main B&H re-direction point for the day, the YRE/ANL delegates were told. Offering as it did easy access to east London, it was certainly plausible. In any case, this is where the ANL and YRE were advised to mobilise. But AFA itself never turned up there. On the day, with the ANL and a large presence of police in place at Old Street station, AFA opted to stand off. Under police surveillance, they gathered near the Angel tube, just one stop away on the Northern Line. Then, just before 5pm, news came through that the main C18 security team had been located by AFA scouts, not near Old Street, but in Bow in the heart of the East End.

After a brief consultation with close colleagues, the AFA chief steward decided to act on the information. The C18 pub was to be hit. Once the decision was taken, with a speed that caught police on the hop, the entire AFA stewards group, now numbering 150, simultaneously emerged from two adjacent pubs and promptly disappeared into the tube network. Of all the anti-fascists, as few as six knew of the destination, which created problems when they alighted, unexpectedly re-emerging out of Bow Road tube station, and headed directly for The Little Driver pub.

Joe: "By now a recurring problem was you never knew who was with you. In a sense, in a mobilisation like this at night, it would be very easy for a couple of plain clothes police to attach themselves to a large group travelling on public transport, without the fear of ever being challenged. The concern was not so much that they could alert the authorities to our intentions in advance, but they could provide damning evidence of conspiracy – by demonstrating some foreknowledge by the organisers at a criminal trial at a later date. In terms of severity of sentence, conspiracy was often more dangerous than the act itself. So here we were, about to attack The Little Driver pub, the C18 nerve centre on the day, packed to the rafters with desperados and there was nothing we could say about it! Instead, we had to lead by example. Luckily, as we came out of the tube there were some scouts on duty, which we immediately got into. This legitimised, if you like, our need for 'retaliation', as well as sending the signal back down the line of the need to prepare for attack."

Alerted by the shouted warning from scouts, C18 poured out of the pub to do battle. In the dimly lit street, all they could possibly make out was that, ten abreast and at least ten deep, in tight formation, was the much hated enemy advancing towards them. A customised Zulu chant rumbled out from the attackers. It is likely the January gloom considerably enhanced the sense of menace exuded. While to the untutored shopper, it must have been an extraordinary sight, for C18 it must surely have carried the hallmarks of a nightmare. So when a distress flare flashed out from within the AFA ranks, hit an overhead bridge and screamed back over the heads of the fast approaching anti-fascists, like indomitable British infantry of yore, they never flinched. C18 did. As more came out of the pub, others broke and ran.

Suddenly, with the AFA front lines less than twenty yards from the pub, police poured from a neighbouring police station to try and head off the anti-fascist attack. Caught by surprise by the numbers, the anti-fascist front line had a split second to make a decision: confront the police, or evade capture and regroup. As the night was young, they instinctively opted for the conservative option.

Denis: "Looking back on the police intervention now, who were obviously on standby to deal with any trouble from C18, ironically, though annoying at the time, it was probably fortunate. They probably did us a favour. Given the history of the organisations, together with a situation where C18 were already being driven back into the pub, clambering over each other to get as far away from the door as they could, but still trapped, it would not have been surprising in the carnage that would have followed if someone was killed."

Joe: "Police vans had already pulled across the road, blocking off our boys. Many of the lads were already corralled, anyway. I was on the opposite side of the road. Suddenly, this fat wobbly figure emerged from between the police vans as if to carry the fight to all 150 of us. It was Charlie Sargent. He was simply throwing a shape thinking everyone was captured by the plod. When he saw us his jaw dropped, he stuttered to a halt and scampered back. You had to laugh. What an idiot.

"With every man for himself, 16-stone boxer 'Big Phil' Edwards, fresh from escaping an attempted murder charge, sought protection by diving into the back of a police car. Only eighteen months earlier, C18 had effectively seized control of the lucrative B&H movement, on the grounds that only with sovereign control of the organisation could it provide it with proper 'protection'. Yet here it now was, itself under the cosh. Who now was to protect the 'protectors'?"

Afterwards, uncensored comments in neo-nazi fanzines like *Rampage* and *British Oi* conveyed a real sense of dismay. "The owners of the back-up hall got scared at the reports of a riot and refused us access, meanwhile two Red gangs were allowed to roam London attacking our people. At Bow Road, the main re-direction point, 200 Reds clashed with C18 and 100 British skins. This led to riot-police attacking nationalists, not the Reds. A similar thing happened at Waterloo with riot police attacking hundreds of skinheads enjoying a quiet drink." And, "By nightfall, London is estimated to have had about 2,000 nationalists there for a gig which is very surprising as the venue would have only held 800 at a squeeze. It is said a gang of tooled-up thugs were ambushing unsuspecting little mobs of skins in full view of our lawmen. Also, the rent-a-mob rabble of the IRA, Red Action, were milling about with balaclavas on, with such items as hammers, etc., on themselves. WHY WEREN'T THEY NICKED?" it whined.

The reference to 'two gangs' in the *Rampage* fanzine is possibly explained by the fact that the main AFA team, having been corralled and then herded on to a train

Riot police outside The Little Driver pub in Bow after the AFA attack on C18 in 1994.

specially commandeered for the purpose, were dispatched to Earls Court in west London as far from their opponents as geographically possible. When passengers asked police what was going on, the explanation provided for the disruption to the trains was that it was 'football related'.

According to police, that should have been that. However, with the immediate danger past, leading C18 member Nicky Cooper drew breath. Apparently eager to impress some wide-eyed young females who had sought out and engaged him and other C18 activists in conversation outside The Little Driver, Cooper, with an eye no doubt to a romantic rendezvous, provided them with details of C18's plan. At Earls Court, AFA organisers (having been briefed by the AFA intelligence officers of C18's plans to re-assemble at Waterloo), presented every appearance to watching police of having called it a day. Even when news reached them that hundreds of ANL supporters who had also been shanghaied on the same train and had rather unwisely baited the riot police, were now taking a bit of a hiding as a result, the militants expressed indifference. Police seemed reassured. Yet the moment police lost concentration AFA slipped away into the night. A police commander later admitted, the ability of the groups 'to find each other was uncanny'.

At Waterloo things quickly went from bad to worse for the Far Right. The apparent 'glassing' of a WPC was an excuse for riot police to launch a full-scale attack on the pub. Joe: "Police just smashed their way through the doors. The level of noise, of smashing, crashing, screams was genuinely awesome. Frankly, police seemed out of control. Skinheads were being dragged out horizontally with coppers holding both legs and arms, and dropped face first on the pavement: seriously over the top." In the midst of such hysteria, the sight of two AFA 'faces' leaning on a railing apparently coolly surveying events was the last straw.

Andy: "By this time it was 9pm, the Bow attack had taken place about four hours earlier. Neither C18 nor the police would have expected to see us again. A couple of us on reconnaissance were standing in the shadow of a bridge, but even in the midst of all the turmoil someone picked us out among a small crowd stood watching. Suddenly, over the din there was an outraged shriek from a mob stood about thirty yards away. Gradually, more and more right-wingers were being alerted, as others grabbed them and pointed over. The level of anxiety at this point was such that it took them what seemed like a couple of minutes to assemble a force to confront just the two of us. As they approached, we walked slowly away down a dark and narrow passage. Deliberately, we never looked back. As they got to the mouth of the alley a girl with them began screaming hysterically, "It's a trap. It's a trap." She repeated it over and over again. This must have totally spooked them as they stopped dead in their tracks as if they had just been warned the alleyway was mined!"

Unlike the Left (although *Searchlight* did feature a photo of the scene outside The Little Driver on the cover of their magazine), the *New Musical Express* of 22nd

January 1994 seemed to recognise the significance of the militant achievement: "A memorial concert for Ian Stuart, the singer with skinhead band Skrewdriver, was cancelled on Saturday following a string of clashes between anti-fascists, police and nazis across London. Anti-Fascist Action said the weekend's events were a complete victory for their protesters, who dogged the nazis' movements throughout the day. The anti-fascists' protests began near Bow Road underground station in east London, where they successfully disrupted Blood & Honour's re-direction point. A group of AFA supporters came within inches of reaching The Little Driver pub where the fascists were assembling, before being forced to retreat by large numbers of mounted and riot police." Meanwhile *Searchlight*, even when condemning AFA for "sectarian obstinacy" for going it alone, was forced to admit The Little Driver had been "a major defeat for C18 and Blood & Honour."

Joe: "Personally I always felt, 'that was it' for them. In terms of lost credibility, particularly on the Right, there could be no coming back for them after that. Worse than being cowardly, they had been shown up as amateurs. Unlike them we made it our business, you see, to 'know your enemy'. We would plot out what they would do, by looking at what we would do given the same circumstances. Our only error was to occasionally overestimate them. But we could always find them by tracking back from where we thought they really ought to be – to where they actually were."

An arrangement three years later, in January 1997, to post a parcel bomb from Denmark to the London AFA address was the nearest C18 ever came to retaliation. It was intercepted at source as a result of an informant, and a Danish neo-nazi and C18 supporter, Thomas Nabka, was arrested and sentenced to eight years. While the resulting publicity briefly returned C18 to the headlines, in truth the militant attack by AFA on The Little Driver had destroyed the credibility of C18, not just in the eyes of anti-fascists and BNP members, but more significantly, in the eyes of the supporters of C18 itself.

3.22
THE MYTH OF COMBAT 18

To fully understand the concept of the 'three-cornered fight' in which militants believed themselves to be involved, it is necessary to first take on board that not everything was as it seemed on the surface. For example, while the re-launch of the ANL in early 1992 saw Left and Right again assume formal battle positions, a re-run of the historic struggle with fascists on one side and anti-fascists on the other, with the authorities somewhere in the middle struggling to keep the sides apart, meant fraternisation was not uncommon. A cursory study of the trajectory followed by C18, its initial relationship with the BNP, then Searchlight, not forgetting the now proven links between various sections of the security services all keen to outdo each other, points to a shadowy world of shifting alliances where double-dealing was regarded as currency.

C18 was originally conceived and sold to the Right as the appropriate riposte to Red Action. Its job, as it saw it, was to destroy or neutralise the physical force opponents of the BNP. A straightforward and understandable enough objective, one would have thought. But there never was any sustained attempt to achieve the declared goal. Instead, within a year of its inception as the pro-active security wing of the BNP, decapitating the leadership of the parent body became the aim.

Searchlight, too, began to exhibit similarly contradictory and schizoid behaviour. Implacably opposed to C18, it was at the same time almost entirely responsible, via exclusive news stories and no less than three documentaries, for bringing the existence of the group to the notice of the public. This exposure was justified on the grounds that C18 was, as Searchlight put it, a terrorist-criminal conspiracy. However, the terrorist conspiracy allegation would be swapped intermittently with the declaration that C18 had from the beginning been set up as a honey trap to ensnare extremists by MI5. An addition to the general intrigue was that, by early 1993, C18, Searchlight (mortified by the arrest of Patrick Hayes) and the security services found in AFA an enemy in common. Gerry Gable had immediately ordered the magazine to begin disassociating itself from the branches they believed were controlled by RA. Following the fatal stabbing of an associate which brought the simmering feud within C18 into the public light, the finger-pointing intensified, with each side accusing the other of working for either Searchlight or the state. In this, at least, both parties appear to have well founded grounds for suspicion.

While standing trial for murder at the Old Bailey, Charlie Sargent was outed as an informant for Special Branch. In a *World in Action* programme that went out in

1998, an undercover policeman who infiltrated C18 says he believed Sargent worked for Special Branch. "I would get a call [from the police]: 'Can you confirm this?' This was before I put any reports in. Someone was getting intelligence to them before I could. I was in no doubt it had to be someone in the top two or three. Then I concluded it had to be Sargent himself, it had to be him" (*Observer*, 5th April 1998)

Actually, it didn't. For, rather remarkably Sargent was far from the only one at leadership level with dubious connections. In 1998 the *Daily Mirror* described another member of the leading triumvirate, Darren Wells, as "a lethal hybrid of football hooligan and fascist thug" (*Daily Mirror*, 12th January 1998). He too, it later emerged, was working with Searchlight and possibly MI5 all along.

The final member of the C18 triumvirate, lynchpin Wilf 'The Beast' Browning, who was routinely portrayed by Searchlight as an irreconcilable national socialist, somewhat inconsistently volunteered to take the witness stand against Sargent in court, on behalf of what C18 referred to as the 'Zionist Occupation Government' (routinely referred to as 'Z.O.G.'). According to Steve Sargent, Charlie's brother, he had also admitted to sitting down with Gable for meetings in "a hotel at the back of Euston station." Was this just black propaganda by an embittered opponent? Perhaps, except intriguingly it was also in a hotel, the Ibis hotel at the back of Euston station, that Pat Hayes and other leading AFA members would meet with Gable to discuss developments prior to Hayes' arrest in April 1993. Someone else to put a question mark against Browning was Tony Lecomber. After one clash with AFA in east London in 1990 in which he, Lecomber, took a "nasty beating", he condemned Browning for deserting him, and accused him of being an out-and-out "coward" (*White Riot*, page 58).

Following the traumatic events at Kensington library, in late 1991, C18 was brought into existence to assemble under one leadership a ready made corps of 'hard men' to protect BNP activities, and proactively confront their AFA/RA nemesis on a regular basis. Nick Ryan, a freelance journalist who had rigorously interviewed C18 activists for a number of feature stories, explained in a later interview what their thinking was at the time: "They felt that talking was not enough and wanted action, this was the end of 1991 – beginning of 1992, a time when the BNP and other extremists were being successfully targeted at public meetings by anti-fascist groups. There were many street confrontations with a group called AFA and its parent organisation Red Action, an extreme left-wing group. It was a dangerous time to be on the Right."

With matchless prose Sargent explained to Nick Ryan the circumstances in which C18 came into being. "The Reds were going around and they were beating the daylights out of the right-wing. They were kicking in doors, petrol-bombing people, and beating old men with hammers [a reference to an attack by anti-fascists on a right-wing meeting in Kensington library during 1992]. Red Action were absolutely battering the Right," recalled Charlie, "We decided we weren't having that and we thought we would do something about it." Which meant? "We fuckin' battered 'em wherever we met until there was no fucker left standing ... now, we don't see them anymore" (*Independent on Sunday*, 1st February 1998).

Like much of C18's propaganda output his statement and objective reality had nothing in common. Far from 'battering the Reds until there was no fucker left standing' the simple fact is that in the five years between 1992 and 1997 the two sides had only met head-on on just four occasions in London, with C18 taking a very poor second prize in three out of four.

It is an undistinguished record that goes some way to explaining why, from the outset, AFA saw no evidence to consider C18 as significant, either politically or physically. This is in spite of the staggering amount of publicity afforded C18 by Searchlight, which caused C18 to briefly become a household name. One of the main reasons for such scepticism was the pronounced lack of calibre at leadership level within C18. Of the main C18 'faces', none had any track record to speak of. Both Browning and Wells, for instance, were total unknowns and, just as significantly, would remain so throughout the five-year campaign.

Charlie Sargent, on the other hand, was a name that was far from unfamiliar. Back in the early 1980s, while a member of the NF, Sargent fell foul of some tough young Red Action members living in the Finchley area. Invariably, whenever their paths crossed, the Reds made a point of giving the chubby Charlie a slap. So humiliated was the future C18 leader by the treatment, he chose to abandon watching his local team, Barnet FC, rather than run the risk of bumping into the RA members. It is true that some years later Charlie did develop a reputation as something of a 'knife merchant' but, as one opponent put it, "the only muscle he ever had, he recruited." So not unnaturally, when Sargent was paraded as the mastermind behind C18, militants were deeply unconvinced; "How could someone like that be taken seriously by anyone?" they asked each other.

Nonetheless London AFA chose to approach the new formation with practised caution. Thus in July 1992, when C18 was announced as security for a public meeting in the Great Portland Street area hosted by controversial historian David Irving, the militants, to the chagrin of other anti-racist groups including Searchlight, refused to mobilise, preferring to view things from afar. Within a matter of weeks, some leading members had a chance to have a far closer study of the new kids on the block than they might have liked.

As the clash occurred in Islington, too, it was more or less inevitable it would instantly pass into C18 legend. Coupled with another 'ferocious' encounter, also in Islington not long after, it looked to many on the Right like the turning of the tide. And it was, in the terms it was presented. But just how C18 found itself facing leading members of AFA with odds of five to one in their favour on the day is an interesting story in itself, which we will come back to.

Target was triumphant. "A superb bit of intelligence-gathering by pro-fascists led to an extremely painful experience for IRA supporting Red Action terrorists recently. On Saturday 8th of August, the day of the IRA's annual 'Troops Out' march in north London, several prominent members of Red Action were placed under surveillance and were eventually followed to their meeting place at the Enkel Arms pub in Seven Sisters Road, Islington. About 12 members were having a pleasant drink when they suffered a full-scale attack by persons unknown. RA's notorious 'hard man' was spotted cowering under a table as broken glass from the windows of the pub came in around him. The pub landlord, a fat Irishman, came outside to fight, but a well-aimed bottle persuaded him it was perhaps marginally safer under the table with Gary. No arrests were made, and the following day the pub strongly resembled a derelict building" (*Target* magazine, summer 1992).

But far from the hit being the result of 'superb intelligence gathering' it was, as Steve Sargent later admitted, a purely chance encounter. "That one was memorable because it wasn't planned. We went up there to photograph the march but when we was in the pub there was some squaddies in there so we started talking to them. They said they were up for it. We were all really pissed up. When the march came we came out of the pub, giving it to them, and a few of them tried to get over but the old Bill got in the middle. Then a group of NF turned up and a mob of Chelsea. No one knew what was going to happen. There were about fifty of us. The geezer was taking photos, well he was going home, but he returned saying: "They're all around the corner in the Enkel Arms." There was a market there. We ran out of things to throw and there was this bloke selling potatoes so we got hold of them and began throwing them at the Paddies. There was no actual fisticuffs, it was all glasses and bottles. A few of the soldiers tried to get into the pub, kicking the door and trying to whack them with pool cues, so it was nearly all just throwing bottles." It is noteworthy that, even by their own accounts with odds of five to one in their favour, C18 did not make any serious attempt, apart from the efforts of some squaddies, to get into the pub and do real damage.

"Those inside the pub," *White Riot* explains, "included some of AFA's top fighters. They, and more particularly the combatants of Red Action, were viewed with some trepidation by many on the Right." In consequence, while C18 were not able to take the pub, or even get close enough to exchange punches, their football mentality of 'taking liberties' in their opponents' manor saw the day remembered as a great victory. AFA saw the day differently as, despite being heavily outnumbered, they held the pub in the face of the onslaught. Even Steve Sargent admired their defiance. "You knew with Red Action, with Gary O'Shea and O'Farrell, that they would have a tear up. I remember that Gary O'Shea just standing there in the pub throwing pool balls. Give him his due, game geezer" (*White Riot: the violent rise and fall of of Combat 18*, by Nick Lowles).

Joe: "If truth be told the whole day was a balls up. What actually happened was a small group of AFA were leafleting the Madness gig in Finsbury Park. Afterwards we decided to have a look to see if any of the opposition had turned up to oppose the Irish Freedom March taking place at the same time around a mile away. The thinking was we might even pick off a few strays. Normally AFA would have mobilised for it properly, but since the hiding the opposition took at Holloway Rd tube a couple of years previously they were distinctly chary of coming into north London at all. Along with half a dozen from DAM, we numbered no more than fifteen. After the leafleting, it was agreed with the DAM we would meet up in a pub called The Enkel Arms situated on the left of Seven Sisters Road, just off the Holloway Road, and the route of the march.

"But for reasons best known to themselves they went into a pub on Holloway Road itself instead. When a mob of Blood & Honour skins walked in they were forced to leave a bit sharpish. Their next pub of choice turned out to be full of C18! Meanwhile directly across the road in The Holloway, Ian Anderson stood with about 60 NF, including what looked like some off duty military. When one of our scout cars came across them, we could see the DAM contingent on foot had managed to attract the attention of the fascists from both pubs. As there was not enough room in the car we told them to make their way to The Enkel."

"When they arrived a couple were muttering that 'we should take them' – meaning C18. They went on to such an extent that Pat even asked me if it was a realistic possibility. So I filled him in on the latest intelligence sightings that pointed to us being out-numbered by about twelve to one. And that was not even counting Blood & Honour. Under normal circumstances we would have decamped, it was the right thing to do. But I was so pissed off with the attitude of some of the DAM I never gave the order. "Fuck it," I thought, "let them see what really happens if everyone acts like them." It was a busy market day. Carl was posted on the corner as lookout, just in case. Some of the other lads were sitting in the sunshine outside the pub. Suddenly Carl shouts: "We're getting it! We're getting it!" I ran to the corner and could see the bobbing heads coming through the crowd of shoppers. Everyone started running around, picking up bottles. One of the boys, Mick F., thought it was a form of street theatre staged for his benefit and was laughing good-naturedly until he was unceremoniously trampled as we dashed for the pub door. He had barely got himself inside as a huge mob of them came flying around the corner. He was still as white as a sheet about half an hour later, thinking about what would have happened had he been caught outside.

"Naturally, as we came crashing through the door, all eyes were on us. There was a row of old Irish boys sitting right under one of the massive windows. I could see what was going to happen. 'Move! Move!' I shouted, 'The windows are coming in!' They were still considering it when a heavy market trader's barrow came crashing through the window almost on to their table. They didn't need to be told twice. One of the lads swore he saw one simply vault the table! Then the other window exploded with a crash. Carl had one door covered. A crate of beer bottles lay at his feet and as a shadow appeared in the doorway he let them have it. There was now a full-scale assault on the main double door but as they tried to come through, Carl potted them through the glass. You could kind of hear them groan. 'Marvellous,' I thought, and then nearly had a heart attack when I realised the other door on the opposite side of the pub was completed unmanned. They could just walk in. 'Stevie!' I screamed, 'Get the fucking shutter!' He jumped to it and managed to pull it half way down before it stuck. 'Good enough,' I thought. After all, who is going to get on his hands and knees to climb under it in the circumstances? A brush was then smashed into the glass in the door and left stuck there. By now Stevie had a hand covering his one good eye in case he was hit in it and blinded for good.

"We began returning fire, so to speak, from inside: anything that came to hand – bottles, glasses, ashtrays. One Irish lad, a boxer on his first day out, started shouting: 'I, I, IRA! I, I, IRA!' Then a tiny little pot man, naked to the waist, began admonishing us in a thick brogue: 'Ah, come on, boys! You're just enticing them now!' Just as he was standing there a bottle smashed out a large portion of window – from the inside. Then another hit a pillar and smashed, again from inside the pub. 'AAA-H! C'-M-O-N NOW!' he berated. Then they were gone. Considering the number of missiles and flying glass about, no one appeared to be too badly hurt, though the pub genuinely looked like a small device had gone off. When the landlady, who had screamed at the top of her voice all the way through the excitement, looked in our direction and commented to one her regulars, 'I think them fellahs might have had something to do with it,' we smiled.

"By now a large crowd had gathered, so as police arrived we slipped out and mingled. Mick F. who, along with some of the DAM, had spent much of the time in the pool-room breaking up pool cues (what good they would have done us if they had got in the pub was anyone's guess) was the subject of fairly wounding banter afterwards. But though the DAM contingent had hardly distinguished itself on the day, they had long been our best allies, and so in the interests of diplomacy nothing was ever said. The real lesson for me was the difference between the fascists and us. If you include the NF and boneheads, they had anything between 100 and 140 at their disposal and they messed up. We would never have squandered such an opportunity."

One of the reasons that AFA was so effective was that it could apparently accommodate recruits from all ideologies and none. Beginning with the re-launch in 1989, alongside Red Action was the orthodox Trotskyist group Workers Power, plus the anarcho-syndicalist Direct Action Movement (DAM). They were later joined by the avowedly Stalinist, Communist Action Group, who despite bitter ideological differences with the larger Communist Party of Great Britain (CPGB) worked happily alongside a contingent from the CPGB at branch level. Elsewhere hunt saboteurs rubbed shoulders with Irish Republicans, who in turn enjoyed the backing of some Protestant-born members of the Para Territorial Army reserve; add in the hundreds of individual members without any party affiliation and it is patchwork quilt that is almost certainly unique. Toss on top the stressful nature of the work, and it is genuinely remarkable that pronounced political divisions did not erupt more often. But as damaging to political unity as any dispute could be, the incident involving C18 demonstrates what disasters lay in store should the rivalries ever be allowed to manifest operationally, as it did then.

There is, for example, a wholly different account of events at The Enkel Arms to the official one. It was published in 2001 in the personal memoirs of a DAM activist writing under the name 'K. Bullstreet'. Entitled *Bash the Fash*, it is all the more intriguing because the author, as he makes clear throughout the pamphlet, held RA activists in the highest esteem.

But he was not present on the day and so had to rely on a hearsay report from one or two in the DAM who were. Looked at objectively it is a fairly implausible story from the get go. A claim is made that 'AFA mobilised' and there is another reference to 'gathering the troops' although the fascists, not known for understatement, put the AFA total involved on the day at just about 'a dozen'. The following recollection reflects how one or two of the DAM members chose to recall events to their colleagues, and exposes the type of fault-lines AFA always needed to guard against.

"In about 1992 Madness were playing a gig in Finsbury Park, north London. Although they are a kosher band, they had one member who was ex-NF, so fascists liked to go to their gigs for a little dance. Or maybe the fascists do have some good taste in music, despite being silly arseholes in every other department. Either way, AFA mobilised because the 'fash' were expected to be there. Red Action, DAM and a few others were holed up in a pub, the Enkel Arms. Some DAM members went scouting and found the fascists in another pub nearby. They nipped back to the Enkel Arms to 'gather the troops'. Unfortunately, there was a lot of dithering by certain people and before you could say 'Freedom for Tooting', the fascists had found the Enkel Arms. In no time bricks were flying through the windows. Uncharacteristically, most of Red Action ran into the back room, leaving the anarchists to defend the place using pool cues, furniture, and those heavy pub ashtrays. In fact our heroes probably smashed more of the pub windows with those ashtrays than the fascists did! There was one hilarious moment when a certain DAM comrade fulfilled a lifetime ambition and used the bar as a springboard just like in those Wild West movies. The cops were there pretty quick just as the anarchists were getting into their stride, but nobody was arrested fortunately." (*Bash the Fash – Anti-Fascist Recollections, 1984–93*, K. Bullstreet, 2001)

By 2001 when this account was published the DAM had long since been wound up. But in 1989 when AFA was re-launched the DAM was by far the largest group nationally, and there was some resentment at Red Action for seeming to hog the limelight. This antipathy was summed up in a throw-away remark by a veteran anarchist, Albert Meltzer, in his autobiography *I Couldn't Paint Golden Angels*, in which he states: "As typical Trots they [RA] had taken [the] key posts in AFA".

Undeniably, there was a feeling that in playing too prominent a role RA had usurped what ought to have been the anarchists' natural authority, especially considering what the DAM had brought to AFA in terms of numbers, not to mention the pull they exerted by re-legitimising AFA (following the Class War fiasco) in eyes of the wider anarchist movement.

Gently bubbling under the surface most of the time, it only threatened to seriously boil over on just one occasion, as a result of a falling out between anarchists and the newly formed RA branch in Glasgow. For the more paranoid this was history repeating itself, with the betrayal of the revolution by 'Stalinists' in the Spanish Civil War the reference point. Such emotions led to wild talk of 'a war on two fronts' (against both the BNP and Red Action), and on a more practical level to a proposal to create 'an anarchist only AFA'. It was of course an attempt to implement that plan at a branch level in Glasgow that had resulted in the fisticuffs to begin with. Luckily within the DAM nationally wiser heads prevailed. Following discussions between the respective leaderships in London, with the highly respected Vince S. (who had always had a soft spot for RA) heading the DAM delegation, any misunderstandings were put to bed and the all-important operational unity maintained. For precisely the same reason, the events that led to the attack on The Enkel Arms were put down to 'a bad day at the office' and never again mentioned.

Outside of the Far Right, the audience most likely to have been fascinated by the description of what really happened at The Enkel Arms were the fellow pupils of eight-year-old, Kieran H. He had been present with his father throughout. On the following Monday, under the working title 'What I did at the weekend', the teacher had invited his fellow pupils to tell the class of their adventures. Mostly this involved an outing to the zoo or a trip to the cinema or some such.

When it came to Kieran's turn he too recounted his day out with his Dad – from start to finish – and with a war reporter's eye for the hair-raising detail!

There is no doubt that in the early days C18 enjoyed a huge amount of goodwill, with almost everyone on the Far Right eager for them to do well. Another clash near Old Street station, on the border of Hackney and Islington, this time between a small C18 band up against what was believed to be a numerically superior Red

Action, briefly surpassed The Enkel in terms of acclaim. In full Churchillian mode, one right-wing journal declared the C18 victory to be their "finest hour".

"Arguably the most ferocious encounter during this period was a street fight between twenty C18 followers and thirty anti-fascists near Old Street, following an Irish Freedom Movement march in south London. After the march anti-fascists and Irish republicans made their way back into the city for a social event that evening: so too did a group of C18, who had been prevented from reaching the march by a heavy cordon of police ... During the evening the two groups met and, though outnumbered, the C18 contingent emerged from a pub armed with pool cues, bottles, glasses and chairs and steamed into the anti-fascists, forcing them back down the street. A ten-minute battle was fought with a variety of makeshift weapons in the complete absence of the police. A group of anarchists arrived a short time after but they too were beaten off. One anti-fascist was caught in the tube station by half a dozen C18 thugs and hit repeatedly with concrete slabs" (*White Riot*, page 5).

The report in *Target*, which described itself as "the quarterly bulletin of Pro-Fascist Action," carried a similar description but with one decisive and all-important alteration. The vanquished were portrayed not as a motley crew of republicans and anarchists but as senior Red Action combatants. And it was precisely because it was leading "members of Red Action who received a severe beating," even with an estimated odds of two to one in their favour, that editor Keith Thompson wrote, no doubt with genuine pride, that "from a Nationalist point of view there is little doubt this was their finest hour."

It was something of a brutal irony that those on the receiving end were not, in fact, the notorious Red Action but renegade AFA members from Hackney who after the clash in The Abbey Arms, and the arrests at Kensington Library in 1991, seemingly felt it safer to strike out as independents. And it was also of course the overall review of nationalist security that took place after the disruption of the Keith Thompson symposium in Kensington that gave rise to C18. Given that experience, little wonder Thompson was initially overjoyed.

But, though thoroughly vicious when allowed, C18 members were very far from being the 'über-nazis' both Thompson and possibly Searchlight wanted and needed them to be. From the very beginning and throughout, the C18 *modus operandi* was always more 'football hooligan' than 'political terrorist'-related. In *White Riot*, Steve Sargent provides a fairly typical scenario: "You'd go into a pub and have a beer, obviously it would be centred around something, if the BNP were doing something or the Reds were doing something, you'd pick a pub in the area and just take it from there. We never had spotters. The Reds did, but we didn't. We always lagged behind them in things like intelligence. The Reds always were better at that sort of thing" (*White Riot*, page 17).

'Better at that sort of thing' was something of an understatement. Professional versus amateur might have been nearer the mark. By now, alongside a wariness on the Left of what C18 was really about, there was a corresponding suspicion on the Right. Some in the BNP began openly to wonder whether C18 was actually employed by State security specifically to destabilise its own operation. Immediately following Beackon's election in September 1993, C18 supporters began to rail against the supposed 'sell-out', and alarm bells began to ring. Moreover, the strategy represented by C18's open support for increased violence was completely at odds with the political analysis of the BNP leadership in waiting. But fearing the possibility of being 'out-nazified', Tyndall himself remained largely silent until an anonymous gloves-off publication called simply *Combat 18* caused him to realise his group was playing host to a fully grown parasite and rival.

In December 1993, a special members' bulletin publicly proscribed C18. "It has come to our notice that representatives of the organisation [C18] have been exploiting their contacts with BNP members and supporters in a deliberate drive to undermine the latter's loyalty to the BNP. The methods used to this purpose have included not only cheap and nasty 'tittle tattle' against BNP personnel, but downright attempted physical violence. In addition to this, Combat 18 seems to have assumed the right to set itself up as the disciplinary enforcement apparatus of the BNP, picking upon party members who for one reason or another have incurred its dislike, and condemning them for acts of 'treachery' against the nationalist cause, then administering 'punishment' to them by random beatings-up.

"Many of those who have read this material and listened to the talk of Combat 18 spokesmen say their language bears a close resemblance to the 'class war' rhetoric of the extreme Left, attempting constantly to divide nationalist from nationalist by exploiting differences of social and educational background. These disruptive tactics have no place in the nationalist movement. Things have now reached a pitch at which the BNP is no longer prepared to tolerate this divisive behaviour, and it is hereby issuing a notice of complete repudiation of Combat 18 and declaring that group to be a hostile organisation. All BNP members who have hitherto maintained links with both sides should be informed that henceforth and with effect from now they must decide where their loyalties lie. If they wish to remain in the BNP they must sever all connections with Combat 18. If they wish to remain with Combat 18 they must consider themselves no longer members of the BNP."

Combat 18 publicly invited readers to ask themselves the question many had been asking themselves in private: "whether Charlie and Steve Sargent are MI5 agents or just poisonous shit-stirrers and completely fucking stupid?" Adding: "Charlie breaks a window and expects you to kill [a million] wogs." And while washing their hands of responsibility for its publication, the political tendency led by Lecomber and Butler was understandably gleeful.

For although over the years C18 had been responsible for a number of attacks on individuals and occasionally managed to push over the odd ANL stall, they never managed to do the business as a stewards group at street level on any sustained basis. Yet to be effective on the street was the declared reason for their existence. But as the BNP leadership knew all too well, despite the hard sell by both C18 and the media, neither had ever been able to report a single C18 success, specifically against those they were set up to crush. It was with bitterness and regret that BNP leader John Tyndall would refer to this elementary failure. Even though he had proscribed C18 in December 1993, time had done nothing to diminish Tyndall's sense of personal betrayal. Eighteen months after the expulsion of C18, not least due to the ever-increasing physical pressure his organisation and by extension he as leader was under, Tyndall increasingly sought succour in denouncing C18's 'inaction against the enemies of nationalism'.

"When three prominent BNP men were seriously injured in savage terrorist attacks in the spring of 1994, the time had surely come for the 'direct action' brigade to show their mettle in the way of retaliatory response. In the event their response was pathetic – inaction was the order of the day" (*Spearhead*, January 1995). And again: "If ever there was a time for Combat 18 to demonstrate its mettle and translate its big talk into deeds, this was the time. Had it been true to its professed policies, its activists would have carried out retaliatory attacks on selected left-wing terrorists or preachers of terrorism, of which there are ample number. Whether or not they actually are proven to have taken part in assaults on the BNP men. But C18 just did nothing."

The anonymous author of the anti-C18 pamphlet put the same accusation in a coarser way. "C18 achievements so far: niggers, Jews, Pakis/other scum sent home in body bags – nil; Main AFA/RA agitators attacked in revenge for attacks on nationalists – nil; Attacks on Searchlight/Gable – nil. Attacks on 'wimmin' – two (London & Halifax); attacks on old Jew-boys windows – one (by the great man himself, Charlie Sargent). Pathetic isn't it? If Charlie and Steve Sargent are so bloody great and C18 under there [sic] command as good as all there [sic] big talk, then how come when a BNP candidate in east London lost an eye that C18 did fuck all? Where was the retaliation? Why didn't C18 wipe out AFA/Red Action? Couldn't they even get ONE of them?"

Despite such credibility problems, *Searchlight* remained steadfast and strangely loyal to how C18 liked to see itself. In January 1994 it warned: "While the anti-fascist movement may be able to hold its own against the nazis on the streets, we cannot deal with bombings and terrorist acts." And its commitment to continuing to sell precisely that image to the public was just as unswerving, but not without cost.

Heedless of the damage to their reputation among committed anti-fascists, at every conceivable opportunity Searchlight saw to it that C18 were relentlessly hyped, not only in the pages of their own magazine but also through the mainstream press and television. Among the highlights, there were two primetime and heavily flagged *World in Action* documentaries in April 1993 and March 1995, separated by a *Dispatches* offering in October 1994 that followed the same breathless format. A propaganda blitz possibly only superseded by having C18 as the lead story and/or centre-page spread in Sunday's best-selling tabloid, the *News of the World*, for most of February 1995. This was a most impressive portfolio, considering the unexceptional raw material they worked with. Client/agent was how Red Action saw the combination. "Though they may on the surface be bitter enemies the de facto relationship remains for the moment more like agent and client. Searchlight have established exclusive rights to the C18 story and so naturally are interested in promoting the notoriety of their protégé ... [T]hat is why Gerry Gable is playing Max Clifford to Charlie Sargent's Antonia de Sancha"* (*Red Action*, issue 71, summer 1995). And even though it ran contrary to everything else it had said as to the nature of C18, Searchlight was not totally averse to co-opting the rumours of state involvement if it added frisson. Ray Hill, at one time a leading British Movement organiser, who had been turned by Searchlight, opened the batting: "To those even more cynical than me and the Searchlight team, I pose the question: is Combat 18 being allowed to exist to service some mad scheme by irresponsible officers in our security services? Sit in a dark room and think about it" (*Searchlight*, September 1994).

In April 1995 it went much further, explaining in a matter of fact fashion what MI5 might have been thinking when it created C18 as a pseudo gang: "The reasons for MI5 wanting to establish another 'honey trap' on the Far Right are understandable and possibly justifiable at the time C18 was created. Stella Rimington had just taken over as director of MI5. With the job came the responsibility for watching Ulster Loyalist paramilitaries in mainland Britain, whom Special Branch had neglected in recent years. It was in these years that some sections of the loyalist UDA and UVF, and their respective killer squads, had started to cooperate with fascists in Britain. Clearly MI5 needed to know the extent of such joint operations. So Combat 18 came into existence" (*Searchlight*, April 1995).

If this were true, why is it that only a month earlier *Searchlight* had been calling for a co-ordinated multi-agency response in order to bring C18 activities to a halt? "All the fears Searchlight and others have expressed to the authorities over the past three years about Combat 18's potential for violence and mayhem were realised when Combat 18 nazis orchestrated the riot at the England versus Ireland football match in Dublin on 15th February. Combat 18 not only advocates serious violence

* A model who had an affair with a Tory Minister, with the media fall-out being managed on her behalf by publicist Max Clifford.

but has the arms with which to carry it out ... [I]f law and order is to prevail, the police and prosecuting authorities must recognise that Combat 18 is an organised criminal gang, and needs a coordinated national response to halt it."

Their absurd insistence that 'law and order' was on the point of collapse resulted from the violence at an international football match between Ireland and England in Dublin in February 1995 which caused the match to be abandoned after twenty minutes. A Searchlight suggestion that the riot may have been planned and that a call to arms had been issued in the C18 fanzine *Putsch* two weeks prior to the game ensured a conspiracy of international proportions.

"As the evening wore on, the TV channels sought to explain the context of and background to the mayhem ... with Miriam O'Callaghan interviewing Rogan Taylor of Liverpool University and Gerry Gable of *Searchlight* magazine about Combat 18 ... the *Einsatzgruppe* of the National Front. 'You really mean this is about politics?' said Miriam with bourgeois incredulity. Well, yes they assured her, it was about politics of a sort. The neo-nazis support the North's Loyalists and they had come to Dublin to 'try and wreck the peace process'" (*Irish Times*, 18th February 1995).

Afterwards, Searchlight crowed, it was "deluged by over 200 media requests for help and information" on C18 as a result of this manipulation. But, as Nick Lowles the editor of *Searchlight* would later admit in his book *White Riot*, not a single member of C18 was actually present. It can be assumed that Searchlight knew of this when they had been lobbying for MI5 to be given the job of dealing with Combat 18. Then after it emerged that it was an MI5 operation all along, Searchlight promptly warned of the threat to democracy "if faceless unanswerable bodies such as MI5 are allowed to run such operations."

Inevitably the militants were scathing. For them the affair asked as many questions of Searchlight's *bona fides* as it did of C18's. "Either they [Searchlight] were promoting MI5 in complete ignorance of the C18 connection, or they were promoting C18 in blissful ignorance of its MI5 origins" (*Red Action*, issue 71, summer 1995).

So just a few weeks after Landsdowne Road, with C18 organising the stewarding for a Loyalist march in central London, Searchlight may have felt it had no choice but to seek to maintain the C18 'super-terrorist' facade. Later, explaining its failure to notify anti-fascist groups of the march, it said it did so "because of the danger of serious violence." In real terms, while the C18 reputation was by now in tatters on either side of the spectrum, the Searchlight synopsis may still have retained some plausibility among the readership of its magazine. One unforeseen consequence of the Searchlight weeding out of the most militant AFA branches from the back of their magazine was that their replacements were worthy but decidedly un-dynamic anti-racist groupings which presented a dismayingly false picture of anti-fascist incapacity. The AFA leadership, in London in particular, were livid when the march went unopposed as a result of the Searchlight sleight of hand, with C18 stewards detouring to attack a Labour Party gathering, with attendant publicity.

Andy: "For us the idea of an emasculated anti-fascism was sending out all the wrong messages. By now we realised we were probably going to have to go through a period of strategic re-evaluation so it was very much in our interests that it appeared 'business as usual' publicly."

Exactly twelve months later, having made certain of their own intelligence, the militants took their revenge. When the English Amalgamated Apprentice Boys of Londonderry (EAABL), along with a Loyalist band from Govan and supporters, backed up by C18 security, duly assembled in Holborn, central London, a large AFA group travelled from Islington to meet them.

Joe: "We knew that the police would be mobbed up at Holborn station so we opted for Russell Square, which though just one stop down would, all importantly, allow us access to our target from the opposite side to the police. The basic plan of attack had already been worked out. However, on the day there was a problem that had been overlooked but was obvious once our people were out of the tube. Russell Square station is deeper than many in London. The maximum the lift carried was probably about forty. We had three times as many. Time was of the essence so there was no way we could wait to ferry everyone up. There was nothing for it but the stairs. There must have been about 200 steps and the heftier 'Brummies' moaned at every one of them. Despite the tension it made some people smile. As the first of us emerged out of Russell Square tube station we were tagged at once by a couple of plainclothes police spotters. One actually ran off, presumably to inform his superiors. What an amateur! By the time he came back with reinforcements, all 120 of us were gone. You see, we had already plotted out the route beforehand and as 'plod' were looking for us in the main drag of Southampton Row, we were approaching our target on Theobald's Road, via Old Gloucester Street, a narrow side street, parallel to it. There was something else as well. Police would have presumed we were heading for C18 at Holborn but we had, in fact, picked a different target. The attack was 'called in' by a senior AFA member in the vicinity who had been doing a circuit of the area in a car."

The AFA stewards communicated by mobile phone: "Where are they? How many? Can we take them?" The final answer was in the affirmative.

Terry: "I was in charge of surveillance on the day. From early on, the immediate area surrounding Holborn tube was saturated with police. The main body of fascists were in a pub called The Princess Louise within spitting distance of them. No chance there. As we were touring the area by car, we suddenly spotted another likely looking crew outside a pub on Theobald's Road. Encouragingly there were no obvious signs of police. I immediately contacted the chief steward and alerted him to the opportunity. As this might be the best chance we would have all day, it was decided to go for it.

"But no sooner had the main body of stewards set off from Holloway Road station, than two vans of police pulled up in a side street around the corner. Did this mean the message had been intercepted? There was no way to alert the boys immediately, as they were travelling on the underground. I knew it was imperative contact was established the second they surfaced. It looked like we would need to abort. We were still circling the area checking both pub and police. The stewards would be arriving any second. Then two things happened at once. First the police drove off. It was back on. In the same second the phone was answered. 'GO!'

"We had pulled into a side street, leading onto Queens Square. We were just in time to see the boys arrive: about 120-strong. They were marching swiftly toward the pub, with not a word being said, and with everyone looking very determined. It was a sight I will personally never forget."

With 300 police on duty in the area (the average police attendance for a Premiership football match), specifically to prevent such an occurrence, speed and surprise were of the essence. Pouring into the side street the AFA group, ten and

The Met's finest prepare to confront anti-fascists at the entrance to the underpass on Theobald's Road, London, 1996.

twelve deep, moved swiftly but silently toward their target. With 50 yards still to go, some young Glasgow Rangers casuals spotted their approach. Assuming this was the infamous, C18 these young 'uns burst into spontaneous and excited applause. By the time they reviewed their decision and screeched a warning it was too late. Exactly two minutes after leaving Russell Square tube the AFA stewards group attacked the Loyalist/C18 overspill in and around the crowded White Hart pub on Theobald's Road.

Astonished bandsmen ("they seemed to come out of nowhere," one told ITN later) found themselves on the defensive as anti-fascists, one using a large sandwich board as cover, tried to batter their way into the pub. Others were picked off in the vicinity of the pub. Terrified C18 casuals were seen to sprint to safety. Loyalist bandsmen employed their standards as spears, while some others produced steak knives. Though inevitably brief due to the proximity of police, it was still fairly bloody. A number of AFA activists were wounded in the exchange but were spirited away to hospitals outside of the area before police arrived. "Four people were arrested after violent clashes before a Loyalist parade through central London on Saturday. Before the march got under way, a number of anti-nazi protesters were involved in scuffles with Loyalists in Holborn. Two men were taken to hospital after a fight in a pub, which left one with a cut to his head and another with a stomach wound" (*Irish World*, 3rd May 1996).

"A bomb scare caused by a suspect vehicle delayed the march in setting off from Lincoln's Inn Field, and Pride of Govan band members required a police escort after being attacked. An estimated 100 counter-demonstrators were cordoned off in Holborn to prevent further clashes" (*Irish Post*, 3rd May 1996).

Despite AFA 'claiming responsibility', the *Observer* referred to the Loyalist/fascist casualties without offering any explanation as to who might have been responsible. "One man was stabbed and three others injured in a brawl before the march." To further add to any initial misunderstanding it went on to print an ANL call for police to ban 'fascists' from marching: "Allowing nazis to march gives them confidence, and confident nazis go out and attack people and commit murders like that of Stephen Lawrence" (*Observer*, 28th April 1996).

Meanwhile, anything but confident, the Loyalists complained bitterly to anybody that would listen. William Moore, General Secretary of the Apprentice Boys of Derry, spoke to the media: "We are here today as British citizens marching in a British city. Our Loyalty is to the Crown ... I think these people do not understand what we are about. This organisation is not racially biased and we welcome anyone into our ranks." By the end of the day, however, that 'anyone' did not appear to include C18. Another member who did not want to be named condemned the White Hart attack as "deplorable" but significantly also insisted fascists "are not welcome anywhere near us."

Even if it eluded the *Observer*, the Loyalists had at least got the message, as did *Searchlight* if its truculent comment later is anything to go by: "The only casualties at this year's Loyalist parade … were some Loyalist bandsmen from Scotland who were drinking with their families in a different pub from the one the nazis were using."

Terry: "After their statement the previous year, Searchlight was trying to suggest we hit the wrong pub. The whole point, of course, was that C18 were meant to be offering security. By damaging those who they were meant to be protecting, we showed them up. Apart from that, evading 300 police and attacking a pub packed with Loyalist Glaswegians in broad daylight sent a powerful message to those watching, including the BNP, that 'we hadn't gone away, you know'."

Two weeks previously in Bolton, a similar attempt by the EAABL/C18 mob to march through the town centre was cancelled by Greater Manchester police following a violent confrontation between Northern Network AFA and C18 stewards. Again, far from preventing trouble, C18 were shown to be a magnet for it. All but washed up as any kind of paramilitary force, before long the C18 leadership had devoted their attentions to making money.

In September 1993, when Ian Stuart Donaldson, founder and leader of the Blood & Honour organisation was killed in a car crash, this unexpected opening at management level saw C18 make their move. They quickly established exclusive control of the organisation's security and political control of the associated music fanzines. Most importantly, they gained control of the B&H purse strings. It was claimed that Charlie Sargent and Wilf Browning dipped into the organisation's finances from the off. Rumour has it that Charlie managed to filter off a figure approaching £80,000 while the ever modest 'Beast' was content with only half as much. These shenanigans soon led to general unrest and certainly did not go down well with fellow fascists. The British Hammerskins described C18's brand of National Socialism as "nothing more than blatant capitalism!" They successfully ripped off a whole number of people: Skrewdriver albums were bootlegged in America and sold as imports while over £10,000 worth of CDs were appropriated from Viking Sounds in Holland.

In 1994 the National Socialist Alliance was created in order to unite a number of small, openly nazi groups like the KKK, British Movement, B&H, etc., all under the supervision of C18. At the same time international links were established with like-minded groups in Europe and North America. This created a virtual C18 monopoly of the nazi music scene, a monopoly that was, moreover, potentially extremely lucrative. For a brief period, due to control of the purse strings, their political influence and income within the Far Right was considerable, but inevitably, given the lack of calibre at leadership level, things soon began to fall apart. By 1996 the discontent created through corrupt activity, combined with attacks on fellow fascists, pooled with their powerlessness against 'the Reds', erupted into open rebellion. The influential *Resistance* and *Nordland* magazines came out against C18 and the floodgates opened. Often quoted, the most damning indictment came from David Lane, then serving a life sentence for involvement in American paramilitary group The Order, "The leadership of C18 are obviously Zionist agents or they are so ignorant they might as well be. It can no longer be tolerated. At the appropriate time the enemy amongst us will face a night of the long knives."

Rapidly, competition internally for control of the CD operation developed into a contest for control of C18 itself, that did appropriately end in murder by 'a long knife'. On 10th February 1996 Martin Cross, a former drummer with Skrewdriver, and Sargent lackey, plunged a knife into the back of fellow C18 member Chris Castle, killing him on the spot. When Michael John Heath, the pathologist, gave evidence in the trial, he told the court the knife wound was two centimetres deeper than the actual blade length, which, despite Castle's heavy leather jacket, led him to conclude "severe force" was used in the killing. Castle had been acting as an intermediary between rival factions in the organisation, one of which was headed by the Sargents, and the other by Wilf Browning, previously Charlie's aide de camp.

What little credibility C18 retained by 1998 was lost entirely with the jailing for life of Sargent in January that year, along with revelations that emerged during the trial that he had been 'touting' for Special Branch, thereby ending any prospect of C18 being held together, even as a business. Nor could it be denied that the relationship between elements of the state and C18 was pretty murky. A *Sunday Times* journalist called Henry McDonald, evidently with close ties to that subterranean world, 'exposed' Sargent as a Special Branch informer. Interestingly, in 1994 the same journalist had claimed "Red Action were run by British Intelligence" (*Irish World*, 3rd June 1994). As with the intention of the *World in Action* documentary, the underlying message was that, as Copsey had observed, militant anti-fascism "should be avoided". But as independent researcher Larry O'Hara put it in his book, *Turning up the Heat*, "There is a world of difference between being the subject of heavy MI5 attention and actually being run by them."

All in all, if the early '90s was "a dangerous time to be on the Right," as Nick Ryan claims, then, if for only marginally different reasons, as events have demonstrated, it was at least as dangerous to be on the Left.

By January 1995 the BNP nationally had had enough, and the policy of 'street warfare' was ditched.

3.23

'NO MORE MARCHES, MEETINGS, PUNCH-UPS'

In political/paramilitary terms, if the C18 demise can be traced back to the events of January 1994, the shock, dismay, and no little delight at their loss of face caused reverberations outside the circles of their own supporters. Across the Far Right, if there were a few who felt mortified, they were more than matched by those who felt politically, and personally, vindicated. Foremost among them were the architects of the BNP victory on the Isle of Dogs, who now saw a window of opportunity to change the course of nationalist history, and jumped through it without hesitation.

Almost immediately after Beackon's election in October 1993, the two chiefly responsible for designing the BNP electoral strategy, Eddy Butler and Tony Lecomber, had come under increased political, personal and even physical attacks from C18 who rather bizarrely accused them of 'selling out'. While there was more than a trace of suspicion at the time that the C18 motivation was state directed, the entire affair had an extremely debilitating effect on the BNP as an organisation, particularly in London, with whole branches falling for the C18 brand of political nihilism. So, what better chance to cut all ties with the past, they must have thought, than at the very moment their militant detractors, those who styled themselves as the conscience of nationalism, were at their least prestigious?

Of course, it may have been a coincidence but on Tuesday 15th March 1994, exactly two months to the day after the shaming of C18 at The Little Driver, Tony Lecomber, who in 1991 was described by a judge as "a dangerous man", addressed a BNP meeting in Newham to which the Press were invited. "The days of street warfare were over," Lecomber told *London Tonight*. There would be "no more marches, meetings, punch-ups." For fascists and anti-fascists alike it was a defining moment. Not that you would know it.

Searchlight, for example, immediately dismissed it as a mere ploy by the BNP to try and appear respectable in the run-up to the local elections the following month. For them, the 'No marches, meetings, punch-ups' strategy would not likely survive the end of the election campaign. "The British National Party's claim that it is moving away from its thuggish street gang image has been slammed as 'hollow' and 'obviously untrue' by anti-fascist campaigners. Peter Brighton, from anti-fascist organisation Searchlight, said Anthony Lecomber has 'a proven track record for violence.' The Searchlight spokesman continued: 'And he is typical of BNP members. They stoke up violence in the streets and then try to reap the benefits in the ballot box, claiming a multi-racial world doesn't work'" (*Ilford Recorder*, 17th March 1994).

With characteristic lack of precision, liberal anti-fascism, possibly because it had so little to do with causing the about face by the BNP, was still unwilling to come to terms with the historic implications of the Lecomber pronouncement a decade later. A chronic inability to 'know your enemy' is reflected by Copsey, who also skates over the implications, going as far as to suggest the BNP absence on London streets thereafter could be put down to rank and file 'demoralisation' following the failure of the party to make an electoral breakthrough in the local elections that May. And if the March 1994 declaration is ever alluded to by the ANL propaganda department at all, it is solely in terms of when 'they', who had been kicked from pillar to post by BNP gangs for the previous four years, had put the BNP to the sword.

Tellingly, the AFA leadership were far more circumspect. Where others saw reason for self-congratulation, militant anti-fascism saw mainly menace, to the extent that within just a matter of months the London AFA leadership had privately concluded that, to remain effective, militant anti-fascism would need to implement a hairpin turn of its own. Thus, in May 1995, when London AFA formally adopted the 'filling the vacuum' strategy, it accepted that physical force anti-fascism had become redundant. It meant that if militant anti-fascism was going to continue to play a decisive role the overall AFA strategy needed to change tack just as decisively as had the BNP. All that was now required was that London convince everyone else.

Across the South East, the BNP response to the 'no more punch-ups' edict was nothing less than immediate, but around the country the response to the order to 'stand down' was initially less than uniform. In the North West, for instance, it seemed to be very much business as usual. But as the body language of the competing groups demonstrated during an extraordinary clash on the steps of Rochdale Town Hall on the night of the local elections on 5th May 1994, the militants now had the whip-hand, and everyone, police included, knew it.

The local elections in Rochdale had been a major push for the BNP. Despite that, they dared not risk calling any meetings, marches, or rallies, and had relied instead on a leafleting and letter-writing campaign to local papers, particularly the *Rochdale Observer*. For AFA, the run-up was much the same as usual: distributing anti-fascist propaganda, coupled with a determination to prevent the BNP doing the same among the windswept housing estates in the hills around the town centre. In the weeks leading up to the election, "a BNP leafleting team narrowly avoided annihilation at the hands of an AFA Stewards Group" and "no BNP leaflets were distributed in Rochdale that day" (*Manchester Red Action*, Bulletin No 9).

On polling day itself AFA was on the prowl from 11am. Yet, though no fascists were spotted, the ANL temporarily fled the area around the polling station in the early evening anyway. At 6.30pm AFA was reinforced by some fresh arrivals that had expectantly taken up position at a pub near the Town Hall. But four and a half hours later the BNP still had not shown their faces, which encouraged the ANL to come back, while the three BNP candidates were smuggled into the count in the back of a police van. That looked to be that, and AFA withdrew – or gave the appearance of doing so. "On cue the BNP ... marched boldly up the Town Hall steps. The ANL response was to meekly step aside and wave their stupid yellow lollipops. At this moment the [80-strong] AFA contingent returned. The BNP fled before the AFA charge, with half of them fighting with police in a panic stricken rush to squeeze through a single door into the safety of the Town Hall itself, while the other half scattered into the ranks of the ANL. The affect of this was to cause the ANL to scatter before the retreating fascists and police in a sort of domino effect" (*Manchester Red Action*, Bulletin No 9).

Jon: "Rochdale Town Hall was probably one of those defining moments for a lot of people involved on both sides. It had been a long day for the core AFA group, between looking for BNP canvass teams and trying to intercept candidates in the late afternoon at their home addresses. There was even an attempt to force our way into [BNP candidate] Christian Jackson's home, such was the frustration! After news came through that the candidates had been smuggled into the Town Hall we had about 60 of our mob who we couldn't justify keeping out any longer. We piled into the transport and we were off. Within a minute or two we got phoned that the fash had surfaced at last: back to the Town Hall. There was a mob of them. This was it and everyone knew it. AFA arrived from three sides. One of the Oldham boys called Priestly says to them, 'This is it boys. Are we gonna stand or what?' while behind him his mates were already busy fighting the police – who were having none of it – in order to get into the hall. The police could see the mayhem, flying bottles and so on, and so were determined to lock it all out. Priestly got whacked. The BNP got a bit of a beating but it was BNP morale that really got kicked into the dirt. AFA then pulled back, taking one or two arrests."

A police spokesman explained to the *Rochdale Observer* that, as a result of two police officers being injured after "bottles were thrown," police ordered the doors "to be kept shut" which he admitted "were only reopened" when AFA withdrew "after 20 minutes." Typically an AFA spokesman offered no apologises: "As far as we are concerned the operation was a complete success" (*Rochdale Observer*, 7th May 1994).

An Asian gang who initially had joined the noisier and more visible ANL picket were much taken by the militant's swashbuckling approach: "Respect to AFA." Later in an interview with the *New Musical Express*, Rochdale rap band Kaliphz echoed the sentiment but went considerably further. "You have to do what AFA do: find the nazis and sort them out ... AFA are the only organisation that goes out there and does something. They make it physically hard for the nazis to move in this country ...This is the one European country where the nazis don't have a firm foothold, and that's because of AFA."

Further clashes in the first six months of 1995, which encapsulated the AFA dominance in Manchester and further afield, seemed to confirm for many BNP members the innate wisdom of the London BNP leadership decision a year earlier. Possibly in tribute to the stranglehold militants in Manchester had established in the city and the North West generally, the Troops Out Movement organisers, following the shock of the huge turnout by Loyalists and fascists in London in 1993, had decided for the first time in twenty years to hold their annual Bloody Sunday commemoration in Manchester. This was a prudent move but unforeseen events appeared almost to conspire against them. It so happened the date of the march, 28th January, coincided with the fifth round of the FA Cup, with the city's two football teams, United and City, quite unusually both being drawn at home. This meant that more than double the normal numbers of police would be required to police these matches, with the result that, instead of the hundreds of police the TOM organisers might normally have expected, all that was on offer was what Manchester police felt it could afford – a couple of dozen special constables!

Initially, for the BNP, who had also flooded into Manchester from the surrounding towns like Burnley, Rochdale, and Middleton, it must have seemed as if Christmas had come early. Reflecting this buoyancy, a group of about forty had gathered in The Clarence pub, less than 150 yards from the marchers' assembly point. In what proved to be a significant fascist counter-mobilisation, others had mobbed up along the route. Fatefully, AFA had also mobilised significant numbers in expectation of trouble. After assessing the scene the chief stewards for the day drew up a battle plan.

Jon: "The basic game plan drawn up by myself and the other chief steward, Denis, was to move into the area of the march, taking a pub on the pivotal crossroads opposite Platt Lane Fields from where the march was taking off. We then divided the 140 or so stewards into three groups, one walking ahead of the march by a hundred yards or so, one to the rear and a group of about 30 'on tour' scouting likely spots in the vicinity. While the lead stewards group filed past The Clarence in a disciplined manner, the BNP congregated there remained silent. But when the actual march came level, thinking the lead AFA group had gone, they gustily opened up with 'Rule Britannia'. Instead of carrying on, the lead group, unnoticed, had U-turned and were now covertly threading their way through the body of the march directly back to The Clarence. Two bars of 'Rule Britannia' in, the AFA stewards bringing up the rear suddenly appear on their left. Emerging from the march I shouted, 'Game On!' and attacked the fascist nearest to me. Our people went straight into them. Hit by a pincer movement, with the march directly in front and a narrow pub door behind, they never stood a chance."

As some fled pulling the door shut behind them, thus locking the less fortunate outside, others fled through the pub into the car park with militants in hot pursuit. The initial encounter, though thunderous, with pub windows being smashed from the inside, had taken less than half a minute. Then the order was given to disengage and move off in anticipation of police intervening. But, unbelievably, as the police and the march continued as if nothing had happened, so it was decided to attack again through a rear door. In what must have been slightly surreal and terrifying experience for the BNP inside, the AFA offensive was accompanied by the rousing music of a Republican flute band which had stopped outside as the main body of the march continued!

With AFA again dispersed into smaller groups, there were further clashes along Oxford Road. With police reinforcements deployed from the matches, AFA returned to the more familiar game of cat and mouse. One BNP outfit was still trailing the march. As a Republican bandsman put it, "It was simply a case of looking at my watch and thinking – any second now." To his delight, the BNP were then ambushed from a side street by the third AFA scouting party.

Jon: "By now fascists were shamelessly identifying their assailants to the police. One in particular was pointing me out to the senior officer who had just arrived to take charge of the mess and I only evaded capture, even with a change of jacket and cap, by ducking into the body of the march. As we entered from the Hulme side, I had rejoined the rest of the AFA group in a pub near Oxford Road Station. Immediately I noticed two more join our number. When it was pointed out they were Special Branch, it was necessary for me to vanish again."

As the march arrived at Albert Square to be addressed by Sinn Fein's Martin McGuinness, fascists again sought to infiltrate the crowd. One proudly announced he was there "to get into the Reds" and produced a St George's flag. A photo of him draped in the flag, but lying senseless, was later described by the *Manchester Evening News* as "chilling" (17th April 1995). From his bird's eye view, McGuinness could see police moving in on the suspects. "Someone should tell those boys they're going to be lifted," he said.

Commenting on the day's events, the Loyalist magazine, *New Ulster Defender*, an organ of the paramilitary Ulster Defence Association, described the activities of "Red Action" as most "sinister". For them there was amusement that "an Irish pub, (yes, an *Irish* pub)" had been wrecked in an attack by what it described as "local Manchester City fans believed to be anti-IRA." Later that evening the landlord of The Clarence was interviewed on Manchester radio, where he claimed over £10,000 worth of damage had been inflicted during the fracas.

Jon: "The pub was a mess, though much of the damage was incurred from 'inside out,' so to speak. I still felt bad, though, as I had been drinking there myself every Sunday for years – it was actually my local!"

Two months later, on 28th April, it was the turn of the BNP in the Midlands to suffer utter humiliation at AFA hands. By this time Kirkby in Ashfield was regarded as the last stronghold of the BNP in the East Midlands. A mass leafting/canvassing was intended to consolidate BNP support on the Coxmore Estate there. Sensing overall victory, the militants were determined to crush the life out of any attempted BNP resurgence. On sight of an 80-strong AFA stewards group, BNP scouts situated in the local High Street simply fled, leading AFA directly to the main body of the BNP. It was later suspected this may have been a police ploy for, on turning a corner, a substantially larger force of police immediately confronted AFA, some mounted, others with dogs. A brief stand-off ensued. Then, without any attempt at negotiation, the anti-fascists were summarily ordered to disperse. Before an appropriate response could be considered, police charged with batons drawn. A number went down, with one lad from Nottingham being set upon by a police dog, and eventually left with a leg broken in five places.

By now, thoroughly alarmed by the consequences for themselves of a vengeful AFA breaking through, the watching BNP simply abandoned their position, in full view of the watching residents they had been hoping to impress. Under heavy police escort, AFA was then forced to the very edge of the estate. News that the BNP were leafleting the High Street led to yet another determined attempt by AFA to break out, which in turn, sparked another baton charge and further injuries. When the furore subsided, the anti-fascists were corralled in the middle of the road, totally blocking the thoroughfare for an hour.

Damian: "Even allowing for the police providing security, the BNP were visibly twitchy and seemed eager to get shot of the leaflets and just get away. Once they left the High Street there were no sightings of them for the rest of the day."

A further indication of the increasing militant self-belief came within days, when a BNP candidate was attacked in his home. For some weeks prior to the local council elections, AFA teams, who had been out leafleting in the Kingstanding area of Birmingham, were informed by a number of sympathisers of the relatively high profile local BNP candidate Keith Axon had begun to adopt, which in turn caused those who shared his views to become ever bolder. At 11.20pm on the night of the count, according to the *Birmingham Evening Mail*, "a gang armed with a knuckle duster and hammer handle burst into Axon's home." A colleague with him "who was struck with the hammer handle suffered a one-and-a-half inch cut to his forehead." The attackers also "caused extensive damage to the flat." Both men were believed to be have been hospitalised. A police spokesman said: "We will be looking to see if the attack was politically motivated" (*Birmingham Evening Mail*, 5th May 1995).

A few months earlier, Devon police were also left wondering if a similar attack on a high profile right-winger was also "politically motivated". The victim on this occasion was a 34-year old NF veteran and Loyalist sympathiser, Mark Cotterill,* who had made headlines in national newspapers the previous year when it was revealed he had been accepted as a member of Torbay Conservatives. In 1992 he had urged Far Right activists to adopt an entryist strategy within the Tory Party. According to a newspaper for the region, "The incident happened shortly before 7pm, when two men forced their way into Mr Cotterill's home in St James Road, Torquay, and attacked him with an iron bar and a knife. He was rushed to Torbay Hospital with severe head injuries, and a police spokesman said he would be in hospital for a considerable time." Two local AFA members were charged with unlawful wounding.

If there was any confusion among police as to who might have been behind the attacks, the BNP leadership would never have been in any doubt. And even though relatively minor incidents in themselves, 'home visits' were an indication of a growing confidence amongst the enemy. When, not long after, Richard Edmunds was mugged in the street and his personal diary containing names and addresses of key BNP members was taken, personal security would likely have been considerably stepped up across the country as a result. For BNP modernisers like Lecomber and, to a lesser degree, Griffin, there must have been a quiet satisfaction in the misfortune of others, as it bore out their prophecy that activity in the physical sphere was "no use", and had become a political dead-end.

From Edinburgh and Glasgow as well, the tone of reports emerging from early '94 to late '95 very much conveyed a sense of anti-fascists mopping up. In truth, the

---

* Mark Cotterill was one of two members of a BNP breakaway group elected as councillors in Blackburn in 2006.

BNP in Scotland had never properly recovered from the catastrophe of the Tyndall visit and the prospects of a physical force revival were not helped when some leading football casuals from both Edinburgh and Glasgow threw in their lot with the militants. This rather unusual alliance had a lot to do with the particular circumstances in Scotland where, largely as a result of Red Action influence, anti-fascist/Republican and BNP/Loyalist battle lines were cemented. A Glasgow Celtic football fanzine with which RA was connected and which was notorious in media circles for its support for the IRA regularly sold 5,000 copies outside the ground. In it, opposition to fascism was made synonymous with support for republicanism. All of this added to the pressure the BNP leadership and members were already under.

"Anti-fascist influence also extended to links with Hibs casuals who, in their own inimitable way, smashed up The Trees pub, favourite drinking den of the BNP and Hearts casuals. As a result of this incident, the brewery sacked the management of the pub and the bar staff who had been exhibiting sympathy for the fascists. Hibs football fans also stumbled upon a BNP leadership meeting in Glasgow, as they passed through the city on their way back to Edinburgh after a Hibs match against Motherwell. The BNP contingent included Steve Cartwright, Scott McLean and Warren Bennett (all leading organisers in Scotland), as well as visitors from London. They were immediately set upon and ended up barricading themselves in the pub's kitchen before being given a police escort to safety. The same group of football supporters were involved in clashes with fascist skins and casuals at the Madness concert in Livingstone in January. Initial reports in the press claimed that the violence was indiscriminate; however, eyewitnesses claim that several groups of casuals and skinheads had united under the BNP's leadership in order to cause as much disruption to the gig as possible and to take on the Hibs casuals. A source close to the action tells us that all hell let loose at the gig with the Hibs boys coming out well on top" (*Red Action*, issue 65).

This tilting of the balance seemed to force the authorities, which would have had no reason to look kindly on the new alliance, into some rather unconventional manoeuvres. In June 1995, when AFA mobilised to confront BNP and Loyalist counter-demonstrators assembling to attack the James Connolly march, "one group (Hibs Casuals) were surrounded early in the morning as they left a flat" which caused the Hibs' intervention to be "effectively neutralised". House arrest is another name for it. Later in the day there was, if anything, an even more bizarre encounter when an AFA contingent was "attacked by at least a dozen casually dressed young men – some of them sporting skinheads – as they made their way to the march. By the casual nature of their dress and their aggressive attitude it was assumed that they must be fascists. The anti-fascists, therefore, defended themselves against the attack. It was only when the tables were turned on the attackers that they apparently decided to 'break cover' and identify themselves as police officers. According to the press reports, four police officers were hospitalised as a result of this incident. The ten anti-fascists arrested and detained for the rest of the weekend at St Leonard's police station, were all subsequently charged under the Criminal Justice and Public Order Act. Among the charges were 'police assault' and 'resisting arrest'" (*Red Action*, issue 72).

Red Action drew some obvious conclusions: "It is obvious which side the forces of law and order are on. Indeed, on past evidence of the JCS march and events, the police have never been neutral. Instead they have taken a pro-active role, harassing individual organisers and those publicans who are still prepared to provide them with venues for meetings … [T]he attempts to criminalise AFA are nothing new. It appears that the police in Scotland are now catching up with (their) English counterparts."

Police partisanship notwithstanding, the steady upping of the ante by the militants across Britain left those BNP regions not yet entirely sold on the idea of an exclusively political 'kampf' feeling increasingly isolated. Unsurprisingly, by the end of 1995, one by one they began to fall in line with the London directive. It would be wrong to pretend that militants in Scotland had it all their own way. One AFA member from Edinburgh was stabbed when passing a pub full of Rangers casuals, simply because his colleague, also an AFA member, was black. One of the nearest

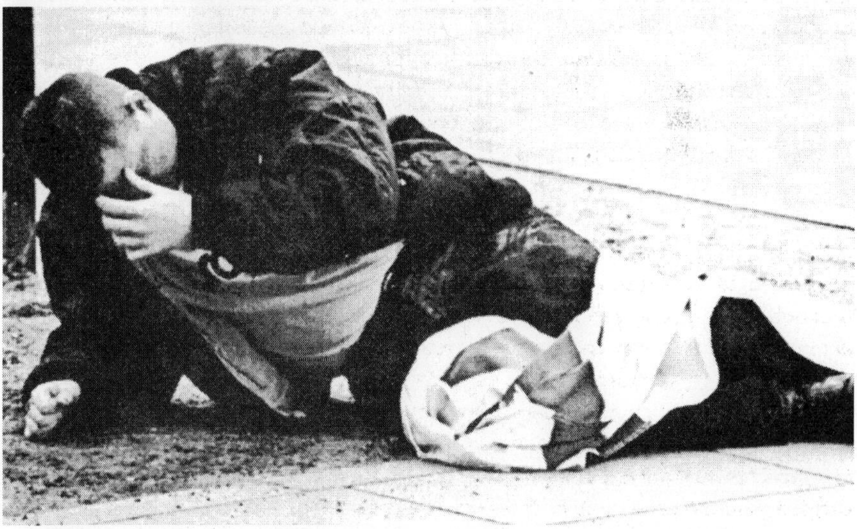

Bloodied and bowed, a right-winger at the Bloody Sunday Commemoration in Manchester on 28th January 1996.

times AFA nationally came to suffering a fatality, happened when a Glasgow AFA member, D., was viciously beaten after being set upon by a gang of BNP supporters as he left the pub. Not realising how seriously injured he was, he made his way home, before collapsing. His mother was woken by the sounds of him drowning in his own blood. A few months later, after returning to the AFA ranks, he was again ambushed. This time his skull was fractured. A metal plate was inserted to repair the damage. Wary of boosting opposition morale, AFA never made anything of the incidents at the time.

3.24

BACK TO SQUARE ONE

Adding to this overall sense of a need for a re-evaluation of strategy and tactics had been the loss of Derek Beackon's seat to Labour in the municipal elections in May 1994. But while the Labour victory saw the ANL popping champagne corks outside the count, in wider terms it was far from being so clear-cut. Firstly, despite, or as some saw it, because of, the ANL campaign, the BNP vote leapt by over 30%; and secondly, while this united front saw the Labour Party returned to power, it was the Labour Party whose often palpable contempt for the working class they claimed to represent, had laid the ground for the fascist breakthrough in the first place.

But what concentrated militants' minds more than anything was the fact that, despite the vast scale of the operation to unseat the BNP, white working class voters on the Isle of Dogs had not been convinced by the anti-fascist arguments, with even the vicar of Christ Church on the Island commenting that the ANL's tactics had been "extremely destructive". For according to the vicar, "like the BNP, they brought in large numbers of people from outside this well-boundaried and insular community to canvass door to door. On weekends near to the May elections there were running battles between rival groups. Islanders hated it, and the ANL got the reputation of being worse than the BNP, who had done their best throughout to seem respectable and to appear as a party of law and order."

Predictably, Copsey sees these comments as interesting, "not least because they reinforce the claim that confrontational anti-fascism can backfire and alienate anti-fascists from the wider community." However, apart from the vicar, there is little else to support the notion of 'running battles'. It is far more likely that the undeniable hostility the ANL provoked among locals was down to their habit of dismissing genuine concerns in regard to housing allocation as 'irrational'. And for a tough working class community their strident demand for the BNP to be 'smashed', without either the capability or intention of doing so would have been equally irksome.

Back in September 1993, when Derek Beackon won the council seat of Millwall with almost 1,500 votes, the priority for the entire Left became the unseating of the BNP, without ever grasping the significance of the fascists' victory, much less the reasons behind it. In 1992 when the BNP secured 20% of the vote there, it was a heavy hint something had gone awry. But nothing was done. Instead the fascists continued to make headway. For instance, there was noticeable anger at the massive investment being poured into the Island's business infrastructure without any working class input or consultation. It was a ready-made opportunity to project 'listening nationalism' as the common sense alternative, which is what happened. As the local vicar admitted, "Many people talked about the vote for the BNP being a protest vote. People felt their needs were ignored. Housing was the main issue. It could just as easily have been schools." His analysis again points to a reality Red Action never tired of spelling out: "The rise of the Far Right across Europe is not the cause of the Left's failure but the consequence of it." Through militant eyes, this initial failing was merely compounded when 'anti-nazism' lined up behind the political status quo. As a result, when a rumour circulated that Militant, who were active on the Isle of Dogs, might be standing against the BNP and, of course, Labour, the AFA leadership were more than interested.

Terry: "The advantage to us of supporting and being identified with candidates in whatever capacity meant we would legitimately have had a reason to be on the Island. And from a Militant point of view, only we could supply the type of muscle needed to protect their canvassers. Anyway, for one reason or another, Militant bottled it. It was a fateful decision as to how militant anti-fascism would develop politically from there on."

Post-May 1994, with the ANL and Searchlight celebrating the Labour accomplishment, leading London militants envisioned the implicit threat in the new BNP strategy and began to consider the need for some form of political response of their own. Officially, however, while the war on the streets outside London still raged, such considerations stayed on the back burner. Of foremost importance was the unity of the organisation, and the concentration on the 'single issue'. Due to the wildly diverse political composition of AFA, even minor tampering could fatally blunt the much-prized cutting edge. That said, in the absence of any organisation moving into these areas to challenge the BNP politically, London made it clear that militant anti-fascism would need to adjust by confronting fascism 'ideologically'. The largely forgotten undertaking from the founding statement would need to be dusted down, if fairly basic anti-fascist objectives were to be fulfilled. To that end London AFA began to prepare the ground by launching a hard-hitting public attack on constitutional anti-fascism and the limitations of single-issue anti-fascism *per se*.

"The Left's sense of triumphalism after the recent elections is not only misplaced, it is perverse. It is also predictable. When the BNP first received 20% of the vote in October '92 it was, the ANL insisted, entirely due 'to a low turn out'. Their subsequent victory only months later, was put down to 'special conditions' on the Isle of Dogs.

"On May 5th this year the turn out was 70%, more than might be expected for a general election, and Beackon's vote went up by 560, an increase of 30% – so much for the 'low turn out' theory. Now we are told that the Labour victory on the Isle of Dogs means that the ANL 'has turned the tide.' Once again reality says otherwise. In the St James' ward of Bethnal Green the BNP candidate polled 653, a 700% increase on the last election. In nearby St Peter's ward they got 889 to Labour's 2,000. In the borough of Newham two BNP candidates collectively polled 906, the equivalent of 80% of the total Labour vote. So much for the theory of 'special conditions' peddled by sections of the media and the Left.

"Prior to Beackon's election *Socialist Worker* had boasted, 'The nazis are on the run ... the ANL have done a brilliant job.' The BNP vote went up again this time by 800. Later, this BNP victory was described as a 'blip'. Some months prior to the launch of the ANL in 1992, its SWP sponsors had dismissed the Far Right 'as no more than a hard core of extremely isolated fanatics.' Today, little more than two years later, 10,000 votes for the BNP across London is being described by the ANL as 'turning the tide'. Unpalatable though it may be for some, the truth is that support for the Far Right is growing steadily and there is little the middle class Left can do about it. There have been too many lies, and as a result the working class is largely immune to their propaganda. In many areas their tactics simply make them an irrelevance, in other areas the only impact is to undo good work previously done by others. Their politics have little resonance in working class areas and the SWP knows it, otherwise, instead of being mere cheerleaders for Labour, they would stand candidates themselves.

"As a result of the ANL/YRE ('If you don't want a fascist for a neighbour, vote Labour') strategy, the BNP is now nationally regarded as the radical, and only, alternative to the establishment parties. The ANL campaign has made a difference: it has increased the Labour vote, but crucially *not* at the expense of the BNP. The politics of the ANL is the politics of the SWP, and the politics of the SWP is still the shrill '60s campus style protest: slogans, placards, and demonstrations. In simple terms, the SWP/ANL combination has been proved a failure; despite endless media promotion and seemingly unlimited resources it has not even curbed the influence of the BNP.

"The BNP can be stopped, and on many occasions up and down the country AFA has physically stopped them. However, we are not blind to the fact that the fight is ideological and accept that the re-emergence of support for the Far Right is a symptom of a deeper malaise. We do not see it as our job to campaign for Labour. It is not AFA's role to argue that change is not needed. The function of anti-fascism is not to see the electoral threat from the Far Right beaten back so that, as happened between 1982–92, Labour and the middle class Left can turn their backs on both the social causes and their own collaboration in the political betrayals that gave rise to the NF and the BNP in the first place.

"The ambition of militant anti-fascism is not simply to see the Far Right defeated and removed from working class areas; the ultimate solution is to see them replaced there. The BNP's attack on Labour is from the Right and is racist, ultra-conservative and anti-working class. Our primary role is to guarantee that a successful challenge to Labour comes *only* from the Left" (AFA leaflet, 1994).

Sometime later when it was publicly acknowledged that AFA could not now hope to stop the BNP entering the political mainstream, this militant guarantee would be revised. Rather than fight to ensure 'a successful challenge to Labour comes only from the Left', the task, as militants now saw it, was to 'ensure a successful challenge does not come only from the Right'.

3.25

DON'T BELIEVE THE HYPE!

From the early 1990s AFA had been working to the principle that it was involved in 'a three-cornered fight' involving the radical Right and the state, but a conservative Left not quite enemy, not quite friend, providing another component. The damage, from a militant perspective, that the ANL had inflicted on anti-fascism has already been detailed. And while AFA had made scathing criticisms of the ANL/ARA/YRE, etc., in *Fighting Talk*, the ANL as an organisation, its initiatives, and most of all its members were largely ignored. But in 1994 when the ANL began to claim responsibility in their propaganda for high-profile AFA victories, such as Waterloo, it was high time for AFA to set the record straight. But there was more at stake than reputation. Publicity-wise, and in terms of trade union branch sponsorship and fundraising generally, it was admitted the ANL were cleaning up. Equally, in terms of benefits and gigs, the ANL were proving effortlessly superior. Tactically this was not a situation AFA could alter by stepping up the fight against the Far Right. Moreover, ANL propaganda was increasingly judged pro-state; more anti-extremist than strictly anti-fascist. All in all, the enduring quarrel with the ANL was not simply about due recognition, for, as far as militants were concerned, the very soul of anti-fascism was at stake.

"The ANL are not our enemies but they are political opponents. Rather than ignore them, as has been our practice, it is time they were treated as such: the ANL needs to be exposed to the ANL. The anti-fascist struggle isn't only the fight against fascism but also involves the fight FOR anti-fascism."

In the same internal document, the advantages of highlighting the systemic failures in the ANL to a specifically ANL audience were outlined. "The ANL has failed. They have exhausted their entire repertoire from the '70s – marches, carnivals, etc. – and the fascists are still coming. Their membership is battered, baffled and demoralised. If we can estimate that we hear of 50% of the attacks, then the ANL/SWP are being turned over on an average of once a week somewhere in the country. The only strategy available to the leadership is to conceal it from the membership in an effort to avoid mass hysteria within the ranks. Their passive compliance brings the whole anti-fascist movement into disrepute.

"The media profile and expensive campaigns and mega-marches are designed only with the intention of creating an anti-fascist franchise. To create the impression that anti-fascism and the ANL/SWP are synonymous and that everything and everybody else is imitative, second rate and counterfeit. We know from the experience of the last two years that the ANL campaign against the BNP, though public, does nothing to damage fascism. Their anti-fascism is seen to be ineffective. In too many areas the unleashing of the ANL provokes sympathy for the BNP in direct proportion to the efforts of the ANL. This antipathy is based directly on class hatred. The more strident the campaign, the more working class alienation, the more damage to the cause of anti-fascism. Because the ANL is seen to be the prototype, everybody is tarred with the same brush. The Left and the media accept this analysis and regard AFA's tactics as excessive, the strategy as deviant and counter-productive. Up to now only the Far Right and the police have a more sophisticated insight. Both they and AFA supporters know that the reverse is the case. The ANL are deviant because you are only properly anti-fascist if you are, from the outset, determined to be effective."

Under the title 'Don't Believe The Hype', the militants' blistering exposé of the ANL record was distributed outside a huge ANL Carnival in Brixton, to the chagrin of the SWP leadership, and later at the SWP annual get together, Marxism 1994. At Brockwell Park, ANL stewards in bibs unwisely attempted to screen out AFA leafleters from Carnival-goers by physically standing in front of them. Within seconds of the entirely predictable fracas erupting, the tactic was hastily abandoned by a now seriously placatory SWP. One SWP full-timer found herself in the awkward position of desperately pleading with police not to arrest an AFA member who they, the police, believed had threatened her and another SWP member, and who now threatened them. "It was all my fault," she repeatedly pleaded. Safe to say, had the AFA member not been black and the ANL carnival been somewhere other than Brixton, such a public display of solidarity would not have been forthcoming.

Generally, the AFA allegations made uncomfortable reading for ANL supporters. For instance, of the thirteen victories the ANL listed in their full colour 'Carnival against the nazis' programme, all but one were either imaginary or down to efforts of other groups, according to AFA forensics:

"Folkestone 17/09/92 – The counter-demo was organised by Kent AFA and supported by Militant and London AFA and the ANL. Militant and AFA were the only groups involved in confrontations on the day. Becontree 15/01/94 – Gig cancelled by police after demonstration. Confrontations on the day involved only YRE and AFA. AFA attacked 150 C18 and Blood & Honour skins in The Little Driver in Bow. There were also clashes involving AFA later in the evening at Waterloo. The Battle of Waterloo 12/09/92 – AFA's most famous victory. 15,000 leaflets were distributed the week before at a rain soaked Unity Carnival. Two days before the event an AFA press release predicted 'maximum disruption ... it will be done peacefully if we are allowed, but we are undaunted by the prospect of physical confrontation and in the end it may be like the Battle of Waterloo…' At one stage five central London stations including Charing Cross and Waterloo were closed 'due to riots'. There were 44 arrests. The ANL? The ANL held a march in Thornton Heath in South London. The European Aryan Festival Derby – Festival closed by the council, beer confiscated by police. Camden 30/04/94 – A 40-strong wedding reception featuring fascist band No Remorse. The ANL, having been on another wild goose chase (on this occasion they had mobilised to stop another Blood & Honour gig in Brixton, no less!), stumbled upon the event when an SWP member went to the pub for a drink. Police were called and the publican closed the pub – locking the fascists in!

"Against the BNP – the ANL claim they've stopped rallies in Bedsworth, Angel tube, Stoke on Trent, Bloxwich, a BNP march in central London and the BNP paper sale in Brick Lane. Bedsworth –YRE counter-demo. ANL present. No BNP sighted. Angel tube – ANL counter-demo, supported by RCP, etc., prevented a small group of fascists exiting from station. BNP rallied at Old Street instead. Stoke on Trent – ANL demo against the NF. No fascists sighted. Bloxwich – BNP stronghold; not even AFA has disrupted fascist activities there. BNP march – despite 2,000 ANL in vicinity of Victoria station, 300 BNP assembled on the concourse and marched to Pimlico where a rally was held. They then dispersed without incident. Brick Lane – it is common knowledge that it was the YRE rather than the ANL who did the business at Brick Lane."

This unexpected AFA propaganda offensive, deliberately targeting ANL supporters, together with the boiling down of the carefully nurtured but largely bogus ANL CV, hit home. In the 1994 Pre-Conference Bulletin, under the title 'Fighting Racism' the SWP Central Committee launched a counter-offensive:

"In the past whenever the nazis attempts to build a mass base have fallen apart, they have turned to terrorist tactics in order to consolidate their core cadre of thugs. So in the late 1970s after the ANL devastated the NF, they turned to vicious attacks on black people and white anti-racists – with attacks on sellers in places like Chapel Market in Islington, and Leeds. The firebombing of the home of our organiser in Newcastle, the driving of a burning car (containing a murdered Asian woman in the boot) into the window of our bookshop in Birmingham. There are signs of a similar turn to vicious thuggery now. In the Leeds/Bradford area there have been a spate of attacks on the homes and cars of our comrades, plus an increase in race attacks on blacks and Asians.

"It is very important we know how to react to such attacks. We cannot simply ignore them. To do so would be to allow the nazi thugs to gain increasing confidence, while creating a climate in which many socialist and black activists felt intimidated from resisting racism. Nor can we deal effectively with them by small groups of our supporters getting involved in physical fights with small groups of theirs. In the late '70s and early '80s some members of the ANL and the SWP made the mistake of following such a strategy. Small squads of them would cruise the streets in cars looking for individual nazis or would try to attack nazis in their homes or pubs. The results of such an approach were disastrous. This 'squadism' fragmented the anti-nazi forces, creating the impression that you had to have paramilitary training and operate in an underground manner to resist the nazis, and narrowing right down the numbers involved in anti-nazi activity. At the same time they created the impression among wider numbers of working class people that the fight was simply between two rival gangs, one from the Right and one from the Left. This isolated us as much as the nazis and it provided the police with an excuse to clamp down on us more than on them. The end result was often the abandonment of our street sales and the setting back of socialist organisation in the area for a number of years. In the end, those who followed these tactics broke with the SWP and the ANL to form groups like AFA and Red Action, who abstain from any socialist activity while engaging in a more or less purely clandestine opposition to the nazis. It is not an experience supporters of the ANL or the SWP anywhere want to repeat."

Read in purely political terms it was an unremarkable document, for the most a reiteration of ANL/SWP custom and practice. However, the rationalisation for sticking to the line is nonetheless breathtakingly dishonest in terms of propaganda and unerringly flawed in terms of projection. From a purely analytical point of view, it seemed to be promising a 'return to thuggery' by the BNP at time when British fascism, under SWP noses, had just undergone a 180-degree turn in terms of strategy. On the propaganda front, the citing of the intervention by the squadists at Chapel Market as 'disastrous' is equally risible, especially as the squadists' involvement came about directly as a result of the SWP Central Committee ordering the local branch to surrender the patch to the NF.

Just as clumsy was the depiction of militant anti-fascism as purely 'clandestine' when, in organising three consecutive Unity Carnivals between 1991–93, the militants had mobilised approximately 25,000 people through these events alone. Repeated marches on Remembrance Day drew in a further and arguably different layer. All told, AFA mobilisations from 1985 onwards brought possibly as many as 40,000 people onto the streets. This, at a time, remember, when the same SWP leadership, along with much of the Left, was insistent neither fascist violence nor race attacks were issues worth bothering about. And formally this remained very much the line right up until a militant show of strength in Bethnal Green on Remembrance Day, November 1991. Two months later the same leadership approved the re-launch of the ANL.

Obviously it was hoped the existence of the ANL would either co-opt or nullify the militants. Instead, to their dismay, AFA was the standard against which the ANL was instantly judged. As galling, SWP leadership pronouncements were openly mocked by everyone from Class War to Searchlight. Under these conditions it was inevitable that anti-AFA propaganda would grow increasingly shrill. Sure enough within a matter of months, AFA slipped from being depicted as 'clandestine and paramilitary' but probably genuinely motivated, to "these people" who, because of their cloak and dagger existence, have become dangerously "depoliticised and sometimes anti-working class" (Julie Waterston,* *Socialist Worker*, 19th November 1994).

Central Committee member, Chris Bambery, took the demonisation a stage further when, in a roundabout way, he drew a moral and political equivalence between the 'working class paramilitaries' on both sides. Using the failures of the German Communist Party (KPD) in the 1930s as a backdrop, he attacked the supposed propensity among the KPD rank and file for the use of 'individual terror', which according to Bambery served to reduce the struggle "not just simply to the minority of workers grouped around the Communist Party but to the young 'hardmen'. There were constant problems with these 'squadists' who glorified a 'laddish' lifestyle. There were reports of bullying within the 'RFB' [Red Front Fighters League]. In one instance, Rosenhaft describes RFB fighters inviting SA men into their tavern to join them for beers at Christmas time. Some 'squadists' even went over to the SA when the KPD tried to modify its line" (*International Socialism*, autumn 1993). Naturally it would not have served Bambery's purpose if he had explained that the invitation to the SA was likely to have been a ruse all along and that it resulted in a beer glass brawl during which one of the SA was fatally stabbed. So he omitted it.

Given the employment of the 'laddish' analogy, there was little doubt as to either the target or the reasoning behind the parable: militant nationalism and militant anti-fascism were historically unprincipled, generally untrustworthy and on occasion indistinguishable from each other. Marxist jargon aside, such pontificating was hardly original. Right-wing revisionists such as the German, Ernest Nolte, had drawn a similar conclusion years previously. "Scum versus Slimebags" was The *Daily Star*'s memorably succinct take on the clash between philosophies (*Daily Star*, 20th September 1993).

In *Socialist Review* in April 1995 there came the first and only public acknowledgement of AFA's existence, albeit followed by the allegation that ARA

---

* In the aftermath of the local election in May 2004, the ANL's main organiser, Julie Waterston, was apparently stood down. This followed an embarrassing outburst during an interview with *Weekly Worker* in which she appeared to suggest that "only the scum on estates vote BNP" (*Weekly Worker*, May 2005).

and AFA were flip sides of the same coin. "The election of Derek Beackon put the anti-racist movement to the test. Both AFA and ARA drew the same conclusions from the rise of racism. They both believed that the white working class is racist and has no role to play in the struggle against the nazis." And, as readers were again reminded, "small groups of street-fighters have never defeated the nazis, as the example of the 1930s and 1970s demonstrate."

It says everything about the uncertainty at the leadership level of the SWP that it was felt necessary to return to the 'violence is futile' argument, introduced in order to explain away SWP passivity in the face of the NF 'turn to terror' fifteen years earlier. For them to use it again in a much-changed situation where it was the 'nazis' who were being 'out-violenced', and by the very same forces the SWP continued to insist were 'apolitical and anti-working class', piled on the contradictions. "In reality AFA's position was more carefully thought out," as Copsey concedes. "According to AFA's class-based analysis, support for fascism was said to come from the disillusioned white working class betrayed by a mediocre Labour Party that had ditched socialism. So without a credible alternative, the working class had no choice but to turn to popular racism by default: 'In the absence of class, race; in the absence of socialism, nationalism'."

In what way did the AFA analysis square with the SWP charge of militant anti-fascism having 'written off the working class'? When this allegation was shown to be redundant, AFA were in turn accused of 'pandering' to the same white working class it had years earlier supposedly written off. And while it might well be argued that physical force alone could never hope to defeat fascism, it is equally true that mass organisations have repeatedly failed for want of a cutting edge. Indeed the recipe that saw the driving back of fascism in Britain in the 1930s and 1970s was the holistic approach that by this time was achieving a similar result in the 1990s.

3.26

BNP – ULTRA CONSERVATIVE

In whatever the context the SWP charge that AFA had 'given up on the white working class' might have been made, it was not sustainable for a moment. Of the multitude of anti-racist, anti-fascist initiatives launched in the 1980s and 1990s it was the militants alone who took the issue of white working class disenchantment seriously. More than that, at the very time the accusation was being made, far from abandoning the working class, AFA was exploring ways in which anti-fascism could be made to reflect contemporary white working class interests.

For instance, when BNP leader John Tyndall stood in an east London parliamentary by-election in July 1994, AFA campaigned with a leaflet entitled *Time For Change?* In it, traditional name-calling was eschewed. Instead there was the beginning of a process to try to re-define fascism and anti-fascism in purely class terms, and, unlike the ANL, in purely modern-day terms. The goal was to re-package anti-fascism as something more than the exclusively 'pro-minority' stereotype which, among other things, militants saw as being responsible for whipping up white working class support for the BNP on the Isle of Dogs a couple of months earlier. Thus BNP policy on race and immigration was ignored, with their policies on housing and welfare spotlighted instead.

"Under this Conservative government, £328,000,000, has been raised by the sale of council houses. At the same time, subsidies to local councils for repairs and new housing have been systematically cut year by year. This policy has condemned hundreds of thousands of working class families, black and white, to live in run down, or temporary accommodation. The BNP's solution? 'Property owners should be given [financial] incentives to let ... council housing subsidies should be eliminated'.

"The Conservatives are dismantling the Welfare State. The BNP would like to see this process accelerate. While Major wonders about 'requiring activity in return for unemployment benefit,' the BNP have no hesitation. The unemployed should be made to work for their dole. 'Social services should not be regarded as an absolute right – social welfare should be earned'."

By dissecting the BNP manifesto in this way, AFA hoped to show that, far from being dangerous and thus glamorous anti-Establishment rebels, stripped down, the philosophy was fundamentally an 'ultra-conservative' one. Thatcher's rather than Hitler's children, if you like. With *Tories in Flight Jackets*, the title of the follow up leaflet, here again was propaganda explicitly devised for white working class consumption. At the same time, from the perspective of a single-issue organisation, 'anti-fascism' was by now being stretched as far as it would go. That this propaganda drive was being implemented as early as July 1994, almost a full year before the BNP retreat from the streets would be widely accepted as permanent even by militants in London, does indicate that the leadership were already looking to Plan B. It would, of course, take many years for Plan B to take physical form. But the Labour team contesting the parliamentary by-election in Barking were given the first indication as to who militants regarded as the real culprits. After an attempt by AFA to leaflet some estates was foiled by police intervention, leading to a number to arrests for obstruction, the main group of militants returned to the town centre.

Attracting the attention of the Labour Party candidate, Margaret Hodge, she initially thanked them for their support before adding smugly, "You're not really needed here, you know." The smiling reply from a leading militant was equally polite but just as cutting: "This may surprise you, but, we're not actually here to support you, either."*

In the meantime, it was still business as usual. When reports of foreign neo-nazi skinheads in and around Carnaby Street reached the anti-fascists in Dagenham they decided that it was an opportunity not to be wasted. Police, however, by now more used to the AFA tactic of partial retreat before appearing again when unsuspected, decided to take no chances. Uniformed officers accompanied them back into London on the train, while Tactical Support Group officers followed in vans. Despite the monitoring of mobile phones of the militants, up to 50 activists evaded police attempts to intercept them. "Two men, believed to be French tourists were hurt yesterday when 60 skinheads ran amok in London's Carnaby Street," the *Independent on Sunday* reported the following morning (5th June 1994).

The so-called 'French tourists' were very probably the FN (Front National) supporting skinheads described in Red Action as "needing the help of a wheelchair and stretcher to get to the ambulance" (*Red Action*, issue 69, autumn 1994). When *Searchlight*, too, reported the clashes as neo-nazi initiated, anti-fascists were most amused. "Reports of skinheads running riot in Carnaby Street in the West End came as no surprise. Shopkeepers were injured and premises damaged during disturbances in which the nazi strength was put at about 50" (*Searchlight*, issue 229, June 1994).

* After the local elections in May 2006, Hodge, by then Cabinet member in the Labour government, discovered to her horror that the BNP would serve as the party of official opposition in Barking Town Hall. Within a year she would shock colleagues by calling for 'indigenous Britons' to be given priority in housing and other services, earning a bouquet of flowers from a gloating BNP.

3.27

BNP IN DENIAL

As much as sections of the Left were shown to have had a vested interest in denying the real motives for the March 1994 bombshell, the BNP leadership, in particular those who championed the retreat from the street, bridled at any hint of militant coercion in their reaching such a historic decision. Time and time again, Tony Lecomber, a BNP veteran of twenty years, took it upon himself to reassure the rank and file of the correctness of the departure from the old ways. And as he repeatedly made clear there could never be any 'turning back'.

In 1997, in order to boost the profile of the 'political tendency' within the party of which he was an integral part, Lecomber launched a new full colour glossy theoretical magazine called *Patriot*. Instantly, and correctly, it was seen by many as a rival and alternative voice to *Spearhead* which was edited and indeed owned by John Tyndall. A couple of years earlier, Tyndall had pulled a major surprise himself by placing NF stalwart but new BNP recruit, Nick Griffin, in the *Spearhead* editorial chair. As Tyndall may have envisaged, Lecomber and Griffin crossed swords almost immediately, or at least appeared to do so. In early 1996 Griffin wrote, "Building a nationalist organisation with the ability to take advantage of the uncertainties of the uncharted economic, social and political waters ahead will, like the developments of a new spirit of the age, be a long process. It will only be slowed by looking for shortcuts, by seeking instant popularity, by trimming policies, proscribing 'provocative' street activities, by trying to pretend that the Holohoax is nothing to do with us. By denying our ideological debt to anti-egalitarian pro-white thinkers and heroes of the past, by cutting ourselves off from our roots and from the lads in boots. We must never forget that at the moment it is more important to control the streets of a city than its council chamber" (*Spearhead*, February 1996).

Lecomber's reply the following month was withering. "What arrant nonsense! For what purpose? If for publicity, to make a name, then the BNP has already done that years ago. All that kind of talk does is keep the BNP a small isolated sect worshipping a long dead God, using long dead invocations and rituals, and, of course, the more that people reject such a stance merely confirms how right the party is to keep them at arms length! It is a self-sustaining cycle of rejection – it has got nothing to do with politics or with a solution to Britain's present problems. Being able to defend party activities, though, is entirely a different matter and everyone should agree with that" (*Spearhead*, March 1996). Tyndall took an obvious delight in playing the role of *éminence grise*; stern and affectionate in turn, metaphorically patting the heads of his protégés, for being 'a little unfair' here, or for failing to choose words more 'precisely' there, while, as he clearly saw it, they squabbled harmlessly on a tier safely below himself.

"He [Tony Lecomber] has at the same time warned that our activists must nevertheless be able to defend themselves on the streets. I would wish to underline that warning. We are on the streets when we are putting out our leaflets, selling our newspapers and canvassing for elections – that much has not changed. Also on the streets are others who will most certainly seek to prevent us from carrying out these functions – that much has not changed either. We must be able to ensure that their intimidation and violence do not succeed. This means that we must have present in close proximity the 'fit young men' to whom Tony Lecomber refers. This is what I think Nick Griffin had in mind when he spoke in his article last month of controlling the streets of a town. I think therefore that Tony Lecomber's criticism of him here is a little unfair – although I will admit that the words used by Mr. Griffin could have been chosen a bit more precisely. The reality is we cannot control the council chambers of any British towns and so it is a waste of time debating the merits of our doing so. On the other hand, we can hope to control the streets of such towns – to the extent that is necessary for our activists to go about their work unmolested. It is vital that we should aspire at least to that degree of control, for if we fail to achieve it there will be many activists who will not wish to venture out onto the streets for fear that we cannot ensure their safety. Tony Lecomber is right in his conclusion..." and so on.

Of course, like many an old tyrant, by the time he realised that in private discussions Griffin and Lecomber had reached agreement, not just on strategy but on how the BNP itself might be re-shaped, he was already on his way out. When Nick Griffin was formally elected as leader in 1999 this put the political tendency firmly in control, and so the project of which *Patriot* was a vital part was wound up, with the final edition coming out in the summer of 2000. In it, Lecomber takes the opportunity to chart the development of the BNP and his considerable role in it, from the early 1980s onward. With evident fondness, he recalls that, in the old days, "whenever the party would meet up in London for activity, a casual observer could be forgiven for mistakenly identifying the BNP assembly as a football firm. Exclusively male, early 20s to mid-30s, casually dressed, hard looking, no passengers. Only the experienced observer would wonder why he couldn't see a single black face. This was the BNP's 'firm'. And truth to tell, when needed, it did the 'business'. While the militant violent Left scored the odd 'success' against the smaller NF or the more ill-disciplined skinheads, at no time did they ever best the BNP, at least in London."

"At least in London" is as near as Lecomber would come to admitting the level of misfortune that had befallen his racial comrades in the Midlands, the North

West, and Scotland. As evidence of the indomitable London BNP he cites an attack on a public anti-racist meeting in Welling, south east London, in June 1989 which was, in Lecomber's own words, put down with the "utmost brutality ... People attending were reported to have jumped out of the first floor windows to escape violence."

Events in Bermondsey in 1991 are also chronicled in extravagant detail, while the Troops Out march from Marble Arch in 1993, when 400 BNP/Ulster Loyalists were arrested, is recalled with puffed-chest satisfaction. Pride of place in the roll of honour, however, is reserved for the attack on a public meeting at Friends House in April 1993, which featured controversial black American preacher and one time American presidential candidate, Al Sharpton. "Walking into the House, the BNP men were the only white people present before marching boldly into the main hall. Sharpton's much-vaunted bodyguards retreated in the face of this determined advance."

Lecomber then quotes directly from *British Nationalist*: "Inside the patriots found themselves outnumbered 30-to-1. But this did not trouble them. It was a settling of accounts. Before anything else could happen, a smoke bomb was hurled into the hall." *British Nationalist* again: "Mass hysteria immediately broke out among the packed hall. Only after the patriots had left the building did a section of the mob rediscover their courage to pour out in pursuit. Great heroism and raw courage was displayed by a number of the patriots who helped each other in the face of overwhelming odds. In the end, everyone got out none the worse for wear ... A full blown riot developed in the BNP men's wake ... While this occurred at the front of the building, two escape exits were flung open at the rear, as a large part of the audience fled, eyes rolling and faces grey with fear." In conclusion he writes: "Let there be no mistake. While we beat the 'Reds' and the party proved itself on the street, the battle was in error. The strategy was mistaken...The macho prestige involved in controlling the streets appealed to those who favoured the 'strong', not to say 'fascist', approach to politics which was why this confrontational strategy was persevered with for so long."

Wary of painting a fascist idyll where the BNP are ever triumphant – 'at least in London' – lest "it might provoke a hankering [among new recruits] for a time they never experienced, I wondered about the wisdom of putting these words in print lest the excitable want to relive those times. I felt I had to, however, for otherwise the reader new to the party now would not fully understand the party's history – and the errors made along the way. The errors have to be recognised so as to avoid the same mistakes, or ever drifting back to those confrontational days."

For the most part, his recall in regard to the examples of BNP derring-do cannot be faulted, particularly as he probably played a pivotal role in their coming about. But these, remember, are specifically listed by him as evidence of the BNP firm 'beating the Reds', when in actual fact, of the victories recorded, not a single one was actually against the 'Reds' – which is to say, against either AFA or RA. Indeed, of the incidents to which Lecomber refers, AFA was present at just one, and then in small and reluctant numbers. Bermondsey was an unequivocal disaster, and no bones were made about it at the time or since. However, at each of the other incidents, militant anti-fascism was quite deliberately not consulted, or simply shut out.

Thus, quite unwittingly, what Lecomber's careful selection achieves is to bring into sharp focus the degree of aggression the BNP was capable of – when militant anti-fascism was deemed not to be a tactical consideration. Put another way, the London BNP 'firm' had learned the hard way to cut loose only when AFA was not in position to exact retribution. All told, it is not too hard to imagine what effect on the extra-parliamentary political order the Far Right would have had in a London that was indeed militant free. An attack in broad daylight on the many-thousand-strong GLC Festival in 1984 by about a hundred skinheads is a guide to how brazen British fascism could be when allowed. In circumstances where there was no organised opposition, the entire Left would have no alternative but to hide.

In deliberately highlighting the potency of the BNP 'firm' (the hard men of the party), Lecomber manages to suggest the existence of a wider, more inclusive political movement or 'nationalist family' from which the 'firm' graduated and which, in turn, could expect to come under the protection of the 'firm'. This may well have been the case with the early National Front but, almost from the beginning, 'hard-looking males' in their 'early 20s to mid-30s' were, and had to be, the make up of almost the entire activist base of the BNP from its birth in 1982 and certainly from when it sought to make inroads in east London in 1990.

This was a result of the mixture of the ideology of the BNP and the militant tactics AFA personified, a combination that meant that, to all intents and purposes, anyone incapable of fight or flight was, and indeed had to be regarded by the Far Right, as 'a passenger'. Thus 'passengers' came to be derided both for being a danger to themselves and, by slowing it down, to the entire 'firm'. In order to avoid presenting a soft target, almost uniformly a BNP recruitment process had to begin with almost all women, and males under 20 or over 40 being weeded out. In real terms, too, there was little or no place for those who came within the approved 20-40 age range, but were from a middle class or orthodox intellectual background.

How the remainder would be assessed was on the basis of how steady they proved under fire. Much of the time this meant accepting the risk of ending up in hospital or jail. As a consequence, for the average BNP activist, being a regular visitor to casualty or magistrate's courts was understood from the beginning to be all part and parcel of everyday BNP political commerce. And even without this pitiless thinning out in the field – a mortality rate that would have impressed a World War

Two infantry battalion – just how debilitating the 'no passengers' maxim was, is best understood by considering the impact if the same restrictions were applied to, say, a 70,000-strong mainstream party like the Liberal Democrats.*

So how very much more disabling must it have been for a fringe party like the BNP, particularly as the process of filing down in order to meet the singular requirement of winning on the streets had to begin prior to the enemy being engaged. "The physiological importance of the strength factor cannot be stated with enough emphasis. Mr and Mrs Joe Public, before they will support something, want to feel assured that it is a real FORCE" (*British Nationalist*, January 1992). Now there is some truth in the statement that people generally only throw their support behind, or ultimately vote for, those with whom they are in agreement, once convinced they will make a difference. But what the BNP meant by 'force' was invariably prefixed by the word 'brute'. Everything about the BNP, including recruits, internal morale, the retention of recruits, electoral performance, as well as its very reason for being, was predicated on Joe Public's acceptance of the BNP as a party of 'power'. If the BNP 'firm' could paralyse, terrorise, or batter a way though the opposition, then it was expected all of the above would fall into place. But of course, if Joe Public is impressed only by candidates with genuine prospects, then the obverse must also apply.

How destructive the correlation really was is illustrated by comparing the following sets of figures. A Searchlight mole, Tim Hepple, who worked at the BNP HQ between 1991 and 92, noted that on average BNP staff sent off about "30 to 40" enquiry packs nationwide "a day" (*At War with Society*, June 1993, page 23). By the standards of many on the Left, a level of interest approximating two hundred potential recruits from the general public per week would have been regarded as extraordinary. Following the showing of the *Fighting Talk* programme on BBC2, AFA, for instance, got around seventy inquiries. However, for the BNP, any gain in volume was offset by everything being sacrificed to the 'war effort'. The level of debilitation is fairly startling. In 1992 the BNP dealt with 10,000 inquiries. In the general election in the same year the total vote for party candidates nationally came in at around 7,000. It is by any standards a fairly remarkable statistical warp, and

* One positive effect of the 'weeding out' process ensured that the sole reliance on those of proven physically robustness would certainly have helped ensure there were no undiscovered dodgy tickers or unusually thin skulls, and thus no more nationalist martyrs like Albert Mariner, a middle-aged NF member who died after a clash involving the NF and mostly black youth in Tottenham. It also helped that the anti-fascists were generally disciplined and followed the 43 Group edict on the level of violence deemed appropriate: "We're not here to kill," a former 43 Group veteran recalls being told before a planned ambush. "We're here to maim" (*Daily Mail*, 14th April 2008).

one that more than anything else gives the lie to the Lecomber claim that the BNP firm did 'the business'.

For, so low was BNP stock in its heartland areas where it, and inevitably AFA, was active, that even die-hard racists there were not convinced that ticking 'BNP' was worthwhile. Equally, as Lecomber insists, had the BNP been a 'real force' and thus all conquering, a revision of the 'marches, meetings, punch-ups' strategy could never have arisen, as it would never have needed to – much less be so publicly accepted as 'a mistake'. Nor would 'errors made along the way' in terms of political presentation and so on, ever have come to be regarded as important, as there would never be anything to gauge them against, and because of that could not have had the remotest chance of being rectified.

In a climate where the BNP was rampant, it is hardly outrageous to suggest it would not have stopped until the very last flicker of resistance was put down with the 'utmost brutality'. In such a climate anything approaching a white flag would have been regarded as nothing but an outrageous betrayal of 'fascist' principle. Safe to say, the announcement of 15th March 1994 was delivered to no such triumphant backdrop. It was not, and could not have been countenanced at all had the situation on the ground not been considered so politically grave. For by then the 'fascist approach' was being persevered with by Tyndall, not as a tactic but as a matter of faith.

There is evidence that some in the 'old guard', Tyndall and Edmonds among them, may genuinely have believed the 1994 announcement was just to earn some respite; a chance to regroup. Certainly, when Tyndall suggested returning to the streets to oppose the Bloody Sunday march in Leicester in January 1996, the 'young Turks' Lecomber and Griffin were so horrified a leadership challenge was immediately posted. Only a humiliating climb down by Tyndall forestalled his immediate departure. To add to Tyndall's isolation, others in the leadership, like press officer Michael Newland, publicly backed the 'political tendency', insisting the adoption of the new strategy was critical not just to the survival of the BNP but also to British nationalism itself. Though not all that much younger that Tyndall, Newland was openly contemptuous of what he referred to as Tyndall's "wartime mindset," a mindset that he claimed worked on the "assumption that the prospect of being attacked would stiffen the sinews of our sturdy British folk. In reality most run a mile."

Veteran nationalist, 'Jack Truman' (a.k.a. Eddy Butler), was hardly less scathing: "It is noticeable that those who most strongly advocate 'red blooded' activism are usually those who live furthest from the likely scenes of the activity. One of the many harmful effects of sending our activists out on this type of activity is that it leads to a high rate of attrition. It is hard enough being a nationalist without inviting all sorts of other trouble upon the heads of young keen activists. How many people around today have been active solidly for five years? Why is this? Is it, as some would have it, that those who drop out are of weak moral fibre? Are they unsteady under fire? Or are we asking the impossible? How many good units have fallen by the wayside due to the young keen organiser going in at the deep end once too often? We must nurture our talent not burn it out. The idea of British nationalism that it should continue to send its troops out over the top for one more push under the command of some unseen staff officer giving orders from far behind the lines is like the analogy of First World War military doctrine, with its stupidity and disregard for lives of its own troops, just plain wrong" (*Patriot*, winter 1997).

One who was ideally placed to gauge the impact of the 'high rate of attrition' on rank and file morale was Tim Hepple. One encounter, he recalls, occurred at Southwark Crown Court in March 1992 when all seven – four AFA, and three BNP members – arrested after the clashes in Brick Lane, turned up in court with their respective entourages. The widely held view of the BNP leadership was that within the confines of the court even AFA "would not try to do anything."

Relatively new to London, Hepple admits he "didn't really know what to expect. But if any of the stories of Red Action were true, I felt that we were a bit undermanned. As we stepped out of the transit van I remember feeling distinctly uneasy and scared even though there were no visible signs of red opposition. Everybody was confident and we were not tooled up. I had told some people not to turn up and help us out on the advice of Edmonds and White. We got into the building and went to find the waiting room outside the courtroom. Present were Simon Biggs, Jim White, Alan Thompson, who braved the Red mob when he arrived late, Paul Williams, Peter, Butler's mate from the ANL attack, myself, Darren Parker, Dave Blezzard, Edmonds, and Milton Ellis the mad postman. Derek Beackon had taken the van and driven to Ken Walsh's flat in east London. We were on the verge of falling asleep outside the courtroom when the first group of left-wingers turned up. These were not very impressive physically, consisting of various people brandishing copies of crap papers like *The Leninist*. Marvellous, we thought, just a rabble of wimpy Reds. The next moment the smiles turned to looks of horror as quite a different group of around twenty large characters turned up. I found this rather amusing to say the least, but I was also rather worried. I remembered none of these would know that I was on their side. I don't know whether or not this was the much-feared Red Action, but I supposed that it was. This was the only time I saw the BNP thugs terrified. They all looked pale and worried and were muttering about the need for reinforcements."

Nor were the rank and file the only ones to fret. Even a dyed-in-the-wool, old-school Mosleyite like Tyndall was, by 1994, frantically signalling for the authorities to do 'something'. Describing Red Action as a "criminal conspiracy" he lambasted "the total failure of the authorities to take any measure against this group or others involved in attacks on BNP members during the May election campaign, [which] suggests that the state security agencies which are supposed to act in defence of democracy are not doing their job very efficiently" (*Spearhead*, July 1994).

Rather unusually, the type of incident to which Tyndall alluded was identified in an article in the *Guardian* on 5th May: "Two weeks ago, Michael Newland, the BNP press officer, was attacked in his north London home by three men, and suffered a broken hand and fractured ankles and knees. Three weeks ago Eddy Butler, the BNP's national elections officer, was slashed across the face. Two candidates and three party workers were also attacked in Newham, east London, and BNP candidate Michael Davison lost an eye."

A strikingly similar report in *The Blackshirt* almost exactly 60 years earlier conveys the quality of pressure the far smaller BNP must have been under. "Within the last month a Blackshirt at Edinburgh has lost the sight of an eye, following a cut from glass caused by a brick through a bus window. A Blackshirt who was at a meeting in Derby is in grave danger of losing the sight of one of his eyes. At Newcastle two men were so seriously injured that they had to receive medical attention for over a week" (*Oswald Mosley*, by Robert Skidelsky, Chaper 19, 'The Beast Unchained').

While the *Guardian* went on to suggest, under Searchlight prompting no doubt, that "some attacks were down to Combat 18," the BNP spokesperson was insistent that all the attacks were "probably the work of a left-wing group called Anti-Fascist Action." More importantly, in providing a snapshot of morale within the BNP in the late-1993/early-1994 period, who did what to whom is largely immaterial, because what emerges is a picture that demolishes Lecomber's fond recollection of an all-conquering BNP.

Indeed, as early as 1992 with the emergence of AFA proper in the Midlands, it may well have begun to dawn on some in the leadership that militant anti-fascism was capable of extending not merely the scope but the duration of the contest to near perpetuity. Taking Weavers Field as the starting point, by April 1994 the BNP had been on the receiving end for a full four years without a break, and with AFA continuing to expand there was no end in sight. And though no BNP members were ever killed, the wearing out of the best of their young militants in the weekly exchanges killed their appetite for the physical struggle. Now, for the old style leadership, street confrontation, as well as being a political act, was also expected to be the means through which the political object desired by the BNP would be delivered. But long before March 1994, street warfare, the 'means', was recognised by some as counter to the political 'object'. In the end it was a simple choice: an abiding loyalty to Mosleyite principles, and with it in time, a straightforward generational defeat as had occurred in the '30s, '40s, '60s and '70s; or the acceptance that if the enemy could not be 'out-terrorised', and because of this, if 'the streets cannot be controlled', the ends may be better served by avoiding such an enemy.

What true fascist could sincerely argue with that if, through the adoption of an alternative euro-nationalist strategy, more cautious, circuitous and less impatient, nationalism emerged substantially nearer its political goals? But for more than a few the dilemma remained that the 'means' were as attractive as the 'ends', and thus what the head knew, the heart contradicted. How psychologically traumatic the 'power for principles' trade-off actually was is demonstrated by Nick Griffin's own uncompromising 1997 statement that "it is more important to control a city's streets than its council chamber." Eventually, when Griffin, too, became politically reborn, he readily accepted, and was not shy of reminding any remaining doubters, how mammoth the 'peace dividend' had proved. "In 1993 a BNP candidate took nine votes in a by-election in Burnley; in May we got 10,000 votes in Burnley."

3.28
FILLING THE VACUUM

It is hardly a surprise when taking into account the level of trauma caused by physical force anti-fascism that, years after the BNP abandoned the streets, this preoccupation with the opposition of the more violent kind would remain. Instructively, too, it would be the 'modernisers' who would spend the next decade periodically looking over their shoulder to scan the horizon for signs of the opposition. Between 1994 and 2004 the BNP leadership would obsessively return to the spectre of militant anti-fascism.

In 1996 at the annual National Rally, current BNP leader Nick Griffin, in what may have been the beginning of his election campaign, ripped up a copy of *Red Action* on stage. He got a standing ovation. The acclaim was hardly surprising as Red Action activists were regarded as "the worst of the lot, total scum," or as a member of BNP GHQ staff once put it: "When you bump into them, you know it's a fight for survival: some of them are even skinheads!" (*At War with Society*, 1993).

Later in the same year, in *Spearhead*, Griffin advanced a more reasoned argument for how the electoral threat being offered by AFA, in the shape of the newly emergent Independent Working Class Association (IWCA), might be extinguished: "The public does not have the slightest reason to be worried about Red Action. Immediately after their crushing defeat in Southwark, the papers of the main Marxist proponents of physical confrontation with nationalists were full of alarm over the way in which the BNP had been able to mobilise popular working class anger against immigration and those who support it. More recently, a different problem has been exercising their strategists, in papers such as *Fighting Talk* and even more so in the internal position papers of Anti-Fascist Action. Their complaint is that, having driven the fascists off the streets and onto the estates, the resulting lack of exciting punch-ups is leading their supporters to drift away and their organisation to atrophy. Their solution to this is to plan to form a political wing to contest seats in council elections so as to provide disillusioned Labour voters with a 'socialist alternative' and so stop them voting BNP. While they are dreaming their pipe-dream, nationalists will note that such a move will expose their key personnel, making it very easy for small groups of dedicated patriots to contact them personally, and through intensive discussions persuade them to leave our candidates, canvassers and leafletters in peace *which is all we need to win*" (our italics).

Predictably, the primary architect of the new strategy, Tony Lecomber, was also at pains to stress publicly, almost as if needing to convince himself most of all, that AFA had "no answer" to "new nationalism." In an article entitled 'Red Front – Spent Force' produced in 1997, he found it necessary to first employ a quote from *Fighting Talk* in order to back up the self-assurance in the title, and then trim it to such a degree that the original proposition was reversed. "We [AFA] cannot actually prevent them [BNP] attempting to enter the mainstream" was how the statement read, following Lecomber's careful editing. Coming from someone like Lecomber who had specifically promised just such a reward, this was on the face of it an admission so satisfyingly succinct as to gladden the heart. Except that when not truncated, the full sentence signalled something altogether different: "We cannot actually prevent them attempting to enter the mainstream, *but we can still deny them* [BNP] *their just reward for doing so by entering the mainstream ourselves*."

After a grudging admission that "on the strength of it, they [AFA] have the right idea in standing for elections in order to offer disillusioned voters a radical alternative other than the BNP," in practice, of course, Lecomber was quick to reassure, "The likely result would be to split the socialist vote and let us in – which is why the rest of the Red rabble remain cheerleaders for Labour. The embryonic IWCA justify this development since Labour doesn't do the working class any favours anyway. Even so, nothing is likely to come of it because AFA, and therefore the IWCA, is too small to have any impact on any election anywhere" (*Spearhead*, December 1997).

Writing in *Patriot* in 1999, under the subtitle 'Red Distress', he again returned to the theme of the AFA 'demise'. Among other things he forecast "a welcome and fully-blown split" in the militant camp, between those "who want to try and turn up at public nationalist [exclusively NF] activities to attack them and those who wish to follow the BNP into the mainstream" (*Patriot*, autumn 1999).

For rival camps that saw an opportunity to grow on the streets at the BNP's expense, he dispensed some fatherly advice. "In the later 1980s and 1990s the BNP encountered stiff opposition from these Reds, but was able to carry on because of the determination of BNP adherents and the numbers that could be mobilised. Today, however aggressive its members, the NF have no such numbers, with marches attracting between 30–60 and these buoyed up from other organisations. The Front tactic of going on the street has also split it internally, with its chairman realising that it is only a matter of time before the diminutive Front comes badly unstuck. It is also known that North London AFA have turned up at several of these marches hoping for an easy target."

Lecomber does not, however, acknowledge that this was a mirror image of the problems that had beset the BNP itself five years earlier. With another disingenuous flourish, he signed off: "What would they [Reds] offer if they did turn their hands to politics? That it's wonderful to be ethnically cleansed? That it's progressive to make women wear veils?" Inevitably, this fixation with what the militants had been capable of infected the BNP as a whole. In 2000 after taking on the guise of a student, *Guardian* journalist Merope Mills joined the Young BNP. She reported they were living in "perpetual fear of being ambushed by its bitter rivals on the far Left" (*Guardian* supplement, 18th July 2000). No prizes for guessing the identity of the bitter rivals to whom she referred.

Rather remarkably, within a few months of making history as the most successful fascist candidate of all time, the centrepiece of Nick Griffin's keynote speech at the BNP 'Red White and Blue' rally in 2001 was the alleged failure of AFA to "fill the space" created by New Labour. "We've got Red Action and people like that saying they are going to fill it, but we don't see them on the streets, we don't see them in the estates, we don't see them helping people on the estates ... we are there and Red Action and AFA and the rest of them are not there. We are the ones filling the space to the left of Labour, where the working class have been neglected for thirty years."

In 2004, on almost exactly the 10th anniversary of the BNP retreat from the streets, Griffin, in a leading article, warned all BNP members "of a sinister game being played to stop the BNP breaking through in June." According to Griffin, the publication of a book called *No Retreat* by an ex-AFA member, Dave Hann, and Searchlight organiser in Manchester, Steve Tilzey, was nothing less than a training manual for neo-squadists. "While superficially little more than the memoirs of a pair of none too bright hooligans, this publication is in fact a training manual in how to operate 'squads' of anti-BNP thugs. The hope is clearly that the know-how in the book will inspire a new generation of leftist street thugs to gear themselves up for vicious attacks on our activities and personnel, as part of a bigger overall drive to stop us breaking through in June."

He went on to describe "so-called Anti-Fascist Action – now effectively a defunct semi-terrorist organisation which used a decade or more ago to specialise in attacking heavily outnumbered nationalists with iron bars." He immediately sought to calm any resulting nerves by explaining why a return to that level violence was "unlikely." There were, he felt, "three key problems that the shadowy figures behind this attempt to revive political violence in Britain have to overcome. The first is that the ranks of the Far Left are now so drastically diminished that they may well not have the pool of support from which an effective direct action gang can emerge or be sustained. The second is that CCTV facilities and DNA testing technology have expanded so massively over recent years that there has never been a less promising time for an amateur left-wing terrorist gang to try to get established."

In making the third point, he quoted directly from the AFA 'Filling the Vacuum' strategy document drawn up almost a decade earlier, emphasising that "It takes two to tango," and in a rare moment of candour acknowledged that "one of the reasons for the collapse of the first AFA was the British National Party's decision to move on from street confrontation."

By 1994 the militant leadership had seen AFA grow effectively from a single branch in London to over forty across the country, but when faced with the possibility that the BNP might indeed be 'moving on from street confrontation' the task of overhauling the existing strategy began. Even with AFA apparently at the peak of its powers, there was a keen awareness within the London leadership that "all our good work in the last decade could be undone by the Isle of Dogs scenario being repeated on a national scale." These and other concerns were raised in a seminal document entitled 'Filling The Vacuum' ('FTV') distributed in early 1995 and outside of London not long afterwards. Among a number of observations was the recognition that "the election of Labour will be a massive shot in the arm for the Far Right" and that "the impetus of the Clause Four controversy will cause a realignment on the Left."

It was also argued that "AFA has long recognised that once the Far Right is allowed to mobilise, is allowed to set the agenda, and has passed a certain point, they begin to control their own destinies – and their opponents'. Once that point is reached it would be useless and possibly counter-productive to rely on a purely anti-fascist stance, primarily because people look to politics for solutions. It might be clear what you stand against, though their understanding of what you stand for will effectively determine their overall response ... [A]n anti-fascist parable, a simple refutation of the 'radical' in nationalism will on its own prove unsatisfactory." Thus, in early 1995, London AFA reached the conclusion that the 'new BNP' already had the potential 'to control its own destiny' when very few in the BNP believed it did.

'FTV': "In straightforward language, it is the politics of the Labour Party that has created the BNP. So, by acting as campaign managers for Labour, the ANL/YRE are prostituting anti-fascism and, instead of being identified with a radical pro-working class position, anti-fascism is seen to be defending the status quo, thereby practically forcing people who want change to vote BNP out of sheer desperation. They are literally driving people into the arms of the BNP. Up to now it's entirely due to the cutting edge of AFA that the passive [BNP] support has remained just that. But it is unrealistic to expect the vacuum to be maintained indefinitely ... in the absence of other suitable candidates it is incumbent on the anti-fascist militants to fill the vacuum themselves."

"Ultimately," it concluded, "the challenge for AFA is not only to destroy the BNP in working class areas but to replace them there ... but to replace them we must not only out-violence them, we must also out-radicalise them."

Intriguingly, at a time London was busily promoting the notion that politics must have primacy for anti-fascism to remain potent, it was not itself placing all the proverbial eggs in the same basket. Concerned at the potential for early electoral incursions by the BNP into areas such as north and west London, previously regarded with good reason as genuinely fascist free zones, the leadership sanctioned 'Operation Zero Tolerance' in late 1996. This involved the setting up of, arguably for the first time, paramilitary style units with the specific purpose of persuading individual BNP activists against the idea of putting their heads over the parapet. In part it was designed to dull BNP ambition in a general way, but also to ensure that the burgeoning of any progressive alternative would not be compromised or distracted by suddenly waking up one fine morning to find the BNP literally on its doorstep. A target of one of the units was Alan Gould, a BNP candidate living in Chingford on the very edge of outer north London.

Gould's ground floor flat was monitored for many hours, over days, weeks and then months. His parents' house was watched. Pubs were visited. AFA loitered in dark corners and parked cars, tramped for miles around the area, night after night. Many schemes were hatched or investigated. Over the months the work became routine in character. A couple of hours might be spent monitoring the flat from a variety of positions on the estate.

All the time the AFA team had only a very poor photograph taken from a local paper. Then in April 1997 Gould appeared on television, filmed at some BNP event. This was recorded and a good video still obtained. Remarkably, though he had been under surveillance on and off for five months, the only time he was actually seen in the flesh during the entire period was the day he was attacked. On the morning the AFA team caught up with him, his parents' house was under close watch and he was seen visiting a paper shop before embarking on the journey home by pedal bike.

It was the weekend before the May elections in 1997. At 7.45am the area was very quiet. The anti-fascists were in position near the estate. After a few minutes he emerged from his flat on foot. He was confronted, knocked to the ground and beaten until he lost consciousness. As the intention was to intimidate rather than maim, he was not badly hurt.

Prior to this, very early one morning a gloved hand had retrieved mail from Gould's letterbox. It included a proxy vote form revealing the name and address of a BNP supporter living nearby. Just before the election the windows were crashed in. 'BNP SCUM' was daubed on the wall for added emphasis. The home of another supporter was spared on the grounds that it was a house-share. Bricks then burst through the glass front door of his parents' house. As a result of the campaign Gould appeared to drop out of the BNP, certainly at a public level, which satisfied the AFA criteria.

As a holding operation for a particular neighbourhood the tactic had its uses. But, albeit similar types of operations in other areas like Hackney took considerably less time, any notion of rolling out such a campaign across the country against a party with thousands of members that would in the not too distant future, as the AFA analysis had correctly anticipated, be putting up hundreds of candidates all over the country at the same time, was demonstratrably impractical.

3.29

IF NOT THIS WAY, HOW? IF NOT US, WHO? IF NOT NOW, WHEN?

Needless to say, what 'out-radicalising' would mean in the context of what had gone before was always likely to be controversial. As pressing for the London leadership was the business of 'selling' the new analysis to the membership nationally. One indication of the sense of urgency felt was that work began at once. With Red Action acting as a bridge between militant anti-fascism and the formally anti-Labour Left, and London AFA taking responsibility for putting the argument to the other regions, meetings were initiated that would continue through the summer. One glaring handicap was that, in many cases, the representatives of both London AFA and RA were sometimes one and the same. And with both Workers Power and the DAM, the signatories to the re-launch in 1989, having departed (Workers Power finding sanctuary within the ANL, while the DAM had dissolved under the weight of internal disputes), this meant that outside of Red Action there was no other network with a national reach that could proselytise among the individual members in the forty-plus branches and beyond.

So, unlike the situation after the 1989 re-launch, the call for a radical switch came to be solely identified with RA, a factor that encouraged opponents of either the strategy and/or Red Action to imply the motivation behind it was self-serving. Almost as great a difficultly was in addressing the many individual militants lacking any ideological compass, which meant each had to be convinced on a personal basis. Among them were anarchists who opposed outright any form of electoral strategy, as well as members of organisations like the Communist Party of Britain who remained steadfastly loyal to New Labour. And whereas the militarist-type focus on the single issue may have been critical in holding things together while the fight was physical, it had given birth to a type of apolitical stubbornness, wary of arguments from whatever quarter that threatened any deviation from the 'up and at 'em' militant signature. In addition, outside of the AFA perimeter, Trotskyism to a man backed Labour. So what remained in terms of numbers and influence was very sparse indeed. To complicate matters further, among the anti-Labour contingent there was not an awful lot of affection for militant anti-fascism, either.

Nonetheless, in the absence of other options, a meeting was called in June 1995 to which the most promising groups were invited. In all, nine groups including the hosts held a five-hour meeting revolving around the core proposition. In all, similar discussions continued for the next six months. London AFA representatives, who, in the meantime, were travelling up and down the country to address AFA branches, were also running into considerable opposition. Ironically, in contrast to the 'political tendency' within the BNP, who for years had to convince the membership that it had lost the battle but could win the war, the political tendency within anti-fascism in presenting exactly the opposite argument, faced as least as many sceptics.

Some simply could not come to terms with the notion that the BNP had or ever would abandon violence as a tactic: "Let's wait and see." Others argued forcibly that "politics should be kept out of the movement", "there was a danger of AFA moving away from its core work and principles" and "our role is to maintain the vacuum, not sit in judgement and decide who is to fill it." Liverpool AFA, while agreeing the "vacuum must be filled," nonetheless argued that for "AFA to become a 'physical wing' or an official part of any particular party/organisation ... isn't the way to go about it." In Edinburgh, anarchists, to the embarrassment and annoyance of the local organiser, implemented a last minute boycott of a face-to-face meeting with a leading London organiser.

In recognition of a growing resistance, three prominent AFA members travelled from London to Sheffield on 23rd September 1995 to address, face-to-face, delegates from all nine Northern Network branches. Over the three hour long meeting the same points surfaced, with the most outspoken criticism being articulated by a Leeds organiser, Simon J. Not long afterwards two documents were distributed among all AFA branches nationally. They advertised some contradictory doubts and grievances against the call for 'a political wing', and were signed by Huddersfield AFA, though London suspected the author was actually Simon J.

This affair could be summed up with the warning: "Throughout Europe the old Left is in meltdown. In France the FN is now the biggest working class party. We can prevent the same happening here, but there is also a possibility to put the whole process into reverse. At the end of the day, it is up to each individual to decide precisely what we intend to do about it. The presumption that we can carry on as before, can survive and remain effective without this 'distraction' from the 'real work' is an illusion. An illusion that has substance only because, up to now, we have been, all of us, almost always on the winning side. Where will the unity of purpose, motivation and recruits spring from if AFA begins to sustain a fraction of the defeats and setbacks sustained by the BNP? Tactically, AFA has always been a step ahead; now would be a bad time to start believing our own propaganda ... The IWCA which has taken twelve months to put together is specifically designed to threaten no one and include everyone ... if we are agreed the vacuum needs to be filled, then the following are the only questions that remain: If not this way, how? If not us, who? If not now, when?"

Just before Christmas 1996, two senior London AFA members sat in on a Northern Network meeting chaired by Simon J. Afterwards the pair got in the car and headed straight back to London. Neither spoke for ten minutes. Looking across, the passenger posed the question. "Well, what did you make of that?" "He's bent," came the reply.

Following an intensive eighteen-month internal investigation Huddersfield and Leeds branches found themselves suspended by the national co-ordinating body. The problem emerged when Simon tried to rope the newly installed AFA organiser in Manchester, John H., into mobilising immediately for an activity in Leeds in 1996. Unconvinced by the arguments, he demanded more information, including the identity of a journalist said to have volunteered the information and deemed to be central to its success. Inexplicably in the circumstances the Leeds organiser flatly refused, citing 'security reasons'. Before long AFA investigators had become convinced that the initial scheme had been part of some Searchlight sting, with AFA personnel in the role of unwitting extras. At a crunch meeting in Huddersfield in Yorkshire in July 1997, core individuals from the region came face to face with two of their accusers. After a number of hours to the consternation of their supporters, Leeds activists Simon J. and Paul B. publicly broke down under cross-questioning, with Simon J. astonishing everyone by adopting a foetal position while still sitting on a chair. Both admitted they had been working to 'a Searchlight agenda' in order, the official report concluded, 'to manipulate AFA from within', which included among other things deliberately leading an 80-strong Northern Network stewards group away from confrontation with the BNP in Leeds in 1995, simply because having the BNP publicly dismantled at that time did not quite fit with a different Searchlight game plan.

Agreeably from a London view point, considering it was it they who had initiated the inquiry, the clinching, and up to then elusive, piece of evidence was volunteered by the highly respected Doncaster-based DAM organiser, Malcolm A. In the early 1990s he had had a personal falling out with a Sheffield based Searchlight operative, also active in the region. Not long afterwards Malcolm A. was publicly identified in the *Searchlight* magazine as a security risk. The individual behind the 'bad-jacketing' was *Searchlight* journalist Nick Lowles. And Nick Lowles was, as Malcolm A. revealed to the meeting, the same individual whose identity the Leeds organisers had sacrificed their own reputations to protect.

Following a meeting of the AFA National Coordinating Committee that pulled together delegates from all the regions, it was decided to suspend not just the individuals involved but both Leeds and Huddersfield branches. Individual members were invited to re-apply on an individual basis. No more than a handful responded. This led to subsequent accusations that London had been heavy-handed, and had basically sunk the ship to get rid of the rats. In truth, without an enemy to directly engage, the Northern Network was already lacking focus. And, for the most part, in rejecting the political analysis forwarded by London, it had already served redundancy papers on itself. By the time the BNP broke through in Burnley in the local elections in 2002 the NN was defunct. Paradoxically, Searchlight, who had spent the following decade busily shoring up the right of centre from the increasing electoral incursions by the BNP, concluded in June 2008 that a political rather than technical/legal solution was indeed the only answer. "Of course on a wider level the BNP needs to be defeated politically. While much of this is outside the remit and capability of Searchlight we will strive to argue that the rise of the BNP is the consequence of the shift to the centre of all the mainstream parties. There can be no disguising this fact" (*Searchlight*, June 2008).

There can be no disguising either that Searchlight's trenchant opposition to this exact viewpoint more than a decade earlier had fractured the organisational potential of the nascent IWCA, and, in demolishing the militant operation, led directly to the BNP getting a free pass across the entire North West. Never the type to look a gift horse in the mouth, the fascists duly turned the region into the first genuine BNP heartland. A fact hammered home with the election of both Nick Griffin and former NF chairman, Andrew Brons, to the European Parliament in 2009.

Exactly thirty years ago the National Front collapsed as a viable electoral entity following a woeful performance in the 1979 general election. Despite being a household name and distributing millions of leaflets, the NF's electoral strategy eschewed canvassing door to door and consequently it failed to put down any roots. The strategy was a disaster and the BNP eventually heeded the lessons. Oddly, the Searchlight strategy played out through the national 'Hope not Hate' campaign is hardly less primitive. With the help of compliant trade unionists and the backing of the *Mirror* newsgroup, it too claims to have distributed millions of leaflets, but as it stands no candidates, the only household name to which it draws attention is of course that of the BNP. And, while claiming to recognise "at a local level, the grievances and insecurities that are giving rise to the BNP in the first place," the only way Searchlight can address the root causes behind the BNP advances is, according to current editor Nick Lowles, to "strive to argue" with its mainstream backers for the critical step change in approach.

'Strive to argue' is a curious little phrase. It brings to mind a memorable line from the film *The Outlaw Josey Wales*, where the character played by Chief Dan George mentions travelling with a delegation of Red Indian chiefs to Washington to directly air their "grievances and insecurities." The advice they were offered by the white man was to "endeavour to persevere."

"We thought about it for a long time – 'endeavour to persevere'. And when we had thought about it long enough, we declared war on the Union."

Sooner rather than later a progressive left will have to declare outright war on conservative anti-fascism too.

EPILOGUE

It used to be received wisdom that in circumstances where a country's parliamentary Right was vibrant, the Far Right could not hope to prosper, and could thus be safely ignored. If such punditry was ever justifiable, it no longer holds true in Europe. In Italy, for example, Berlusconi's populist Forza Italia comfortably found accommodation at ministerial level for representatives of both the Far Right National Alliance, and the even more flamboyant reactionary Lega Nord. In Austria, it was the conservative Right and the Far Right in the shape of the Freedom Party who shared power at the expense of the Social Democrats. In France, it was Le Pen who, at the expense of the Socialists, came second to Jacques Chirac, a Gaullist, in the run off for President in 2002.

Only if these signals are utterly disregarded can conventional conservatism be regarded as a reliable bulwark against extremism. For, as is evident from even recent history, if circumstances prove judicious, it can as easily become an ally. Given the history of the pre-war years this may not be much of a revelation but, nevertheless, it does mean another canon of constitutional anti-fascism needs revising: fascism can mean something other than an exclusively violent reaction to social democratic ascendancy.

Even now it is still fashionable to see the emergence of this new fascism as a backlash against multicultural success, rather than the result of unalloyed socialist failure. Such wrong-headedness, naturally enough, is accompanied by complacent propaganda, which still presents the Euro-nationalist as the opposite of the popular will, and criminal, anti-democratic and anti-social by nature. It is necessary for those who hold this view to be incontrovertible to close their eyes to the discomfiting actuality that much of the vote for fascism across Europe has come from the previous constituency of the Left. In France, in what was known as the 'Red Belt', where support for a post-war Communist Party seemed inborn, the vote goes just as doggedly to the Front National.

The contradictions don't end there. In the French presidential elections in June 2002, it was not the Right but 1.5 million organised by the Left, who took to the streets in protest at finding themselves losing out in the democratic argument. This was an impressive turn-out by any standards, and was widely hailed almost immediately as a truer reflection of the popular will than the four times as many who ticked FN in the election. Such self-delusion is bad enough but arguably what is even worse is that the show of force was a substitute for the type of day-to-day campaigning on impoverished estates that was once a benchmark of the Left and is now part and parcel of Euro-nationalism everywhere. "We're on the landings and no one else is," is how one FN supporter put it. A statement AFA recognised from the late 1990's would soon apply in Britain too.

In Burnley in May 2002 this scenario was played out on a smaller scale when an 80-strong ANL picket outside the Town Hall denounced the BNP and the 10,000 voting for it inside as 'undemocratic'. That the party with the closest ties to the ANL had roughly the same level of support in Burnley as the ANL had activists, merely reinforced the feeling of a liberal Left floundering. In order to highlight the inconsistency, the BNP launched the Pro-Democracy League in 2004, hoping to counter the propaganda of the Anti-Nazi League. Not long afterwards the ANL was wound up.

Plainly this ability to outflank the liberal Left did not happen overnight but is a result of a protracted series of almost unimaginable blunders stretching back decades. The result is that today, where the liberal Left continues to ignore working class concerns and has priorities other than immediate working class interests, Euro-nationalism is capable and more than happy to 'fill the vacuum'. And in the scenario described, where it is the radical Right that comes to be accepted as the anti-establishment alternative, anti-fascism cannot, and cannot be expected to, deliver acceptable anti-fascist solutions. After all, if through a feeling of abandonment the bottom 40% of society are won to the arguments of the Far Right, who can be relied upon to fight fascism with any conviction? The state? The media? Liberal anti-fascism?

Hardly, as to a large extent the state/media/multicultural/liberal combination has already failed, not just in Britain. France, Austria, Italy and Holland and a host of other countries bear witness to the impotence of that consensus. And while the continued demonisation of the nationalist Right can certainly retard, if only to a limited degree, what it cannot do is pretend to represent a political remedy. Nor is it the case that the anti-extremist poultice in which the strategy is wrapped is in itself safe or benign. Among a multitude of sins there are the inherent errors of exaggeration, one-sidedness, and outright lies. All of which, to a population already deeply alienated by the mainstream parties, risks casting the target in a positive light.

The main danger in over-reaching is the risk of converting those that are no more than sympathisers into a world-view-accepting hard-core, a patent already evident from the ANL campaign on the Isle of Dogs in 1994 that caused a 30% rise in electoral support for the BNP there in just six months. But even where strident counter-propaganda leaves negative residue, as the trajectory of the European Right illustrates, and as *Searchlight* admits, unvarying vilification is doomed to the law of diminishing returns. Which is probably why Nigel Copsey in his summing up calls for a period of 'reflection' by anti-fascism in Britain. He poses the questions as follows: "What happens if an extreme-Right party emerges like the Front National in the 1980s, that immunises itself against charges of nazism? Even if a hidden core of fascism can be exposed, what happens when, with generational shift, the strength of anti-nazi feeling and the memory of war fades?"

Ironically, by the time he posed the question in 1999 his prediction had already come to pass. He just didn't see it, which is why the "practical lesson" he recommends all anti-fascists to take on board ("Any collective response must be rooted firmly in the local community along the lines of Tyne & Wear Anti-Fascist Association") looked pitifully inadequate just a couple of years later. A reality forcefully brought home in 2003, when to the background of claims of victory from TWAFA the BNP took 14% of votes across Sunderland. Ultimately, for the anti-racist projects championed by Copsey to have political purchase would require the BNP to restrict itself to contesting seats in those areas inhabited by a substantial number of ethnic minorities. Not unexpectedly, their electoral strategy is exactly the opposite.

Another factor not often taken into consideration is that, in total, ethnic minorities make up substantially less than 10% of the UK population, so what possible relevance could the NMP and TWAFA, or schemes modelled on it, have for the rest or – as the Far Right would have it – the opposing 90% of Britons? It is exactly this blind-spot that damns the Searchlight analysis too. It is surely now evident that Euro-nationalism will not be stopped by consensus-friendly cross-class and, all importantly, apolitical half-measures. If the battle for working class hearts and minds is to be won, Euro-nationalism will need to be challenged head-on by just as compelling and grand a narrative. Surely this should be an inescapable reality by now. "The BNP does not get votes because it is especially gifted at articulating the fears of white, working class and lower class Britons; it gets them because it is the only party that specifically targets that group" (*Observer* editorial, 23rd April 2006).

But by and large this particular penny has yet to drop. When BNP potential first emerged in Oldham in 2001, many pundits, unwilling to come to terms with the nature and scale of the problem, promptly demanded New Labour 'refocus'. They addressed the threat as if it was all a matter of political will, while closing their eyes to the absence of an activist base by which to deliver the non-existent New Labour programme for working class communities to begin with.

Thoroughly wrong-footed by the unexpected turns of events, a united Left, with the blessings of the ANL, first thought to present a 'socialist alternative'. However the entire electoral impact of the Socialist Alliance would be limited to just one seat in Burnley in 2002 where, through taking a few dozen votes, it caused another council seat to go to the BNP. Thereafter, the ANL largely reverted to backing Labour, or failing that, the Liberal Democrats: a policy that inevitably ended in calls for anti-fascists to vote Tory. "People should realise that in some places the most effective way to get the BNP out is for people to vote Tory. The Tories themselves must put up a fight [there] even if they don't think they can win" (Trevor Phillips, chairman of the Commission for Racial Equality, 16th September 2003).

In due course this marriage of convenience must too end in divorce. This is because a conspicuous contradiction in tail-ending the mainstream 'anti-nazi' parties is the tendency for the political centre when under pressure to tack to the right, thereby seeking to assimilate all that is radical in the extremist agenda at the expense of moving rightwards itself. For instance, a major factor in the election of French President Sarkozy in 2007 was a result of his brazen appeal to ultra-right voters. But, as has long been identified in other parts of mainland Europe, such a ploy is not always even a short-term success, with voters showing a continued preference for 'the original over the copy'.

So barring an implosion, does this mean the BNP will have a free run? Well, yes and no. As we have seen since 1994, their climb to prominence has been a near vertical one, with the negative, anti-extremist parable exemplified by legal anti-fascism, in the shape of first the ANL and then 'Unite against Fascism', lacking both resonance and credibility as an electoral deterrent. Thus, it follows, if the 'drift' is to be anchored it will be achieved only by a counter-analysis and philosophy – targeting exactly the same constituency where the BNP has greatest appeal. As said, the FN once boasted, "We're on the landings and no one else is." This simple lesson has been staring the European Left in the face since the emergence of the FN as a truly national force in 1985, and it has uniformly and wilfully refused to act on it.

In 2002 a number of the pilot schemes set up by the IWCA broke surface with candidates appearing in disparate areas such as Havering in Essex, Hackney in east London, Oxford, south Islington and inner city Glasgow. An average return overall of 25 per cent of the vote, plus the actual election of the first IWCA councillor caused a sharp intake of breath amongst the orthodox Left. Though welcomed in some quarters, it was widely regarded in others as an impertinent display and a rebuke to the feeble efforts of far larger and better funded groupings, such as Arthur Scargill's Socialist Labour Party or the Socialist Alliance who, despite standing many hundreds of candidates, managed double figures on only the very odd occasion. Logically, it ought to have given pause for thought, but within just a matter of days the secretary of the Socialist Alliance announced, "We have nothing to learn from the IWCA."

With the BNP taking three seats in Burnley in the same election the ratio between the rivals stood at three to one in favour of the BNP. In 2004 when the IWCA candidate received the backing of 50,000 voters in the London Mayoral election, it bore reasonable comparison to the 80,000 the BNP had attracted when it too first stood in 2000. But the BNP was not standing still either as the 50% increase in its own vote demonstrated.

And so by 2006 when the IWCA had amassed four councillors, the BNP had something like 54 and the smaller organisation was fast disappearing in the BNP wing mirrors. On top of this, the aggregate turnout of around 60% in the general elections in 2001 and 2005 points to the alarming scale of, in particular, working class political disaffection in 21st century Britain. Amongst many poorer neighbourhoods this loss of faith is not only in the mainstream parties, but also in the value of representative politics altogether. Accordingly, with the mainstream parties increasingly clubbing together in the neo-liberal centre, the greater the potential legroom for radical elements on their flanks. Which is one of the principle reasons for deep establishment unease. "As the Westminster parties cluster ever closer together, there's a rumble in the margins from right and left, which has all the signs of getting louder and more troublesome" (*Red Pepper*, issue 156, Oct/Nov 2007).

Eventually, this now undeniable electoral void, first flagged by AFA in 1995, will of course be filled. And shaping the future is the prize for whoever achieves it. With an annual expenditure of around £750,000 by 2008 (even prior to the £5 million expenses windfall from the European Union), the national profile enjoyed by the BNP puts it in pole position. In their wildest dreams the IWCA could never have hoped to match such resources. Crucially, however, a strategy for challenging the BNP on even the meanest of landings is now in place. And as a study by the radical left magazine *Red Pepper*, into the success of the party's methods on the vast and troubled Blackbird Leys estate, put it: "Take note of the IWCA – it is as good a place as any to start thinking about possible outcomes" (*Red Pepper*, issue 156, Oct/Nov 2007).

One possible outcome is that the BNP continue their advance. Another possible outcome is that the wider left, trade unionists and even straightforward democrats reach the same conclusion as the militants, and finally set about the task of bringing the marginalised working class in from the political cold. This is what the militants believe must now happen. And, as we have shown at critical junctures, they have been proved right before.

But with nationalist prerogative dictating across much of the continent already, the very nature of democracy, not just in Britain but also in Europe, may depend on them being right again.

APPENDIX: ABBREVIATIONS

AFA Anti Fascist Action

ANL Anti Nazi League

ANLMK1 Anti Nazi League 1977–1982

ANLMK2 Anti Nazi League 1992–2003

ARA Anti Racist Alliance

ARAFA Anti-Racist Anti-Fascist Action

ARAFCC Anti-Racist, Anti-Fascist Co-ordinating Committee

B&H Blood and Honour

BNP British National Party

C18 Combat 18

CPGB Communist Party of Great Britain

CSB Cable Street Beat

CW Class War

DAM Direct Action Movement

GCARA Greenwich Campaign Against Racist Attacks

GLC Greater London Council

ICF Inter City Firm (West Ham football hooligans)

ILOL Independent Loyal Orange Lodge

IWCA Independent Working Class Association

NF National Front

NMP Newham Monitoring Project

RA Red Action

RCP Revolutionary Communist Party

SWP Socialist Workers Party

TOM Troops Out Movement

TSG Territorial Support Group

UDA Ulster Defence Association

WIA World in Action

WP Workers Power

YRE Youth against Racism in Europe

INDEX

ANARCHISTS IN THE SPANISH REVOLUTION
by José Peirats

This is the most comprehensive history of the Spanish Civil War (1936–39) and the role played by the CNT-FAI, anarcho-syndicalists and anarchists. Included is a brief survey of the working class movement in Spain, and the political struggles which were a prelude to the Civil War.

£11.95 (including postage and packing) *ISBN 0 900384 53 0*

ABOUT ANARCHISM by Nicolas Walter

The case for anarchism as a pragmatic political philosophy is explained in this classic work by Nicolas Walter, who was a writer, journalist and active protester against the power of the state. It has often been reprinted and translated into many languages, including Japanese, Serbo-Croat, Chinese, Polish and Russian. Introduction by Natasha Walter.

£3.50 (including postage and packing) *ISBN 0 900384 90 5*

MAY DAYS: BARCELONA 1937 by Augustin Souchy, José Peirats, Burnett Bolloten and Emma Goldman

Eyewitness reports of the crushing counter-revolution from Augustin Souchy, José Peirats, Burnett Bolloten and Emma Goldman. This 'minor' incident in the Spanish Civil War claimed more casualties than in the first week of the military uprising in Barcelona in July 1936.

£5.95 (including postage and packing) *ISBN 0 900384 39 5*

ANARCHIST QUIZ BOOK by Martin Howard
illustrated by Paul Petard

Some say that it should not be the highest priority of a revolutionary movement to ask itself obscure questions, but it is fun, and if it encourages an inquiring mind to find out more, then all the better. So agitate, educate and organise, all in a handy question and answer format!

£5.00 (including postage and packing) *ISBN 1 904491 07 3*

ANARCHY IN ACTION by Colin Ward

Not a book for those who have spent a lifetime pondering the problems of anarchism, but for those who either had no idea of what the word implied or knew exactly what it implied and rejected it, considering that it had no relevance for the modern world. It is about the many ways in which people organise themselves in any kind of human society.

£7.50 (including postage and packing) *ISBN 0 900384 20 4*

ABC OF ANARCHISM by Alexander Berkman

"Government remains strong because people think political authority and legal compulsion necessary. Capitalism will continue as long as such an economic system is considered adequate and just ... progress consists of abolishing what man has outlived and substituting in its place a more suitable environment."

£6.00 (including postage and packing) *ISBN 0 900384 03 4*

ZAPATA OF MEXICO by Peter E. Newell

Zapata fought for the rights of local communities and became the purest embodiment of the Mexican Revolution. Today the indigenous rebel army in Chiapas, the Zapatista Army of National Liberation (EZLN), continue the struggle against the same social ills that Zapata fought, and take their inspiration from his life and struggle.

£9.50 (including postage and packing) *ISBN 1 9004491 05 7*

HISTORY OF THE MAKHNOVIST MOVEMENT by Peter Arshinov

During the Russian Revolution the old order was swept away, but the Bolsheviks were developing their own brutal repression. Makhno's struggle with both the old and the new oppressors is as significant now as it was then, and this is undoubtedly the most important source work available.

£9.90 (including postage and packing) *ISBN 1 900384 40 9*

A SUMMER IN THE PARK by Tony Allen

"What stuns is Tony's enthusiasm to pick himself and his art apart, to dwell (fully and healthily) on his many shortcomings and failures as a Hyde Park orator, and in so doing he throws up more insights into the performer's art than any other book I know... I plead we get more summers" (Ken Campbell)

£8.50 (including postage and packing) *ISBN 1 904491 04 9*

AT THE CAFÉ: CONVERSATIONS ON ANARCHISM by Errico Malatesta

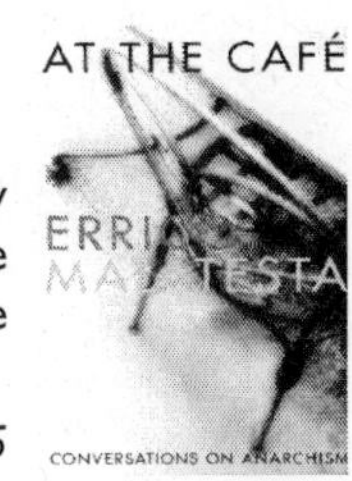

While Malatesta was hiding from the police he took the risk of regularly visiting a café in Ancona, Italy. The conversations he had there became the basis for this book. In this first English translation, he analyses the arguments for and against anarchism in his usual commonsense style.

£7.50 (including postage and packing) *ISBN 1 904491 06 5*